'History as it should be – informed and judicious, but conveyed with zest, purpose and enviable clarity. Peel and Twomey weave the myriad strands of Australia's story into a thoroughly absorbing read' – Stuart Ward, Professor, University of Copenhagen.

'An energetic and multifaceted history of Australia that illuminates a rich national story interlinked within an international context ... the book achieves its aim of rendering Australia's past, and the challenges the country has faced and met, with aplomb.' – Patricia O'Brien, Visiting Associate Professor, Georgetown University, USA

From the very first settlers of thousands of years ago to the great migrations of more recent centuries, through to the more anxious border controls of the present day, the story of Australia – and its place in the world – is one shaped by movement and mobility.

A History of Australia here brings to life the ideas, hopes and journeys of Australians' past and present. Drawing on political debate, official reports, intellectual discussion and popular culture, it weaves together a vivid, multi-dimensional history that frames key cultural, social, political and economic events and issues against the wider global context. Comprehensive in both its chronological and geographical reach, this is essential reading for all those seeking an authoritative and engaging overview of Australian history.

MARK PEEL is Professor of Modern Cultural and Social History and Head of History at the University of Liverpool, and was formerly Professor of History at Monash University, Australia.

CHRISTINA TWOMEY is Associate Professor of History at Monash University, Australia.

PALGRAVE ESSENTIAL HISTORIES

General Editor: Jeremy Black

This series of compact, readable and informative national histories is designed to appeal to anyone wishing to gain a broad understanding of a country's history.

Published

A History of the Low Countries   *Paul Arblaster*
A History of Italy   *Claudia Baldoli*
A History of Russia   *Roger Bartlett*
A History of Spain (2nd edn)   *Simon Barton*
A History of the British Isles (2nd edn)   *Jeremy Black*
A History of Israel   *Ahron Bregman*
A History of Ireland   *Mike Cronin*
A History of Greece   *Nicholas Doumanis*
A History of the Pacific Islands   *Steven Roger Fischer*
A History of Korea   *Kyung Moon Hwang*
A History of the United States (3rd edn)   *Philip Jenkins*
A History of Denmark (2nd edn)   *Knud J.V. Jespersen*
A History of the Baltic States   *Andres Kasekamp*
A History of Australia   *Mark Peel and Christina Twomey*
A History of Poland (2nd edn)   *Anita J. Prazmowska*
A History of India (2nd edn)   *Peter Robb*
A History of China (3rd edn)   *J. A.G. Roberts*
A History of Germany   *Peter Wende*

A History of Australia

Mark Peel
Christina Twomey

palgrave
macmillan

First published 2011 by
PALGRAVE MACMILLAN

Palgrave Macmillan in the UK is an imprint of Macmillan Publishers
Limited, registered in England, company number 785998, of Houndmills,
Basingstoke, Hampshire RG21 6XS.

Palgrave Macmillan in the US is a division of St Martin's Press LLC,
175 Fifth Avenue, New York, NY 10010.

Palgrave Macmillan is the global academic imprint of the above companies
and has companies and representatives throughout the world.

Palgrave® and Macmillan® are registered trademarks in the United States,
the United Kingdom, Europe and other countries

ISBN 978–0–230–00163–3   hardback
ISBN 978–0–230–00164–0   paperback

This book is printed on paper suitable for recycling and made from fully
managed and sustained forest sources. Logging, pulping and manufacturing
processes are expected to conform to the environmental regulations of
the country of origin.

A catalogue record for this book is available from the British Library.

A catalog record for this book is available from the Library of Congress.

10 9 8 7 6 5 4 3 2 1
20 19 18 17 16 15 14 13 12 11

Printed in China

For Scott – M. P.
For my Australian girls: Grace, Isobel and Maeve – C. T.

Contents

List of Illustrations

List of Maps, Tables and Figures

MAPS

TABLES

FIGURES

Acknowledgements

A History of Australia is the product of a collaboration that both of us have enjoyed. We have used the federation of the colonies into the Commonwealth of Australia in 1901 as our 'hinge', with Mark Peel writing the first eight chapters and Christina Twomey the latter seven, but we also discussed and debated each other's contributions and the themes of the book as a whole during our time together in Monash University's School of Historical Studies. While Mark's move to a chair at the University of Liverpool at the beginning of 2010 stretched those discussions over a rather larger distance than the two doors along a corridor that used to separate us, it in no way prevented the book benefiting from our continued cooperation.

We would like to thank our colleagues in the former School, especially the members of our research group who read drafts of chapters: Barbara Caine, Jane Drakard, Leah Garrett, David Garrioch, Michael Hau, Clare Monagle, Alistair Thomson and Beatrice Trefalt. Lynette Russell was a tremendously helpful reader of the first chapter. Monash cartographer Toby Wood drew the maps and Lachlan Grant was a reliably painstaking checker of facts, dates and figures. The proposal to write *A History of Australia* was first made by former Palgrave Macmillan editor Terka Acton, and we remain grateful to her for entrusting the task. Jeremy Black also provided very useful advice at the beginning of the journey, and the two manuscript reviewers matched generosity with rigour in the most helpful possible way. Kate Haines, Jenni Burnell and Felicity Noble have been both very patient and inordinately helpful during the inevitable struggle to bring the manuscript in on time (which we didn't manage), within the word limit (also slightly overstepped) and without anyone suffering a breakdown (triumph at last).

Finally, we would like to thank our partners, Scott Evans and Andrew May, for their willingness to listen and give frequent assurance. Christina's parents Peter and Sandra Twomey helped in many ways, most particularly by having the children for sleepovers during the school holidays. Her daughters, Grace, Isobel and Maeve, are only just beginning their own journey as Australians; it will be interesting to see the futures they make.

ACKNOWLEDGEMENTS FOR ILLUSTRATIONS

The authors and publishers wish to thank the following for permission to use their material:

The Australian War Memorial for Illustration 10.1 on p. 168, and Illustration 12.1 on p. 210.
John Oxley Library, State Library of Queensland, for Illustration 2.1 on p. 16.
The National Archives of Australia for Illustration 11.1 on p. 182, and Illustration 13.1 on p. 223.
The National Library of Australia for Illustration 1.1 on p. 12, and Illustration 14.1 on p. 233.
The National Library of Australia, Rex Nan Kivell Collection for Illustration 3.1 on p. 29, Illustration 4.1 on p. 48, Illustration 5.1 on p. 59, and Illustration 6.1 on p. 76.
Geoff Pryor and the National Library of Australia for the Illustration 15.1 on p. 264.
The State Library of Victoria for Illustration 7.1 on p. 99, and Illustration 8.1 on p. 131.

Every effort has been made to trace the copyright holders, but if any have been inadvertently overlooked, the authors and publishers will be pleased to make the necessary arrangements at the first opportunity.

Introduction

Australia is a large country that became a small nation. Roughly equivalent in area to the United States, or Europe without Russia and the Ukraine, its modern history has been characterised by the fact – and the anxiety – of its relatively small population. In 1901, at the nation's founding, there were fewer than four million Australians. More than a century later, there are over twenty-one million, about the same as Sri Lanka or Romania. Only half-Arctic Canada and glaciered Iceland are as thinly settled. Yet Australians have often wanted their nation to assume a level of global significance greater than such numbers might warrant. They have been and remain relentlessly comparative, eager for the news, products and celebrities that flow from the imagined centre of the world, anxious about how they and their progress are being measured, unsure as to whether their new world is as yet an improvement on the old. Australia's history must always take heed of its larger context, because for much of its European history, at least, Australians were such eager participants in the global traffic of ideas and people and so preoccupied with their place and future in the world.

Writing Australia's history means facing a series of challenges, not least an unfortunate conviction that nothing much happened. According to one view, the relatively brief yet intense interruption of European conquest and convicts provides a rare moment of excitement in an otherwise tedious story, which is punctuated again in the twentieth century by war and occasional political crisis. Among Australians, this is a view too often endorsed by poor teaching or inexpert storytelling, as well as by an obsessive focus upon a few moments and themes of Australia's history – especially the ill-fated landing at Gallipoli in 1915 – rather than a longer view. For people living in other places, it is a conclusion encouraged by the seeming absence of some of the nation-building landmarks they expect to see: revolutions and wars of independence, secession or separation, or the bloody tumults of political challenge.

In that light, it is important to begin with a question: what makes Australia's history fascinating? One answer is the ways in which its first people shaped and reshaped their country, and their meetings with the newcomers who would propel that country in a new direction. The encounters between eighteenth-century British and Aboriginal people came at a significant moment in the longer history of Europe's expansion and are an especially good example of the momentum of misunderstanding that so often accompanied it. Another answer is that Australia's dramas were often subtle and ambivalent. This is a place marked strongly by aspirations that may not seem immediately revolutionary but are no less interesting for that. It was and is a highly mobile society, a population full of migrants and movers and sojourners who have had to work out – with more or less success – the practical tolerances that allow people to live together. Far from the centre of the world, Australia was and is an anxiously experimental society, a place of invention and innovation, emulation and nervous introspection, a place where some people could forget where they came from, while others made the best of themselves and still others longed only to return else-where. It was and is a place where some hierarchies – faith, caste and birth, for instance – seemed less important and could be relaxed, while others – especially race – were fashioned with a detail exceeding almost every other nation.

As is true of other places, from Canada and the United States to Argentina, South Africa and New Zealand, Australia's European history is the history of a self-consciously new society. Embedded at its heart are the hopes and fears of novelty, the sense of possibility and the tremors of anxiety that accompanied the making of the future. Here, it always seemed more possible that the future could be different, for Australians as individuals and Australians as a people, because the threads of tradition were frayed by distance. But making a different future also carried risks: would and could Australia rise above its Old World past? Could it improve and strengthen its inheritance? Or would Australia, so far from the solid foundations of the European past, fail and decline? In many ways, Australians have tended to live with one eye looking forward and one eye cast nervously back. It makes for a fascinating interplay between dream and doubt, fear and confidence. This is a past that the Australians of the twenty-first century need to better understand, in its black and white and its shades of grey. It is also a past in which people who live elsewhere can find the characteristic dramas of new societies.

It might seem that this will be the history of thinkers and nation-builders. But for everyone who came, Australia was a new land, and all of them imagined it before they arrived. For its first explorers, visiting and eventually settling into the inlets and river mouths of the northern coast fifty or sixty thousand years ago, and for the Europeans who 'found' Terra Australis in the seventeenth and eighteenth centuries, first by chance and then by design, Australia would have different meanings and different prospects. How might this land have appeared to the people who first tracked inland, or to the transported convict and the press-ganged sailor of that first European settlement at Sydney Cove? To the hopeful German migrant or the Chinese gold seeker of the 1850s? To the conscripted Pacific Island labourer of the 1870s? To the young Englishwoman drawn by the Empire Settlement Scheme of the 1920s? To the Italian migrant or the Vietnamese refugee? All imagined their future here, whether or not their passage was willing and whether or not they really intended to stay. Australia might be a new home, a place to serve a purpose or to serve one's time. These people also made Australia's future.

In this history of Australia, we trace how Australians imagined, debated and made their future. We begin with the first people, who changed Australia more dramatically and over a longer time than has usually been acknowledged. In Australia's European history, the hinge is the moment of Federation and the turn of a new century in 1901, which shifted Australia from an assemblage of colonies to a nation in its own right.

As ever, history's drama lies in the fact that the people of the past don't know what happens next. Like us, they must create the future unaware of what lies around the corner. We are most interested in the ways that ideas about Australia's future were changed by powerful events and new possibilities, by arguments, debates, agreements and disagreements. We are interested in Australians' hopes and fears; as they argued about what come next, they discussed what was and what had been, and they pondered over the identities and relationships of men and women, different races and different classes. They wondered what Australia could and should be, and they advanced Australia down different and sometimes incompatible paths. This means that Australia's history, like the history of any other nation, is about what happened and what did not happen. It is about paths taken and not taken, futures that did and did not come to be.

1

First People

The question of how and where to begin the nation's story once seemed relatively straightforward: history commenced when 'civilisation' arrived in Australia during the last part of the eighteenth century. It has taken a long time, but few would now question the fact that Australia's history began a good deal earlier, with its first people. That this has become a fact also suggests something of the distance that many Australians have travelled, especially in the last two generations.

During much of the twentieth century, Aboriginal people often remained disappointingly 'primitive' to their white interpreters, even to those who struggled to support them and refused to accept, let alone celebrate, their apparent demise. They were treated with pity or contempt, too rarely with respect. But a thoughtful few began to listen to the continent's original occupiers in a different way. Some archaeologists and anthropologists began to provide evidence for a different story, about a culture almost destroyed by European violence, diseases and ignorance. They began to understand the rich ethnographic record of communities that had preserved oral traditions past the rupture of the Europeans and into the twentieth century. They laid a path that historians could follow. Some descriptions were overly romantic, portraying a kind of splendid 'stone age' isolation or a society somehow frozen in a 'never never' time; they forgot that Aboriginal people radically reshaped the environments in which they lived. Against the idea that the first people had been dominated and determined by their environment, scholars began to emphasise dynamic interactions. Aboriginal people became the active discoverers and users of the land, and comparing their struggles and successes with those of other human societies made clear the extent of their triumphs.

Archaeologists examined the history of other places – eastern North America, Peru, Melanesia, or north-western Europe during the Mesolithic period – and began to develop a longer-term and more comparative understanding of Australia's human history. They showed that humans had been here longer than commonly assumed, at least forty thousand years, probably sixty thousand years and perhaps more. Historical demographers rethought the size of the pre-1788 population, more than doubling the earlier guesses by estimating that perhaps a million or more people lived on the continent around the time of Cook's voyages. The carrying capacity of the land was reinterpreted, and scientists began to understand the successful food management systems that had sustained human life. The evidence of ritual burial, and the use of materials such as ochre that had to be transported to the burial sites, suggested that Australia's first people were among the most rather than the least sophisticated of humans. Ethnographers and historians began to argue that judgements about the size, diversity and complexity of the societies that existed in Australia could no longer be based only upon what was discovered by Europeans in the late eighteenth century, amidst the onslaught of terrible epidemics and disruptions. We had to find new and better ways of understanding how they had lived.

Those who listened also heard of the diversity of Aboriginal culture and languages, the complex structure of family and social ties rooted in relationships to land, and the intricacies of laws and customs. They heard stories of the beginning, the Dreaming, and began to comprehend how the Aboriginal landscape was sung and told into meaning and recognised by the signs of spirits passing and resting. Among a non-literate people, life's origins and purposes were told and retold in ceremonies of song and verse and in visualisations such as rock art or sand painting. The story of Australia's discovery could include new characters, people who had revolutionised the land and its plant and animal life just as surely as any other group of humans. Aboriginal farming and hunting, especially the use of fire, had dramatic effects on the ecology of forests, plains and coasts. Different Aboriginal clans specialised in particular forms of agriculture, developed or appropriated specific tools, and traded with the peoples of New Guinea or the Macassans of Indonesia.

Our understanding of the people who had met the European explorers – and of what had happened on this frontier between them – was enriched and deepened by empathy and listening. Acknowledging the complexity of those first meetings made for a more engrossing story. As had been true in the history of North America, it meant turning the story around in order to see the Europeans as strangers. It meant looking out from, not into, Aboriginal country. It meant returning to some of the founding moments, such as the encounter at

2

Botany Bay in 1770, and insisting that Aboriginal people were central actors, with their own ideas, beliefs and interests. To look at Europeans from an Aboriginal point of view was to try and imagine what it was to see strange humans and strange contraptions, and to imagine the conversations that rippled up and down the coast about people who seemed to understand neither warning nor welcome. Instead of telling the story through English eyes – of 'natives' whom botanist Joseph Banks assumed to be 'disputing our landing' – it meant asking what was made of the English by the men who came to the shore, only to be shot at with a musket? What did the children who were hidden behind a shield make of these strangers? Or the women whose shelters were broken into, and returned to find lances and fishing poles and even cooked food stolen, with only 'beads, ribbands, cloths etc.' left as 'presents'? What about the people who shouted 'wooroo, wooroo', which in all likelihood was a rather impolite version of 'go away', or those who walked 'leisurely away till our people were tired of following them', or those who shrank from Europeans with 'extreme fear or disgust'?[1] The key to telling the story differently lay in recognising the diversity of possible reactions, and refusing to see the Eora people as simple characters in a short-lived drama. Some showed great curiosity and interest. What did they think when the English sailed away? Eighteen years later, when the English came again, this time in greater number, what memories and stories shaped the response? How did the people of Sydney Cove welcome or attempt to ward off the strangers? What did they try to tell them?

Telling true stories about Australia's first people has demanded imagination and inventiveness. It has meant using myths and stories, as well as the material record, to describe people who recorded their past in song, dance and ritual. We have to try to see the land through their eyes, with whatever materials and methods we have. Archaeologists and historians have continued to gather and interpret evidence, adding further regional variations, deepening our sense of change over time and adding further depth and complexity to our sense of the Aboriginal past. It is important to recognise, too, that concentrated archaeological and historical research on Australia's pre-European past is only thirty or forty years old. Fundamental shifts may yet occur in the timing of particular stages, and in future people's understandings of the nature of the civilisations that existed on this continent for the vast majority of its human history. It is a challenge. Yet even with so much destroyed, or still to be found, and even with so much almost forgotten, it is a fundamentally important story to tell and the only place to begin.[2]

MIGRATION AND OCCUPATION

Of the world's great migrations, it is one of the least known. The first people to live in Australia travelled by sea, some ninety or one hundred kilometres, to explore the waterways and inlets of the islands that lay across the Timor trough, at a time when lower sea levels joined Australia with New Guinea and Tasmania. In fact, these lands have been connected for around eighty per cent of the region's human history. The travellers came with a purpose of settling, with previous generations having already moved down through the islands of Indonesia. As for those who peopled Ice Age Europe at the same time, or North and South America in a later period, migration to Australia stemmed from a mix of perceived possibilities and the pressures of famine, conflict and environmental change. One path led through Sulawesi to New Guinea and Cape York Peninsula, another via Timor to the north-west coast. Either or both were used. Both demanded relatively short but difficult ocean voyages and frequent water crossings; while Africa, Europe and Asia could be settled by walking, Australia was the first continent that set humans a more demanding task, which involved some degree of coordination, planning and risk. There is little doubt that its peopling was intentional.

These first migrations brought humans from Southeast Asia into a very different world, with a distinctive and long-isolated marsupial fauna. Placental mammals were rare, with only rats and bats having made it from Asia before human help brought in new species, beginning with the dingo. The climate was milder and wetter than it is today, until a significant shift some thirty-five thousand years ago saw falling temperatures and rainfall; as the Northern Hemisphere was iced, Australia became colder and more arid. The great central deserts were laid down. Around fifteen thousand years ago, temperatures and sea levels rose; by six thousand years ago, Tasmania and New Guinea were no longer joined to the continent, and the El-Niño-Southern Oscillation emerged and began to produce its alternating droughts and rains.

The pattern of human occupation is still a matter of some debate. An older hypothesis suggested a relatively static population, and slow social, economic and cultural change, following a relatively rapid occupation occurring over a few thousand years. In this model, Australia's first people were largely dominated by the changes in their environment. A later model, however, assumes a much more dynamic process of expanding population, intensifying use and management of resources, and the development of more complex relationships between more differentiated groups; here, the first people are much more active agents in their own transformation.

Much remains unclear, including the paths taken by the first occupiers. Some archaeologists argue for a coastal colonisation, in which people used waterways to move into the interior, while others suggest that people arrived first in the northern savannah and then fanned out through the then better-watered western deserts, as well as the forests along the eastern coast. Given the age of the human remains found at sites such as Lake Mungo in New South Wales – up to forty thousand years – the occupation of these areas must have taken place relatively soon after the initial settlement of the northern coasts. The colder highlands of the south-east were perhaps the last area to be intensively peopled. Given changing patterns of aridity, the continent probably combined areas of constant settlement – or ecological 'refuges' – joined by corridors, and areas of fluctuating occupation, such as the great deserts of the north-west and centre. In the driest time – from about twenty-five thousand years ago until about eighteen thousand years ago – Australia's first people may have contracted into better-watered areas, such as Cape York and Arnhem Land, and abandoned areas further from rivers and the coast. But even in the deserts, to which Aboriginal people had success-fully adapted within ten or twenty thousand years, occupation continued through even the driest millennia. Some settled areas lost their lakes and waterways, and with them their people, only to be re-occupied once water returned. Strong chains of contact and connection persisted down the eastern coast, and across the 'top end' to the western coast, even during the most unfavourable climatic periods.

The most contentious issue is the impact of human occupation on the continent's animals, especially its megafauna, which included a three-metre tall kangaroo, a two-tonne wombat, a sheep-sized echidna, a flight-less bird (*Genyornis*) that was twice the size of an emu, and a marsupial lion. On the evidence, all were extinct by around twenty thousand years ago, but there are different arguments as to why and how quickly. One privileges climate change and increasing aridity, and the likelihood that people and some megafaunal species co-existed for thousands of years, especially in the south-eastern parts of the continent where rainfall was more reliable. Another argument – vigorously espoused by some histo-rians and just as emphatically criticised by others – points to a much more sudden and dramatic human impact through hunting and the use of fire. The disagreement is difficult to resolve, not least because the areas in which megafauna lasted longest were also those in which the shatter-ing impact of European disease and occupation meant that little direct evidence of pre-European patterns survived. Later excavations, including one at Cuddie Springs in New South Wales, have shown that humans and megafauna did co-exist; in some areas, extinctions seem to have been rapid, while in others, megafauna survived longer. The best explanation seems to be that Australian megafauna were particularly vulnerable to new kinds of predators and to human-induced changes in vegetation. With the onset of a period of aridity about twenty-five thousand years ago, their fate was sealed. Larger animals, and animals with relatively specialised diets, either died out or evolved smaller versions, while smaller animals that could adapt to a wider variety of ecological conditions survived.

It is an uncontested proposition that Australia's first people used fire both for hunting and for what later ethnographic studies described as 'clearing up' or 'improving' their country. Burning was shaped by seasons, ritual and local knowledge. It made travel and hunting easier. By creating newer growth around water, for instance, burning attracted grazing kangaroo. Burning the land fundamentally changed Australia's flora, thinning out once thick forests, reducing arboreal diversity and privileging plants – such as eucalypts and the chenopod scrub that dominates areas like the Nullarbor Plain – that could survive or even benefit from frequent fire. Before humans, Australia's flora was adapted to drought; after humans, it adapted to fire. Among the best evidence we have for the impact of Aboriginal fire are the landscapes that lost their fire-stick shapers: in coastal western Tasmania, for instance, rainforest began resuming its former place once Aboriginal people had been driven from the land, while further inland, what had been plains reverted to scrub once their burning regime ceased.

SHAPING THE ENVIRONMENT

At the end of the Pleistocene period, about fifteen thousands years ago, humans had formed the landscape and the animal life that Europeans would later 'discover'. People were most numerous along the northern, eastern and south-eastern coasts; Tasmania was less densely settled than the mainland, and the central deserts probably supported the smallest populations of all. Of course, these landscapes were very diverse, and posed distinctive challenges to their human occupiers: what was true of coastal people was not true for desert people, and differences were just as profound between the tropical and subtropical north and the colder south. While there were continuing migrations and contact throughout most of the continent, Tasmania became more isolated once the land bridge was cut, a contention strengthened by the survival of the

Tasmanian tiger, a marsupial predator that, on the mainland, lost its ecological niche to dingoes. Tasmania's Aboriginal people also followed their own path, abandoning some practices – including the use of bone tools – and developing others, especially the use of highly specialised rock products quarried on the west coast and carried inland. It seems they gradually stopped eating fish, and made much greater use of the seals and sea birds that proved better sources of fat and energy.

By the eighteenth century, there were over two hundred distinctive languages spoken in Australia, though the importance of inter-group networks means that many of the first people were bilingual or multilingual. Some Aboriginal societies were highly mobile, others were more sedentary, especially in the kinder seasons of autumn and winter. Beach people were oriented to the sea, and their dugong- and turtle-hunting, canoeing and fishing gave them very different lives from hill people who might live only a hundred or so kilometres inland. In the deserts, people moved between waterholes. Along inland rivers, they gathered at billabongs. On the coasts, they built huts for enduring the northern summer's wet season or the south-east's winter storms.

It is important to try to understand Australia's first human societies in context and in their own terms. It is also important to move beyond meaningless and often ridiculous comparisons that privilege certain kinds of ingenuities and inventions – the wheel is a good example – over others, such as efficient canoes, bird-snares or fishing traps. Indeed, careful examination of some sites has indicated a much higher degree of environmental manipulation than had previously been assumed: at Toolondo, in western Victoria, for example, drainage systems first observed by Europeans in the 1840s included large artificial channels that drained swamps and allowed the harvesting of eels and other fish at collecting points. The drains also served to retain water – and the eels that lived in it – during droughts. At nearby Lake Condah, there was a complex system of fish traps. We must start by asking what Aboriginal people did, rather than what they did not.

It is just as vital to see Australia's first people as actors, and to reduce the distance that has often been assumed to separate these so-called hunting gathering groups from the 'agricultural' societies of Europe. To do so means casting them in a drama about decisions and choices, a drama in which they shaped and reshaped their environment. The first people were – and had to be – resilient, resourceful and adaptive. They were hunters, gatherers, foragers, fishers and farmers in particularly demanding environments. They faced hunger in hard times, and reliance upon one kind of food could bring disaster. Managing those demands meant

7

developing technological responses: the manufacturing of portable and durable tools, for instance, and the exchange of tool-making techniques with other groups. Variations in resources also encouraged adaptive foraging, so that people broadened their diets to take in insects, nuts and seeds. Fruit, roots, tubers and vegetables had to be found, processed and, where possible, propagated. In tropical areas, yams and coconut trees were planted around camping places, and many groups seeded yams and other useful plants in areas outside their normal range. In the arid deserts, fruit was dried and stored, and seeds were turned into breads and biscuits for easy transport. Fish, eels and animal meat were dried and wrapped in leaves. Aboriginal people made use of more than half of Australia's plant species for staple food. Survival depended upon and reinforced an intense study of local ecologies, climates and food reserves and, in turn, the development of strong traditions to guide the successful exploitation of resources. Put simply, you had to know where everything was or would be, or the people with whom you lived might not survive. There was a lot to know, and this meant that those presumed to have knowledge and wisdom, especially elders, held considerable weight.

Emphasising their dynamic use of the environment has also led to a re-evaluation of the complex relationships that must have existed between the different family, kin and language groups who lived in different parts of the continent. Communal feasting and exchange rested upon the organising of food surpluses and in turn food storage, while decisions about labour, and the distinctive contributions that men and women, or old and young, might make to collective fortunes, were just as important in mobile societies as in sedentary agricultural ones. Work and ritual were both organised around gender differences. Later observers sometimes noted the strong reliance of men upon women's almost constant labour, and comparisons with other similar societies suggest that Aboriginal women played the major role in most activities, including fishing; only the hunting of large animals was an exclusively male pursuit. If men provided meat, women provided most of the rest of the food. Some goods were exchanged and traded, and different groups specialised in the acquisition and production of particular items: ochre, special stones for axes or for seed-grinding, shells, wooden weapons and pituri, a mixture of nicotine-containing leaves and ash. There is also strong evidence of cultural exchange, with ceremonial forms and rituals being adapted and revised along travel routes. All the while, particular forms of food – yams in some northern areas, cycad seeds along the Gulf of Carpenteria, fish along the eastern reefs, or eels further south – took on great importance as markers of membership and place.

Aboriginal people used the resources of their environments to make meaning and identity, as well as food.

Overall, Australia's first people did relatively and perhaps remarkably well. They developed flexible economies that could withstand the ups and downs of a somewhat capricious environment. In the ten thousand or so years preceding European arrival, when the evidence is most solid, their living standards, diets and health were probably little different from those of ordinary people in Europe and may have exceeded them. Infant mortality was high, but Aboriginal adults would usually expect to see their fortieth and perhaps their fiftieth year, which roughly equalled the life expectancy of Europeans. Their social organisation rested upon families and clans that wrapped each individual into strong networks of obligation and kinship. Some groups were patrilineal, descending from a male ancestor; others were matrilineal and traced descent through mothers. In these networks, as was true in other human groups at this time, lost biological family members were replaced by fictive ones, restoring accepted patterns of authority and responsibility based upon age, gender and role. If the most intimate relations were with a band of perhaps two or three dozen people, a broader link joined such groups into clans with a shared ancestral history and a country based on a focal point of origin. All of this established the significance of knowing who you were in terms of the people with whom you were linked, and it emphasised lines of descent and identification. This further strengthened the hand of older people, and with it the power of tradition and acceptance. But the evidence of material culture suggests that this did not weaken the capacity for innovation and inventiveness. By commonly agreed measures – living standards, longevity and adaptability – Australia's first people were probably among the most successful of the billion or so humans who lived on the earth in 1770.

CIVILISATION

Aboriginal people lived in a world of their own making, and they understood, shaped and celebrated that world in increasingly diverse ways. Over hundreds of generations, boundaries between groups turned into differences of language and customary practice. Evidence suggests that while some of those boundaries were fluid and relatively open, others were more tense and had a history of antagonism. Even those could be porous at particular times; in dry years, different people might be allowed to cross a boundary to find water.

In Victoria, for instance, the Kulin people of the central and western districts and the Kurnai people of the south-east seem to have had little contact and a good deal of conflict; Kulin influence – over language, tool-making and art – spread north to the Murray and Darling basins, among the Tjapwurong groups, and west into South Australia, but did not spread east into Kulin country. There was also a clear boundary between the patrilineal Kulin and the matrilineal Mara peoples of the south-western coast, but this boundary seems to have been characterised by greater ceremonial and social interaction than was true of the Kulin–Kurnai division. The control of interaction and the creation of identity also sparked more complex cultural differentiation in art and technology. In times and places of scarcity or competition over territory, or in conflicts over sexual and family relation-ships, differences – and a concern for the power of enemies' sorcery and malevolence – sparked hostilities, abductions and even killings. Again, we need to be careful about making too many assumptions, but in Australia, as was also true in much of North and South America, hostilities were normally enacted in highly ritualised forms of combat, arbitration, compen-sation and treaty-making, and within clear boundaries that ruled out the kind of escalating slaughter that characterised European warfare.

Ancestry and group identification were the most crucial aspects of belonging. Stories of creation still trace lines of descent to female and male spirit ancestors, the makers of mountains and rivers, and the namers of plants and animals, who taught the people their Law. Among the people of the north, there is Imberombera, who arrived on the Arnhem Land coast with her children, yams and roots, Djan'kawu, a man and his two sisters who brought sacred objects from Bralgu, the island of the spirits, and found fresh water by plunging a digging stick into the ground, Giroo Gurrll, part man and part eel, Waramurungundji, who came from the north-west by canoe, and the giant Rainbow Serpent, who formed the rivers and gorges as she wound through the soil. In the south, there is Ngurunderi, who established the Law. In Tasmania, Laler created kangaroos, while Moinee, defeated in heavenly battle by Dromemerdeenne, came to earth. Joined by his wife, he made the first man, Parlevar.

In terms of understanding stories of origin, our evidence is much stronger for the Holocene period (from about fifteen thousand years ago), and for certain areas and groups. It is important not to imagine or portray Aboriginal people as homogenous and static, and it is possible that the cultural forms best known to us through the work of archaeologists and anthropologists are the product of major cultural changes in the last five or six thousand years. However, their different cultures and faiths had some strong similarities, and they shared significant common ground with those of other peoples in other continents whose fortunes relied as heavily upon the bounties of the earth. In general, Aboriginal people made sense of the world through beliefs summarised as The Dreaming. This was not a single belief: different groups had different dreamings. But the common elements are crucial: life emerged from – and returns to – earth and water; the world was formed by ancestral beings with whom all people share kinship; there was a point of origin or creation, and at that point began a law that defined both the relationships between all things and the ways in which humans should live. Accordingly, these stories told of great ancestors who had created both the world and the means of life, who taught humans how to do things, and who continued to exist in spiritual form. Their every action and decision – walking, sleeping, digging – formed the landscape that people would come to inhabit. The ancestral places of creation and rest were linked by lines of movement, song and story. Some Dreaming beings stayed in place, others travelled, but the entire world was informed and explained by their presence. Individuals were affiliated from birth with specific beings and with the other people of their Dreaming. Through their Dreaming, people had country: sometimes land, sometimes land and sea. They shared a place and a time. They were centred by sites of great significance, which had to be maintained and celebrated through rituals of song, dance, painting and the sharing of wisdom. Some symbols and rituals were public, but others were very secret.

Aboriginal people lived in a world of intense symbolism and meaning. Culture was shaped by the desire to honour and please those who held human fates in their hands, by a fear of the evils that carelessness and disrespect might unleash, and by a preoccupation with the fertility of people and land. In stories about rising seas and failing land, for instance, the greed and foolishness of humans was blamed: in one South Australian region, the medicine man Gumuduk made salt water inundate the country of the people who had kidnapped him and his rain-causing bone. The events of life – birth, coming of age, marriage, death – were of great moment and demanded elaborate marking of passage. There was much vital information, and many secrets, that had to be stored and passed down.

These were cultures – or different forms of a similar culture – that emphasised interdependence, and the ties that bound people together. They also aimed to mould people's relationships with the natural world through rituals that would alter the elements and affect the behaviour of animals. As such, they emerged from – and in turn helped people understand – the particular challenges and opportunities of Australia's environment. These were cultures full of possibilities, which etched, painted and carved their meanings into rock in a very similar way to the earliest inhabitants of Europe. At Koonalda, on the Nullarbor Plain, or in the Snowy River Cave in eastern Victoria, or at Mount Gambier in South Australia, there are carvings that stretch back tens of thousands of years, while the rock art of Arnhem Land is held by some archaeologists to be the most prolific and complex in the world. There are representations of humans and animals, along with narrative compositions of dancing and hunting, while later developments included the so-called X-ray paintings, in which external and internal features are displayed, or the highly detailed Wandjina art of the Kimberley. Art re-enacted the great and small events that had shaped the world and gave it meaning. So did architecture; in Victoria, northern Queensland and other places, Aboriginal people constructed mounds from rocks or shells that served as monuments and markers and expressed again their intricate mapping of the land.

Based on all that we now know, it is not unreasonable to suggest that Europeans largely failed to understand the societies they encountered in the seventeenth, eighteenth and nineteenth centuries. This was not because those societies were primitive or inferior, but because they were richer in cultural than material creativity. Europeans came looking for the wrong kind of civilisation. Disappointed by what they saw, they assumed civilisation itself was absent.

Illustration 1.1   An example of rock art from the Northern Kimberley
Source: Gordon Donkin collection of photographic slides, National Library of Australia, nla.pic-vn3821624.

1770

The patterns of Aboriginal life were complex and dynamic. Australia's first societies produced their conservatives and pessimists, alongside their optimists, wanderers and puzzlers. Within the last few thousand years before Europeans found their Great South Land, it is likely that its first people experienced a slightly less variable climate. There is strong evidence that one major language group spread across the central deserts from the west, while in the east, increasing population meant the occupation of more places, less mobility, and a greater degree of permanent or semi-permanent occupation. Archaeologists and historians generally agree on an increasingly intensive occupation of the continent, with new types of tools, weapons and artefacts, greater use of food processing and the settling of a wider range of sites and offshore islands. The use of local materials produced more technological differentiation and with it reasons for exchange. Eighteenth-century evidence suggests that highly populated areas with relatively stable resources, such as the Sydney Basin, saw considerable interaction between different groups, following kin and Dreaming links, as well as more ceremonies and dances. At the same time, those groups were also defining their language and cultural boundaries more sharply. Rock art supports this claim, with a trend towards more regionalised styles. In other parts of the continent, such as Groote Eylandt and the islands off the northern coast and in the Torres Strait, people were developing more regular interactions with outsiders, as Macassan fishing fleets seeking trepang (sea cucumber) carried away and brought in sandalwood, pottery, glass, pearls and shark tail. There was strong Indonesian influence in the Kimberley and Arnhem Land, and even stronger links between New Guinea and Cape York. Australia's first people were always selective. They took some things – fish hooks, skin drums, canoes – and not others: pigs, or bows and arrows, for instance.

In almost every part of Australia, the first people lived in their country. The Aboriginal societies of Australia were not dormant, or backward, or awaiting the arrival of the Europeans so that history could begin. They were not waiting for discovery, and they were making a future that did not depend upon European ideas, goods or knowledge. They would meet – but only some would survive – the shock about to come.

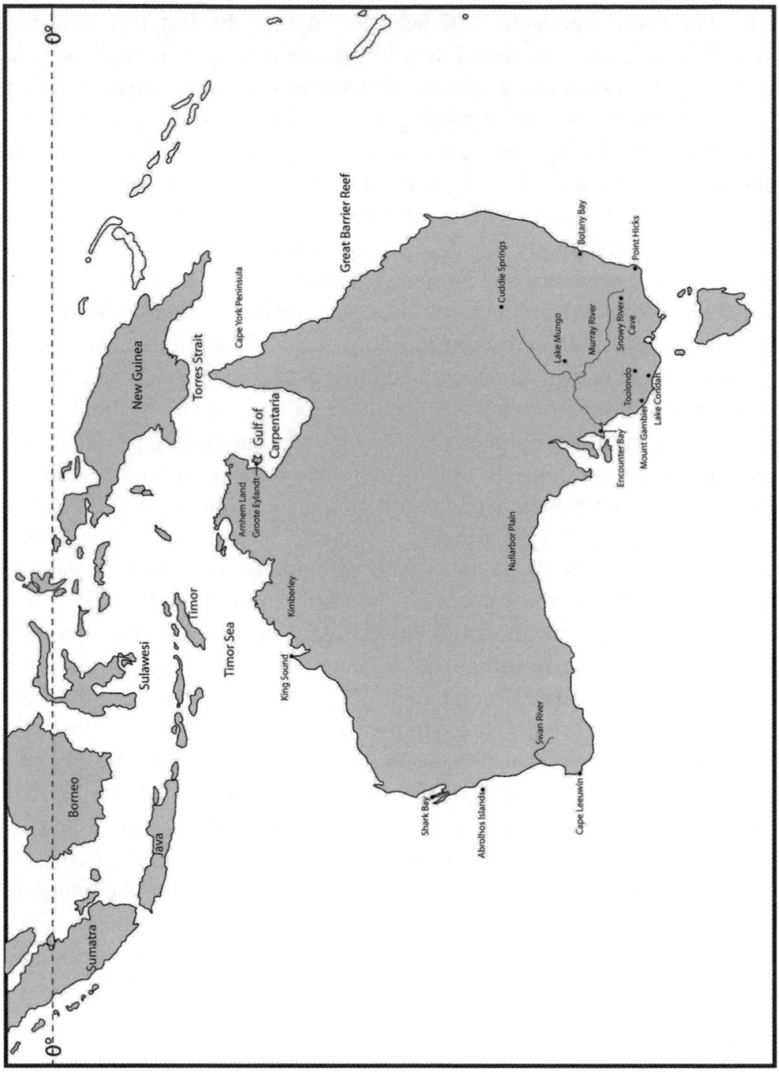

Map 1 Australia before Europeans

2

. . . .

The Great South Land: 1500–1800

The usually violent possession of other people's land took Europeans across the Atlantic and into Africa and Asia during the fifteenth and sixteenth centuries. In time, seamen would begin to stumble upon Australia's north-west coast. While some were victims of weather or miscalculation, others were more deliberate in their search for islands of gold and other riches south of Asia. They could draw upon the uncertain descriptions of Chinese, Arab and Greek cartographers, as well as the suppositions – if not the actual arrival – of Portuguese sailors. The 1494 papal demarcation of the globe, which gave Spain most of the Americas, also granted them possessions in the Spice Islands, so Spanish ships struck out westward from Peru and Panama in search of a 'continent towards the south'.[1] Expecting to find a populous and fertile territory, they first encountered the Moluccas and New Guinea. By 1550, French priest Pierre Desceliers' world map included a southern land illustrated with strange inhabitants and stranger creatures, and Nicholas Desliens showed it again in 1566, labelling it 'Java la Grande' and using its empty heart as the place for the scroll bearing his name. These and other maps were enticements, tailored to increase the thirst for expansion that had come to characterise the competition between Europe's empires and newly divorced faiths. Yet the actual outlines of the Great South Land remained unclear. When Spanish explorer Luis Váez de Torres travelled along New Guinea's southern coast in 1606, kidnapping 'natives' and claiming territory for his king, he probably sighted Australia, but did not recognise the distant shore as anything more than another island.

With their rich East Indies trade to defend against competitors, and occupying the most southerly of Asia's European bases, the Dutch became most interested in *Terra Australis*. First encounters, though, suggested few prospects. In 1606, Captain Willem Janszoon was reported to have said of Cape York that 'there was no good to be done

Illustration 2.1 A map of Australia from Nicholas Vallard's Atlas, 1547
Source: John Oxley Library, State Library of Queensland, Image number: 696149.

there', and from 1616 other Dutchmen – Dirk Hartog, Frederick de Houtman, Jan Carstenzoon, Willem Van Colster, Pieter Nuyts and François Thijssen – added further features and Dutch honorifics to the emerging European map of Australia.[2] But they could offer no cogent reasons to land there. Those who arrived did so inadvertently; when the British ship *Tryall* ran onto reefs off Western Australia in 1622, for example, less than a third of the crew made it back to Java. In 1629 the Dutch ship *Batavia* was wrecked in the Abrolhos Islands and its captain, Francisco Pelsaert, sailed to Batavia to organise a rescue. Some of the crew left behind then massacred other survivors before being overcome and executed by their returning captain. In a telling indication of what this strange coast was thought to merit, two of the mutineers were marooned on the mainland. The Dutch were persistent, though Abel Tasman's voyages in 1642 and 1644 produced little further joy for his sponsors in the Dutch East India Company, save an island named for the Batavia Governor-General Anthony Van Diemen. Further shipwrecks – and the ensuing search for survivors – stranded more Dutchmen on the western coast in the 1650s and the 1690s. Willem de Vlamingh surveyed the Swan River in 1697, and Martin Van Delft visited Melville Island and the Cobourg Peninsula in 1705.

English adventurer William Dampier made two visits to the continent now known as 'New Holland'. In the 1680s, Dampier joined one
of the global raiding parties that was picking at the edges of Spain's
increasingly precarious empire. Leaving Manila and the Spice Islands,
he spent part of 1688 in and around King Sound on the north-western
coast. Well-written accounts of adventuring were very popular in the late
seventeenth century and, following the publication of his *New Voyage
Around the World* in 1697, Dampier was given another opportunity to
see New Holland, this time as a British explorer with the blessing of the
Admiralty and command of HMS *Roebuck*. His 1699 visit encompassed
a greater amount of coastline, but did little to shake his unfavourable
opinion. Arid and barren, this new land scarcely supported 'the misera-
blest People in the world', with 'the most unpleasant Looks and the worst
Features of any People that ever I saw, tho' I have seen great variety of
Savages'. Europeans had not often been more disappointed by the people
they encountered, though even here Dampier strove to find evidence of a
recognisable social order: among these New Hollanders, he reported in
A Voyage to New Holland, there was at least one 'who by his appearance
and carriage ... seemed to be the chief of them, and a kind of prince
or captain'.[3] But in general these 'savages' showed nothing that might
excite Englishmen – or Dutchmen – interested in useful commodities,
profits and potential customers. With its northern and western coasts
inscribed on European maps, along with fragments of the southern coast
and Van Diemen's Land, New Holland and its people were left alone.

ENTER BRITAIN

The British occupation of Australia awaited a changing conception and
form of empire, in which even apparently barren territory had more purpose.
Exploitation and commerce were not abandoned, but the usefulness of land
was also measured in its strategic bulk and location, and the prospects it
afforded for imperial growth. William Dampier's accounts of New Holland,
along with the records of earlier explorers and adventurers, were re-read
in the light of a desire to possess, occupy and make use of the lands they
described. At the same time, European Australia's beginnings reflected the
growing interest in the sciences of natural order and natural history. It is
important to remember that the advance guard of British conquest was made
up of floating laboratories and botanical collections, not just ships of war.

Scientists also planted flags and inscribed names, and their interest in
recording, picturing and sampling new landscapes never implied their

Table 2.1 Major European explorations, 1600–1802

Year(s)	Leader	Where
1606	Willem Janszoon	Gulf of Carpentaria and Cape York Peninsula
1606	Luis Váez de Torres	Torres Strait and New Guinea
1615	Willem Schouten	New Guinea
1616	Dirk Hartog	Shark Bay area, Western Australia
1619	Frederick de Houtman	Coast of Western Australia
1623	Jan Cartenszoon	Gulf of Carpentaria and Groote Eylandt
1627	François Thijssen	Southern coast
1642–4	Abel Tasman	Van Diemen's Land and northern coast of Australia
1688	William Dampier	King Sound
1696–7	Willem de Vlamingh	Rottnest Island and Swan River, Western Australia
1699–1701	William Dampier	Coast of Western Australia and New Guinea
1770	James Cook	Eastern coast, Great Barrier Reef and Torres Strait
1772	Marc-Joseph Marion Dufresne	Tasmania
1773	Tobias Furneaux	South and east coasts of Tasmania
1777	James Cook	Southern Tasmania
1788	Jean-François de La Pérouse	Botany Bay
1792–3	Antoine Raymond Joseph de Bruni d'Entrecasteaux	Southern coast of Australia and Tasmania
1796	Matthew Flinders	Coastline around Sydney
1798–9	Matthew Flinders and George Bass	Circumnavigated Tasmania
1801–2	Nicolas Baudin	Western and southern coasts
1801–2	John Murray	Bass Strait and Port Phillip
1801–2	Matthew Flinders	Circumnavigation of Australia

Source: Michael Pearson, Great Southern Land: The Maritime Exploration of Terra Australis (Canberra: Environment Australia, 2005), pp. 20–8, at www.nla.gov.au/exhibitions/southland/All_Voyages.pdf.

future preservation. As in North America – which was, of course, the conquering and colonising experience that Britons knew best – claiming the land signalled an intention to change it. Indeed, their sense of North America's history led eighteenth-century Britons to imagine their empire as possessing distinctive traits and capacities, especially in regard to settlement. Compared with Spain's great tributary empires of silver mines and slaves, or the unsuccessful faltering of New France, or the fortified trading posts of the Dutch and the Swedes, Britons laid down sturdy, thriving and agricultural civilisations. Theirs was an empire charted by explorers and conquerors, but secured for the future by settlers. For all of the colonies produced by Europe's relentless expansion from the fifteenth to the nineteenth centuries, much depended upon timing and the competition between empire-seekers. It very much mattered that it was the eighteenth-century British, and not the Spanish or the Dutch, who decided to move beyond coastal reconnaissance in Australia. The imagined future of those supposedly unclaimed lands rested on a new kind of union between science, governance and empire, which was at this stage most strongly developed in Britain.

The voyage that would claim Australia for Britain exemplified this union. It was developed and advocated by the Royal Society and the Admiralty, and combined an expedition to the South Seas to observe the transit of Venus at Tahiti with an extension of the voyage to the west, in order to determine the existence and scope of the southern continent. As leader, the Society suggested Alexander Dalrymple, of the East India Company, who had emphasised the importance of Torres' findings in *An Account of the Discoveries Made in the South Pacifick Ocean, Previous to 1764* and brought the issue to the attention of Joseph Banks, already a noted naturalist, who returned to London in 1767 from expeditions to Newfoundland and Labrador. Dalrymple wished to command the voyage, but the Admiralty insisted on one of its own. It chose James Cook, a young lieutenant and veteran of the Seven Years' War. After participating in the siege of Quebec in 1759, Cook impressed his naval superiors with his surveying and cartographic capacities, particularly his mapping of the almost impossibly jagged coast of Newfoundland between 1763 and 1767. He was the ideal man for a voyage dedicated in large part to observation and mapping. The Society urged the inclusion of Banks, 'a Gentleman ... well versed in natural history'. He was joined on the expedition's ship, the *Endeavour*, by two naturalists (a Swede, Daniel Solander and a Finn, Herman Spöring), an astronomer (Charles Green) and the artists Alexander Buchan and Sydney Parkinson, as well as two of his family's Lincolnshire tenants and two 'Negro servants'.

The party furnished itself with the materials for natural science: 'a fine Library of Natural History' was taken on board, as well as 'all manner of devices for catching and preserving insects and fish', 'a strange apparatus understood to be made from a telescope, which, put into the water, enables the viewer to see the bottom with amazing clarity' and 'many cases of bottles and stoppers' to 'preserve specimens in Spirits'.[4]

The *Endeavour* completed its observations at Tahiti and, sailing westward, encountered and circumnavigated the islands of New Zealand, of which Cook took formal possession in ceremonies of tree carving and naming. Cook resolved to 'steer to the Westward until we fall in with the East coast of New Holland' and on April 19, 1770, one of his lieutenants, Zachary Hicks, sighted the point that would bear his name.[5] The *Endeavour* followed the coastline, seeking safe harbours. It made landfall in late April at what became called Botany Bay, giving the further stamp of science to the coast. Further landings were made to the north, before the ship entered into the passages and shoals that separated the coast and the Great Barrier Reef. Damaged by a reef in June, the *Endeavour* was beached and repaired, and then proceeded, rounding and naming Cape York before hoisting 'English Coulers' at what Cook called Possession Island.[6]

As Cook found in this journey along its eastern coast, the southern continent contained sufficient oddities to occupy his natural scientists and their artists. Before taking possession of a land he decided was sufficiently promising to label New South Wales, Cook did what British explorers imagined they should do. He mapped and took soundings, so that others might follow. He landed, and to mark his arrival he broke the silence of as yet 'unused' shores with axes and guns. He and his crew forayed into the bush, to hunt and shoot mostly unrecognisable animals and birds; one 'Beast', the kangaroo, proved particularly interesting and, as Joseph Banks reported, 'dress'd for our dinners, prov'd excellent meat'.[7] The ship's hogs feasted and fell ill from unusual vegetation. Cook also pondered the future. It was to be one, he supposed, of agriculture and civilised settlement. He was sure that the country 'doth not produce any one thing that can become an Article in trade to invite Europeans to fix a settlement upon it', but by the same token 'this Eastern side is not that barren and Miserable country that Dampier and others have discribed the western side to be'. Cook claimed that 'most sorts of Grain, Fruit, Roots &ca of every kind would flourish here' and that cattle would also do well. This was a land 'in the pure state of Nature', he wrote, which could be transformed by the 'the Industry of Man'.[8]

Cook established sovereignty over the country in the name of George III, and signalled its future as a British landscape. He had separated New Holland from New Guinea, found both where land did and did not exist, and added the east coast to Europe's map of the southern continent. He met great praise upon his return to England, though it was Joseph Banks more than Cook who became the public hero of the voyage. Banks was a little more circumspect about the land's potential; in his journal, he had decided within a day of the first sighting that its 'gentle sloping hills' had 'the appearance of the highest fertility' and 'seemed to be cloth'd with trees of no mean size'.[9] But after several weeks he concluded that 'barren it may justly be call'd and in a very high degree'. He spent some days 'botanising' but with varying degrees of success; he also took his greyhound into the forests to hunt small animals. There was 'no want of trees', he reported, 'but all of a very hard nature'. He concluded that 'New Holland, tho' in every respect the most barren countrey I have seen, is not so bad but that between the productions of sea and Land a company of People who should have the misfortune of being shipwreck'd upon it might support themselves'.[10] It was a less than glowing endorsement.

DISCOVERING THE INHABITANTS

Cook always followed proper dictates. In claiming sovereignty of the land, he did not ignore or preclude the questions that international law and custom asked about the status of new territories. He was also fully aware that the land was inhabited. The nature and degree of that habitation were crucial questions, which much affected how and by what means possession could be claimed. From the fifteenth century onwards, dealings with Indigenous peoples had been a subject of much debate among European colonisers, whether in the Americas, Africa or the Pacific. The fact that people inhabited those territories meant something in law, faith and practice. There were differences between legal possession and illegal seizure, and religious authorities had made clear that Indigenous people had both souls and reason. In any encounter with a newly discovered people, there were questions to be asked and answered.

Certainly, the men on the *Endeavour* took a very different view of New Hollanders to that of Dampier seventy years before. These were humans in British eyes, though not particularly industrious or civilised ones. Striving to place them in a hierarchy his readers would comprehend,

21

Banks reported that they 'were blacker than any we have seen in the Voyage tho' by no means negroes'.[11] It was not that they were lazy, more that to European eyes they rested too lightly upon their landscape, using rather than subduing it. Cook emphasised that they knew 'nothing of Cultivation' and Banks described the country as 'thinly inhabited'.[12] But that did not strip them of their rights, especially when their land was to be possessed by a civilised and civilising people – such as the British – who expected to decide the complicated issue of their status on the basis of careful, judicious observation. That is why the voyage of exploration and discovery was so important: it set in train the process of gathering and managing evidence that was so crucial in deciding the future of any territorial acquisition. The short ceremony at Possession Island in 1770 did not forever resolve questions about who owned the land called New South Wales; it simply concluded that no other European power should hope to establish itself there.

Cook, Banks and the other Europeans on this voyage often showed their impatience with the Indigenous peoples they met, and their willingness to use force at the slightest provocation made them churlish and even danger-ous temporary neighbours for the people who already lived along this coast. These were people they misunderstood, in large part because they assumed the absence of attributes – leadership, faith, authority, a sense of ownership – rather than the possibility of their different expression. They were not disposed to respect moral and cultural differences and their own accounts of their time in New South Wales make clear that they were often hostile and usually clumsy. But their reports were not without favour. Cook wrote of the inhabitants that while 'they may appear to some to be the most wretched people upon Earth ... in reality they are far more happier than we Europeans'. They lived, he wrote 'in a Tranquility which is not disturb'd by the Inequality of Condition; the earth and sea of their own accord furnishes them with all things necessary for life'.[13] Indeed, comparisons with Europeans could take a turn in their favour. Banks called them 'happy' and 'content with little nay almost nothing'. But where nineteenth-century Australians would see a lack of possessions as evidence of savagery, eighteenth-century Britons could see the 'natives' in a more positive light, as people 'removed from the anxieties attending upon riches'. 'From them', Banks argued, 'appear how small are the real wants of human nature'.[14] Not for the first time, non-Europeans could be held up as an example of what Europeans were sacrificing to undue luxury and vice. At the same time, Cook, Banks and others accorded the New Hollanders some prospect for improvement. It would take another forty or fifty years for Australia's Indigenous people to be regarded as irredeemable.

COMPLETING THE PICTURE

James Cook would return to the Pacific and Antarctic Oceans between 1772 and 1777 to further establish the boundaries of *Terra Australis*. From 1785, French navigators began their own Pacific expeditions. The first, by Jean-François de Galaup, Comte de La Pérouse, mirrored Cook's emphasis on science and carried astronomers, geologists, mathematicians and physicists alongside its natural scientists. It arrived at Botany Bay just after Arthur Phillip's First Fleet. The meeting was courteous enough, and the British ship *Sirius* carried La Pérouse's journals back to London, whence they were sent to Paris. Heading for New Caledonia, the French expedition was wrecked in the Santa Cruz Islands. In 1801, the French arrived again, when Nicolas Baudin and Jacques Hamelin captained two ships (carrying nine zoologists and botanists) and travelled westward along the southern coast. In Encounter Bay, in what became South Australia, the French met Matthew Flinders, sent by the British Admiralty to complete the exploration of the southern coastline from west to east. Flinders had already made his reputation – and earned his name on geographical features – by exploring the coastline around Sydney and establishing that Van Diemen's Land was an island. Now, as he touched down along the coastlines between Cape Leeuwin and the settlement at Sydney, proceeded north along Cook's route, and then sailed west, south and east to return to Sydney, he completed the first undisputable European circumnavigation. It was Flinders' view that the 'whole island' he had established should be called Australia, 'as being more agreeable to the ear, and an assimilation to the names of the other great portions of the earth', but popular usage – and his publisher's conservatism – gave his subsequent book the title *A Voyage to Terra Australis*.[15] Flinders died in 1814, but his name for the continent was endorsed by the then Governor of New South Wales, Lachlan Macquarie, who recommended its use to the Colonial Office. In 1824 – not such a long time in the complicated world of British administration – the Admiralty decreed that the continent and country was officially and forever to be known as Australia.

Explorations sparked the imaginations of other explorers, who in turn shaped the perceptions of those who would decide what to do next. Expeditions were one thing. The decision to follow them with conquerors and settlers was another. In 1770, and still in 1785, the place and role of New South Wales in Britain's empire was a matter for debate. The question of the rights of the people who already lived there was not yet settled. Nor was the shape of its future.

3

Britain's Prison: Convicts, Settlers and Indigenous People, 1788–1802

In the middle of January 1788, the First Fleet arrived at the place James Cook had labelled Botany Bay. There were eleven ships, and the more than one thousand people on them had spent nearly eight months on their voyage from Portsmouth. Their leader, Captain-General and Governor-in-Chief was Arthur Phillip of the Royal Navy. He carried the literal and figurative seeds of a new colony, including cattle, sheep, goats and hogs, and an 'Assortment of Tools and Utensils'. He also carried instructions that specified his most immediate objectives: securing his people 'from any attacks or Interruptions of the Natives', 'the preservation and safety of the Public Stores' and the 'Cultivation of the Land'. Phillip was directed to use 'every proper degree of economy' and to transmit accounts to the Treasury so that 'the propriety or expediency of granting further supplies' might be ascertained. He was further enjoined to send a 'small Establishment' to Norfolk Island, more than a thousand kilometres into the Pacific, in order to 'prevent its being occupied by the subjects of any other European power'.[1] The Island's timber and flax resources made this double colonisation all the more attractive.

Phillip's initial explorations of the recommended site, Botany Bay, made clear its limitations. The soil was poor and dry, there was no reliable source of water, and the site felt too exposed, no small matter when other European powers were considered a potential threat. Phillip chose to move the colony north, to Port Jackson. On January 26, 1788, the First Fleet unloaded itself on the shore, named Sydney Cove in honour of the British Home Secretary. Two weeks later, on 7 February, the entire colony was assembled to hear the reading of the royal commission. There was a triple discharge of muskets – one of the most frequent acts

24

of the first Europeans was to fire guns to break the silence that always seemed to accompany civilisation's absence – and an address by Phillip to the Marines. He then addressed the convicts, telling them that 'by industry and good behaviour, they might in time regain the advantages and estimation in society of which they had deprived themselves' and that the 'infant community' was an excellent place for reformation, being 'removed almost entirely from every temptation to guilt'. Having already witnessed what he described as 'illegal intercourse between the sexes' and a 'general profligacy of manners', he also strongly recommended marriage.[2] The officials and officers then had dinner.

In time, Phillip would remember 'the contemplation of order and useful arrangement, arising gradually out of tumult and confusion' as 'large spaces are opened, plans are formed, lines marked, and a prospect at least of future regularity is clearly discerned'.[3] Yet the order he had been sent to impose took some time to achieve, and it was not the pastured Englishness imagined by James Cook back in 1770. Cook's version of New South Wales' prospects had been supplanted in British minds by another: an appropriately far-flung end of the earth for unwanted felons. America's Revolution had robbed Britain of its usual place of banishment; as Britain's gaols and even the convict hulks moored on the Thames filled with thieves and brigands, New South Wales became the replacement. Joseph Banks had first promoted the idea in the late 1770s, and it was then taken up by James Matra, who had sailed on the *Endeavour* as a midshipman. These were important opinions, and what they suggested solved an important problem. Whatever the other attractions – timber for British masts, a possible home for the thousands of loyalists displaced by the new United States, nearness to the lucrative East Asian trade, or a means of staring down the inquisitive French – it was Britain's need for a new overseas gaol that mattered most, especially given the substantial cost and difficulties involved in transporting convicts half-way around the world. At the time of its creation, this was New South Wales' most important potential contribution to the ambitions and functions of Britain's empire.

THE PEOPLE OF SYDNEY COVE

The first white settlers were more than seven hundred male and female convicts (including nearly two dozen of their children), the two hundred and fifty Marines who would guard them, some of them bringing wives and children, and the officers and officials who would plan, develop and regulate the penal colony. New South Wales was not the product of adventurers and mavericks, but of administrators, surveyors and people accustomed to doing their duty, along with people who had broken the law. They had come to Sydney Cove together, but the first Europeans in New South Wales could trace many different journeys. There were Irish and Germans, Welsh and Scottish, as well as English. There were Catholics and Jews, Anglicans and Nonconformists. Some were lifelong servants of empire, such as the Hanoverian surveyor Augustus Alt, who laid out Sydney and the new settlement at Parramatta, twenty-five kilometres upstream from the cove, or John White, a navy surgeon with ten year's experience who organised the hospital and preserved many of the convicts against scurvy, dysentery and the effects of their long confinement, while also keeping a journal and collecting specimens of birds, animals and plants.

These men, and others who came to New South Wales, had spent years in imperial work, in Africa, the West Indies, North America, or India. Some of the marines, too, were long-term builders and defenders of Britain's empire: David Collins, who had been at Bunker Hill in 1775, was the new colony's Judge Advocate, responsible for creating a legal system. He would, within two decades, write *An Account of the English Colony in New South Wales*, found a new colony in Van Diemen's Land and become its Lieutenant-Governor. George Dawes, wounded during the American War of Independence, came to the colony as an engineer and surveyor, built an astronomical observatory, made maps, built batteries at the entrance to Sydney Cove and explored the mountains that ended Sydney's coastal plain. He also made careful study of the local people, whom he knew as Eora: their term for 'here in this place', which they used to tell the outsiders where they were, was misunderstood by the British as a statement of identity. Dawes left the colony in 1791, after conflict with Phillip. He spent more than forty years in further service to the empire, first in Sierra Leone and later in Antigua. Captain-Lieutenant Watkin Tench, whose journals are one of the most significant sources of information about the colony's first years, had been imprisoned by the Americans in Philadelphia in 1778 and later served in the West Indies. His was no accidental writing career; before leaving on the First Fleet, he arranged with the London publishing house Debretts to write a book. His *Narrative of the Expedition to Botany Bay* appeared in 1789, securing three editions and translation into French, German, Dutch and Swedish; *A Complete Account of the Settlement at Port Jackson* followed in 1793.

While we know less about those who failed or faltered, late eighteenth-century careers and aspirations could clearly be very fluid, especially on the relatively blank canvas of New South Wales. Reverend Richard Johnson, for example, was thirty-five years old, and had graduated from

Cambridge University in 1784 before being appointed as Chaplain to New South Wales. Johnson became one of the colony's most successful farmers, built his own church, and, with his wife, taught the colony's children. One of Principal Surgeon White's assistants, William Balmain, combined surgery and hospital maintenance with terms as a magistrate – in both Norfolk Island and Sydney – and as Registrar of Exports and Imports, land acquisition, the buying and selling of rum, the supervision of orphanages, captaincy in the Sydney Loyal Association, the private chartering of a trade ship to India and small commissions earned as the Sydney agent of a London trading company. He also managed to fight – and survive – a duel with White, and successfully treat Arthur Phillip's wound from a 'native spear' in September 1790.

The largest single group, of course, were the convicts. The First Fleet's cargo was the first of many. It included some who prevailed and prospered, and others who quickly died or struggled to adapt to what were often terrible circumstances. There was Esther Abrahams, convicted for stealing lace, sixteen years old and the mother of a ten-month-old daughter, who would live with George Johnston, a Marine lieutenant, and eventually receive land in her own right. On the *Friendship* was Elizabeth Thackery, about twenty and from Manchester, a stealer of handkerchiefs, placed in irons at times during the voyage, who would serve her time, move to Van Diemen's Land, and marry. There were men of enterprise, like James Squire, a remarkably unsuccessful Surrey thief and a very successful brewer and seller of liquors after the expiration of his sentence. Or James Ruse, transported from Cornwall for stealing watches, who would develop a successful farm at Rose Hill and receive the first grant of land in 1792. There were teenagers; Matthew Everingham, the servant of a London attorney, was convicted of stealing two books and had spent three years in the Thames hulks before being selected for transportation at the age of seventeen. And there were convicts who would use their resourcefulness to different ends, such as Mary Bryant, a thief who would in 1791 undertake a remarkable journey from Sydney to Timor in a stolen boat, eventually reach London and be pardoned. More troubling still was the West Indian John Caesar, who took to the bush in 1789, returned, absconded again, was sent to Norfolk Island, came back to Sydney, ran away again, this time forming a runaway gang, and was eventually pursued and killed in 1796.

Between 1788 and the ending of transportation in the middle of the nineteenth century, around 160,000 convicts were sent to the Australian colonies, about half of those directly to New South Wales. About twenty-five thousand were women. More than forty thousand were Irish and Catholic at a time when either quality invited prejudiced disdain, and a particularly high proportion – around twenty per cent – of the Irish were women. Not all convicts came from the British Isles: perhaps one in fifty came from Italy, Sweden, Denmark and other European countries or were, in the language used by a colonial official, 'Negroes, Malays, Mohammedans, Hottentots, Asiatics' or 'Pagans' from Jamaica, Malta, Calcutta, French Canada, the Cape Colony, Mauritius or Gibraltar. Hundreds were West Indian servants accused of stealing from their London masters and mistresses; others were British-born 'coloureds' who worked as cooks, footmen, maids and servants.

If Britain's elite assumed that the problem of overcrowded gaols could be solved only by transportation, few could even begin to acknowledge that the crimes filling those gaols stemmed mostly from poverty and inequality. Eighteenth-century Britons and Irish lived in a world where the poor – the great majority of the population – paid a heavy price for their frailties or failings and in which women, children and the vast army of unskilled labourers were always vulnerable to disaster. This was a population criminalised by desperate necessity, not depravity. They were incarcerated for the sins – and sometimes the protests – that stemmed from persistent need, and sometimes for taking things that fifty or a hundred years before had been the property of everyone. They were also incarcerated because Britain's legal codes generated large numbers of criminals who did not merit death but for whom there was as yet neither another effective punishment nor a 'penitentiary'. Banishment – first to the Americas and then to New South Wales – was a useful middle ground between hanging and freedom.

Evaluations of the convicts' backgrounds and character have taken an interesting course, which traces Australians' changing sense of their past. In the nineteenth century and well into the twentieth, a convict heritage was frequently a source of shame, except where transportation could be portrayed as a matter of political conscience, or as one of the many injuries suffered by the Irish, the Scots and the Welsh at the hands of the English. This was a past more often denied than embraced; it was a 'convict stain' that few Australians wanted to own, especially in places such as Tasmania where the proportion of people with convict ancestors was relatively high. Schoolbooks and historical accounts assured Australians that any legacy the convicts might have left had been overcome; they were merged in with the pioneers and settlers, and their stain was washed away by the flood of free emigrants during the 1850s. Of convict women, often described in the surviving sources as actual or potential prostitutes, the less said the better.

Novelists, poets and historians began to break that silence in the 1950s and 1960s, installing the convicts at the beginning of a more triumphantly

Illustration 3.1 'Convicts Embarking for Botany Bay', early 1800s
Source: Rex Nan Kivell Collection NK228, National Library of Australia, nla.
pic-an56012547.

independent national story: as victims of Britain's class-bound cruelties, the convicts were merely the first of those who left behind an old country's dark satanic mills for a new life, more prosperous and successful than they could otherwise have enjoyed. Their fate was deplored as a prime example of British injustice; eventually, it seemed that almost every convict had stolen no more than a handkerchief, at worst. Convict women were also reclaimed and rehabilitated, as the victims of injustice and sexual subjugation. By the 1980s, convicts were the subjects of a flourishing genealogy, and to be descended from one was becoming a source of pride. With the publication of Robert Hughes' highly successful and deliciously overstated *A Fatal Shore*, everyone knew just whose side to be on. At the beginning of the twenty-first century, an impossibly high proportion of the Australian-born population claims – perhaps yearns for – convict forebears.

Historians have located the truth somewhere in between the gloomy anxieties of the past and the righteous indignations of the present. It has been important to question the contemporary sources that portrayed convicts as all of one type, often emphasising their depravity or, among the women, their sexual impropriety, and to look for evidence that provides a more accurate picture of their origins and circumstances. Most of New South Wales' convicts had committed some form of theft; a few were forgers, frauds or insubordinate soldiers and sailors. A very small proportion were 'political' prisoners who had taken part in protests or dared to form trade unions. Convicts were a mix of first and repeat offenders. Around a quarter had been transported for life, the rest for seven or sometimes fourteen years. They were largely young – only one in seven was thirty-five or older when they arrived – and mostly unmarried. Many had been displaced by the powerful storms of Britain's agricultural and industrial revolutions and suffered from the rapid fluctuations of largely unregulated markets for labour and the materials of life. Careful analysis of convict lives and personal histories, much of it gathered in the musters taken as they arrived, suggests that they were particularly likely to come from that group of people who were already mobile; having been dislodged from villages into Britain's growing towns and cities, they were part of a new urban working class. On the evidence, they were more literate and skilled than average Britons. Like the thousands of foreign-born transportees, many were already migrants and many brought useful capacities to the new colony, capacities that would in time prove very important. As the colony's most important source of labour and enterprise, convicts built the fabric of the free society they would inhabit once emancipated and in which their children would be educated and find their way. Almost from the first, they had a hand in determining what New South Wales might become.

SETTLING CONVICT SYDNEY

Whatever the qualities of the convicts, Sydney Cove very nearly became a disaster. It is a common feature of Britain's first settlements – Roanoke Island and the first Virginian settlement at Jamestown are the obvious comparisons – that first fleets are too slowly followed by second and third convoys to feed and replenish them. Food was a problem from the first; the Europeans identified little of the native fauna and flora as edible, despite some attempts by the Eora people to educate them. Few of the convicts – and fewer of the marines and officials – had farming experience, the cattle brought from the Cape strayed into the bush, and hunting parties were insufficient to feed the thousand or more people, most of whom were put to heavy labour. With starvation a growing possibility, Phillip sent the *Sirius* to Cape Town for supplies and introduced rationing. In early 1789, seven of the marines were tried and executed for robbing the stores, and rations were reduced by one-third in November. There was drought, and a movement of marines and convicts to Norfolk Island was organised to relieve the pressure at Sydney. With the *Sirius* wrecked off the island in March, 1790, and further ration reductions, HMS *Supply* was sent to Batavia in April. People starved, and they stole.

In June came the Second Fleet. It carried rations and the first detachments of the recently-formed New South Wales Corps, but of the thousand convicts who had left England, 267 had died and nearly five hundred were too sick to leave the ships. No more 'horrid spectacles' had been seen in New South Wales than these emaciated and lice-tormented survivors, many of them carried into a tented temporary hospital near the landing place.[4] The masters and naval agents of the Third Fleet, which arrived between July and October in 1791, managed to kill fewer of their charges, and after some initial shortages – and yet another supply mission, this time to Calcutta – the extra labour of another 1800 convicts would prove crucial in making the settlement sustainable.

Survival encouraged consideration of the future. If this was to be a gaol, what did that mean in practice? In the Americas, which had received perhaps fifty thousand convicts between the *Transportation Act* (or *Piracy Act*) of 1717 and the outbreak of the American Revolution, criminals had been sold as servants to farmers and planters. Yet Arthur Phillip's instructions suggested a rather different nature and scope for this new penal society. This was to be a prison, but an ideal and cost-efficient one that would morally improve its inmates. Phillips's instructions were clear: he was to ensure the transplanting and development of a British society in New South Wales. This included the 'due observance of Religion and good order', encouraging more women to accompany ships to the new settlement (so long as the ships' officers did not 'exercise any compulsive measures, or make use of fallacious pretences'), and the direction that emancipated male convicts were to receive a grant of land (fifty acres for married men, and a further ten acres for each child) 'free of all Fees, Taxes [and] Quit Rents' for ten years, along with further donations of provisions, tools, seeds and livestock to ensure a viable beginning.[5] From 1792, Phillip was permitted to make land grants to the marines. He also begged British authorities to allow and encourage the migration of free settlers. The first – five single men and two families, comprising three farmers, a millwright, a gardener, a black-smith and a baker – arrived in 1793. They were the first unconvicted and non-serving Britons to be given free passage to the Australian colonies.

By the middle of the 1790s, and with increasing momentum after 1800, the convict system mixed together various forms of servitude, with some convicts labouring on roads, buildings and other public works, some assigned to free settlers or marines as domestic and farm servants, and still others trusted to run farms, work as surveyors and serve as a colonial police force. Whatever their status, most convicts survived as best they could. People who are not free have always resisted the terms of their bondage, and so did Australia's convicts, at least within the ambit of what was reasonable. They negotiated, bargained and lied. They worked slowly and ineptly for bad and cruel employers, more willingly for those who treated them well. They complained about poor treatment and used gossip and scandal to blacken reputations. They tattooed themselves, believing that they possessed their bodies if nothing else. Assigned to private settlers, they regarded themselves as temporary servants, not slaves, and they insisted on their rights. In time, convicts were allowed a 'ticket of leave', a combined probation and work release that allowed them to sell their labour, marry or bring their families out from Britain. Further good behaviour could bring a conditional pardon. The majority of convicts repeated the basic social, moral and emotional patterns of the society that sent them, but also refashioned them in a place that allowed conventions to be challenged and fixed social positions to be overcome.

Convicts were agents of their own fortune, at least to some extent: if they were not powerful, they did not totally lack power, and most imag-ined themselves as maintaining the rights of freeborn Britons. The first civil action in New South Wales was taken by two convicts of the First Fleet, Henry and Susannah Kable, against a captain, Duncan Sinclair. They claimed that a parcel of goods worth fifteen pounds and belonging to them had been plundered while on board his transport. In England, they would have been unable to sue because they had been sentenced to death and, even though the sentence was reduced to transportation, the felony attaint persisted, and barred them from holding property, giving evidence or suing in court. In New South Wales, they were not only allowed to sue, but did so successfully, Judge Advocate Collins finding 'for the Plaintiff, to the Value stated by him in the Complaint'.[6] New South Wales was British, but even at this very early stage of its invention it was not Britain.

Clearly, this was to be a permanent and agricultural settlement, in which the incarcerated, most of whom were transported for set periods and not for life, would be remade, especially as farmers and farmers' wives. New South Wales was an exile, but one that could end. The tension between rehabilitation and punishment would dominate early colonial life, along with two other very important questions: for whose benefit the convicts might be employed, and the precise meaning of freedom in a society made up of those who weren't free, those who had been made free, and those who had never lost their freedom. The convicts, sent to what seemed the ends of the earth, were meant to suffer their expulsion. They lived in a penal colony, which, once it could feed itself, wavered between a possible reward for good conduct and a certain retribution for bad behaviour. Their world included daily spectacles of punishment and shame, men and women wearing iron collars, and streets trod by chain gangs.

All of this bears remembering in assessing the nature of convict society. Convicts suffered privations and punishments before, during and after transportation. They were exiled from their homelands and sent further than anyone had ever been sent before. Some made successes of their lives, or simply prevailed long enough to be freed, no small victory given the rigours of English gaols, the hulks, the voyage and the raw new colony. Some returned to Britain, their sentences served, and tried to re-place themselves within what they had known before. Others stayed on, unable to afford or perhaps to contemplate a return. But many failed. The traumas of punishment and detachment were strong and their imprint could ruin lives. If we remember the men and women who survived convictism, and those who gained freedoms and benefits from transportation they would never have enjoyed in Britain, we need also to remember those who did not, as well as the drifters, inebriates and loners who never could mend what had been torn.

There were others who could never accept their station and their fate, who rebelled or simply said 'no more'. For them, there were greater cruelties still. They were hanged in public, or they were flogged to the limit of what they could bear and then flogged again. Bloodied convicts were paraded through the streets. They were branded and had their heads shaved or were put into leg irons. For women who re-offended and proved 'delinquent', as well as those who could not be found assignment as servants, there was the confinement and hard labour of the Female Factory at Parramatta.

There was more organised and violent resistance, most notably the uprising at Castle Hill in 1804, when convicts, including some who had been involved in the Irish Rebellion of 1798, seized arms and ammunition and gathered for a march on Parramatta. Overcome by a contingent of the New South Wales Corps, some were executed, and others were flogged and sent to the Coal River chain gang. Convicts rebelled in other ways. Some absconded, hard as that was in a small and surveillant settlement. Some tried their luck with the local people, or disappeared into the unfamiliar bush, often to return when they could find neither escape nor sustenance. The most adventurous dreamed of places where people lived unchained, unlashed and free of masters, and fled Sydney or Parramatta to find them.

POSSESSION AND OWNERSHIP

Neither James Cook nor Arthur Phillip would have agreed with the contention that British sovereignty meant that the people already existing in New South Wales would relinquish all rights to the land. Certainly, as no other European power occupied the land, there were no legal or moral barriers, in British minds, to the act of taking possession. The descriptions of Aboriginal life made by James Cook, Arthur Phillip, Watkin Tench and others mixed positive with negative, though they always underscored the inferiority of the people they encountered. They were ruled by the assumption that Europeans were civilised Christians and 'natives' were not. Yet the precise nature, status and future of those people were not decided once and for all in 1770 or 1788. Important questions remained, and awaited the more thorough investigation that actual occupation would allow. Phillip's instructions were clear on this point: he was 'to endeavour by every possible means to open an Intercourse with the Natives and to conciliate their affections, enjoining all Our Subjects to live in amity and kindness with them'. Phillip was also to punish any Britons who should 'wantonly destroy' or give 'any unnecessary Interruption' to them. Finally, he was to 'endeavour to procure an account of the Numbers inhabiting the Neighbourhood of the intended settlement and report your opinion . . . in what manner Our Intercourse with these people may be turned to the advantage of this country'.[7] This set of directions signalled Britain's right to possess and occupy the land. It provided those who already lived there with limited options, and it ensured that British interests would play the leading part in whatever decisions were made about their future. But it remained, for that moment, open to debate.

Two questions were immediately important: how numerous were the inhabitants, and what kind of people were they, in terms of customs, habits, faith and intelligence? If they were very few, and mere savage nomads, then there were few barriers to a properly conducted occupation. But if they were larger in number, and closer to Europeans than William Dampier or Joseph Banks or even James Cook had described, the conduct of that occupation would need to be different. On the first question, the local people were more numerous than expected. On the second, First Fleet officers like Watkin Tench recognised that if they were not yet 'enlightened by revelation and chastened by reason', they might be capable of it. They manifested, Tench wrote, 'consciousness of a superior power' and belief in the immortality of the soul; more important, when attending a church, 'they always preserved profound silence and decency, as if conscious that some religious ceremony on our side was performing'. Tench argued that on issues of advancement and acquisitions, 'they certainly rank very low', but also that they 'possess a considerable portion of that acumen, or sharpness of intellect, which bespeaks genius'.[8] Moreover, even if their footprint upon the land was not quite what a European would call 'settled', they did seem to have a sense of possession, at least in common, and a strong identification with particular country or what Tench called 'their own pale'.[9]

These early moments of contact were a mix of apprehension and curiosity. The people of New South Wales were not easily drawn into the 'intercourse' recommended by the King, and Phillip and others recognised that this stemmed in part from their dislike and possibly their contempt for the British arrivals. At times, the British recognised their own clumsiness, or despaired at the ways in which the convicts and even the marines acted stupidly, criminally and in haste. These were fraught and complicated interactions, so people both grabbed at instances of apparent understanding and tended to assume the worst of any misunderstanding. The British found it difficult to explain a 'civilisation' they took for granted as superior. A few had greater insight. Phillip, in particular, and despite being the victim of a ritual punishment spearing that injured his shoulder in September, 1790, seemed to grasp the fact that the people of Port Jackson had every reason to resent the British; 'they think perhaps', he wrote, 'that we cannot teach them any thing of sufficient value to make them amends for our encroachments'.[10] But Phillip's eagerness to fulfil his duties also led him into his own clumsiness, such as kidnapping local men Bennelong and Colbee in an attempt to ensure a conversation from which languages and customs might be ascertained. Assaults upon the colony sparked punitive expeditions, with little thought to what bands of armed Britons might signify to the Eora and against the advice of those, like William Dawes, who had begun to argue that such military incursions tended to inflame rather than cool the tensions that rumbled through Port Jackson in the first years of its occupation.

At this time, there was no final, authoritative decision on the questions of ownership. It would not, in the end, matter, because it was already becoming clear that some Britons would refuse to recognise that the Eora or other Aboriginal people had any right to land or indeed to remain where Europeans wished to go. It was also becoming clear that they would engage in violent rather than legal dispossession, and then expect the law and its enforcers to protect what they had gained. Later European Australians would derive much comfort from the convenient fiction that Aboriginal people were savages who did not own the land and had to give way before the necessary advance of civilisation. A careful assessment of the evidence, especially the words written down by the Britons of the First Fleet, makes clear that the momentum of misunderstanding, revenge and retaliation that turned Australia's frontiers into a killing zone for so much of the nineteenth century stemmed from choices and decisions, not from inevitabilities.

Of course, the story of that frontier – as it first emerged along the shores of Port Jackson and as it moved north, south and inland – must also be told from the other side, with Indigenous people as actors rather than passive bystanders. It is difficult to imagine the shock that must have accompanied the arrival of the Europeans among a people who may well have believed that they and the close-by groups with whom they traded and spoke were alone on the earth. Who were these strangers, and from where had they come? What should be their welcome, or their warning? Some tried to explain how things were done, and the best ways to live in a land they knew best. The people of Port Jackson danced and chanted, trying to explain by providing maps and histories in song. They wondered at the ineptitude of the strangers, and at their peculiar customs. These newcomers were clumsy, and often destructive. Some of them stole, and had little sense of boundaries, and few seemed to understand the basic principles of hospitality and reciprocation. They were needy and inflexible, and even the most careful of them was prone to ignorance. The shock of their arrival was compounded by the diseases they carried: smallpox and measles almost destroyed some of the clans around Sydney, while sexual contact – sometimes willing, sometimes not – brought gonorrhoea and syphilis. Europeans disrupted hunting and fishing territories, put up fences and spoiled waterholes. Little wonder, as Phillip found, that local people's dislike of Europeans tended to increase upon 'discovering that [we] intend to remain among them'.[11]

MEETING THE BRITISH

Aboriginal reactions to this invasion were as complex as any other people confronted by occupying Europeans. Some were curious, adapting

European tools and metals, going out to meet and bargain with the new arrivals, taking advantage of new foods like flour and new hunting animals, like cows and sheep, which lacked the agility of the kangaroo. Others drew back and kept away. For some, the arrival of strangers brought novelty; young people, more daring and less nervous, became negotiators and 'translators' and influential before their time. Others found Europeans dangerously uncontrolled and quick to violence.

In general, Aboriginal people tried to incorporate Europeans within their own ways of living in the world, and into accepted systems of exchange and hospitality. They also tried to negotiate with them along the established lines of mutual respect for territory, which meant trying to minimise, contain and, when necessary, ritualistically express inter-group conflict. In some places, they suggested that Europeans might live in a hunting plain, or along a watercourse, but they expected this to mean continued common access to the resources that were found there. If there was one thing that a number of observers noted, it was the very great consternation caused to Indigenous people by fences, and by what fences symbolised, as well as the ferocity with which the British defended them.

The evidence suggests that the people of New South Wales, first the Eora, the Carigal and the Dharug, and then the other people of the nearby coasts and hills, initially tried as best they could to accommodate a troublesome and very needy group of newcomers, whose numbers increased with each of the ships that landed at the place they knew as Warrung. As such, their experience and approach was very similar to the other peoples who first encountered the English in North America, such as the Powhatan in Tenakomakah (Virginia) or the Algonquian tribes in Massachusetts Bay. Uncertain at first, these societies also tried to accommodate the new arrivals, but gradually became less welcoming as the disruptions caused by Europeans increased. Many observers in New South Wales noted that Aboriginal people were rarely impressed by European life and expressed little desire to assimilate into European society. It is more likely that they expected the British to eventually depart, or, in adapting themselves to the land, to recognise the superiority of Aboriginal ways. But that prospect receded as settlers, convicts and soldiers kept arriving, and as Aboriginal people realised that the newcomers did not wish to share the land, but to own it and occupy it for themselves. Once that discovery was told and retold up and down the Aboriginal side of the frontier, there could be little hope of bargaining with these invaders. They were here to stay, and so were their fences, their guns and their possessive habits. In the end, these two civilisations could not share the same country because one refused to share the bounties and fruits of the land.

As also occurred in Virginia and Massachusetts Bay, the realisation of European permanence came at the very moment when the full impact of their diseases made it difficult to drive them away. In New South Wales, strong traditions of self-sufficiency and occasional hostilities between different clans and family groups also made a full-fledged defence of land more difficult. But if there was no full-scale assault upon the colony at Sydney Cove, or the farms and huts strung out along Port Jackson to Parramatta, there was certainly resistance. All of the observers – whether or not they were sympathetic – recognised that the Eora and others defended their territory, even if that defence took a form and strategy that the British could not always recognise. Warnings and symbolic assaults were escalated by British reactions, and by 1792, Pemulwuy and other resisters were engaged in a sustained campaign against the settlers. Pemulwuy was, Judge Advocate Collins noted, 'a most active enemy', though Collins also recognised that much of the trouble was caused by the settlers' misconduct, clumsiness and ignorance.[12] Against their enemy, the British adopted the practice they had used in North America: the collective punishment of the Bediagal people by military force, whatever the extent of their involvement and however understandable their hostility. There was the organised violence of punitive raids and the disorganised violence of settlers with guns and a presumed license to shoot.

After leading a raid on a government farm in 1797, Pemulwuy was tracked, wounded and captured, but escaped. In 1801, he was outlawed and a reward was offered for his death or capture. Pemulwuy was finally shot by settlers during the winter of 1802. His head was cut off and, it was reported, sent to Governor Philip King and then to England. Indigenous resistance did not end, and would flare along each and every frontier for generations to come. But as the story of Pemulwuy's fate was shared, and as the clans and families looked east from their country into the British colony, they must have known that things had changed. Whatever they thought of British customs and goods, and whether or not they wanted to live among or near them, they realised that savagery had entered their land.

4

. . . .

Free and Unfree: Reforming New South Wales, 1803–29

In 1803, New South Wales founded a new colony in southern Van Diemen's Land. With the French still hovering, it seemed sensible to occupy the continent's southern fringe, and Lieutenant John Bowen led a small party to Risdon on the Derwent River. One month later, David Collins, who was commissioned to form a settlement on Bass Strait, arrived in Port Philip Bay. Unimpressed by his first site, near what is now Sorrento, and finding his second, near today's Frankston, almost as unwelcoming, Collins reloaded his ship with hundreds of convicts and soldiers and sailed south for Van Diemen's Land. Selecting a site several miles south of Risdon, Collins founded Hobart Town in February 1804. The Risdon settlement was abandoned six months later, and Lieutenant Bowen left. As at Sydney, Hobart's first years were difficult; it was another starving time.

Whatever Collins' difficulties, and Bowen's disappointment, expansion was perhaps the least taxing of the challenges that faced New South Wales as the colony entered its second and then third decades. The work of forming an efficient and effective colony continued, but the meanings of freedom and unfreedom – which were always of major significance in a penal society – were persistent sources of anxiety. A society of gaoled was also a society of gaolers, but with more and more free settlers, some of them men of considerable wealth, it was also a society of those who wished to use the gaoled for profit. In time, it would become a society in which some wished to soften the legacy of forced transportation, and even bring that form of gaoling to an end.

EARLY SYDNEY

By the end of Sydney's first decade, voluntary migrants were arriving from Britain, while some of the gaolers and guards, and some of those they had once guarded, were leaving once their sentence or service was ended. Former prisoners, termed 'emancipists', were taking up grants of land and labour, and some were assigned their own convicts in turn. Native-born children added another complication to the social structure. At this time, when relatively few were free, the economic and political opportunities afforded by freedom were great indeed, something realised by men like John Macarthur, who resigned his post as Superintendent of public works in 1796 and took up more than eighty hectares near Parramatta to farm and begin his breeding of sheep. Macarthur's pugnacious attitude made him a dangerous enemy to anyone who stood against his plans for the future of the colony, but he was not without his supporters.

In the hiatus between Arthur Phillip's departure in 1792 and new Governor John Hunter's arrival in 1795, the officers of the New South Wales Corps began reconstructing New South Wales. They established a form of military rule and steered the still battling colony towards a system of publicly funded free enterprise based partly on farming – the Corps received land grants as well as convict labour – and partly on rum, which, in the absence of sufficient coinage, had become the colony's chief means of exchange. If the Corps controlled the courts and the public stores, and the Corps controlled the rum, then they controlled the colony. There was little anyone could do against them. Governor Hunter tried and failed; recalled to Britain in 1800, he rather pointedly remarked that he 'could not have had less comfort, although he would certainly have had greater peace of mind, had he spent the time in a penitentiary'.[1] The Corps also defeated the next appointee, Philip Gidley King, who encouraged agricultural experiments and further exploration and favoured the granting of opportunities to the emancipists. He tried to control the illicit manufacture and trade of alcohol. He also tried to deal with John Macarthur, who had wounded a superior officer during a duel and was sent to England to stand trial in 1801. Undaunted, Macarthur spent several years rebuilding his London social and political connections. He resigned his commission in 1805 and returned to the colony, bearing a grant of twenty square kilometres in which to continue his wool-breeding enterprise.

Even at the beginning of this new century, Australians tended to imagine and debate their future in light of what they knew about other parts of the British world. John Macarthur was particularly concerned that New South Wales develop along the lines of the former North American colonies, where convicts were used as labour in enterprises that would generate public and especially private wealth. In Macarthur's mind, the colony would and should depend upon its entrepreneurs and honourable gentlemen. Such men would need governments to maintain the supply of cheap and compliant labour and protect private property. Macarthur attempted to resolve the colony's problems of authority and legitimacy in his own terms. He desired economic success, but he also wanted a stable social and political hierarchy, in which inferiors obeyed their betters and where those never gaoled – who would become known as the exclusives – maintained their advantages over the emancipists. In his eyes, the future of New South Wales ultimately depended upon the extent to which it protected the economic and social fortunes of enterprising people such as him.

Not for the last time in the Australian colonies, however, local initiative went too far. The battle over beginnings was not to be decided by the New South Wales Corps, and those planning the future of the colony in London desired a balance between private and public interests that better suited the existing and potential interests of Great Britain. They had not intended that the colony become a kind of militarised distillery, and they were troubled by the growing conflict between the governors and colonists over land leases and property rights. Where Hunter and King had tried to accommodate clashing interests, new governor William Bligh asserted his prerogative. At the same time, he slurred the reputations of the New South Wales Corps; in a society where honour and regard were a man's most important possessions, this was risky indeed.

So, in January 1808, the Corps marched on Government House and placed Bligh under house arrest. It was a coup d'état. The fingerprints of John Macarthur, whose wife Elizabeth famously described Bligh as 'violent, rash [and] tyrannical', were fairly obvious to everyone.[2] That Bligh had his moments of maverick and martinet behaviour was no news to his superiors in London, but this was sedition, however much Macarthur claimed to be defending the colony's liberties. Undermining governors was one thing; actually deposing them was quite another. Bligh would not give in; told to sail HMS *Porpoise* back to London in early 1809, he instead went to Hobart to gain the support of Lieutenant-Governor Collins. Collins refused. Bligh floated in the harbour. Macarthur and his supporters ruled Sydney. Tiring of the Corps and the disruptions in New South Wales, the Colonial Office recalled both Bligh and the Corps, and sent in another regiment, the commanding officer of which would become Governor. In early 1810, nearly two years after Bligh was deposed, Lachlan Macquarie was instated. The rule of law was restored, and the colonists were reminded of British authority.

Matters of honour were at stake in this conflict, and so was the future of New South Wales. Part of the battle took place in Australia, but part of it continued in London; John Macarthur had gone there in March, 1809, and, knowing that he would be arrested if he returned to Sydney, spent eight years in England. His was an unusual situation, but it signals the continuing links between the small but growing colonial elite and the empire's centre. People like Macarthur would for a long time live in and between two worlds, despite the great distance of the four- or five-month voyage. Poorer migrants – and most of the convicts – left England knowing they might never return. The soldiers and military men would survey, build and protect Britain's offshoots wherever they were sent. But elites accepted no such severing. Their sons were sent to English public schools. They travelled to London securing favours, negotiating trade and exchange, attending clubs and seeking advantageous marriages for their daughters. They studied law. They had relatives, friends and useful acquaintances at the empire's heart and in some of its other branches: the Cape, India, Canada or Singapore. The empire's networks were sustained over very long distances, not least because they were very important resources in the struggle for social and economic position in Sydney.

Macarthur was finally allowed to return in 1817, without apologising or acknowledging any impropriety. He found Sydney somewhat changed. The growing hunger for farms and the growing number of people able to take up land grants had pushed the colonists north and south along the coast and the rivers, and up against the Blue Mountains to the west. In 1813, a way was found through the mountains by a sample of the colony's social layers: free settler Gregory Blaxland, soldier and landowner William Lawson and William Wentworth, born at sea to convict parents but, courtesy of his father's landholdings, educated in London and already a substantial landowner along the Nepean River. By 1820, farmers, sheep and shepherds were pouring into the breach and fanning out into the western plains. Further north, former Navy lieutenant and now surveyor-general John Oxley found both dry scrub and flooded swamp along New South Wales' northern rivers in 1817, writing of its 'dreary uniformity . . . which wearies one more than I am able to express' and concluding that 'the interior of this vast country is a marsh and uninhabitable'.[3] He had better fortune in 1818, coming upon the Liverpool Plains, and in 1823 and 1824, when he explored south-eastern Queensland and named the Brisbane River.

Reluctant to permit uncontrolled expansion, the colonial government would have preferred to confine colonists to a limited range. Their version of settlement involved a closer and more managed expansion, focused on towns and outposts such as Bathurst, which was established in 1815. As had also been true in North America, imperial planning lagged too far behind colonial ambition and land hunger; by the time Governor Darling announced the boundaries of prescribed settlement in 1826, there were already hundreds of farmers living beyond them. There was little that authorities in Sydney, let alone London, could do to prevent the adventurous and the greedy from simply occupying territory. They seized the moment and took the land. They pushed the frontier into the bush, setting in train a persistent tension between these 'squatters' and those who came after them that would dominate colonial politics for decades to come. They created problems for colonial officials in Sydney, who in turn struggled to meet their instructions from London. They also sparked conflicts with Aboriginal people up and down the unstable limits of European incursion. In some places, there were negotiations and compensation for land deals. Whether or not the Indigenous people who made them were aware of what the settlers intended, all of these deals lacked any authority. In other places, of course, no such deals were struck; the settlers simply took the land and held it by weight of arms. Whether by supposed negotiation or by force, the land was taken, and those who now claimed to own it expected their rights to be defended. They created a problem that would, in time, have to be addressed.

A PLACE OF PUNISHMENT

Sydney was also changing. Governor Lachlan Macquarie (1810–21) used his power and the labour of his convicts – alongside contracts with locally powerful businessmen – to create buildings and vistas that better suited a colonial city. His vision was of an improved and improving place, its work and prospects represented in solid architecture as well as in good order, church attendance and the proper conduct of business. This was to be a civil landscape, and Macquarie's projects – complete and incomplete – are significant: new barracks for the army and the convicts, a hospital, a 'domain' of open space and a garden, parks, sites for churches, a new Government House, names for Sydney's piggledy streets and five planned towns along the Hawkesbury River. He tried to bring civilising regulation to the economy, too, and encouraged the development of the Bank of New South Wales. He also had faith in redemption, and believed that the colony's future had to depend in part on those who were becoming or would become free. Macquarie's support of the emancipists brought him talented officials, architects, magistrates and surgeons, but it hardly endeared him to men like John Macarthur.

Ideal colonies are expensive, and while the Governor's apparent liking for emancipists riled some of Sydney's elite, it was the costs of public works and the supposed self-indulgence of his vision that brought him undone in London. Macquarie survived a first report, by a Select Committee, in 1812, but was damaged by a second, undertaken by John Thomas Bigge in 1819 and 1820 and published in 1822 and 1823. Lord Bathurst, the Secretary of State for the Colonies, directed Bigge to determine how New South Wales could be managed and 'made adequate to the Objects of its original Institution' as a penal colony. The need was made more pressing by an upsurge in the number of transported convicts following the end of the Napoleonic Wars in 1815, and by the fear in Britain that transportation might be losing some of its deterrent power. Whatever the relationships being built in Sydney's complicated social landscape, men of power and wealth in Britain were determined to prevent crime by ensuring that potential criminals were terrorised by the severity of punishment. Transportation grew still more during the 1820s, partly as the result of British courts reducing their recourse to hanging; with Britain's prison system still underdeveloped, this meant more use of exile to Australia. The convicts were a little different too: the postwar stream had fewer women – only one in eight compared to around a quarter in the first twenty years – and more Irish.

Partly from the momentum established by earlier governors, and partly from Bigge's recommendations, the convict system in New South Wales shifted into a different balance between labour and incarceration under the stewardship of Thomas Brisbane (1821–5). Bigge reaffirmed the primary objective of the colony as a place of punishment. For most would come redemption: Bigge proposed that the 'moral ascendancy' of free over convict be reinforced, and argued that greater assignment of convicts to private masters would both reduce the costs of the system and ensure that convicts could benefit from the reforming example of their superiors. For the recalcitrant and those who re-offended, however, New South Wales would become a more horrible place. The penal colony generated its own places of exile within exile, with the development or re-use of prisons for those who could not be reformed and who, in the words of a later governor, Ralph Darling (1825–31), should be 'worked in irons' and suffer 'the extremest punishment short of death'.[4] These sites of 'secondary punishment' were to be characterised by stringency and brutality. Their isolation would signal their occupants' exile unto death, and make their escape impossible. In New South Wales, Port Macquarie on the north coast was one such place. In western Van Diemen's Land, the Macquarie Harbour Penal Station was set up on Sarah Island in 1822; convicts worked in its shipyards to pay their way until the station was replaced by Port Arthur on the east coast in the early 1830s. Norfolk Island, abandoned in 1814, was reoccupied in 1825 as what Brisbane called the *'nec plus ultra* [nothing further beyond] of Convict degradation'.[5]

Harsh punishment did not prevent strife; on these terrible fringes of the convict system, it probably made violence even easier for convicts to contemplate. Some of the men being transferred from Macquarie Harbour in 1834 managed to capture a ship and sail to Chile, and other, less dramatic flights augmented the ranks of the escapees roaming through the bush in New South Wales and Van Diemen's Land. Runaways and absconders had always been a problem, but by the 1820s, their growing numbers created new alarm about 'bush-rangers'. In a still raw society, in which fears about threatening outsiders – both ex-convicts and Aboriginal people – ensured that most people were armed, guns were relatively easy to steal. Authorities feared more than stealing: Governors Brisbane and Darling sent armed patrols into the bush and offered rewards for the capture of ringleaders. The problem, of course, was that while draconian systems produced fearful compliance, they also kept producing rebels, especially when rules proved unfair. In 1829, near Bathurst, convict Ralph Entwistle was flogged at the order of the police magistrate because he and a companion had been swimming naked in a river at the very moment that Governor Darling was riding by. While there was no evidence that the Governor's delicate eyes had actually glimpsed the affront of a naked convict, the men were flogged anyway. Entwistle was also denied the ticket of leave to which he had almost become entitled. In the spring of 1830, having nursed his grievance and gathered supporters among other assigned convicts, he became the head of a bushranging gang. They were captured in October, and ten, including Entwistle, were publicly hanged at Bathurst in November.

Convict women, who endured their own kind of exile in the female factories, also made trouble: in 1827, the inmates of Parramatta's Factory escalated their demand for better food and conditions into a riot. There were further disturbances in 1831 and 1833, in part spurred by the women's fury at having their heads shaved in punishment. The control of convict women grew more rather than less stringent, however, especially as assumptions about the viciousness of a few hardened into a conviction that all were in some sense depraved. Earlier, women had a number of ways to leave the Female Factory, but by the 1830s, the only possible door was legal marriage. New female factories were created in Van Diemen's Land; the George Town factory assigned coarse dresses to its inmates, with the worst classes of offenders forced to wear special marking on their sleeves and backs. In Hobart, the *Town Courier* reported 'much insubordination' at the female factory in 1826, including attempts at escape by breaking down walls. The Launceston factory, completed in 1834, had even greater problems; its superintendent reported being 'obliged to carry pistols' and having had 'my shirt torn from my back'. In 1842, its inmates rebelled and took possession of the prison. Described as 'Amazonian' by a local reporter, the women 'fought like demons' but were eventually compelled to capitulate when constables and men conscripted from the convict barracks broke through the walls.[6]

EMANCIPISTS AND A NEW BRITANNIA

To the growing number of emancipists who had made their way out of the convict system, some of Bigge's recommendations had another unsettling feature. They seemed to ignore the growing complexity of condition and ancestry in New South Wales. In and around Sydney, in the western plains and in Van Diemen's Land, an emerging emancipist elite, encouraged by former Governor Macquarie's faith in their redemption, feared that their efforts to reduce the burden carried by those with a convict past – or indeed by convicts' children – might be damaged by the new governors. It was important to convince them, and perhaps even more the British authorities who sent them, that ex-convicts and their children could not only overcome that legacy, but were valuable members of an emerging new society. Perhaps the best-known child of convicts, William Wentworth, wrote in his poem 'Australasia' that 'land of my hope! soon may this early blot, amid thy growing honours, be forgot', while also suggesting that this 'last-born infant' might be 'a new Britannia in another world'. If it wasn't elegant rhyming, it was a forceful reinterpretation of Australia's future.

Earlier, in 1819, Wentworth had published a book about New South Wales, with a telling subtitle: *With a Particular Enumeration of the Advantages Which These Colonies Offer for Emigration and Their Superiority in Many Respects Over Those Possessed by the United States of America*. Competition for imperial favour would continue for much of the nineteenth century: 'native' Australians endeavoured to find the best possible comparisons with Canada, or the Cape Colony, or New Zealand, and to find the best way to lure migrants into ships making the long voyage to Australia rather than the much shorter one to New York,

Boston, Halifax or Montreal. The reference to the United States certainly suggested a different version of Australia, in which visions of abundance and development might supplant those of gaols and criminals. But Wentworth's book was also directed at a country in which the loss of the American colonies just forty years earlier still rankled, and its suggestions about elected assemblies and the extension of British freedoms, such as trial by jury, reminded Britons of what could happen when colonial interests were overshadowed by imperial ones. Wentworth encouraged other promoters of free migration, some of whom set up private companies to raise funds, recruit families and settle them on farming land north of Sydney and west of Launceston.

During the 1820s, Wentworth and others also tried to promote and extend those parts of Bigge's reports that proposed the development of more 'normal' British freedoms and institutions. Under Governor Brisbane, and in the *New South Wales Act* of 1823, the colony gained a Supreme Court, a Chief Justice and a Legislative Council; the Council's five members were to be appointed by the Governor, but it was a start. The Council was increased to fourteen members by another act in 1828, which also decreed that all laws and statutes in force in England would apply in New South Wales. The first Chief Justice, Francis Forbes, also extended the practice of trial by jury rather than by a panel of military officers. That right was removed from the colonies in 1828; its reinstatement, alongside those other 'imprescriptive rights of Englishmen' – a free press and taxation by representation – became the focus of public meetings, pamphlets and speeches. In 1834, a speaker at one meeting in Hobart reminded his audience that 'the fountain of power is in the people' not 'a petty Aristocracy'.[7] Nineteenth-century Australians lived in a world of ideas, concepts and words derived from decades of debate in Britain, Europe and the United States. If they sounded at times like American or even French revolutionaries, or the liberal voices in Britain's parliament, it was because they understood themselves as part of that same political and social landscape and the same process of reform.

Still, it remained difficult to reconcile a version of Australia devoted to the extension and perhaps the expansion of English liberties, rights and civilisation with the visible harshness of convictism, or the fact that two in every five of the people in New South Wales were in literal or figurative chains. And the convict transports kept coming. This was still a penal society, though the growth of the assignment system, tickets of leave and the secondary punishment centres scattered most of the convicts throughout mainland New South Wales and Van Diemen's Land and took others out of sight – if not out of mind – on isolated

47

Illustration 4.1   'The First Parliament of Botany Bay in High Debate', 1786
Source: Rex Nan Kivell Collection NK1345, National Library of Australia, nla.
pic-an6589643.

islands and pinched peninsulas. But this was still a place for public
spectacles of punishment. During one year, 1835, a quarter of the
convicts in New South Wales were flogged at least once. There were
fifty public hangings a year. This was a still militarised community,
full of soldiers and police, courts martial and armed patrols. Within a
decade, the people of New South Wales would be debating how best to
end their convict days. As they did, it was this time, the time of Brisbane
and Darling, which became the shaded past New South Wales would
have to overcome.

5

New Australias: 1829–49

In the 1830s and 1840s, New South Wales and Van Diemen's Land – established as a separate colony in 1825 – edged further into the 'unsettled' lands. Australia's geography remained something of an exciting unknown; based upon previous experience, especially in North America, its explorers expected to find great lakes, powerful rivers and alpine mountains. The early impressions of Cook and Banks now seemed too enthusiastic; as the later explorer Charles Sturt put it in 1833, what appeared to 'those distinguished individuals' an 'earthly paradise' was 'abandoned by the early settlers as unfit for occupation'.[1]

But horizons always promise something more. In New South Wales, explorers pressed into the interior, to show the directions in which the colony might expand, and perhaps to find an inland sea or continent-dividing strait to which all those rivers flowing west might lead. They wanted to open up the country, breaking its supposed stillness with gunshot and axe strikes and possessing it with names and markings. Seeking the patronage of governors, but often financing their expeditions from personal funds or the benevolence of friends, young men struck out to the west. In 1824, Hamilton Hume and William Hovell established an overland route southwest from Sydney. In 1828 and 1829, Charles Sturt and Hume tracked the northern rivers of New South Wales; the puzzle of the western-flowing waters was not resolved, so in 1829 and 1830, Sturt travelled down the Murrumbidgee. Excited by the larger river – the Murray – into which it flowed, and by the junction of another large river, the Darling, he tracked it to its ultimately disappointing mouth of sandbars, mud flats and shoals. No fine estuary, just a place of 'impracticability and inutility'.[2]

Even successful explorers made their mistakes – Hume and Hovell thought they were at Western Port but were actually near Corio Bay, some sixty kilometres distant, in 1824 – and expeditions named for leaders did not always register the significance of the assigned convicts, servants and Aboriginal guides who accompanied them. But successful explorers, after naming a few features after themselves, also traced political and imperial pedigrees upon the land: by the 1850s, Australia would be known for Britain's sovereigns (Victoria), sovereign's wives (Adelaide), prime ministers (Melbourne), colonial secretaries (Hobart and Murray) and governors (Brisbane, Darling and Bourke). Explorers wrote detailed books, dedicating them to people who had been helpful in the past or might help with future ambitions. But even the successful could be defeated by what one called 'the general sterility of Australia'.[3] The names they gave places seemed sometimes like retaliation: Victoria has a Mount Disappointment and a Mount Difficult, and both Victoria and New South Wales have a Mount Hopeless.

Around Australia's edges, there were new possibilities. Not all were planned, named and surveyed. Sealers, whalers and mutton-birders made camps along known and unknown shores, mingling with Aboriginal people and sometimes staying with them. The new Australias that were forming were not yet fixed upon one future, though all would share the problems of precarious beginnings. By 1830, Van Diemen's Land, which some argued had been left to turn into a wild and lawless place of convicts, deserters, 'natives', bushrangers and beleaguered settlers, had been returned by military force to its penal purpose. In time, it would generate its own offshoots, on its north coast and the islands, and later in what would become Victoria. Hobart Town would also become one of the world's great whaling ports during the 1830s and 1840s. But Australia's most durable convict colony it would remain: when transportation was suspended to an increasingly resistant New South Wales in 1840, the stream was redirected to Van Diemen's Land, with more than five thousand – nearly a tenth of the entire population – arriving in 1842 alone. The colony's convict-ness would be asserted again in 1847, when Britain proposed ending the convict system in New South Wales and transferring any remaining prisoners south. There were protests and anti-transportation leagues, and the last convicts arrived in 1853, but even changing its name to Tasmania in 1856 could not prevent Van Diemen's Land remaining the place of convict Australia's most horrible incarnation, real or imagined. Little wonder that novelist Marcus Clarke chose Tasmania as the setting for his 1874 story of injustice and brutality, *For the Term of His Natural Life*. Tasmanians, more than any other Australians and for a longer time, would live with the convict stain.

Another convict place was created by New South Wales, at Moreton Bay. By the end of 1824, there was a depot at Redcliffe, but this was abandoned by the autumn of 1825 in favour of a site further up the Brisbane River. Unhappy with the first name, Edenglassie (an inelegant mashing of Edinburgh and Glasgow), officials decided that the names of river and settlement should concur. Also intended for retrograde convicts, this colony worked them on docks and roads, and in timber-cutting, and barred free settlers. About twelve hundred convicts, soldiers and officials lived there by 1831, but as convicts' sentences expired, they left for Sydney and were not replaced. Moreton Bay's future as anything more than a slowly shrinking prison would depend upon the settlement of free farmers and the mapping, surveying and selling of land, a process Andrew Petrie would undertake from 1837. The penal settlement ended in 1839.

To the south, there was sporadic settlement along the north coast of Bass Strait including a short-lived convict station at Western Port that was primarily intended to see off the renewed French inquisitiveness of Rear Admiral Jules Dumont d'Urville. During the 1820s, farmers in Van Diemen's Land expressed interest in a northward migration, but all requests were refused. Undeterred, and eager to exploit land that seemed promising to several visitors, a group of Launceston pastoralists and investors decided to form the Port Phillip Association and strike out for Portland Bay. The Henty family settled there – quite illegally – in late 1834, and were discovered by a surprised explorer Thomas Mitchell in 1836. It was neither the first nor the last time that Australia's colonists moved ahead of official settlement and simply took land, confident that governments would eventually recognise and protect them. In the meantime, John Batman had undertaken another illegal occupation, compounding the mischief by negotiating a treaty with the Kulin people for the use of the land. Batman was well pleased, having noted in his journal that 'the Land was as good as Land could be' and that he wanted to 'get if possible on friendly footing with them'.[4] Batman left for Launceston to gather up a larger expedition; as he prepared, a second group organised by John Pascoe Fawkner sailed from Launceston and unloaded itself at the north end of the bay. Batman showed up several days later, and the two parties decided to share the spoils. In the eyes of colonial governors, of course, the disposition of Port Phillip's land was theirs to decide, but frustrations in Sydney could not uproot the settlement that became Melbourne. Governor Bourke sent a magistrate and military commander. Gridded and surveyed, Melbourne was incorporated as a town in 1841 and grew steadily on the proceeds of wool. Sometimes labelled 'Australia Felix' to signify its agricultural promise, the Port Phillip District first tried to separate from New South Wales in 1840. The separation was finally achieved by an act of the British Parliament in 1850 and legislation passed by the New South Wales Legislative Council in 1851.

THE SWAN RIVER AND SOUTH AUSTRALIA

Other colonial ventures aimed to set themselves upon a different footing altogether. They would begin free of convictism and they would build different versions of Britain in the new land. In the continent's western half, a first establishment at King George Sound in 1826 was more military outpost than settlement. The western coast had not so far impressed most of its European visitors, though fears that the French might try to establish themselves there made some kind of colony more urgent. Captain James Stirling had the necessary enthusiasm and political connections, and his proposal for a free colony at Swan River was accepted in 1828. In the winter of 1829, the British arrived, founding the port at Fremantle and the main settlement at Perth. One of the early arrivals, Mrs Dance, chopped down a small tree as part of the founding ceremony. The new colony depended upon settlers with money, such as Thomas Peel, who would receive large land grants and bring bonded labouring families with them to create a largely self-sufficient agricultural settlement. It was not a success. The soil was sandy, crops did not take, and Stirling was forced to buy food in Batavia, India, Cape Town and Van Diemen's Land. Land clearing proved more difficult than anticipated, and too much cheap land meant that some of the agricultural labourers progressed up the social scale a little too rapidly, leaving no one to work the farms. Reports of the colony's poor prospects diverted some intending migrants to the Cape or New South Wales; Britain's migrations were always shaped by the tendency for fervent claims to create disappointment. Others who arrived drifted south and east, taking land around Bunbury, Augusta and Albany. The free colony experiment lasted only until 1846, when continuing problems encouraged an offer to Britain: just as transportation was ending in New South Wales and Van Diemen's Land, Western Australia would take British convicts, nine thousand of them between 1850 and 1868. At the colony's request, all were male, and only a very few had been convicted of rebellion or other political crime. Another request – that they not be convicted of serious crimes – was honoured only for the first few voyages.[5]

Yet plans for 'systematic colonisation', or the migration of English society in idealised microcosm – landowners, labourers, and wives – were not abandoned. The installing of new communities in the Australian colonies took on a different purpose during the 1820s and 1830s, as increasingly overpopulated Britain became the first imperial power to embrace rather than fear the loss of numbers by emigration. If Australia had first been a place for the exiled, it might now become

Table 5.1 Migrant and convict arrivals, 1820–50

	Convicts	Free migrants	Total
1821–30	32,390 (74%)	11,200 (26%)	43,590
1831–40	50,690 (43%)	66,400 (57%)	117,090
1841–50	33,325 (23%)	108,950 (77%)	142,275
Total	116,405 (38%)	186,550 (62%)	302,955

Source: W. Vamplew (ed.) *Australians: Historical Statistics* (Sydney: Fairfax, Syme and Weldon Associates, 1987), p. 4.

a place in which Britons could build ideal agricultural settlements. Australian advocates such as Presbyterian minister John Dunmore Lang drew upon the ideas advanced in Britain by Edward Gibbon Wakefield. Wanting to avoid both labour problems and the use of convicts, Wakefield proposed that land be sold, not freely granted, and the money raised be used to carry free labourers to the colony. They would work for wages and, with land prices kept high by the colonial authorities, provide labour for several years before they could afford to purchase their own properties. There must also be women and children, for ideal colonies would build upon and nourish ideal households. The image was one of a concentrated, limited and organised colony, which would have a proper social hierarchy – and reward for strenuous effort – from the beginning. Compared to the convict societies, with their wild, ever-spreading frontiers and their tribes of unmarried men, this would be a true slice of England.

Wakefield's vision was best expressed in the plans for South Australia, first settled in 1836, though he would also be influential in Canada and New Zealand during the 1840s and 1850s. By 1840, the South Australian Colonization Commission had carried more than twelve thousand people – including thirty-five hundred women and forty-seven hundred children – to the colony. Another sixteen hundred had paid their own way. If the closely settled ideal was not fully realised, South Australia benefited nonetheless from its degree of prior organisation, from the greater proportion of its settlers who brought agricultural and building skills, and especially from Colonel William Light's ability – relatively uncommon among the first founders of Australian settlements – to insist upon a site that provided reasonable drainage, fertile land and fresh water. His grid plan for the new city of Adelaide was a mirror of 1830s preoccupations, imagining not just blocks for building but park-lands, public buildings and vistas, a botanical garden and an Aboriginal

Reserve. The new colony still struggled, and was almost bankrupt in 1840. An *Act to provide for the better Government of South Australia* was passed by the British Parliament in 1842: it established a Legislative Council, secured the colony's debts and turned a £155,000 government loan into a gift. This, along with good harvests, John Ridley's new reaping machine for wheat and the discovery of copper at Kapunda and Burra, secured South Australia's future.

BRITONS AND AUSTRALIANS

In these new colonies, as well as in New South Wales and Van Diemen's Land, the social and cultural patterns of Britain were moulded to different ambitions and possibilities. So far from the empire's centre, there would always be innovation and making do, especially in those tools of communication, transport and farming that were difficult to import whole and had to be rebuilt on the ground. Australia's migrants wanted the freedom to prosper, and their relatively high levels of literacy suggest they came from that slice of British society that balanced the costs of the longer and more permanent journey to Australasia (rather than, say, North America) against the possibility of greater success, for their children if not for themselves. They were aspiring and they were also, by and large, assisted. Governments worried over the numbers of women, skilled workers and agriculturalists, and actively augmented the migrant stream by way of bounties, free passages and financial rewards. Strong chains of migration brought particular groups in large numbers: Lowland Scots, especially from Lanarkshire and Midlothian, for example, as well as Cornish miners. Its officials and agents having described a better future, government would have much to answer for if hopes were dashed.

Among the baggage nineteenth-century migrants carried across the sea, there were few more significant items than their faith. There were a few English-born Jews, but most were different kinds of Christians, a not unimportant fact in an age when denomination was not simply about doctrine but shaped belief and behaviour, including children's schooling and the choice of partners in marriage and business. Most people also drew their friends from among their congregation. Religion was also a crucial component of civilisation, and was always expected to play a major role in civilising the new land.

Yet in religious matters, distant Australia delivered a relatively large degree of tolerance, if more by muddled uncertainty than deliberate intention. While ardent advocates tried their best to spark disputes between and within denominations, there was little appetite for the importing of Britain's battles over establishment and disestablishment. If the baggage of faith was carried to Australia, not all of it was unpacked. Adherents of the Church of England might have hoped for an established church, and British authorities tended to act and speak as if it was, but growing demands for rights of political representation were accompanied by calls for religious toleration. In any event, by the 1820s, large numbers of Scottish Presbyterians and English and Welsh Nonconformists – Methodists, especially, but also Congregationalists and Baptists by the 1830s – ensured that any attempt to create special privileges would not succeed, especially in South Australia and Victoria, where the proportion of non-Anglicans was particularly high. In 1833, New South Wales Governor Richard Bourke reported that 'the inclination of these Colonists, which keeps pace with the Spirit of the Age, is decidedly adverse to such an Institution'.[6] Tolerance extended also to German 'Old Lutherans', who faced persecution for refusing to conform to the merger of the Lutheran and Reformed churches in Prussia. Seeking to leave in 1835, their timing was ideal for the South Australian Company, whose Nonconformist traditions made them very sympathetic to religious oppression; George Fife Angas declared the colony 'a place of refuge for pious dissenters'.[7] The opposition to establishment also allowed Catholics greater freedom in the Australian colonies, with recognition afforded them nearly a decade before the British Parliament passed the *Catholic Relief Act* in 1829. Sydney had two Catholic chaplains and by 1842 its first archbishop, John Bede Polding, and there were separate sees in Hobart Town, Adelaide, Perth, Melbourne and Maitland by 1847.

The colonies were sectarian, and debates about crucial matters – particularly the funding of separate education – relied upon and reinforced strong suspicions, especially between Catholics and Protestants. Men seeking election might play the sectarian card. Yet while there was never a formal separation of church and state, colonial governments practiced neutrality, or at least roughly equal treatment; as Bourke put it, people of 'different persuasions' should see government 'as their common protector and friend'.[8] In 1836, the *Church Act* settled the thorny issue of aid for religious schools by declaring that all of the major Christian denominations would receive the same consideration. Faith remained a vital force in people's lives, and a reason for prejudice and ill-treatment against those who lived in error, but even here, colonial distance tended to increase rates of intermarriage and decrease most divisions. The Australian colonies were products of the nineteenth and not the seventeenth century, and they generated neither new religions nor exclusive utopias. This was, as James Macarthur argued in 1843, a place that realised 'enlightened and truly pious sentiments', where 'all British subjects of whatever Christian persuasion' could live 'upon a footing of general equality'.[9]

THE LAND: CLAIMING, TAKING AND DEFENDING

All through the 1830s and 1840s, Australians debated the ethics of possession and dispossession. The talk was vigorous and important, for it measured in part what might be the colonies' future status and reputation in the world. As settlers collided with Aboriginal people on each and every frontier, and as each colony's founders and governors tried to bring some order to its hoped-for progress, the people who were taking the land made choices. Their descendants might claim they were driven by inexorable forces, or simply played out the inevitable triumph of a superior civilisation. At the time, and based upon the evidence, settlers and officials not only knew that they were deciding the future of the people who already lived in Australia, but also that this future was not cast in stone. In seeking friendly relations with the people of Port Phillip, John Batman also wrote a document of exchange in which the people he called 'Chiefs' were 'possessed of the whole of the Country' under discussion.[10] In South Australia, the founders promised not just a better kind of colony, but a more organised treatment of the Indigenous peoples; the King's Letters Patent issued by King William IV in 1836 made clear that nothing contained in them 'shall affect or be construed to affect the rights of any Aboriginal Natives of the said Province to the actual occupation or enjoyment in their own Persons or in the Persons of their Descendants of any Lands therein now actually occupied or enjoyed by such Natives'. Here, and elsewhere, the 'Natives' were subjects of the Crown, and accorded its due protection.

But here, of course, was the problem. Even if they were the monarch's subjects, what did words like possession, occupation and enjoyment actually mean, and upon what evidence were they to be established and, if necessary, defended? If they listened, settlers knew that Aboriginal people had a strong sense of rights over territory. The first explorers certainly saw it, and they used the obvious word: as James Stirling reported to Governor Darling of the Swan River people in 1827, 'they seemed angry at our invasion of their Territory'.[11] Or, as Van Diemen's Land Governor George Arthur advised the Secretary of State for War and the Colonies in 1832, 'each tribe claims some portion of territory, which they consider peculiarly their own'.[12] The evidence was extensive and hard to refute. Those responsible for the law were particularly likely to grasp these facts. In Western Australia, George Fletcher Moore, the Advocate General, understood the words of a local man, Yagan, in these terms:

> You came to our country; you have driven us from our haunts, and disturbed us in our occupations; as we walk in our own country, we are fired upon by the white men; why should the white men treat us so?[13]

Moore might have put words into Yagan's mouth, but he was confident that he understood the concepts. Yagan's deeds were even more forceful, and his destruction was telling. Captured for making retaliatory attacks upon settlers, he was exiled to Carnac Island in 1832, but escaped and continued his resistance. Declared outlaw in 1833 for the killing of two settlers – both of whom had previously been convicted for assaulting Aboriginal people – Yagan was shot and killed. His companion Midgegooroo had already been captured and executed by firing squad. Yagan's marked skin was stripped from his back as a trophy, and he was beheaded. His head was taken to England and displayed as an anthropological 'curiosity'. Later buried in a Liverpool cemetery, the head was only exhumed in 1997, and taken back to Australia by a delegation of Noongar people.

Up and down this and other frontiers, everyone realised that the taking of the land, and its transformation into fenced and guarded property, imperilled relations between colonists and Aboriginal people. It disrupted hunting, fishing and agriculture and increased Aboriginal reliance upon rations of flour and other food. When tensions led to violence, reprisal followed upon reprisal, and settlers, in particular, were always ready to explore new forms of savagery, with collective punishment for individual misdeeds and spectacular deterrence, such as instant and public floggings of Aboriginal men and women. The pressure also heightened conflicts between different Aboriginal clans and dialect groups; in these savage times, Aboriginal sometimes killed Aboriginal as the war over land intensified.

In Van Diemen's Land, the sporadic but severe conflicts that became known as the Black War rumbled through the 1820s, with dozens dead on either side; it was ended when Governor George Arthur declared martial law in 1828 and then attempted to push the 'formidable and

57

troublesome' Aboriginal people ahead of a 'black line' so they could be contained and captured. There were clashes, and there were killings, on the Victorian coast, around Bathurst, and everywhere the squatters pressed into the interior of New South Wales. The settlers along these frontiers, wanting secure possession and safety, sought a relatively free hand with – but protection from – the people they were dispossessing. Effectively, they wanted to be left alone when defending themselves, and protected when under attack. It was not the law, and it was not justice, but it was very often the way. And we know from settlers' letters and other accounts that some of them said it was wrong and admitted they had seized land that was not theirs for the taking. Indeed, some of them knew they were in the middle of what they described as a war; as one Van Diemen's Land settler wrote, they 'look upon us as enemies – as invaders – as oppressors and persecutors – [and] resist our invasion'. They were, he continued, 'an injured nation, defending in their own way, their rightful possessions, which have been torn from them by force'.[14]

Official policy struggled with the formation and especially the application of law. The Colonial Office might have liked concentrated and controlled settlement, but wandering sheep and a mobile population made this a difficult policy to enforce. Sparked in part by the use of maverick treaties, deals and exchanges, including Batman's, Governor Bourke issued a proclamation in late 1835 declaring them void. By reasserting, in very strong terms, the notion that only the Crown could sell or assign land that was vacant, he made clear that individual settlers could not purchase land from Aboriginal people and implied that Aboriginal people could not sell what already belonged to the Crown. In one sense, Bourke's proclamation did not entirely settle the issue, as it was not entirely clear if he meant to include 'the Aboriginal Natives' among those considered as 'trespassers' through illegal occupation. He was also following precedents first established elsewhere, and especially in North America, where eighteenth-century proclamations preventing the purchase of land from Indians were intended to protect the Crown and Indians alike from the fraudulent loss of land. The law was also developing a stronger stand on 'aboriginal title', developing a practice that acknowledged the tenure of Indigenous people but, by declaring that tenure 'uncivilised', granting the Crown the right to extinguish it. Settlers could not buy land from Aboriginal people, in other words, but the Crown – represented by the Governor – could take it away from them and then sell or give it to settlers. There would be further debate on the question of Aboriginal possession, and criticism of Britain's failure to

Illustration 5.1 'Governor Davey's [*sic*] Proclamation to the Aborigines', 1829

Source: Rex Nan Kivell Collection NK9916, National Library of Australia, nla. pic-an7878675.

predict or provide solutions for the problem of Aboriginal land rights. In local areas, there was talk of compensation, but few could agree on how much or who might pay it. But in a very important way, and whatever the ongoing discussion, the practical outcomes on the Aboriginal side of the frontier were now no longer in dispute.

More difficult still was the issue of how to police the application of the law. If lawmakers and governors adopted a policy of controlling conflict, settlers at the colonies' edges carried out their own policy of winning the land, through conflict if necessary, and defending it by force. Certainly, some settlers faced the consequences of particularly egregious acts of fraud, violence and murder, most famously in the aftermath of the 1838 massacre of twenty-eight Aboriginal adults and children by a free settler and eleven convicts at Myall Creek in New South Wales. The massacre was an example of random collective punishment: because some Aboriginal people had stolen cattle, all Aboriginal people faced retaliation. At the urging of his attorney-general, Governor George Gipps ordered an investigation, and the eleven convicts were charged with murder (the free settler remained uncaptured). The first trial resulted in acquittal, but in a second, for the murder of one of the children who was killed, seven men were found guilty of what Justice Burton described as 'a fearful barbarity which perhaps had rarely been equalled'.[15] They were hanged.

PROTECTION AND DESTRUCTION

So the law could work. But the continuing violence along the frontier made clear that colonial law and authority were not respected there. The problem was even more pressing as British attitudes towards the larger question of protecting Indigenous people and the specific nature of Australian settlement began to shift in line with a more general concern for the fate of the weak and defenceless. While slaves, or overworked children in textile factories, were among the more notable objects of this new emphasis on protection, reform and pity, colonised peoples, and especially the Australian Aborigines, were also joining the cast of forlorn characters. By 1837, there were dedicated missionary societies, and an Aborigines' Protection Society, which would over the succeeding decades consider and bewail the conditions of the Aboriginal people, as well as the Maori, the Canadian Indians, and the people of Africa, New Guinea, Melanesia and Polynesia. Their mission, broadly, was 'to ensure the safety and elevation of the uncivilized natives of those parts of the

Globe on which British Colonies or settlements are formed'.[16] As this implies, the plight of Australia's first people would be put into a global context, something of no small importance to colonists deeply conscious of their status and reputation in the British world and beyond.

This was an evangelical movement, rooted in faith and the conviction that the duties of the true believer included raising up, not exploiting and abusing, the unfortunate and the ignorant. The violent conflicts in the Australian colonies were always going to capture their attention. Indeed, some Britons were beginning to ask who the barbarians in their colonies actually were. If settlers could not be controlled, then perhaps Aboriginal people would need to be protected from them, perhaps even sheltered and kept away. And by protecting and removing Aboriginal people, reformers would also protect white people from the sinful temptations and moral damage of the violent and uncontrolled frontier. They could colonise with a clearer conscience, and repair the damage that unchristian colonising did to white souls.

This wasn't simply an issue in Australia. In 1837, a British House of Commons Select Committee on Aborigines, chaired by veteran anti-slavery campaigner Thomas Fowell Buxton, wrote a report drawing upon the work of missionaries and other observers in the Cape Colony and other British possessions. It condemned the ruthless and violent exploitation and expropriation that was taking place, asserted that Indigenous people had a right to land, and provided a rather different history of settlement: 'Europeans have entered their borders uninvited', it argued, 'and, when there, have not only acted as if they were undoubted lords of the soil, but have punished the natives as aggressors if they have evinced a disposition to live in their own country'. Their criticism could not have been sharper: 'the land has been taken from them without the assertion of any title other than that of superior force'.[17] The point of this was not to preserve 'native' society intact. Humanitarians in Britain and its colonies always assumed that the best future for all people lay in their acceptance of Christian faith and British civilisation. The point was to protect those societies long enough that their members could make that transition in peace and good order. As a first step, the Committee recommended the appointment of Protectors of Aborigines, who would help prevent acts of cruelty and oppression and stand with their charges against the encroaches of the settlers.

In Australia, one task was to bear witness to what was happening along the frontier, and to found missions to signal the arrival of conscience and faith. Another was to try to conciliate, bringing ethics to the relationship between settlers and 'natives' and thereby reforming the degraded souls of the former and bringing Christianity to the latter. In Van Diemen's Land, Quakers James Backhouse and George Walker toured the island and then left for further missionary work in Mauritius and South Africa; Backhouse returned to London to write and publish an account encouraging greater protection, while Walker came back to Hobart Town to work as a draper and a banker and for the temperance cause. In the west, the West Australian Missionary Society, established in London in 1835, sent Louis Gustiniani. Horrified by the scale of the violence, he tried to defend Aboriginal people in court, but left after two years dismayed at the weakness of Christian conscience among the settlers. Catholics, too, did evangelical work, with an 1843 mission on Queensland's Stradbroke Island – though abandoned by 1847 – one of the first attempts in that colony to ensure healthy competition with Protestants for souls.

The spirit and practice of Aboriginal protection were pursued most vigorously in South Australia, where medical doctors Matthew Moorhouse and William Wyatt took the lead, as well as in Port Phillip. In Van Diemen's Land, George Robinson, a builder by trade who had migrated to Hobart in 1824, responded to an advertisement from Governor Arthur seeking a man of good character who could take charge of the Aboriginal camp at Bruny Island, to which they had been expelled. Robinson then re-invented himself as the 'protector' of all the colony's Aboriginal people, using conciliation and the promise of security, safety and food to remove them from the firing lines of the Black War and take them to Flinders Island off the northern coast. By 1835, most were at the new Wybalenna settlement. As it began to assume the features of a prison rather than a refuge, Robinson left, to take up the role of Protector of Aborigines in Port Phillip. For ten years, until the Protectorate was abolished in 1849, Robinson travelled among the Aboriginal people of the western half of the district, doing much good for later historians with his careful descriptions, but able to do little for the 'original occupants of the soil', as he called them; 'the past and present state of the Aborigines is one of annihilation or destruction', he lamented in his journal. He wrote of a 'hapless race', 'poor creatures [who] are worse treated than slaves', of people 'made use of' and 'destroyed with impunity' and of actions that 'would not be allowed in civilized society'. Whatever agency Robinson and other protectors might once have felt, they commonly became overwhelmed.[18] And in a decade when anti-slavery sentiment was growing rapidly, the use of the word 'slaves' said something of the problem's urgency.

The struggle over land wasn't over. It would flare again and again. But by the 1840s, even well-intentioned whites began to regard Aborigines as objects of pity, as people who deserved the protective hand of civilisation but who could no longer expect either justice or compensation for the loss of their land and their living. As was true for Native Americans, Australia's Aboriginal people would increasingly face a choice. They could live within settler society – just – but only by becoming un-Aboriginal. Or they could live outside, and face the continuing threat of dispossession and violence by people who never kept their promises, people their own authorities and governors could not control.

Australia's settlers would continue inventing Aboriginal people as savages. In some minds, that justified their destruction. In 1846 and 1847, responding to a rumour that a white woman had either been captured by or lost among the Kurnai people of Gippsland, west of Melbourne, expeditions of settlers and native police set out into the bush to find her and to punish any and all of those who might be holding her. She was never found, probably because she never existed. The number of Kurnai dead was estimated to be at least fifty by the Commissioner for Crown Lands, Charles Tyers. A local squatter, Henry Meyrick, wrote to his family in 1846: 'no wild beast of the forest was ever hunted down with such unsparing perseverance', he began. And those doing the hunting knew it was unlawful: 'these things are kept very secret as the penalty would certainly be hanging'. Meyrick concluded that the Aboriginal people 'will very shortly be extinct'.[19]

Meyrick was wrong, of course, about extinction. Aboriginal people survived, even in the places people thought they wouldn't, and their survival, like the survival of native Americans and Canadians, is one of the great stories of the last two centuries. They survived, and they would prevail, to tell the people who came after that the most important thing about the settlers was not the superiority of their civilisation but the ferocity of their intent.

COLONIAL LIVES AND FORTUNES

Along with the fate of the Aborigines, other questions regarding the nature of the civilisation taking shape in Australia came to the fore during the 1840s. There was as yet no definitive future, with penal and non-penal colonies, and the coexistence of convicts, emancipists and 'exclusivist' free settlers, still suggesting the possibility of different paths. New Zealand was proclaimed a separate colony in 1840, leaving four: New South Wales, Van Diemen's Land, South Australia and Western Australia. Further exploratory journeys connected the British dots; Edward

Eyre struck north from Adelaide, found salt lakes and retreated from Mount Hopeless. He then struck west, traversing the southern coastline into Western Australia. International traveller Pawel Strzelecki surveyed Gippsland, explored the Australian Alps and the Snowy Mountains, and ensured spelling dilemmas for most future Australians by naming the highest peak after Polish patriot Tadeusz Kosciuszko. Clement Hodgkinson surveyed the land between Port Macquarie and Brisbane in 1841 and 1842, and returned to the colonies some years later to help plan Melbourne's grand public gardens. Charles Sturt set out again, from Adelaide this time, looking for whatever might lie at the continent's centre. He found the Simpson Desert's dunes and turned back. The northern coast saw a series of unsuccessful British settlements; Port Essington was founded in 1838 and visited by HMS *Beagle*, but its diseases, heat and an 1839 cyclone's storm surge made it an unattractive option for free migrants, and it was abandoned in 1849. The most adventurous explorer was Prussian Ludwig Leichhardt. His first journey, more than three thousand miles between Moreton Bay and Port Essington, was a great success. Emboldened, he meant his second journey to take him across the continent to Perth, but it faltered in the face of rain and fever. He set out again in 1848 with only minimal supplies, apparently believing that he and his companions could live off the country. Their remains were never found.

Australians lived in a largely migrant, mobile and malleable society, which made for a mix of highly successful and highly unsuccessful lives. The privileges of birth and fortune were less apparent than in Britain, and it took a generation or two to build the large houses that would symbolise distinction and the exclusive schools that would preserve it. But the costs of failure were greater too, and those impoverished by age, debility or desertion could find themselves cast adrift in a place with few of the statutory protections, such as the Poor Law, afforded them in the old country. For a few, land acquisition, squatting or a skill brought high rewards, while for others the traumatic legacy of transportation blighted their lives. Most ordinary people probably lived slightly better than their compatriots in Britain. They ate more, suffered less environmental pollution, and worked in strenuous but often less dangerous occupations. They did not necessarily have more money, but the cost of significant resources – land and housing, in particular – was much less, and the supply of basic foods was more secure. Their houses were a little larger, and spaced further apart, and people in Queensland and New South Wales were already discovering the benefits of adapting the Indian verandah to shield rooms from the sun. One of the most important possessions was a horse, and there were nearly a quarter of a million of them in the colonies by 1850. Hard to transport by sea, the number of horses grew by natural increase rather than by importation. Most horses were workers, but by the end of the 1830s, horse racing was already a major occupation in the cities and towns.

There were more improving pursuits, many of them available in the mechanics institutes founded in Hobart Town, Sydney, Adelaide, Melbourne and Brisbane by 1842. Often the most impressive secular building in the town, they sponsored lectures and debates, provided a place for dramatic performances, and built free libraries. The skilled workers who frequented them were also quick to form labour unions, despite the legal uncertainties of such 'combinations'. They struggled to survive in the 1840s, with a sharp economic depression brought on by the collapse of speculative pastoral investments and the falling global price for Australian wool. Banks failed, new immigrants were destituted, and government spending fell by two-thirds. The hard times encouraged the growth of mutual assistance and protection societies to insure people against any future bust.

One estimate is that a child who migrated from Britain to Australia around 1820 probably enjoyed between ten and twenty extra years of life on average. Better diets and health in childhood and adolescence meant healthier babies as colonial women reproduced in the 1830s and 1840s, and the survival of a greater proportion of babies and children created the same kind of explosive population growth – six, eight or even ten per cent per year, counting births and migrant arrivals – that was occurring in

Table 5.2 Vital statistics of the European population, 1851

Population	437,665
Number of births	15,784
Birth rate (per 1,000 people)	36.1
Number of deaths	5,878
Death rate (per 1,000 people)	13.4
Number of marriages	4,677
Marriage rate (per 1,000 people)	10.7
% of population female	41.3
% rate of annual population growth	8.0

Source: W. Vamplew (ed.) *Australians: Historical Statistics* (Sydney: Fairfax, Syme and Weldon Associates, 1987), p. 44; Australian Bureau of Statistics, 'Australian Historical Population Statistics, 2006' (3105.0.65.001), at http://www.abs.gov.au/AUSSTATS/abs@. nsf/DetailsPage/3105.0.65.0012006.

the United States and Canada. Frontier life had its problems. Australian babies were vulnerable to the 'summer sickness' of contaminated water, and Australian women's death rates in childbirth were little better than those in Europe.

By 1850, as Table 5.2 shows, there were more than four hundred thousand white Australians, a number that had doubled since 1840. Around half of them lived in New South Wales, with around seventy thousand each in the Port Phillip district and Van Diemen's Land, sixty thousand in South Australia, and just four or five thousand in Western Australia. At some point in the previous decade, they had probably overtaken the number of Aboriginal people, who were suffering the great population decline caused by disease, immiseration, cultural dislocation and violence.

Australians lived at the edge of the British world, but they were not disconnected from its centres or from its other edges in New Zealand, southern Africa, India, Singapore, Canada or China. Ships brought migrants, goods and letters, and carried back people – children to British schools, tourists and retirees – as well as colonial produce. There was great eagerness for news; colonial newspapers carried stories from Britain, though they were weeks or months old, until the arrival of new

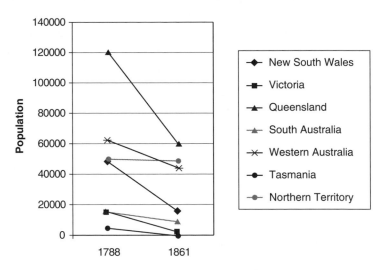

Figure 5.1   Estimated decline of the Aboriginal population, 1788–1861

Source: L. R. Smith, *The Aboriginal Population of Australia* (Canberra: Australian National University Press, 1980).

distance-conquering communication technologies in the second half of the nineteenth century. English political and cultural disputes were closely followed and often mirrored in the colonies, sometimes being overlaid by those that derived from Australia's particularities.

But if they were of the British world, they were more likely to feel a sense of growing difference from Britons 'back home', and with this came increasing arguments about what kind of British society Australia might and should become. Migrant and native-born expressed their differences in words, some of them borrowed from Aboriginal languages, others from Welsh or Gaelic, some of them drawing upon regional, marginal and sometimes underworld dialects in England. All mixed up, and with a good dose of Irish words and inflections, these were the beginnings of Australian accents. The native-born adopted more or less gentle put-downs as identifiers: one was cornstalks, which suggested lanky and premature growth. The difference was also described as 'currency' (local) and 'sterling' (born in Britain). A former surgeon superintendent, Peter Cunningham, wrote: 'our Currency lads and lasses are a fine interesting race, and do honour to the country whence they originated', he reported, adding 'the Currencies grow up tall and slender, like the Americans, and are generally remarkable for that Gothic peculiarity of fair hair and blue eyes'.[20] If the compliments were tongue in cheek, they were seized upon by the native-born; in the nineteenth century, to be compared to the Americans was to say something very encouraging about your future.

A FUTURE FREEDOM

By the 1840s a good many colonists believed their society to be in transition, and were picturing the kind of world in which they wanted to live. Once a place of exile, theirs was now the land of the second chance. Since the turn of the new century, ideas about human potential and capacity had shifted, and there was increasing focus – in the Old World as well as the New – on reformability and education. There was less emphasis on fate, more on prevention, planning and insurance. If new and better environments might generate self- and collective improvement, then perhaps these Australian colonies could even outdo or improve Britain. Caroline Chisholm and other proponents of assisted free migration had, after all, suggested that any 'ardent desire' among Britons 'to escape the continual struggle they endure' would be fulfilled in Australia.[21] Promises of abundance and freedom, taken at their word, were powerful pulls for

67

people in Britain's cities and farms. They made Australia seem a place in which those ordinary women and men might rise. For those who knew they were born to rule, however, transition brought insecurity and doubt, especially about the virtue and the character of former convicts and those only one generation removed from their vices.

There was still the problem of the largest and most obvious legacy of British rule: convictism itself. The colonists might grant that the convict system had changed, and that more enlightened governors – Richard Bourke in New South Wales, to take one example – had begun to ameliorate some of its effects and, by providing more liberal rights for the freed, were hastening their transformation into good British subjects. The newer outposts such as Port Arthur were more penitentiary than before, taking on the new and more rational disciplinary models, such as solitary confinement and self-reflection, that were being discussed in British, American and French penal theory. Juvenile offenders were sent to the separate reforming prison at Point Puer. But exclusives such as James Mudie could also keep insisting, as he did in his book *Felonry in New South Wales*, that 'the admission of freed convicts, whether by pardon or expiry of their sentences, to the same social and legal rights as the emigrants, is not only a subject of discussion, but of bitter and well-grounded complaint'.[22] Mudie was not a man lost for words when it came to convict calumny:

A very large proportion of the population, indeed, consists of branches lopped for their rottenness from the tree of British freedom, venerable for its grandeur and antiquity, whom the outraged soil of England, shuddering at their crimes, has expelled, and whom she has with just abhorrence cast forth from her shores. ... No absurdity, then, can be greater, nothing can be more anti-British, either as to the spirit of British law, or as to the tone of British feeling and morals, than to suppose that the emancipated convicts of New South Wales are entitled to claim the same consideration in society, or the same rights and immunities, as those claimed by or granted to the free and respectable settlers.[23]

But as British political and public opinion shifted, the changing facts of the convict system in the Australian colonies mattered less and less. While the great majority of convicts worked for settlers or on government works and were not locked up, it was the confined and the flogged who dominated the way people imagined that system. While most ex-convicts settled into something like ordinary life – indeed this was a crucial component of the colonists' arguments about their potential – it was the degraded, scarred bushrangers who were thought its typical products. Norfolk Island was convictism gone too far; atrocity generated mutiny and in turn more atrocity, even after penal reformer Alexander Maconochie had tried to reduce degrading punishments and introduce a probation system between 1840 and 1844. A report by Bishop Robert Wilson to the House of Lords in 1846 brought some remedy and the beginnings of the convicts' removal.

The ultimate insult, in a way, was that the very Parliament that had first allowed Australia to be made convict had, by the middle of the 1830s, decided that convictism had been its downfall. A parliamentary select committee led by William Molesworth declared in 1838 that transportation had degraded and corrupted the colonies (and the colonists). The signs of that degradation ran the gamut from the shortage of women to the perversion of civilised relationships between employers and employees in an assignment system it condemned as akin to slavery. As was also true of critiques of American slavery, the effect upon the brutalised was matched by the effect upon the oppressor. They recommended an immediate end to transportation, at least for New South Wales. In one sense, the colonists had obtained something that many had wanted: no more convict transports and some hope that the colony could overcome its convict origins. But the Molesworth committee also exacerbated the problem of reputation; peripheral Australia has always been a place interested in what others make of it, and here was decisive proof that the empire's centre saw this still as a somewhat blighted edge.

Many colonists had always lived with two images of themselves. On the one hand, they were 'a rising generation', most definitely on a par with the people of any other British colony and able to turn the new land into a potential paradise. On the other, they feared that theirs might well a degraded society only ever moments away from relapsing into the vicious habits of its first, and involuntary, British and Irish migrants. It was difficult to demand no more convicts, who they said brought in crime and vice, while at the same time insisting that theirs was not a criminalised and vicious society. Resolving that tension, and imagining a brighter future, sparked significant arguments during the 1830s and 1840s. One tactic was to argue that convicts could and did reform, and that they and their children would fill the country's 'vast solitudes with a numerous, industrious and virtuous agricultural population'.[24] Another was to insist that the currency lads – though not, of course, the lasses – could participate in their own governance. The desire for separation – fulfilled in Victoria but delayed for Queensland until 1859 – was one aspect of the determination to make political institutions more responsive to local aspirations. In 1842, New South Wales won an expanded legislature, of whom two thirds would be elected, but this was not yet representative government, as the Governor could withhold assent to any of its legislation and answered only to the Colonial Office in London. A further act in 1850 – *for the better Government of Her Majesty's Australian Colonies* – broadened the franchise and empowered the Governor to establish a parliament of two houses in New South Wales, and created for Van Diemen's Land the partly representative government that New South Wales had been granted in 1842.

These demands for self-control also reflected another argument emerging out of the decay of convictism: what was holding the colonies back was not their mixed inheritance but the uncaring and arbitrary rule of the British government and their appointed leaders. Convicts were still being sent to Van Diemen's Land; there was a moratorium in 1846, but more ships came between 1848 and 1853, some of them bearing Irish rebels. Convicts and 'exiles' – men given conditional pardons if they agreed to be transported to Australia – also arrived in Port Phillip after 1841. While Britain was now building gaols, and transporting a smaller proportion of its criminals, opinion in the colonies had turned decisively against further voyages.

By the end of the 1840s, it was clear that many Australians could no longer accept the contradiction between a hopeful and expansive future and the continuing use of 'their' land as a home for felonious Britons. From a public meeting in Launceston in 1849 came an Australasian Anti-Transportation League. After the Van Diemen's Land elections of 1851, all sixteen seats in the Council were held by anti-transportationists. The decision to resume transportation to New South Wales and Port Phillip in the late 1840s was the final straw. It was a 'flagrant invasion of the rights of British freemen'; having 'just emerged from a state of vassalage' the colony would once again be 'sunk into this wretched and degraded condition'.[25] Poet Charles Harpur railed against the 'windy shows of Aristocracy', especially because there were squatting and wealthy elements in the Legislative Council – including William Wentworth – who had been urging transportation's resumption in order to maintain the supply of assigned labour. The people of Sydney were less happy, and tried to prevent the unloading of the convict ship *Hashemy*. The people of Melbourne tried to blockade their port; as one newspaper writer put it, 'we should duck the scoundrels if they attempt to set foot in a country of free men, and send them back as they came to the greater scoundrels who dared to send them'.[26] More clearly still came this statement: 'as far as the colonists of

New South Wales are concerned, the Transportation Question is settled – settled fully and finally – settled for ever'.[27]

Significantly, *The People's Advocate* argued that renewed transportation 'could have no other effect but to degrade us in the eyes of the world'. And, just as tellingly, the people of the eastern colonies ignored the fact that Western Australia had just become a convict colony. But with that exception, this was a national movement, and one in which the House of Lords was warned that it faced another Massachusetts. It was prudent to back down, and the British government did. There was much celebration; in 1853, when its last convict ship had arrived, Van Diemen's Land gave all of its schoolchildren a special medallion. It would celebrate again in 1856, with the grant of self-government and a new name – Tasmania – that drew attention away from its convict past.

For some people in these colonies, imagining tomorrow was beginning to mean looking to a new society and to an Australian future. They would develop the balance between inventiveness and novelty, on the one hand, and uncertain emulation and a concern with the eyes of the world, on the other, that would continue to characterise ideas about Australia and its present and future place in the world. Around 1850, it was clear that this would be a British world, though one, perhaps, in which British virtues might overcome British vices. Yet that optimism would always be tinged with the continuing anxieties of the convict past, especially in a society about to be shaken by the rush for gold.

6

. . . .

The Golden Lands: 1850–68

On the first day of July in 1851, the new colony of Victoria was established. Within a few weeks, Victoria would become one of the most important places in the world, and it would remain so for a few years. The discovery of gold in Australia – first in New South Wales and then, more spectacularly, in Victoria – was not accidental. After the great rush began in California in 1848, people who knew the land, or who had identified likely fields by reading the numerous descriptive accounts of colonies, went looking for gold, and governments promised rich rewards to anyone who could discover a viable field. Edward Hargraves, who arrived in Sydney in 1832, sold up and went to California in 1849. He came back in 1851, bringing American techniques to districts he was sure would contain gold. Hargraves, John Lister and William Tom found it, at Ophir near Bathurst. Hargraves announced its location to the newspapers in May, securing for himself the £10,000 reward, and started Australia's first rush. July brought new and larger discoveries, first at Anderson's Creek and then at Clunes and Ballarat. Castlemaine surpassed them, and was itself bettered by Bendigo. There were finds at Beechworth in 1852, at Bright in 1853 and then at Walhalla in 1862. The first prospectors picked nuggets from the ground; after the alluvial goal was exhausted, miners sank shafts. Australia had gold fever.

Gold rushes were the most absorbing global fascination of the last half of the nineteenth century. After California and Victoria, there were significant rushes at Kiandra, Lambing Flat, Young and Forbes in the early 1860s. Smaller rushes occurred in Queensland, at Gympie in the 1860s and at Palmer River in the 1870s. There were rushes in Canada's British Columbia in the 1850s and 1860s, and in Otago in New Zealand in the 1860s, while the great rush of the 1880s was to the Witwatersrand in South Africa. The last rushes – better characterised as stampedes, so rapid had communication and transportation become – were at Western Australia's Kalgoorlie and Canada's Yukon in the 1890s.

Gold rushes dramatically changed the societies that hosted them. They brought in tens of thousands of people, some to look and dig for gold, others to feed, launder, entertain and police the diggers. Some stayed, and built the towns around the diggings, while others followed the trail of gold: Australians who had gone to California came back, accompanied by Americans, only to leave again, often as unwealthy as they came. Thousands walked from South Australia, or sailed from Van Diemen's Land. Rapid immigration transformed Victoria into a colony challenging and then overcoming New South Wales in a battle over colonial supremacy; between 1851 and 1860, half a million people left Britain and Ireland for Australia, and more than half of those landed in Melbourne and other Victorian ports. Ballarat, Bendigo and the other towns attracted more than forty thousand of the other great gold travellers of the nineteenth century, the Chinese. The rushes also brought in some sixty thousand Europeans, ten thousand North Americans and five thousand New Zealanders. They put Australia, and especially Victoria, at the centre of the globe: one-third of the world's gold was found in Victoria, and Melbourne was for a time the world's fastest-growing city, matched only by America's prairie boomtown, Chicago, and another city built on gold, San Francisco. Such rapid movements created the same kinds of problems in every gold rush society: as tens and even hundreds of thousands of people swamped the fields, they came into conflict with Indigenous people, with established settlers and with each other.

Every gold rush raised the same questions about the future. Those questions were perhaps especially urgent in the Australian colonies,

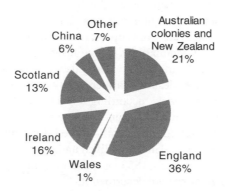

Figure 6.1   Birthplaces of the Victorian population, 1857

Sourc: Australian Bureau of Statistics, 'Australian Historical Population Statistics, 2006' (3105.0.65.001), at http://www.abs.gov.au.

where the rushes occurred only sixty years after the first British occupation. In the United States and Canada, gold revolutionised relatively distant peripheries such as California; in Australia, it shook and turned over the most populous and prosperous colonies. For patriots such as John Dunmore Lang, gold was proof that Australia would and could become 'queen' of its hemisphere by first matching and then speeding past the United States. In his more optimistic moments, Lang even foresaw a United Provinces of Australia, incorporating New Zealand and governing a western Pacific Empire, its flag adorned with a kangaroo and seven stars. Lang was more enthusiastic than most, but everyone agreed that finding goldfields confirmed a providential intent. Australia could be remade by gold. If some could make fortunes, all could benefit from the returns. The migrants, in the tens of thousands, would swamp any remnant convict stain. Money would build great cities, and the evidence for that lay in the grand town halls, avenues and botanical gardens of the gold towns. The discovery of gold in such abundance confirmed that the new land was destined to be a great nation, and on the back of gold arose both the first forecasts of a federated union of the Australian colonies and a more vigorous agitation about the rights and freedoms of the colonial population.

THE GOLDEN REVOLUTION

Yet fantasies about gold were matched, and sometimes outweighed, by fears about the disorderly society it brought in its train. Gold turned the world upside down, stripping established towns of their people and building shanty settlements along creeks. The cities seemed suddenly bereft of workers and even shopkeepers; ships could not sail for want of sailors, all but two of Melbourne's police resigned to try gold-seeking, there was a shortage of carts and horses, and even apparently respectable people – 'responsible tradesmen, farmers, clerks of every grade and not a few of the superior classes', according to Victoria's Governor Charles LaTrobe – set off in search of fortune.[1] There was a significant growth in the numbers of deserted wives and children, for which the colonies' charities were ill prepared. Hundreds lived under canvas on Emerald Hill in Melbourne. John Sherer's 1853 pastiche of contemporary accounts, *The Gold Finder of Australia*, described it:

> In fact, everything had assumed a revolutionary character. The very human countenance had changed, from the golden dreams which, day

and night, were continually haunting the imaginations of the victims of the prevailing mania ... I shall leave it to your imagination to picture to itself the state of society in which such transitions ... are daily occurring, and in which even female servants are hardly to be found willing to undertake the domestic duties of a family.[2]

The miners were, in many eyes, rather wild characters. They seemed footloose and vagrant, holding little stake in whatever society gave them gold. As they poured into Victoria from other colonies and from over-seas, their goldfields began to look like the frontier and convict socie-ties some colonists had wanted to leave behind: unformed, uncivilised and unstable, full of men in tents and shanties without the tempering influence of women, family and home. There were 'sly grog' shops, prostitutes and gambling, and tents flying flags and banners with politi-cal proclamations. If later writers would romanticise the lone male, be he bushman or miner, most opinion in the 1850s saw isolated men as a mounting social and moral problem. Some of the visual depictions of the goldfields were more warning than celebration: the works of Samuel T. Gill, which became widely popular in 1853, showed 'The lucky digger that returned' nestled back home with wife and child but also 'The unlucky digger that never returned' as an abandoned and decomposing corpse. As one writer warned in 1853, 'a community of men is a herd of selfishness and brutality'.[3] Observers of the fields were rather too prone to dismiss the place that women had made for themselves within the gold economy, but their anxieties reveal the absolutely central place that gender balance played in nineteenth-century understandings of civilisa-tion. Following gold, Caroline Chisholm's urgings as to the importance of women and children in the migrant stream took on a new legitimacy.

Gold was arbitrary. Few made much, but many made a little. Gold elevated people suddenly and disrupted the supposed link between wealth and character; if the only real talent of the rich was taking advantage of good fortune, then the argument that they had somehow deserved their social and political advantages seemed more tenuous. Much was made of the diggers' financial irresponsibility, and the illegitimacy of wealth without morality. There were reports that diggers were burning money, and stories of 'digger weddings' that aped the finery of their betters. Sherer expressed something of the ambivalence of rapid wealth:

All the aristocratic feelings and associations of the old country are at once annihilated. Plebianism of the rankest, and, in many instances, of the lowest kind, at present dwells in Australia; and as riches are

Illustration 6.1   'Unlucky Digger that never returned', 1852

Source: Rex Nan Kivell Collection NK586/48, National Library of Australia, nla. pic-an7537607.

now becoming the test of a man's position, it is vain to have any pretensions whatever unless you are supported by that powerful auxiliary. It is not what you were but what you are that is the criterion – as, indeed, it ought to be – by which you are judged; and although your father might have been my Lord of England-all-over, it goes for nothing in this equalising colony of gold and beef and mutton.[4]

In the nineteenth century, no less than the twentieth, Australians sometimes measured themselves by the calibre of the celebrities who visited them. Numerous important people came to see the goldfields and examine these newest examples of imperial fortune: Robert Cecil, the future British prime minister, actually found them more orderly and civilised than he had imagined. At its height, though, the worst fears of those concerned by gold's fever were realised in the 1855 arrival of Lola Montez, famous alike for her affair with King Ludwig of Bavaria, her cigar-smoking, her general bohemianism and her skills as an entertainer. Lola's dancing – and especially her most famous contortion, the Spider Dance – enraged Melbourne's *Argus* newspaper, which declared it a 'most libertinish and indelicate performance' and 'utterly subversive to all ideas of public morality'.[5] Happily, Governor and Lady Hotham, along with numerous dignitaries, were able to witness it without incident.

As was true in California and other gold rush societies, the arrival of Chinese miners generated further anxieties. By 1855, there were fifteen thousand in Victoria – perhaps one in ten of the people on the fields – and by 1858, there were forty thousand in the colonies. All but a few hundred were men. Often highly successful diggers, Chinese migrants developed strong fraternal organisations and services. Many were enmeshed in networks of debt and obligation that stretched back to southern China. The other miners sometimes respected their industry, and the relationships on the fields themselves were always more complicated and intermixed than outsiders saw; far from being a closed or insular community, the Chinese miners were sometimes veteran and bilingual gold-seekers. But there were also frequent assaults and assertions of European superiority, in part because the Chinese were seen to be 'hoarders' who had no commitment to the colonies and simply wanted to take their riches back home; as one French woman observer wrote, the English 'beat them and chase them on the pretext that they don't spend all that they earn and because they eat rice'.[6] The complaints about them mostly stemmed from antipathy to the cultural and religious practices of a 'pagan race' and the charge that 'coolies' were being used to bring down the price of labour.

REBELLION

In their dealings with the Chinese, and each other, the miners were disorderly. Those observing the fields ignored the preachers' tents and open-air services that showed evidence of faith, or showed too little respect for the fact that many miners managed to cooperate and resolve disputes over claims despite inevitable competition. In rough communal justice, thieves and claim-jumpers might be exiled and marched off the field or flogged. But stealing was a constant temptation. Unprotected at first by police, and living in a place where one's fortune could very easily be stolen, most diggers armed themselves, and gunshot became one of the most common sounds of the fields. The fields had the usual characteristics of a well-armed population: high rates of accidental shooting, as well as a few homicides, and the blurring of the differences between perpetrators and potential victims. Diggers could not always be told apart from the bushrangers and thieves who preyed on them.

The fields were troubled, and the difficulties of creating and maintaining order were very real. Victoria Governor LaTrobe faced severe financial constraints, and the hostility of Victoria's squatter-dominated Legislative Council; the license paid by miners was one of his few means of paying for police or providing the fields with roads and other public services. In late 1851, he proposed to increase the fee to £3; at angry meetings, especially at Forest Creek and Golden Point, miners used a language of tyranny. They stressed the link between taxation and representation, and the rights of British men to resist oppression and injustice. Anyone who knew the history of Britain's North American colonies should have understood the depth of their feeling.

The fields bubbled and sometimes boiled over, with renewed agitation – and a petition demanding reduced license fees and land reform – in the Bendigo Red Ribbon Rebellion in 1853. At Castlemaine, a meeting on Agitation Hill, in full view of the government and police camp, warned miners and goldfield residents to 'demand your rights, otherwise you will live and die all slaves'. There was talk of revolution and retribution, and there was anger at the 'oppressions' and clumsiness of the police; the people, one speaker claimed, will 'oppose the authorities, crumble them to the dust as useless worms, and chivalrously demand their individual liberties'.[7] The language and the sentiments were plain, but colonial officials, not least the new Governor Charles Hotham, failed to comprehend the miners' complaints about arbitrary policing, even though men were fined and sometimes chained up for not carrying their license.

Grievance usually sparks into rebellion when events prove to people they have no option and their fears of an oppressive conspiracy have some foundation in truth. At Ballarat, in October, November and December 1854, the clumsy handling of a murder and a retaliatory arson proved such a spark. Matters were not improved by the police's decision to harass the servant of a Catholic priest in a strongly Irish community. The miners formed the Ballarat Reform League to demand justice and a series of other measures – such as the vote – that would transform their status and see them treated as the free men they thought they were. They sent a deputation to the Governor, which was rejected. A detachment of troops arrived. The miners met, ostentatiously showing the 'Southern

Cross', a non-British flag, and decided to burn their licenses. With a new license hunt, anger grew, and became more militant. Hundreds pledged allegiance to their new standard, and marched to the Eureka diggings, where they built a rough stockade. Early on the morning of 3 December, troops and police attacked the stockade. It was over quickly, though some of the troops burned tents and nearby stores as well as dismantling the battlements. More than twenty diggers were killed. Thirteen of the survivors were later tried for sedition, but the scale of public revulsion – and the government's misjudgement of the public support the miners would receive – ensured that all were found not guilty of the charge.

The events on the goldfields show the importance that nineteenth-century people attached to justice, representation and protection. Miners were demanding what they saw as their rights. That they used the language of English Chartism, Irish rebellion and American freedom is hardly surprising, for a good many of them were English Chartists, Irish rebels, and either white Americans imbued with their nation's republican tradition or African-Americans speaking of slavery. The goldfields brought together various political traditions that agreed on the threat of corruption and conspiracy and demanded the political empowerment of ordinary men. In one sense, the demands of the Ballarat Reform League were distinctly colonial, but they also shared much with a global language of rights and justice: manhood suffrage, secret ballots and the abolition of property qualifications for members of parliament, as well as the specific issues of goldfield law and administration.

They won concessions. Even before the events at Eureka, Governor Hotham had instituted an inquiry. The Gold Fields Royal Commission abolished the licenses, and created a miner's right: for one pound a year, you could mine gold and vote in the elections. While no direct changes were made to Victoria's new constitution, ratified in 1855, the first parliament passed laws that created full manhood suffrage and secret ballots and removed property qualifications for the lower house. It also passed a Chinese immigration act, which imposed a head tax on any Chinese migrant entering a Victorian port and restricted the number of Chinese who could arrive on any one ship. It was a short-sighted measure; the Chinese simply had to land at ports in South Australia or New South Wales to avoid it. Nor did it abate fears of a future dominated by uncomfortably proximate 'Asiatics'. In 1856, a nervous satirist wrote a story in the *Melbourne Punch* set in the year 2000, 'the centenary anniversary of the establishment of a Mongolian dynasty in Victoria', when 'British chain-gangs' were working the mines. There was a new Select Committee in 1857, which took as its aim 'to effectively prevent the gold fields of Australia Felix from becoming the property of the Emperor of China and of the Mongolian and tartar hordes of Asia'.[8] Adult Chinese men were forced to pay an additional residence tax and were denied the right to take legal action to defend their property or mining claims.

Anti-Chinese agitation grew louder on the fields; expulsive violence exploded at Buckland River in 1857 and Ararat in 1858 before culminating at Lambing Flat in New South Wales in 1861, when a mob of thousands, with banners unfurled and a brass band playing 'Rule Britannia', drove the Chinese from the field. In all cases, the police, hastily-appointed Chinese Protectors and some sympathetic miners won some control, but the pressure for restriction or exclusion was escalating, as Miners Protective Leagues and other bodies railed against 'the Mongol race'. The Chinese lost both ways. If they were the victims of disorderly miners or exploitative employers, they had to be restricted for their own protection. But white Australians also had to be protected from them. Either justified their penalisation, restriction and even removal. They were not silenced, and they made their own protests. But what the Australians of the 1850s had begun to thread together – preserving their civilisation and the whiteness of their land – would become even more tightly connected in the decades that followed.

GOVERNING A NEW WORLD

Conflicts over rights, liberties and opportunities were not confined to the goldfields. Australian colonists would everywhere debate very similar issues to those that dominated other nineteenth-century societies: mobility, property, political rights, the extent of public responsibility for education and self-improvement, the boundaries between governmental and private provision and the place of faith. Their debates found expression in colonial newspapers, which wore their political colours less hesitantly than they would in the twentieth-century; liberals and reformers read the *South Australian Advertiser* or Melbourne's *Age*, while Victorian conservatives preferred *The Argus*. Their debates would be made particularly fraught and interesting, however, by the fact that they lived in what they saw as a new world. That meant an eagerness and capacity for change, alongside a degree of nervousness about the political and social consequences of straying too far from the British template. After all, most colonists were not attempting to create something entirely new in Australia, and the divisions between them were mainly based on different interpretations of agreed and fundamental principles.

One abiding issue was the question of who should govern. For conservatives, especially those concerned to protect the advantages of the wealthier squatters, it was important to limit popular influence. They feared too much popular rule; government should represent 'interests' – of which the largest and most important was 'the pastoral' – and reflect the unequal stakes that people had in their society. Their preference was for a government of men esteemed by birth, property or wealth, not a 'mindless' democracy of self-interest. As they designed colonial constitutions in the early 1850s, especially in New South Wales, those who felt they had a right to rule tried to create a colonial aristocracy, which would sit in an unelected upper house mirroring the British House of Lords, with property qualifications limiting the franchise. One of their leaders, William Wentworth, now reconciled with his former exclusivist foes, was particularly insistent upon having a British and not a 'Yankee' constitution, and developing the hereditary principle that distinguished them. Without this, he warned, the 'elective element' in government would be uncontrollable.[9]

These were perfectly logical extensions of his personal views, but they were deeply unpopular among the great bulk of the colonial population. This kind of political exclusion could not be manufactured or defended in a newer, mobile and migrant society. The debates over the New South Wales Constitution Bill showed the depth of people's attachment to the idea of broadly based political participation. And if Wentworth spoke for one kind of European tradition, advocates such as Daniel Deniehy, like Wentworth the son of convicts who had prospered in New South Wales, spoke for another. They demanded full manhood suffrage, and they ridiculed Wentworth's colonial peerage as 'a bunyip aristocracy'. If many colonists followed Deniehy into a demand for democratic representation, fewer followed him into republicanism and the idea of a direct severing of links to Britain. They may have assumed that a republic would eventually come about, but their own experience showed them that it was possible to argue for and develop relatively democratic and open government in the colonies without an American-style separation. They argued that if Britain accepted their demand for responsible self-government, there would be no need for a republic; conversely, as Launceston newspaper editor John West argued, 'if responsible government be refused – if the fair claims of Australia be disregarded, in our heart we believe that in less than two years she will be a republic'.[10]

For the majority of Australian colonists, there was no necessary tension between what they understood as independence and the continuing influence of Britain. The constitutions that created responsible government in every colony except Western Australia in 1855 and 1856, and in the new colony of Queensland in 1859, gave legislative precedence and supremacy to Britain. They also imposed various degrees of property qualification, though the relative wealth and high wages of colonists compared to Britons meant that property restrictions based on British standards actually disenfranchised relatively few Australians. In the middle of the nineteenth century, few agreed with Lang that allegiance to Britain and to Australia were incompatible. They were 'Austral-Britons', in equal measure independent and loyal. And with the passing of the *Electoral Reform Act* of 1858, New South Wales essentially achieved full manhood suffrage and the secret ballot. Victoria and South Australia had instituted the secret ballot in 1856. Victoria abolished all property qualifications for elections to its lower house in 1857, and in 1856 South Australia abolished plural voting by property-owners in different electorates, making it one of the world's first one man-one vote electorates. However, by installing upper houses with significant property qualifications, the founders of responsible government in the colonies created the grounds for dispute, deadlock and profoundly undemocratic outcomes as lower and upper houses struggled over almost every important question.

Another major issue that created conflict in the 1850s and dominated reformist politics in the 1860s was access to land. In a new and migrant society, access to land symbolised access to opportunity. There was growing anger among the majority about the minority who had grabbed land and had their possession turned into legal occupation and then ownership under Crown leases and licenses during and after the 1830s. Deniehy was particularly riled by 'pompous tyrant squatters ... whose cattle graze on lands stolen from the people by government connivance'; opposition to the 'squattocracy' united gold diggers, townspeople and those convinced that Australia's best future lay in something more like equality of opportunity.[11]

The remedy was legislation to encourage closer agricultural settlement and a fairer distribution of land by allowing 'free selection' before survey. The selectors would, in other words, be empowered to purchase land occupied by squatters once the latter's leases expired. There were strong similarities – not surprising given the shared circumstances of rapid pastoral and agricultural expansion – with the *Homestead Act* of the United States. The issue was a relatively minor one in Tasmania, Western Australia and South Australia. Legislation was somewhat – and eventually – successful in Victoria, especially after further refinements gave small selectors more protection in the 1870s. But in New South Wales and Queensland similar acts led to a scramble for possession, in which squatters used their power to guard the land, employed agents as 'dummy selectors', paid cash to outbid selectors at auctions, used every loophole they could, and bought up failed farms to further consolidate their holdings. The strength of their self-interest, and the material and political advantages they brought to the process of selection, meant that only very careful, considered and strong legislation could have worked. It was not until the 1880s that something like that finally was put into effect.

COLONIAL DIFFERENCES

Debates over rights, freedoms and the shape of the future were also evident in other issues during the 1860s. The last convict landed in Western Australia in 1868, freeing the way for the extension of that same limited form of local representation first seen in New South Wales in the 1840s. The colony would not have full responsible government until 1890. In Australian cities, the movement attempting to realise British socialist Robert Owen's maxim of 'eight hours labour, eight hours rest, eight hours recreation' was particularly strong in the buoyant and labour-scarce 1850s, with significant victories for building workers and a few other skilled trades. By the end of the 1850s, an economic bust weakened their position; in Sydney, there was enough concern over its impact that a parliamentary committee recommended the temporary imposition of higher duties on imports to raise funds and protect employment. This protectionist policy, seen as temporary in New South Wales, lodged more firmly in Victoria. A division that would come to dominate differences between the colonies in the last quarter of the nineteenth century widened in 1865, when the Victorian parliament passed a bill providing for a tariff of ten per cent to protect its industries, and in 1871, when the tariff was expanded and raised. Suspicions between the colonies did not prevent the discussion of eventual federation, and by the end of the 1860s there had already been inter-colonial conferences. One, on mail services, featured a lively speech about Australia's future federated greatness by Henry Parkes, who would become the primary advocate of union in New South Wales. But at this point, a lot of other people in New South Wales saw talk of federation as Victorian talk; in the language of families and siblings that they used to describe their relationships, Victoria was a younger sister trying to force her older and wiser sister's hand.

There was intense discussion about education, especially in light of its function in a society where talent, character and the thirst for

83

self-improvement, not birthright or unearned largesse, were meant to determine individual fortunes. In line with American ideas, Australians assumed that good schools might build good citizens. As a result of the gold rush migrations, and as school attendances rose during the 1850s and 1860s, literacy rates were among the highest in the world: around ninety per cent for both men and women. At this point, most children went either to the public Board schools or to separate schools run by religious denominations or private teachers, and relatively few attended any kind of high school. Boarding schools were too expensive for most, costing perhaps a quarter or a third of the average wage for a tradesman; the Catholic system provided a cheaper alternative, as did a few government-run but fee-paying state high schools, especially in New South Wales. For well-off Australians, there were grammar schools that aped their British models, but even here Australian schools moved rather more quickly to the utilitarian side of the scale, adding modern languages such as French and German, as well as 'mercantile' and 'commercial' subjects like bookkeeping. The 1860s and 1870s also saw much interest in technical education and colleges for mining, agriculture and industry.

The job of government was to educate younger children, especially those from the lower social ranks. During the 1850s and 1860s, the system worked well enough, using textbooks based upon the Irish National Readers (written for the mixed faith Irish population, they seemed a good choice for the mixed faith colonies). But disputes between faiths, the inefficiency of 'dual' public and private systems and the rapid expansion of the school-age population as the gold rush migrants' children grew up, encouraged all of the colonial governments to institute what Victoria's *Education Act* of 1872 celebrated as 'free, compulsory and secular' education for children aged between six and fifteen. Free and secular it became, so Catholic and Irish children, in particular, moved even more strongly into their own system, and the wealthy chose schools that kept out the lower orders with fees. The Irish readers contained rather too many references to faith, and were replaced by the rigorously secular Royal Readers. State aid for denominational schools ended in 1874.

What had been clear for some time was that the established church would continue to find its status much reduced in Australia. In 1861, the New South Wales Supreme Court ruled that the Church of England was one of a number of religious groups and had no claim to precedence over the others. As nominal Anglicans were perhaps a bare majority of the population, it seemed a fair point. Catholics recruited priests, monks and nuns from Europe – and especially Ireland – for teaching, nursing and missionary work. Sectarian feelings ran strong, especially in Melbourne, but they did not and could not prevent Catholics holding high position. Baptists and Congregationalists were a strong force in Adelaide, as were Presbyterians in Melbourne, and German Lutherans maintained their churches and language in parts of South Australia and Queensland. Australians rarely matched the enthusiasm of the Americans, but revival tours with vigorous preaching backed up by massed choirs stirred up city and country people alike, most notably when William 'California' Taylor roared through for the Methodists in the 1860s. But for the most part, Australians shared a form of religious commingling in which Christianity in general – and Protestantism in particular – were presumed preferable and dominant but not in need of strenuous legal reinforcement.

Overall, this was a period in which the people of the Australian colonies still tended to depict themselves as strapping but somewhat ungainly youths. Nervous members of colonial elites identified a need for order, temperance and the supervision of an unruly colonial population, and their desire for monumental expression of stability is evident in the public libraries, learned societies, museums, parks, universities and parliamentary buildings established during the 1850s and 1860s. But working people wanted improvement as well, and there were plenty of savings clubs and fraternal societies to protect their investments. Protesting miners, workers and smallholders occasionally used a radical language, but most wanted inclusion in an orderly British society, not its overthrow. The resolution they found to the problems and opportunities of rapid growth rested upon a distinctive Australian blend of principles. On the one hand, government should ensure that people were free to pursue and enjoy prosperity and to improve their positions. On the other, it should protect them from the risks of change and the consequences of competition, and ensure that others' improvement did not come at their cost. In a difficult environment and an unstable economy, colonists wanted two good things, the freedom to succeed and protection from failure, and they did not always recognise the potential contradiction between them.

EXPANDING AND EXHIBITING

If the feverish thirst for gold had taught them anything, colonists now imagined Australia's destiny in more fulsome terms. This could be a British society, but it would be an improved and improving one, and might surpass even America in size and strength. The colonies had separated from New South Wales and from Britain. There was responsible government, a degree of democratic qualification and participation achieved in few other societies, and the beginnings of an attempt to open up the land. Gold had generated wealth, and would help fund the future. The rushes had brought a share of wild-eyed adventurers, but the great majority of Australia's gold-era migrants were literate, skilled and possessed more wealth than the far greater numbers who made the much cheaper Atlantic crossing to Canada or the United States.

This greater degree of independence brought its own anxieties. The continent itself seemed still unfinished, and its capacity to defeat investigation was vividly realised by the disappearance of Robert Burke and William Wills, who left Melbourne in 1860, reached the Gulf of Carpentaria and then ran out of luck and supplies on the return journey. Relief expeditions were mounted, and found the only survivor, John King, a twenty-two year old Irish soldier who had spent time on India's Northwest Frontier and had been kept alive by the local Aboriginal people. John McDouall Stuart had better fortune, though in his travels across South Australia's deserts in 1859 he rather over-confidently described them as 'wonderful country'.[12] In the 1860s, Stuart tried, failed, tried again, failed, tried again and finally succeeded in 1862, travelling from South Australia to the north coast, which also laid out a possible route for the overseas telegraph to come to Adelaide. The settlement of Palmerston at Port Darwin, founded in 1869, became Australia's telegraphic connection point with the world.

With self-government came concerns about self-defence. In the 1850s, the Crimean War led to fears – however unlikely they might seem in hindsight – of a Russian attack, and a flurry of fort-building on various headlands. The French were still about too. Gunboats at the ready, they declared Tahiti a protectorate in 1842 and, more threateningly, took possession of New Caledonia in 1853. Napoleon III rather liked the idea of a Pacific empire; to the great chagrin of Austral-Britons, his government also decided to use the island for – of all things – a penal colony.

Having achieved a prominent position at London's 1862 Great Exhibition, Victoria hosted the Intercolonial Exhibition of Australasia in 1866. Director of the Botanic Gardens, Ferdinand Von Mueller, wrote a major new work on Australian vegetation, and each colony contributed a series of products, mechanical devices and manufactures. The Grand Introductory Concert featured a band and chorus of some eight hundred performers; reserved seats (for which evening dress was required) were five shillings, while a seat in the back cost two shillings and sixpence. As the Exhibition's guide noted, the products and skills 'prove in a most striking manner not only the general existence of a highly-cultivated intelligence amongst the people of these colonies, but show a strongly-marked progress of refinement'. There were nearly three thousand exhibits, half from Victoria and more than seven hundred from Tasmania. New South Wales could manage only 273 – courtesy, the guide fumed, of 'the coldness of a few politically bilious individuals' – and Queensland just 36 (the same as New Caledonia), largely because much of its exhibition was already being despatched to Paris for the great Exposition Universelle of 1867.[13] The Exhibition's earnest displays of 'public spirit, intelligence and industry' were meant to be 'suggestive of a future time when the Australian colonies will be great and prosperous States, rivalling European kingdoms in all that is worthy of rivalry'.[14] For the coming people of the Antipodes, no future expectations were too grand.

It was with great excitement, then, that thousands of people welcomed Queen Victoria's second son, Prince Alfred. Arriving from the Cape Colony in October 1867, he toured Adelaide, Melbourne, Sydney, Hobart and Brisbane. Here, indeed, was proof of a coming of age, that the monarch would send one of her sons, and a relatively important one at that, even if she regarded him as vague, touchy and wilful. The Catholic *Freeman's Journal* lampooned the pleasure cruise of a 'young Anglo-German gentleman'.[15] But this was Irish sarcasm, and most Australians eagerly awaited a chance to see a member of the ruling family. But in an instant, colonial excitement would give way to deep, dark despair.

7

At the Forefront of the Race: 1868–88

Prince Alfred survived the bullet of his would-be assassin. It was fired into his back, but missed his spine. The news could hardly be believed, the Legislative Council of New South Wales doubting its veracity until there was confirmation from detectives. In the crowd at Clontarf, 'women and men fainted and sobbed', wrote Elizabeth Rickets Hall, for whom the outrage seemed 'too deep and grave even for words'. The criminal 'was nearly torn to pieces on the spot and with difficulty saved from Lynch law'.[1] The people of Sydney found immediate comfort in the fact that the villain, Henry O'Farrell, was from Victoria. The people of all the colonies found further comfort in the news that he was Irish, and therefore almost certainly one of the Fenian terrorists. Irish rebels there were in Australia, including some recently transported to Western Australia. But it is unlikely that any organisation would have found much use for O'Farrell. He was virulently anti-British, but also most likely insane, by the definitions common in the nineteenth century. It did him little good. Tried and sentenced, he died by hanging within five weeks of the shooting.

There was deep shame. A day after the shooting, twenty thousand people attended an Indignation Meeting in Sydney, and within a week almost every Australian town or city had followed the lead. Country people used the still novel technology of the telegraph to send in their expressions of horror. Perhaps the most common refrain was that 'the whole colony has been wounded' by a crime that would 'shadow our reputation'.[2] Emotions ran strong. Henry Parkes, the Colonial Secretary, was sure that a Fenian conspiracy had injured the prince, even though O'Farrell made clear in his confession that he had acted alone. The New South Wales Parliament passed the *Treason Felony Act*; it would now be an offence to refuse to toast the Queen or to use any language that was disrespectful towards her. The incident re-energised Australian sectarianism; disloyalty became Irish and Catholic, and for decades Australian Catholics would be closely watched for signs of radical, republican or anti-monarchical thought (a small number of girls at an Albury convent school who failed to stand for *God Save the Queen* created much excitement in 1870, for example). It also made sure that the rituals of an Austral-British and imperial culture, and the royal personages who most clearly represented them, were more firmly embedded at the centre of Australian life.

COLONIAL ANTICIPATIONS

The shooting revived concerns about the convict inheritance and the debilitating presence of possibly inferior breeds. Nineteenth-century Australians were always caught between self-confidence and fears that they might prove inferior to the task of spreading and improving British civilisation; it was possible, after all, that Australians might just as easily deteriorate as rise. The quality of the population was one issue. Another was the possible effect of the continent itself. There were humorous asides about the effects of an 'inverted' hemisphere upon manners and morals, the strangeness of roundabout seasons, cartoons of 'Topsy Turvy Land' and, from 'The Land of Contrarieties', the claim that 'there vice is virtue, virtue vice, and all that's vile is voted nice'.[3] Novelist Marcus Clarke was more influential; his satiric description of an 'Australasian' modified by climate appeared in 1877:

> The average Australian will be a tall, coarse, strong-jawed, greedy, pushing, talented man, excelling in swimming and horsemanship. His religion will be a form of Presbyterianism; his national policy a democracy tempered by the rate of exchange. His wife will be a thin, narrow woman, very fond of dress and idleness, caring little for her children, but without sufficient brain-power to sin with zest. In five hundred years, unless recruited from foreign nations, the breed will be extinct; but in that five hundred years, it will have changed the face of Nature, and swallowed up all our contemporary civilisation.[4]

But Clarke's humour was more than matched by scientific speculations that Australia's inferior soil and hot climate would lead to 'an inevitable degeneration of the Anglo-Saxon stock'. As nineteenth-century Europeans developed iron laws about the relationships between soil, culture and racial development – which held as an inviolable truth that 'the physique, intelligence and morale of a race are determined by the geological conditions of the country it inhabits' – some of their colonists had cause to worry.[5] In some minds, the lowly status of the Aboriginal people was proof enough of that. When you also considered some of the native mammals, with their strange features and retarded habits, the picture only darkened. The duck-billed platypus might be a natural wonder, or a marvellous curiosity. Or it might be a sign of just how far Antipodean nature could fall.

Little wonder that many colonists strove to mould their character and their future around imported models. Gentility was measured by British standards of dress, behaviour, education and manners. In thousands of colonial gardens, European plants and flowers struggled against a hotter sun and drier climate. There were horticultural books to help guide the way, and during the 1860s and 1870s, 'acclimatisation' societies intro-duced European animals and plants to the continent. The first emerged in Victoria in 1861. There was a nostalgia for the familiar, the huntable and the commercially viable, but there was also a conviction that a landscape not yet Europeanised was in some sense deficient. The aim was clear; Dr George Bennett of Sydney claimed the introduction of animals and plants 'will impart life and beauty to our plains' and 'fill our lakes and rivers with beautiful objects of nature'.[6] Acclimatisation went hand in hand with the development of zoological gardens for native and imported animals; the New South Wales Zoological Society, for instance, listed its aims as 'the introduction and acclimatisation of song birds and game' in 1879, and the Adelaide Zoo was created by the Acclimatisation Society of South Australia in 1883.[7] Birds were sent to towns like Bathurst, Goulburn and Maitland, where they could be released to fill the forests and to break what one natural scientist called in 1862 the 'present savage silence'.[8] Salmon, trout, perch and carp were put into colonial rivers, where they rapidly reduced the size of native populations. The botanist Ferdinand Von Mueller thought blackberry would be a good idea. There were intra-colonial transfers, too: kookaburras were introduced, with little success, to New Zealand and Fiji, and with much more success to the area around Perth. Victoria sent four possums to New Zealand in 1863, where they began their disastrous trail through native forests. Among the most successful acclimatisers were rabbits – colonists even poisoned native predators to ensure their successful spread – and foxes.

Landscape artists and nature poets are among the best indicators of how an environment is perceived. In Australia during the 1830s and 1840s, Augustus Earle, John Glover and Conrad Martens had grappled with the light and the difficult task of painting eucalypts while remain-ing true to English conventions. Their landscapes were not European, but could contain Europeans, their horses and their haystacks, as well as the more recognisably unusual features of Australian flora and, in some examples, Aboriginal subjects. In the 1860s, the colonies could claim some 'natural' if not 'national' poets in Henry Kendall and Adam Lindsay Gordon, while painters Eugene Von Guerard and especially Louis Buvelot shifted the adaptation of European landscape conventions further towards accuracy of colour and form. Their ambivalence about the strangeness and the wonder of Australian country was mirrored even among ardent acclimatisationists; the same society stocking New South Wales with starlings also pressured the colonial parliament to pass an act protecting native birds.

The science of 'stock', 'breed' and 'blood' spurred anxieties about the likely future of the colonies, but it could also provide anxiety's antidote. European science was in the middle of several decades of fascination with racial hierarchies and histories and had proved to its own satisfaction that race was the single most powerful force in human 'evolution'. Australians eagerly grasped the logical conclusion: their racial inheritance would prevail. As popular novelist Rolf Boldrewood predicted, 'Australia may eventually produce a type of the highest physical and mental vigour possible to the race'; indeed, 'the Great South Land' would so develop those 'root-qualities of the race' that it would carry forward 'the great Aryan stock'.[9] Australian nationalism came to rest on the confident foundations of racial superiority and improvement. As would be true for decades to come, it was decidedly comparative, with colonial eyes likely to be cast across the Pacific to the United States as another 'great white nation'. Indeed, Australians were more and more likely to believe that their nation, which lacked America's racial diversity, would be one of the few that might become and remain truly 'white'.

DETERMINING THE ABORIGINAL FUTURE

In a science that proved the natural triumph of 'Aryans', there were casualties. The status of the Irish remained ambivalent, and there were some who held that Catholics as a whole were a different breed as well as a different faith. The Chinese and the 'Hindoos' were clearly a stage below the European, though industrious in their own way. Indeed, one of the burdens of racial superiority was to manage and control these inferior people, and to prevent the sullying of European stock through what was termed 'racial mixing'. Australia's Aboriginal people were often placed among the lowest on a racial ladder that put Anglo-Saxons at its top and so based every judgement on what most favoured them. There were practical consequences too. Australians, along with Californians, led the world in immigration restriction activism by the 1880s, their aim squarely on the Chinese. Sinophobia had diminished somewhat with the passing of the gold rushes, and the poll taxes and other anti-Chinese laws were repealed in the 1860s. But by the middle of the 1870s, feelings and protests against 'Celestials' and 'Mongols' were growing once more, fuelled in part by a trade unionist conviction that inferior people such as these were too easily exploited and underpaid, and the colonies began to reinstate severe restrictions and even total exclusions on Chinese immigration.

The implications for Australia's Aboriginal people were even more profound. Clearly doomed in what schoolmaster and writer Alexander Sutherland called European 'obedience to natural laws over which they have no control', they deserved sympathy.[10] There were even thoughts that they were vanishing and might become cultural oddities and museum pieces. It was a strange belief, because Aboriginal people were everywhere. Along the edges of settlement, graziers used the people they had displaced as labour on sheep and cattle stations, often for rations rather than payment. Aboriginal women and girls provided a good deal of the colonies' domestic labour and cooking. Some industries – pearling and bêche-de-mer farming are perhaps the best examples – were heavily reliant on Aboriginal labour. Aboriginal men were hired – or simply used – as guides and trackers, or as 'native police'. All through the colonies, Aboriginal families and groups found whatever space they could for a compromised, damaged and yet never-surrendered culture. They sought work and food, continued to bargain with pastoralists over access to land and tracks, and tried to establish some secure basis for future life.

Depending upon where they lived, Aboriginal people had to contend with two different approaches to their future. On the frontier, the momentum of violence and dispossession was repeated across Queensland, the Northern Territory and Western Australia. The shock troops of settlement were human and animal, as water- and vegetation-hungry cattle, sheep and rabbits moved out into more and more marginal land. Conflicts over land, water and hunting sparked everywhere; there were killings in retaliation and there were killings in anticipation. The improved weapons of the 1860s and 1870s probably increased Aboriginal casualties. Expeditions to 'disperse' and punish 'natives' set out into the Western Australian Kimberley, central Queensland, the Gulf country and Arnhem Land, and along the telegraph track between Alice Springs and Darwin. The costs of resistance were high. A bullock speared or a horse stolen by any Aboriginal person made every Aboriginal subject to violent payback, sometimes at the hands of the native police. From the 1860s until the 1920s, conflict was probably most violent in areas such as north-western Queensland and the northern parts of Western Australia, where the struggle over land was more prolonged and the outcome made more uncertain by smaller numbers of settlers.

In the areas settled most quickly and densely by white settlers, Aboriginal people were, from the late 1850s, subjected to another approach: 'protection' by means of forced relocation, concentration and segregation. As was true in North America, this achieved two objectives. First, it established the fact of complete and permanent dispossession and made clear that Aboriginal people would now live where they were told, in groups that could be supervised and controlled. Second, it promised to protect those remnant populations from the exploitation, violence and liquor of settlers; protection and reservation policy always allowed that Aboriginal people – or native Americans – had been the victims more than the villains, though it offered no remedy for their loss of land and livelihood and it often blamed the problem on Aboriginal weakness. With concentration and segregation, it was also easier to imagine a process of 'elevating and improving' at least some of the beneficiaries. Protection was always followed by segmentation, and in particular the development of legislation and practice, based upon ludicrous measurements of blood, heritage and 'stock', to identify those who had some hope of assimilating into white society or the children who had not yet been 'lost'. It was also crucial that protectors control marriage, reproduction and child-rearing.

The process is well illustrated in Victoria. In 1858, a government select committee recommended a system of reserves, having found that the colony's Indigenous population, 'being weak and ignorant, even for savages', had failed to match New Zealand's Maori in forcing the 'new occupiers of their country to provide for them'.[11] It also established a Board for the Protection of Aborigines in 1869. The Board found that while it would not be practical or humane 'to compel the old natives against their inclinations to abandon the localities where they were born' it was necessary to remove the newer generation into stations and schools.[12] In 1886, a further *Aborigines' Protection Act* allowed the removal from reserves – and from the rations, work and clothing they provided – of any person aged less than thirty-four and categorised as not 'full blood', including children. Protection could never mask its cruel accounting.

Things would not always go smoothly, because Aboriginal people often came to regard reserves and rations as theirs by right; concentration and segregation could also produce resistance and rebellion. Indeed, having been brought together into missions such as Victoria's Coranderrk, Aboriginal residents developed the idea that they should be able to manage themselves. Other Aboriginal people purchased small selections, or tried to argue for possession of inalienable and crown land. As a member of the Victorian Parliament acknowledged in an 1876 debate, some of the Coranderrk people 'could read, write, and argue, and put forward their opinions on various subjects in a most intelligent manner', with some even claiming that 'it was the duty of the State to support them'.[13] Despite such risks, other colonies followed Victoria's pattern: Protection Boards were established in New South Wales in 1883 and in Western Australia in 1886, and Queensland passed a Protection Act in 1897. In South Australia, which had made the Commissioner of Crown Lands responsible for the care of Aboriginal people in 1856, and in the Northern Territory, protection came somewhat later, in 1911 and 1910 respectively. Around the edges of the government system were built faith-based missions, such as Lutheran Hermannsburg near Alice Springs or Presbyterian Mapoon on Cape York in Queensland, while Aboriginal people set up farms at places like Cummeragunja on the Murray River. It is possible that the reserves and missions saved some Indigenous communities from an even worse fate, while also ridding colonial settlements of a problem they did not want to see nor face. But they always signalled the determination to immobilise Aboriginal people in places not of their own choosing.

In Tasmania, there was no assumed need to protect a race that had supposedly vanished. The forty-seven people who remained on Flinders Island in 1847 were removed again, to Oyster Cove, south of Hobart. By 1873, only one woman, Truganini, remained, and she died in 1876, misidentified then and often still now as the 'last of the Tasmanians'. People in other colonies sometimes wondered if their Aboriginal people might also die out, but there were differences of opinion on the cause. In his four-volume work *The Australian Race*, one-time squatter and inspector of stock Edward Curr argued 'the White race seems destined, not to absorb, but to exterminate the Blacks of Australia'.[14] Others at the time, and later generations – even into the twenty-first century – preferred a more benign and less violent process. Australia's native tribes, Alexander Sutherland wrote, were 'poorly recuperative' in the face of 'a divine law that [Europeans] are to emigrate and form for themselves new homes in waste land'. He continued, in a regretful fantasy:

Yet will there ever cling a pathos round the story of a vanishing race; and when we think of the agile forms that once held dominion over these widely forested lands; when we see them vanishing with terrible speed to be but a memory of the past, the contrast affects our feelings, even though our intellects refuse to be moved, recognizing the working of a law above that which man makes for himself.[15]

AUSTRALIAN LIVES

However inaccurate his playful prescriptions, Marcus Clarke had captured something of the change in Australians during the 1870s and 1880s. As the large gold rush generation aged and reproduced, the colonies steadily moved towards a native-born majority. Their children were a bulge in the population similar to the twentieth century's baby boom; in 1871, every third Australian was a child of twelve or younger, and more than half of the population were aged under twenty. By the 1880s, Australians, like Europeans and North Americans, were limiting their families – four or five pregnancies rather than eight or nine – and sending their children to school into their teens. The birth rate almost halved within just one generation, in part because Australians were world leaders in the use of contraceptives, including the new rubber condoms, despite campaigns to ban advertising and information.

There were undoubted challenges, including killer epidemics of childhood diseases, especially of measles, scarlet fever and diphtheria, and different colonies were struck by smallpox. Typhoid – also called colonial fever – was endemic by 1850 and remained threatening into the 1880s, and tropical diseases also became established in Queensland and the Northern Territory. As rural areas filled up with bullocks, so cities filled with thousands of horses, and city streets with their manure. Melbourne, occasionally lampooned as 'Smelbourne' because of the stink of sewerage, offal and food manufacturing, was on a par with other great cities when it came to death rates from typhoid. There, too, infant death rates were much higher, especially from 'convulsions', 'atrophy' and teething, most of which was probably weanling diarrhoea. As coal consumption soared in the 1860s and 1870s, cities grew smoky and even more unhealthy.

Yet most of these largely British people benefited from their long migration. Australians were comparatively healthy; the infant mortality rate – about one baby in ten – was almost half that in the cities of England, and colonial children and adults enjoyed the better health that higher relative incomes brought. A person born in the 1860s who survived infancy and childhood could expect to see the age of fifty and

Table 7.1 Population growth, 1851–91

	1851	1861	1871	1881	1891
New South Wales	197,265	357,362	516,704	777,025	1,153,170
Van Diemen's Land/ Tasmania	69,187	89,908	101,900	117,770	151,150
Western Australia	7,186	15,936	25,447	30,156	53,177
South Australia	66,538	130,812	188,644	285,971	324,721
Victoria	97,489	539,764	746,450	873,965	1,158,372
Queensland		34,367	121,743	221,849	400,395
Australia*	437,665	1,168,149	1,700,888	2,306,736	3,240,985

* Aboriginal and Torres Strait Islander people are not included in these figures.

Source: Australian Bureau of Statistics, 'Australian Historical Population Statistics, 2006' (3105.0.65.001), at http://www.abs.gov.au.

was likely to reach sixty. Australians were among the greatest eaters of meat on the planet, and had unusually good access to milk and butter. All that protein made Australians comparatively tall: women averaged around 160 centimetres (around five feet two inches), while men were about fourteen centimetres (five inches) taller.

Australians ate well, and drank a lot. Their beer, which used cane sugar, was rather different from the English variety and its uneven quality caused a good deal of anguish until the introduction of pure yeast strains for fermentation in the 1880s. With access to markets, city diets were less monotonous than country ones, and included nineteenth-century fast foods like fried fish, and even a few imported delicacies from Malaya, India and China, to add to flour, potatoes, bread, tea and bacon. By the middle of the 1880s, diets would be expanded significantly by refrigerated transport, but even earlier visitors were impressed by the range of foods ordinary people consumed, which included oranges and bananas, eggs and cheese, and lamb as well as mutton, the great staple of the nineteenth-century British world. City and country people grew, ate and preserved vegetables and fruit. With refined white flour in the 1860s came sweet biscuits and cakes. Increased income always meant more meat and more sugar, and Australians were great enthusiasts for both.

Despite an emerging conviction that Australia's essence might live in its bush, a steadily growing proportion of Australians lived in town, making it one of the most urbanised countries in the world. Both Melbourne and Sydney were very large cities by international standards, but the trend was just as apparent in the growth of Brisbane and Adelaide, or of smaller but substantial towns such as Launceston, Geelong, Toowoomba or Bathurst. In the nineteenth-century world, high levels of urbanisation also meant high levels of literacy and a thirst for news; by 1883, when the colonies could claim several hundred active dailies and weeklies, British visitor Richard Twopeny would label Australia 'the land of newspapers'.[16]

Taken as a whole, Australians were among the richest people on the earth. Their houses and cottages were relatively large, often made of brick and stone, and they could afford some of the newer possessions, such as wood or gas stoves, iron cooking utensils and even the new 'instantaneous water heaters' that burned pine cones, twigs and wood chips. By 1891, a third of Australians lived in homes they owned or were purchasing. Wages were comparatively high, because labour was comparatively scarce, and colonial elites assured would-be migrants that 'to the operative classes, Australia is a veritable land of promise'.[17]

Table 7.2 Population of capital cities, 1871–91

		1871	1881	1891
New South Wales	Sydney	134,736	220,894	383,283
	% of total colony	26	28	33
Tasmania	Hobart	19,092	21,118	33,450
	% of total colony	19	18	22
Western Australia	Perth	5,007	5,044	8,447
	% of total colony	20	17	16
South Australia	Adelaide	27,208	38,479	37,837
	% of total colony	14	14	12
Victoria	Melbourne	191,449	262,389	474,440
	% of total colony	26	30	41
Queensland	Brisbane	19,413	37,053	101,554
	% of total colony	16	17	25

Source: W. Vamplew (ed.) *Australians: Historical Statistics* (Sydney: Fairfax, Syme and Weldon Associates, 1987), p. 41.

THE EIGHT HOURS DEMONSTRATION.

Illustration 7.1 'The Eight Hours Demonstration', 1879

Source: LaTrobe Pictures Collection, State Library of Victoria, IAN12/05/79/77.

Though most male workers laboured for fifty hours a week, with only Sunday for rest, and women carried the double burdens of hard domestic labour and paid work woven in and around childbirth and childrearing, observers were also impressed by the Australian appetite for leisure, especially organised sport. If proof of Australian men's imperial capacities were needed, the 1877 victory of a Combined Australian Eleven in the 'Grand Combination Match' of cricket in Melbourne would do. But reputation was a fragile thing. A controversial umpiring decision caused a riot at a match in Sydney in 1879. Australian dignity was restored by its victory over an English side in London in 1882.

By the 1860s, a distinctive brand of football – 'Australasian Rules' became one term for it – was spreading from Victoria into South Australia, Tasmania and Western Australia; its progress was halted in Queensland and New South Wales by the prior popularity of rugby. Sport was very popular, and attendances grew as more workers began to achieve a half-day on Saturdays. The colonies managed to develop other pastimes – especially cricket and horseracing – without creating different versions. Indeed, horseracing was the only truly national sport in the 1870s and in 1879, the Melbourne Cup, first run in 1861, became the occasion for a public holiday in the nation's then largest city.

Australia was also becoming easier to come to and get around in, as clipper ships cut the time of journeys from Europe and North America, and paddle-steamers, rapid coach services and then railways moved towns and cities closer together in time. As steam cut the practical distances between Europe, America and Australia, global celebrities were easier to attract, and a new group of entrepreneurs fuelled and fed Australians' desire for famous travellers, from African explorer Henry Stanley and American author Mark Twain to one of the most celebrated women of the nineteenth century, Sarah Bernhardt. Every colony had railways by 1871, and within twenty years rural settlement was rearranged into thin strips of connection between the major ports and cities. The wheat belt took shape inland, and the coastal farming areas shifted towards dairying and horticulture or, in Queensland, sugar. Here, as in other technological changes, government ownership or funding was a crucial factor in rapid development; in Australia, public authorities often assumed the risk and initiative that private companies provided in more populated places such as the United States. Trains meant timetables, which in turn meant keeping more accurate time and – eventually, from 1892 – establishing standard time zones to replace the local mean times that had made Sydney time, Melbourne time, Albury time and Townsville time all different. By the 1880s, the telegraph, the telephone and accurate timekeeping transformed business and commercial relationships. Their rapid success in Australia, something that was also true of domestic appliances and farming equipment, signalled an important lasting characteristic: Australians were innovators and inventors, particularly in agriculture and mining, but they were even more enthusiastic about the rapid adaptation of overseas technologies. There are few innovations in the last two centuries – from domestic refrigerators to mobile phones – that have not had their most rapid take-up in Australia.

A HARD COUNTRY

This was a land of promise, perhaps, though not of guarantees. Most of Australia's capitals were spared the great fires and floods that destroyed cities in Europe and North America; Brisbane lived closest to the edge of disaster through flood and cyclone. Yet the less spectacular insecurities of life created their share of misery and poverty. There was charity, but in a land of supposed plenty, in which people were meant to look out for themselves, it was often meanly measured and grudgingly given. Average wages may have been high, but many working people faced seasonal lay-offs and short time because so much of the work in farming, construction, transport and manufacturing was casual or subject to the weather. Life's dangers and frailties could overwhelm even the most careful; this was a hard country in which to be poor, deserted, old, infirm, alone or unwell. The dangers of alcoholism encouraged new concerns for sobriety, with coffee palaces and the 'temperance hotels' trying to draw city people into less intoxicated pursuits. Prosperous some Australians may have been, but thousands of others filled orphanages and asylums for the destitute.

Detailed investigations into the lives of ordinary Australians revealed the extent and the implications of economic and social inequality; it came as some surprise to proponents of the 'coming man', from the 1850s onwards, to find that Melbourne and Sydney, in particular, were developing slums and urban blight to match those of London, Paris and Manchester. One Melbourne doctor reported that 'nothing I have ever witnessed in the West Riding of Yorkshire and in South Lancashire equalled in repulsiveness what I found in Melbourne'.[18] In Brisbane, sewerage from the prosperous households on the numerous hills washed down into the poorer households in the valleys and river flats, with tropical rains forming vile lakes throughout the wet season. In Sydney, too, there was much concern with the disease of 'larrikinism' as young toughs stalked the city's streets. Petty thievery and thuggery were not unusual in any nineteenth-century city, though the sensational trial – and hangings of four larrikins – that followed an alleged mass rape at Sydney's Mount Rennie in 1886 gave Australians something of the outraged thrill that increasingly greeted urban criminality.

Compared to Britons, Australians were noted for their egalitarian manner by the 1860s and 1870s, something shown in their relative lack of deference and in the dignity that was afforded ordinary aspirations. Yet this did not mean that social and cultural distinctions were unimportant. Private clubs and private schools ensured that the wealthy would not have to spend too much time with their inferiors, and the thirst for imperial honours became greater, if anything, the further one travelled from the centre of the empire. Australian elites had a broader range of social origins than was true in Europe but, as was true in North America, the very fluidity and newness of social caste made maintaining the rules of division even more important.

Australia's inland had its own social and economic fissures. If gold began a long economic boom, wool maintained it. Squatters chose the less negative term 'pastoralists' and reinvented themselves as a kind of pioneering squire. Some farmers were wealthy, and others did well enough, but small farmers on marginal land struggled to do more than survive. In Victoria and South Australia, the wheat belt farms of the 1870s and 1880s showed that legislatures could make access easier for smallholders, but that did not protect them from unwinnable odds. While the coming great droughts and erosions of the 1890s would finish off many selectors, their hard times were already endemic by 1880.

During the 1860s, bushranging and other kinds of rural banditry flourished in New South Wales, with Frank Gardiner, Johnny Gilbert, Ben Hall and others picking off gold escorts and mail coaches. When they came into violent conflict with police and trackers, they were hunted down as outlaws. If much of their thieving was indiscriminate and petty, the last wave of bushranging in Victoria in the 1870s also expressed the grievances of poorer rural Australians about policing, the impounding of cattle, and ownership of the land. Ned Kelly was a thief, but one who more than others pointed out the prejudices visited upon him as a poor man and a Catholic. As his conflicts with police escalated, to the point of murder and then the shoot-out at Glenrowan, Kelly increasingly styled himself a victim of injustice and persecution. In his long and self-defending manifesto, written at Jerilderie but not rediscovered until 1930, he fumed that 'it will pay the Government to give those people who are suffering innocence, justice and liberty. If not

I will be compelled to show some colonial strategem which will open the eyes of not only the Victorian Police, and inhabitants, but also the whole British Army.'[19] Ned's notoriety was helped by improved graphic and news technologies, which put his picture into illustrated newspapers and updates on his trial onto every newsstand. After his execution in 1880, his story was told in weekly parts and was quickly turned into myth. He was a product of grievance, but he was also one of the first to be subjected to a new kind of celebrity.

LOCAL LIVES

Whether or not bushrangers showed the darker side of the coming Australian, doubts and misgivings belied the apparent confidence of an expanding colonial society during the last half of the nineteenth century. At this point, however, each colony pressed on with its own development and, in turn, its own version of the future. That each colony laid its railways to different gauges was one of the best examples that they did not really consider the longer-term problems that might be produced by their rivalries. Each parliament directed public money to the task of securing that colony's prosperity and each political elite tended to nourish and protect its own fortunes. It was an approach to the future beset with difficulties, notably booms and busts of investment and speculation in pastoral industries, railways, mining and urban land values. Some of the wealthy managed to pool their money through prudent marriages, but fortunes were as often spectacularly lost as gained. And fortunes lost were sometimes replenished from public funds, as when colonial governments had to pick up the pieces of failed private railway companies. Visiting English social reformer Beatrice Webb's later and rather sniffy description of colonial politicians as 'a mean, undignified set of little property owners' was unfair, but not completely inaccurate.[20]

Colonists still lived very local lives. There were shared dilemmas and possibilities, but there were also strong disagreements and powerful feelings of distance. Two colonies – New South Wales and Victoria – assumed that they would set the course into the future. Victoria tended to see itself as Australia's progressive leader and booming Melbourne as its prosperous vanguard. The colony boomed on the back of the gold rush migrants and their children and the city became Australia's financial heart. With five international exhibitions to its name, the most extravagant in 1880, a reputation as one of the largest and finest cities in the Empire, and a growth rate that saw it rival the new great American metropolis of Chicago, the city awaited only a suitable moniker. English journalist George Sala delivered 'Marvellous Melbourne'. Victoria's development, however, rested on borrowings, which in turn rested on confidence. By the end of the 1880s its fortunes would begin to turn.

As well as expressing colonial pride, Victoria's leaders increasingly rallied around the idea of 'protectionism', which tied Australia's future economic and social development to the protection of local farmers and industries by tariff barriers. They understood this to be a distinctive kind of political economy, defended by newspaper editor David Syme in *Outlines of an Industrial Science* in 1876, which would also bring social and intellectual progress. It also demanded an extension of government beyond its mid-nineteenth-century limits. It was not popular with the large landowners and money interests that dominated the colony's upper house, and their bitter opposition created crisis after crisis in Victoria's parliament. Protectionist policies would also find support in the smaller colonies, where tariffs seemed to nourish industries and provided crucial revenue for public works.

New South Wales was industrialising too, especially in and around Sydney, but it stuck with the British policy of free trade and *laissez-faire*. The differences in actual rates of development were relatively minor, but the battle between free trade and protection quickly became a battle between New South Wales and Victoria and between two faiths, each holding firm to its vision of the future. The dominant figures in New South Wales, especially Henry Parkes, who served as premier five times between 1872 and 1889, saw protectionism as a parochial and short-sighted mistake that pandered to popular misunderstandings of good policy and contradicted the direction of the Empire. The customs posts along the Murray River, collecting Victoria's tariffs from New South Wales producers, was an infuriating symbol of the southern colony's madness.

Other colonies took paths more or less in between the two monoliths. Tasmania grew more slowly than the rest and moved less quickly away from its function and form as a penal society. Whatever distance it achieved in reality – and discoveries of tin, gold, lead and eventually copper promised to turn its economy towards mining – was somewhat dented by its continuing reputation both for the apparent destruction of its Aboriginal people, who were used around the world as an example of unrestrained colonial excess, and for brutality, especially when Marcus Clarke's 1874 novel *For the Term of his Natural Life* added cannibalism to the mix of images associated with Tasmanian convicts.

Western Australia's convict past had ended; sheep grazing spread into new areas such as the Pilbara and the Murchison in the 1860s and 1870s,

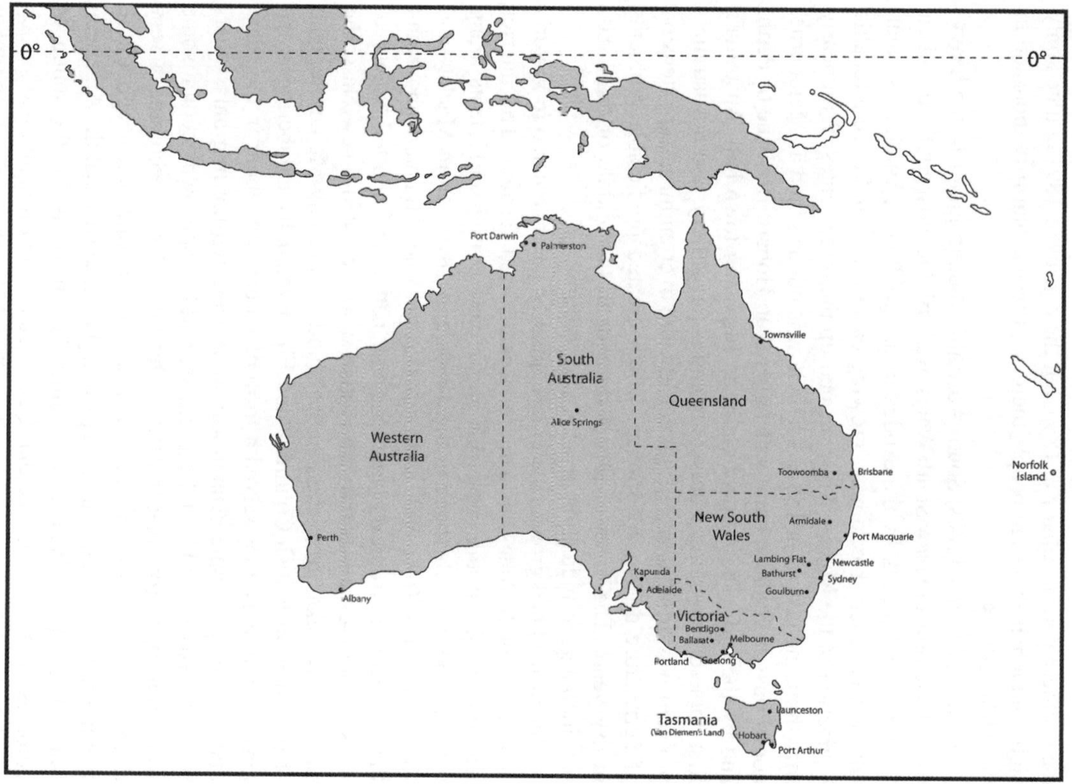

Map 2 The Australian colonies in 1870

while explorers walked through parts of the continent as yet unknown to its European settlers. In 1889, Western Australia finally gained self-government with the passing of the bill granting a constitution in 1890. Perth was connected by telegraph to Adelaide in 1877 and by railway to the southern port of Albany in 1889, but the census of 1891 counted only eight and a half thousand people there, and fewer than fifty thousand in the whole colony.

In the 1870s and 1880s, South Australia, though junior to the heavyweight Victoria and New South Wales, was still the most civilised of their 'sisters'. First shrunk by the exodus to the goldfields, South Australian wheat was better able to meet growing eastern demand once a reliable navigation of the Murray River opened up the trade routes. With nearly fifty thousand people in 1881, Adelaide was not as grand as Melbourne, nor as busy as Sydney, but it was larger than Hobart, Brisbane or Perth, and by the early 1880s could claim an imposing town hall, Australia's first horse-drawn trams, a university and an art gallery. South Australia's problem was drought or, more precisely, the over-enthusiastic extension of agriculture during good years, which created predictable problems in dry years. The onset of severe drought in the middle of the 1880s provided a good indication of what was to come.

Queensland had grown much more quickly and, compared to Victoria and New South Wales, in a more decentralised fashion. The interior was run by sheep and cattle, but sugar cane strung settlements along the coast north of Brisbane in the 1860s and 1870s, from Mackay and Rockhampton to Townsville and Cairns. Sugar's need for hard labour, and the link between tropical plantations and 'native' or imported 'coloured' workers, long-established in the British world, created a new class: the so-called Kanakas from the Pacific Islands, especially Melanesia, who also worked in British Columbia and Fiji. Eventually numbering in the tens of thousands, they served a form of indentured labour in the sugar and also the pineapple plantations; some were willing migrants, others were tricked or lured by false promise, and by their own account some were kidnapped (or 'blackbirded'). Queensland was becoming a very different place, a vast expanse of tropical and subtropical agriculture that might develop along its own path in the same way that the American South had. Henry Parkes, discussing the prospects for the union of colonies in 1879, suggested that Queensland might remain outside such a union 'because her capabilities of soil and climate so clearly mark her out for a colonizing career dissimilar from that of her elder sisters'.[21] At this point, this great leader of the movement that would achieve federation in 1901 thought it possible that Australia might be formed from New South Wales, Victoria and South Australia alone, leaving others – small Tasmania, underdeveloped Western Australia and plantation Queensland – outside the national fold. The issue became even more difficult in the 1880s, once the Queensland government led by Samuel Griffith moved to restrict the importation and even the use of 'coloured' labour. The planters of its northern half began to agitate for separation, with the idea of forming a new colony with a capital at Townsville. If it were to join an Australia more or more concerned about remaining white, north Queensland would face a hard choice about its future.

DEBATING UNION

If there were forces keeping the colonies apart, what might pull them together? Almost everyone acknowledged that there would be benefits from a national union – perhaps even a regional one including New Zealand and Fiji – and younger, native-born Australians were becoming more used to the inter-colonial connections that new forms of communication and transport were encouraging. After 1871, there was also a vigorous nationalising body, the Australian Natives Association, which began as a friendly society but quickly took on the broader mantle of civic improvement, native-born pride and federation. Some of the earliest inter-colonial conferences focused on the tasks a union might better accomplish, such as mail services, customs and trade. Yet the differences sometimes seemed insurmountable. As ever, Australians cast about for international models, but their lessons were ambivalent. Germany had been formed by a dominating Prussia. Canada was a more promising example, though Switzerland's 1848 federation had only followed a small-scale civil war. The United States was certainly a strong federation, but Australians were very conscious of its terrible civil war. And some political theorists argued that federations just might not work at the vast scale of a continent.

Changes in the way Britain managed its empire created some of the momentum. With the rise of Prussia and then a unified Germany, and intensifying competition between European empires in Africa and elsewhere, the British government preferred colonies that would accept responsibility for their own defence, releasing its troops and its funds for more immediate challenges. The withdrawal of the last British troops from Australia in 1870 symbolised this shift. But by the 1870s, British proponents of a 'new imperialism' were also arguing that colonial self-government and a form of independence could be achieved without separation; an empire of self-sufficient Anglo-Saxon colonies would be more powerful and sustainable. It was a decisive rejection of any necessary link between political federation and separation from the empire. Australia could have legislative independence without severing itself from the crown.

At the same time, greater independence from Britain threw questions about colonial security into a much sharper focus and encouraged ideas of defensive union. Ever since the French seizure of New Caledonia in 1853, Australians had wondered about the possibility of European conflict in the South Pacific and the brakes this might place upon Australia's own territorial ambitions. Another inter-colonial conference in 1870 focused on colonial defence. In 1881, a further meeting discussed tariffs, as well as the advantages of federation for another issue: how best to restrict the immigration of the Chinese. German and French adventures in the 1880s sharpened the sense of threat. Anxious that 'the unappropriated parts of the world are rapidly being seized upon', colonial politicians urged action.[22] They were not passive bystanders, and demanded British protection for missionaries and merchants. In 1883, sure that Germany was about to seize them, Queensland annexed south-eastern New Guinea and surrounding islands. This attempt to force Britain's hand was overruled by Britain; the natives, Queensland Premier Thomas McIlwraith was told, had given no indication of wanting to have their land occupied, nor of any willingness to contribute more 'coloured labour' to Queensland's plantations. It was a sharp reminder that colonial parliaments could not determine matters beyond their own borders. It was also a less than serious protection of 'native' rights; within eighteen months, Germany had taken possession of the north-eastern part of the island and Britain declared the south-eastern part a protectorate. Britain's refusal to support Queensland's action, and its apparent, if tacit, support of German ambitions, linked the issues of federation and defence more strongly in people's minds, and encouraged the view that a single, national voice in imperial affairs might not be a bad thing.

The next intercolonial conference, in 1883, created a Federal Council, the first national body to have any powers at all. They were limited, being restricted mainly to extradition and the regulation of fisheries, but the meetings of the council provided an important venue in which to imagine and rehearse feasible federal government. The Council was weakened by New South Wales' decision not to join a body regarded by some of its most powerful leaders – including Henry Parkes – as a Victorian plot to 'mend her condition at our expense'.[23]

The colonies pulled together and pulled apart. The Australian Natives Association held a great meeting at Melbourne's Town Hall in 1884.

New South Wales sent troops to the Sudan in 1885. They weren't asked for, and arrived too late to be of any particular use, but the gesture was enthusiastically endorsed by most Australians, not least because in the face of Britain's wavering, the colony demonstrated a willingness for its young men to die in a British cause. The celebrations for Queen Victoria's Golden Jubilee in 1887 were another opportunity for displays of colonial attachment to empire; though Sydney was somewhat embarrassed by eruptions of anti-British sentiment at some meetings, the planting of trees and the building of statues was nothing less than enthusiastic. In 1888, another intercolonial conference agreed to a common policy restricting further Chinese immigration and movement between colonies, and preventing any further naturalisation of Chinese people already resident in Australia.

In 1888, as New South Wales marked its centenary, the Australian race could be celebrated in all manner of ways. Anxieties were stilled by the rapid growth of colonial cities, the development of modern and compulsory education systems, and the number of elevating public edifices. In fact, Australia's boom was about to bust, but that wasn't yet clear in 1888, and it seemed that this was not a pinnacle but part of a constantly rising slope. Victoria and the other colonies were not completely enthusiastic about the celebrations – 'Sydney's birthday' was the sniffy response of some Melburnians – though few could question the scale of New South Wales' ambitions. They included plans for a mausoleum, State House and museum (which would include a display of Aboriginal customs, languages and ethnological characteristics). They also proposed a gigantic statue of 'Australasia' astride Sydney's heads. Sadly, it was never built. While Sydney pondered grandiose statuary, Melbourne staged a Centennial International Exhibition, which opened in August. If some of the audience fell asleep during Henry John King's great – and very long – Centennial Cantata, they would enjoy rather more the first Australian performances of symphonies by Schubert, Brahms and Schumann, as well as every Beethoven symphony. Few could disagree that Anniversary Day marked not just the birth of a British nation, but also the foundations of Australia's 'empire'. As the winner of an essay competition urged, 'Australia, as a nation, must be Queen of the Southern Hemisphere' and 'a civilisation of the highest type'.[24] The coming race had surely been tested and proved, and they would create a nation and an empire to rival any other.

8

. . . .

A Truly New World: 1888–1901

From the late 1880s until the federation of the colonies into the new Commonwealth of Australia in 1901, debates about the future were particularly intense. These debates expressed different versions of the new nation and its possibilities. While some sort of federation always seemed the most likely outcome, its timing and nature were less clear-cut. Looking back from such a culminating event, people tended to assume that it had to happen. Nationalists preferred their nation to have been there all along, just waiting for the moment of its birth. They smoothed out the rough edges of a process that never looked as certain to those who carried it out. Nor was federation simply a matter of colonial leaders discussing the model they wanted. Their role was undeniable, especially in negotiating the rivalries between and within the colonies. But they were conscious, too, of the different Australias that colonial people had in their heads. These represented a variety of dreams and hopes, as well as anxieties about the future of their country. Federation built upon an emerging sense of nationhood that, in the context of economic and strategic uncertainty, mixed together aspirations and fears. There were questions about the place of the new nation in the empire, the meaning of independence, and future relationships with the United States – clearly the next great global power – or newer rivals such as Japan. For insecure labourers and rural workers, fears of hardship raised hopes of a new and more protective nation. A new generation of native-born women dreamed of a society that might exemplify progress, and in which female citizens would take their proper place in the making of the future. And there were serious questions about the kind of civilisation Australians should aim to build. What should the new nation aim to be? What example might it show to the world? For what might it be known? Australians hoped they would succeed, yet remained anxious they might fail.

LOOKING INTO THE FUTURE

It is hardly surprising, of course, that Australian writers and readers participated so enthusiastically in the futurist fantasies that were such an important feature of world literature in the years between 1880 and 1914. A few Australian writers followed the track of gothic horror re-popularised by Bram Stoker's *Dracula*, or the 'scientific romances' of H. G. Wells and Jules Verne. The cities' dark and thrilling underside was explored, too, in Fergus Hume's *The Mystery of a Hansom Cab* and similar tales. A mix of utopianism and socialism was more common. While none gained the fame of American Edward Bellamy's *Looking Backward* or William Morris' British response *News from Nowhere*, Australian writers expressed a similar interest in speculative fiction, which was heightened by the combination of a century's end, the struggle to overcome a deep economic depression, and the possibility of nationhood. Like Bellamy, Melbourne clergyman Horace Tucker (in his 1894 novel *The New Arcadia*) believed that the scientific and technological possibilities of the late nineteenth century promised a society of such abundance that antagonisms based on unfulfilled want would be reconciled, and replaced by a spirit of 'Co-operation'. Australia might, in fact, be a natural location for the rise and triumph of socialism. For some writers, a cooperative reconstruction would need preliminary destruction, as in David Andrade's *The Melbourne Riots* (1892) or Samuel Rosa's *The Coming Terror* (1894), while William Lane's *The Working Man's Paradise* (1892) showed Australia as a continent almost quivering in socialist anticipation:

> All the world over it was the same, two great ideas were crystallising, two great parties were forming, the lists were being cleared by combats such as this for the ultimate death-struggle between two great principles which could not always exist side by side. The robbed were beginning to understand the robbery; the workers were beginning to turn upon the drones; the dominance of the squatter, the mine-owner, the ship-owner, the land-owner, the shareholder, was being challenged; this was not the end, but surely it was the beginning of the end.[1]

A distinctive Australian twist on the futurist theme appeared in three kinds of stories popular in the last two decades of the century. One genre told of lost civilisations in the desert, as in G. Firth Scott's *The Last Lemurian* (1898) and Ernest Favenc's *The Secret of the Australian Desert* (1895); in the same vein, Robert Potter's *The Germ Growers* (1892) used the still believable notion of an 'unknown' interior as the setting for an alien invasion (six years before Wells developed a similar theme in *The War of the Worlds*). Ripping yarns of uneven quality they might have been, and they drew heavily upon such successful works as Henry Rider Haggard's *She* and *King Solomon's Mines*, but their depictions of empires undone by volcanic eruptions and earth-moving catastrophes also hinted at the fragility of civilisations, especially in such a 'savage' and even 'primeval' land. A second genre focused on invasion, and particularly the threat posed to white Australia by the 'yellow' races to its north; William Lane contributed *White or Yellow? A Story of the Race-War of A. D. 1908*, serialised in the weekly magazine *Boomerang* during 1887, which was followed by Kenneth Mackay's *The Yellow Wave* in 1895. A third genre explored present and future relationships between men and women. Rosa Praed's *Fugitive Anne* (1903) fused this theme with the 'lost race' fantasy, its modern and independent heroine emphasising the possibilities for women in an unsettled and perhaps unsettling land. More developed futurist novels – especially Henrietta Dugdale's *A Few Hours in a Far-Off Age* (1883) and Catherine Helen Spence's *A Week in the Future* (1889) – established the possible significance of Australia as a site for women's progress, and emphasised that any Australian utopia had to tackle women's oppression. Fantasies these may have been, but in the fantasies of a particular place and time we often find the themes and issues that people were taking most seriously and that they found most interesting and exciting. After all, these were intensely realistic speculations, about a people whose future demanded political action in the here and now.

A SENSE OF NATIONALITY

It is a commonplace to suggest that the colonists became self-consciously 'Australian' in the last few decades of the nineteenth century. To understand the eventual creation of the nation, it is first necessary to understand how some Australians became convinced – and then strove to convince others – that theirs was or in some sense could be a distinctive and even superior civilisation. Nationalism always expresses a feeling of, and perhaps a desire for, distinction. It establishes distance, in Australia's case from Britain as a parent and from other British colonies and the United States as siblings. It does not rule out what is held in common – such as language, or faith, or political structures – but it searches for aspects of culture and behaviour that suggest improvement or superiority, and it often finds comfort in competition and comparison.

Certainly, talk of nationality increased during the 1880s. Australian Natives Association member George Meudell urged 'Australia for the Australians' in 1882, and the *Bulletin*, a Sydney-based magazine that would become the ardent nationalists' favourite, adopted the phrase as its masthead. Artists and writers began to identify more confidently a distinctive Australian ethos in the common people and the commonplaces of 'the bush'. The painters of the Heidelberg School strove to capture Australia's bright, squinting light; artists such as Arthur Streeton and Tom Roberts also revelled in the beauties of Sydney and its harbour. They placed Australians in a more accurately realised landscape, in which shearers, pioneers, rail-splitters and swagmen became the 'real' Australians. If these were the archetypes, the actual heroes were often world-beating sportsmen – such as the sculler Henry Searle, for whose funeral in 1889 tens of thousands of people packed Sydney – or world-renowned horses, such as the New Zealand-born Carbine, which won the Sydney and Melbourne Cups in 1890.

Essayists, poets and editors were busy inventing stories of an undeferential, egalitarian and self-reliant people whose fiercely democratic temper set them against what the *Bulletin* often called 'the new order of plutocrats'. The story was as romantic and fanciful as are most of those defining nations. Many of those producing it knew little of the bush and those who did, like poet Henry Lawson or novelist Joseph Furphy, were usually careful not to ascribe heroic qualities to everyone who happened to live there. It was an anti-urban story produced by and for the urban people who formed the great majority of Australians. In fiction, Rolf Boldrewood's *Robbery Under Arms*, first serialised in Sydney and then published in London in 1888, used Australian vernacular and distinctively Australian characters. Andrew 'Banjo' Paterson, a Sydney solicitor, became a sensation during the 1890s with poems such as 'Clancy of the Overflow', 'The Man from Ironbark' and 'The Man from Snowy River'. 'In Defence of the Bush', Paterson's response to Lawson's starkly realist 'Up the Country', contrasted the Australian-ness of the bush with the city's 'ceaseless tramp of feet' and 'squalid street and square'. In the same decades as Americans embraced the cowboy, Australians placed their nationality in the hands of the bushman. They also began to measure him in capitals, as the Bush and the Bushman.

Australians were rethinking their relationship with the country. Thousands became 'field naturalists', or went tramping in those parts of the bush they could reach by bicycle or train. As people's sense of the value, purposes and future of Australia shifted, they founded and joined nature conservation and wildlife protection societies. There was a stronger sense of its fragility, with moves to protect native plants and grasses and the establishment of Victoria's Water Conservancy Board in 1881. The country had to be changed, irrigated, harvested and made useful, but some of it was becoming more beautiful in its own terms and could be preserved. The first national park, south of Sydney, created in 1879, was a place for recreation amidst beauty, rather than strict protection, but it nonetheless signalled a change of heart. In the 1880s, nature photography also grew, with a photographic survey of Victoria and, in 1889, the first photographs of Uluru.

It was not that Australia's bush or native animals suddenly became less strange. But they did become, to a growing proportion of the population, more important and more valuable because they were different. With Australia now indisputably settled, difference could become a matter of pride rather than anxiety. Nature was beginning to be nationalised. Australians embraced the wattle, with the ladies' committee of the Adelaide Australian Natives Association among the first to form a Wattle Blossom League – and create a Wattle Blossom Banner – in 1890. The kangaroo and the emu would eventually appear as a coat of arms. Koalas, still being shot in the thousands for their pelts, slowly became something other than an oddity. The adults of the 1880s and 1890s began a transition that their children would largely realise in the new century. Indeed, children's books helped develop the ideas of independence and national promise, as well as embracing native flora and fauna, beginning with Ethel Turner's adventure story *Seven Little Australians* (1894) and Ethel Pedley's *Dot and the Kangaroo* (1899), in which native animals befriended a lost child. For one 'native', however, there was no embrace. The Australians being celebrated in the 1880s and 1890s did not include Aboriginal people.

The celebration of Australian-ness could extend into a questioning or even a rejection of Britain's continuing influence. Republican movements re-emerged in Queensland, Victoria and New South Wales in the late 1880s and early 1890s, some to express the idea that a New World Australia would only be possible if links with Old World Britain were severed, others taking to its logical conclusion a distaste for aristocracy, and especially for the hereditary privilege and gross inequalities the British monarchy was seen to symbolise. The *Bulletin*'s writers were especially savage in their denunciations, and in Henry Lawson they found their poet. In 'A Song of the Republic', he urged Australians to 'banish from under your bonny skies, those old-world errors and wrongs and lies' and to choose between 'the Land that belongs to the lord and the Queen' and 'the Land that belongs to you'. In an 1887 essay he ridiculed the idea that Australia needed Britain's protection: 'the only protection Australia needs', he argued, 'is from the landlordism, the title-worship, the class distinctions and privileges, the oppression of the poor, the monarchy, and all the dust-covered customs that England has humped out of the middle ages where she properly belongs'.[2] There was a growing sense that Australia should also protect itself from Britain's military and imperial adventures; by the time of South Africa's Boer War, Australians were being warned against involvement, even though every colony sent a contingent and more than twelve thousand men served there. Yet this was agitation against one war, not all wars; indeed, some of the critics were eager for Australians to find and fight their own wars, against 'Asiatics' and invaders from the north. In Lawson's words it was only from wars that nation arise and are 'aroused from their dream of ease'.[3]

But even if they criticised Britain and its monarch, few Australians were republicans, even among the Irish and Catholics who had most to dislike about Britain's dominion. By the 1890s, most Australians combined some form of nationalism with continuing loyalty to Britain. Their sense of difference from the 'mother country' did not preclude belonging to its empire and feeling pride in its achievements (or, indeed, wanting to defend it when the time came). Imperial conferences, coinciding with Victoria's great jubilees in 1887 and 1897, promised the colonies a greater sense of involvement in a more collective empire. Australians were better Britons, not non-Britons. In Australia, people who would be held back by Britain's class structures and religious intolerances could rise and prosper. As writer Joseph Furphy had his character Tom Collins insist, Australians were meritocratic, in principle and in practice: 'I acknowledge no aristocracy except one of service and self-sacrifice', he wrote, 'in which he that is chief shall be servant, and he that is greatest of all, servant of all'.[4]

For all their emphasis on Australia for the Australians, too, the *Bulletin* and other magazines also told Australians about their place in the world, keeping them abreast of political and social developments that would shape the coming century. Australians remained intensely interested in global questions, and in measuring their reputation among the leading countries of the world. And when an Australian did well – even spectacularly well, as was true of the great operatic soprano and prima donna Nellie Melba – the promise of this coming civilisation was satisfyingly assured. It might need to make its own explanations to the world: there was an *Australian Slang Dictionary* and a guidebook, *Austral English*, to help the uninitiated by 1898. Yet this remained a less than complete confidence, and questions continued. Bernard O'Dowd, winner of a 1900 prize for poetry, asked whether Australia was a 'will o' wisp on marshy quest', or a 'new demesne for Mammon to infest', or, perhaps, 'lurks millennial Eden 'neath your face?'[5] Few Australians could have quoted O'Dowd's poem by heart, but there is no doubt that he captured something of their anxious confidence at century's turn.

THREE PRINCIPLES

In 1899, the *Bulletin*'s literary editor A. G. Stephens wrote an article, 'A Word for Australia', in which he listed the 'three essentials' of national life for the soon-to-be federation. The first was the 'transference of population from city to country, where independent homesteads can be established', so that Australia's cities – 'huge cancers' in which 'health and strength are sapped; the habit of productive labour is lost; and the character of the people sensibly deteriorates' might be 'extirpated'. Issues of national vitality loomed large in turn-of-the-century minds, and with them came questions about the tendency for the 'unproductive' labour and pleasures of cities to unman men. The second essential was

Table 8.1 Vital statistics of the white population, 1851 and 1901

	1851	1901
Population	437,665	3,773,801
Number of births	15,784	102,945
Birth rate (per 1,000 people)	36.1	27.3
Number of deaths	5,878	46,330
Death rate (per 1,000 people)	13.4	12.3
Number of marriages	4,677	27,753
Marriage rate (per 1,000 people)	10.7	7.4
% of population female	41.3	47.6
% rate of annual population growth	8.0	1.6
% population aged 0–14		35.1
% of population aged 15–29		27.8
% of population aged 30–64		33.1
% of population more than 65		4.0
Infant mortality rate (per 1,000 births)		103.6
Life expectancy at birth (women)		58.8
Life expectancy at birth (men)		55.2

Source: W. Vamplew (ed.) *Australians: Historical Statistics* (Sydney: Fairfax, Syme and Weldon Associates, 1987), pp. 26, 45, 50 & 56; Australian Bureau of Statistics, 'Australian Historical Population Statistics, 2006' (3105.0.65.001), at http://www.abs.gov.au.

'the preservation of the race [and] the purification of the national blood', which meant the permanent exclusion of 'Asiatics' and 'South Sea Islanders'. The third was 'equalisation of fortunes', which would include plans to 'tax the rich for the benefit of the poor', 'ensure to some extent a re-distribution of wealth at each generation' and 'place education within the reach of all, [and] capital within the reach of the industrious'.[6]

Table 8.1 shows that by century's end Australia was becoming a more settled country, with slower rates of growth and a more balanced population. As Australians looked to the future in the 1890s, a future that a growing number assumed would mean the creation of a nation, they vigorously debated what kind of nation it should be. Stephens' 'essentials' tell us something of the point that debate had reached by 1900. While historians differ a little on their characterisation, it is possible to speak of three principles underlying this debate. The first was progress. Australians tended to agree that theirs should be an improving country, something Stephens again captured succinctly in his wish that 'it be the pride of every Australian boy to become a better man than his father, of every Australian girl to become a better woman than her mother, of every Australian father and mother to rear children better than themselves'. Progress, as this suggests, was very much occupied with questions of gender and generation. If there was a sense of excitement, there was also a degree of anxiety, which stemmed in part from the shock of a deep economic depression, severe labour conflicts and a series of savage El Niño droughts. From this came a second principle: protection, but in a form that extended to the safety and security of citizens, capturing something of what Stephens termed 'equalisation of fortunes'.

The third and in many ways least contentious principle was purity of race. To these nation-makers, white Australia was an ideal and an achievable reality. Australians believed that they could, through immigration restriction and the removal of all non-white people, such as the Pacific Island labourers in Queensland, create a white nation. The silence on Aboriginal Australians is a telling indication of just how precarious their ultimate future was presumed to be. Australia's racial distinction is important. What was woven together – a white Australia, progress, and national pride – cannot now be pulled apart to make the past more palatable.

Yet it must also be understood for what it was, and for the fact – however strange it might seem now – that progress was seen to depend upon racial exclusion. Race was central in people's minds, and formed a crucial component of their sense of history, identity and future possibility. White Australia was a highly popular idea. People's understanding of the past told them that 'mixed' societies were economically and socially backward, that 'coloured labour' undercut the wages and conditions that allowed men to live dignified lives and that racial inferiors were incapable of enjoying the benefits of democracy and self-government. In that sense, purity underpinned progress and protection. Those speaking in favour of white Australia often disavowed racial hatred or antipathy. They did not understand themselves in that way. In their own minds, they were not anti-Chinese, but anti-degeneration. They saw themselves as realists. They were convinced that white and coloured could not co-exist and they were unable to imagine how two races could share a space without the inferior contaminating and dragging down the superior. And in imagining their future, Australians looked across the Pacific to the nation many had always reckoned their chief competitor and perhaps ally. As Victorian Alfred Deakin, one of the finest political minds of his generation, argued in a speech to the new parliament in 1901:

> We should be false to the lessons taught us in the great republic of the west; we should be false to the never-to-be-forgotten teachings from the experience of the United States, of difficulties only partially conquered by the blood of their best and bravest; we should be absolutely blind to and unpardonably neglectful of our obligations, if we fail to lay those lessons to heart.[7]

With no history of slavery, and with a commitment to repatriate its racial others back to their homes, Australia would in fact be able to achieve what America had not and could not: a degree of whiteness that its citizens assumed would guarantee social, political and economic progress.

WOMEN AND THE FUTURE

If purity was relatively uncontroversial, progress and protection were more contentious. In terms of the first, Australian feminists ensured that the future of women assumed a particular significance. They described themselves as part of the Woman Movement, and mixed their feminism with concerns about social purity, cruelty, charity, the protection of children and temperance, and sometimes a belief in cooperation and socialism. Temperance was perhaps strongest of all, with the powerful Women's Christian Temperance Union based upon a solid and long-standing tradition of campaigns against public drinking and drunkenness in which women supplanted men as the chief actors by the 1880s.

Theirs was a feminism of writing, lobbying and advocacy, leagues and associations, hard political work and constant activism. In was led in Melbourne by Annette Bear-Crawford and Vida Goldstein, in Sydney by Maybanke Anderson, Rose Scott and Mary Windeyer, in Perth by Edith Cowan, in Brisbane by Leontine Cooper and in Adelaide by Mary Lee, while Jessie Rooke and Georgina Kermode organised Tasmania.

Australian feminists shared with their global counterparts a commitment to highlighting the ills caused by women's oppression. They drew upon and contributed to a shared sense of injustice, and some travelled widely within a feminist world, speaking and listening to suffragists in London, progressives in New York and fellow WCTU members in Chicago. Together, they criticised the brakes applied to women's freedoms, educations and aspirations, the unjust divorce and property laws that essentially turned married women into their husbands' dependents, the denial of political participation, the problems of male excess, and the double standards that penalised women's infidelities while forgiving men's. Women trade unionists and labour activists – such as Adelaide's Augusta Zadow, Brisbane's Emma Miller and Sydney's Rose Summerfield – also highlighted the sometimes-appalling conditions endured by working women and the need for factory inspectors. Miles Franklin contributed a distinctive Australian heroine, Sybylla Melvin in *My Brilliant Career*, and magazines and newspapers began to speak about 'the Australian girl' as a different, more independent woman than her English cousins.

It was time for women to emerge from silence. Henrietta Dugdale's futuristic novel had a humorous museum of antiquities and an exhibit on 'The Age of Blood and Malevolence' (the nineteenth century). One of the young visitors was shocked to hear of what went on in that unenlightened age:

> The males of these primitive people … those poor vain creatures, with much assumption of wisdom, though still very apelike in various ways, made laws affecting women's liberty, property, and even her children, without consulting her, her happiness, or any higher feeling than their own self-love, comfort and aboriginal greed. In short, the women up to past the nineteenth century were really slaves in all but the name.[8]

In one of the most interesting of the fantasy novels, Mary Moore-Bentley's *A Woman of Mars*, the woman, Vesta, is sent to Earth to emancipate its women and regenerate the human race. She starts in Sydney, and within five years, the movement she inspires makes Australia the wonder of the civilised world, with its perfect and rational organisation of industry, its bicycle-riding women and its subordination of individual needs to those of the race. Utopia is threatened by Lord Beauclerc, a licentious fiend, and his seductive – and Asian-appearing – sidekick Judith. But they are overcome by the forces of reason, and women regain their natural dominance as the shapers of the best imaginable future.

Though in less fantastic terms, Australian feminists also emphasised the importance of women's empowerment for the progress of a new nation. Progress would be most rapid, Sydney feminist Louisa Lawson urged, if everyone agreed that 'the life and work of every woman is just as essential to the good of the community as that of every man'[9] Next to the coming man might stand a New Woman. She would need expanded opportunities for professional training and employment, and reformed marriage and divorce laws. If Australia was truly to represent the highest development of civilisation, and the Anglo-Saxon race, its women would need to be elevated onto a more equal footing with men, and protected from any evils and injustices that dimmed their moral, civic and social influence. Direct participation in politics was one means to that end; South Australian women won the vote in 1894, as did Western Australian women in 1899. Yet the New Woman would do more than vote. She would, Rose Scott argued, 'inspire man' so that 'the safeguards of the nation will then rest on the individual conscience of its women', while the more forthright Lawson insisted: 'follow man no longer as his slave; step forward as his peer; advance, and if he does not keep pace, be his leader in progress'.[10]

In the lead-up to federation, and well beyond it, feminists developed the logical extension of long-established ideas about women's moral superiority and civilising mission. There had always been concerns that a society of unbalanced gender was subject to discord and decline. If proposals for easier divorces and more equality in marriage, or for laws to curb men's drunkenness and immorality, stepped on a few male toes, the assumption that women had special responsibilities for social change and forming the future still held strong. Perhaps even more than in other countries, new world women saw themselves as the best direc-tors of social progress, which meant protecting and empowering women while also encouraging change among men. It was a proposition that Australian feminists used to good effect, and in the new century, as in the 1890s, they would use it to argue for much more than the vote.

Any conversation about womanhood is also and always a conver-sation about manhood. The New Woman got short shrift from some nervous men, who assumed that defending the interests of men and

Table 8.2   Votes for women

1869	*Women permitted to vote in Wyoming Territory, USA*
1893	*Equal voting rights for New Zealand women*
	Referendum approving female suffrage passed in Colorado, USA
1894	All women in South Australia given State voting rights
1895	*Women in Utah, USA, gain vote by constitutional amendment*
1896	*Women in Idaho, USA, gain vote by constitutional amendment*
1899	Women (excluding Aboriginal women) in Western Australia given State voting rights
1902	All women in New South Wales given State voting rights
	Women (excluding Aboriginal women in Western Australia and Queensland) given Federal voting rights
1903	All women in Tasmania given State voting rights
1904	Women (excluding Aboriginal women) in Queensland given State voting rights
1906	*Female suffrage in Finland*
1908	All women in Victoria given State voting rights
1913	*Female suffrage in Norway*
1915	*Female suffrage in Denmark and Iceland*
1916	*Women in Alberta, Manitoba and Saskatchewan get the vote*
1918	*British women aged 30 or older get the vote*
	Canadian women (except those living in Quebec) get the vote
	Female suffrage in Germany, Latvia, Poland, Estonia and Russia
1919	*Dutch women get the vote*
1920	*Full female suffrage in the United States*
1928	*Equal voting rights for British women*
1962	Aboriginal women given Federal voting rights and State voting rights in Western Australia and Queensland

Source: http://www.womenaustralia.info; 'International Woman Suffrage Timeline', at http://womenshistory.about.com; Audrey Oldfield, *Woman suffrage in Australia: A gift or a struggle?* (Melbourne: Cambridge University Press, 1992), pp. 64–5.

the interests of Australia were one and the same. Some of the writers inventing 'bushmen' were worried enough about the effects of feisty women on manliness to link the New Woman and national decline. Other men worried about the potential effects of all these strong women on the coming generation of boys, and the fitness of Australia's men for their national duties would become the subject of vigorous debate after 1901. Yet the evidence suggests that a fair proportion of Australian men agreed – at least in some ways – with the proposition that a progressive civilisation was in part measured by the freedoms and status accorded its women. Though some goals were not achieved, and while the gains of a new womanhood were less clear for working women, Australian feminists had certainly sparked a discussion that meant that the 'founding fathers' of federation would talk not just about political structures, but also about the male and female citizens who should inhabit them.

DEPRESSION AND CONFLICT

The other issue dominating colonial societies in the decade before federation was the growing antagonism between classes, and the ideas about protection that these conflicts helped promote, especially as droughts and depression savaged all of the colonies in the 1890s. There were specific conflicts about the nature of workers' entitlements, but these always reflected broader concerns about the distribution of wealth and the extent of inequality. In 1883, a writer in the *Bulletin* described 'the new order of plutocrats' and argued that 'the masses everywhere arraign the social codes which permit such monstrous and iniquitous disparities to exist'.[11] The 1880s seemed buoyant enough, with most of the colonies experiencing rapid growth, but its benefits were uneven, and large numbers of urban and rural workers were left disgruntled by low wages and poor conditions. They sought some insurance against disaster in the friendly societies; for a regular payment, members received allowances when unable to work and a decent funeral when they died. Conflicts over land lingered, and in the 1880s many small farmers – such as those later sketched by Queensland writer Steele Rudd in *On Our Selection* – were already mired in hard times. Trade unions formed associations and met in inter-colonial congresses, while more militant activists, versed in European and American socialist and radical literature, talked of more direct political action. As ever, they took careful note of international conversations, and imagined ways of educating Australians to new ideas, from Henry George's single tax through co-operative land settlement and free thought to the varieties of French anarchism.

By the early 1890s, the colonial economies, which had rested too much on British and colonial government investment and on short-term speculations, were tottering. Melbourne's land boom collapsed in 1888, and the severe drought in the same year exposed the fragility of the over-expanded pastoral economy, especially in South Australia and New South Wales. By 1893, banks were crashing in Victoria and Queensland as British investors pulled away from a rickety financial system. In the early part of that year, thirteen of the colonies' twenty-two banks closed their doors, though only two actually failed. What followed was that downward spiral of anxiety and fear so characteristic of economic depressions. Not for the last time, Australia's problems were heightened by its dependence on the equally depressed economies of Europe and North America. In the cities, unemployment soared, and private charities were overwhelmed by the weight of need. Brisbane's miseries were compounded by 1893's severe flood. A timely gold rush insulated Western Australia, but in every other colony economic collapse revealed just how close to poverty's edge most small farmers and urban workers lived. Perhaps a third of the population was unemployed.

The depression had a marked psychological and physical effect upon the generation that endured it. It revealed how unequally the prosperity of the 1870s and 1880s had been shared. Though it lifted in the middle of the 1890s, its ending merged with the beginning of what became known as the Federation Drought, which lasted until 1905. Fifteen years of hard times. Sheep and cattle numbers more than halved, but desperate grazing in the marginal areas of South Australia, Queensland and New South Wales did lasting damage to the land. Neither people nor money flowed into the colonies from Britain. With less wealth came less tax and the dereliction of public works and services, as government spending fell by forty per cent. For a time, banks became more conservative, but they lost a good deal of esteem and were frequently charged with accusations of carelessness and even class robbery. Some of the Gold Rush generation, now in their sixties and seventies, lost all of their savings and their homes. Less nourished as children, Australians born during the 1890s were shorter on average than their parents. The future seemed suspended. Marriage and fertility rates fell; the proportion of men and women who never married was higher in 1901 than in the 1980s.

The early years of the 1890s also revealed deep fractures within colonial society, and sometimes created levels of conflict close to warfare. Aggrieved by the denial of longstanding claims, marine officers went on strike in Melbourne in 1890, and were quickly supported by seamen, wharf labourers and coal miners who refused to dig for non-union ships. Their employers seized upon the chance for a fight, and used 'scab' labour to undermine and defeat the strike within a few months. Confronting less organised employers, the shearers of Queensland and New South Wales won some concessions in 1890, and declared they would no longer shear next to non-union workers. Their employers formed the Pastoralists Federal Council and their counter-offensive in 1891 shattered the union. These confrontations, and the lock-out at the mining town of Broken Hill in 1892, involved battles between strikers, scabs, police and hastily-mobilised 'special forces' armed with guns and batons. This, and the arrest of strike leaders, taught unionists that as long as the forces of 'law and order' were in the hands of employer-friendly politicians, few gains could be won or defended. The argument that the workers' future depended on securing their own representation began to make more sense; if more proof was needed, a further employer attack on the shearers in 1894 led to violent confrontations throughout Queensland and New South Wales, in which the police and the troopers again intervened against the union.

A PARTY OF LABOUR

What then of the 'rising civilisation'? The class confrontations and economic anxieties of the 1890s savaged the colonies' confidence. They revealed deep antagonisms and divisions, which surpassed inter-colonial rivalries, or the long-running debate about free trade. Trade union newspapers showed images of devilish and murderous bosses and talked of monopolists and speculators and blood-sucking lawyers, while the opponents of unionism and socialism depicted strikers as overbearing thugs holding the country to ransom. There was a war of words, pitting patriots against radicals and law and order against anarchy, and a war of threatened and actual violence. If a socialist paradise had not arrived, it seemed to some that the class cataclysm that preceded it certainly had.

There were various ways forward. For some, the inevitability of socialism remained a guiding hope. Australians would need to make themselves worthy of that ideal, but the 'New Order' was surely coming. Cartoons showed the imminent triumph of socialism, its chariot sweeping the plutocrats from the stage of history. In a 'new unionism' devoted to solving the labour problem, William Spence and others identified 'what will really be a revolution in our social system ... that the rest of the world will not be slow to follow'.[12] For William Lane, the struggle between socialism and capitalism could be furthered only by a utopian separation and a New Australia; with writer Mary Gilmore, activist Rose Summerfield and more than two hundred others, he left for Paraguay in 1893.

It was more common to try to find a solution within Australia and without revolution. Compared with other industrialising and conflict-ridden societies, especially the United States, Australian unions and labour activists faced less repression from governments. They survived the strikes in strong enough shape to look for alternatives and to form a labour party, and there was sufficient faith in the possibilities of mainstream political activism to make socialism, democracy and parliamentary representation seem like mutually reinforcing rather than contradictory aims. Australia's progress could be reignited through political activity, especially the development of an organisation that could better reflect the progressive spirit and wishes of the ordinary people and could be bound – or pledged – to platforms and principles in which they had some say. By the 1880s, each colonial parliament had its own factions and coalitions, often formed around powerful political personalities, but there were no great national political organisations such as the Democrats and the Republicans in America. There were liberals and conservatives, free traders and protectionists. From the early 1890s, colonial politics were reshaped by the rise of a new force – the Labor Party – and the non-Labor groups it helped to spark. Their names were telling: in South Australia, to take one example, the rising Labor Party's opponent called itself the National Defence League.

Labor's rise was dramatic. It brought together urban and rural workers, and its strongest support in its first decade often came from outside the cities. In New South Wales' 1891 election, on a platform emphasising democratic reform – such as the abolition of plural voting and the creation of equal electoral districts – and a range of labour and socialist interests – from a national bank to the stamping of all Chinese-made furniture – Labor candidates took a quarter of the seats. Further successes were made by South Australia's United Labor Party in 1891 and in Queensland in 1893. In Queensland, as in New South Wales, Labor members assisted either free-traders or protectionists to form governments in return for concessions, especially on voting and parliamentary reform. Electoral support for labour platforms also emboldened reforming liberals such as South Australia's Charles Kingston to legislate for workers' compensation, factory regulation and old age pensions. In 1899, Queensland's Labor Party was the first of its kind in the world to form a very brief minority government (it lasted a week). In Western Australia, a Coolgardie trade union congress formed a labour party in 1899, and six of its members were elected to parliament a year later. In Victoria, the rise of Labor was slowed by the strength of liberalism and protectionism, especially under the highly popular – and astute – Alfred Deakin, while in Tasmania, the trades and labour councils also tended to throw their weight behind existing reform politicians such as Andrew Inglis Clark.

As the joining of Labor and progressive forces in these colonies showed, the 1890s saw more than an electoral shift. There was a changing expectation of governance. To many Australians, if the strikes, the

droughts and the depression had revealed anything, it was their vulnerability. Governments could be engines of economic development, but
they might also be protectors and equalisers, serving the interests and
securing the safety of all of their citizens. A strong link was being forged
between entitlement, political participation and legislative consideration.
For all but the staunchest conservatives, the future had to be different,
not more of the same. Workers needed protection from exploitation,
from the threat the unemployed posed to jobs and wages, and from the
supposed servility of 'non-white' labour. Farmers and rural labourers
needed protection against droughts, tumbling prices and the power of
large landowners. Liberals and progressives wanted less conflict. If
they did not endorse socialism, they initiated or welcomed democratic
reforms, the idea of arbitration for industrial disputes, the principle of
government investment and regulation, and the overarching idea that
government should be an active and not a passive force. Australia and
New Zealand both adopted a more forceful system of compulsory arbitration for industrial disputes than any other country in the world. It was
from those same principles that quicker strides were made in public
health and services, the provision of sewerage and clean water, and the
regulation of food and milk. If people supported capitalism, which most
of them did, they did not support it unrestrained and unmanaged. They
wanted it civilised.

A writer in the radical Queensland journal *Boomerang* came up with
this description in 1888:

> We don't want another Rome, or another England. We only want an
> Australia, a new nation, a glorious republic, a free state, a country
> from which injustice shall be banished and in which every citizen
> shall do his duty and injure none other while protected from injury
> to himself.[13]

Almost everyone in the 1890s would have found one thing with which
to disagree in that statement. But almost everyone would have warmed
to one or more of its principles.

FEDERATION?

The question remained whether there would be a nation. In the midst
of depression and conflict, and persistent inter-colonial suspicions, it is
perhaps surprising that the separate colonies managed to federate into

the Commonwealth of Australia by 1901. Federation resulted from a mix of motives. Ideas about national destiny, or the economic sway of a nation compared to six colonies, made a good deal of sense. People worried about defence saw a safer future in federation, with a national government raising a stronger army and navy. Merchants and manufacturers were tired of the complexities of inter-colonial commerce. Others held federation up as a fitting culmination to progress since the gaining of self-government in the 1850s, and there was also the advantage of a national approach to immigration restriction and the repatriation of racial inferiors. For the Australian Natives Association, nothing less than federation would prove that the native-born were worthy, and that stereotypes of Australians as uncouth and inferior were unwarranted.

But ambition was tempered by apprehension. Less populous states feared domination by New South Wales and Victoria, while New South Wales and Victoria feared each other as rivals divided by the still powerful issue – and even more powerful symbolism – of free trade versus protection. As in any nation-making exercise, there were very difficult questions. Where would contentious powers – like raising money – be located? What compensation might the colonies receive for the loss of customs duties and other taxes? If a constitution left out some powers and duties, would the states or the federal government retain them? Would the rules of qualification for voting mirror the most progressive – such as South Australia's – or the least? How American, or British, should the political system be, or would Canada or Switzerland be a better model? If there were to be two houses, what might be their respective powers? Radicals and nationalists in the eastern mainland states dismissed the 'abominable heresy of State Rights' and an upper house 'dominated by reactionaries from Western Australia and Tasmania'.[14] They also thought most proposed models did not go far enough in reducing British influence. Based on their experience of the blocking power of upper houses in each of the colonies, socialists and unionists worried that the upper house would simply push aside social and political reforms. Conservatives worried about delegating too much power to a distant national legislature, especially one elected by the majority of the citizens, including women and the poor; new political institutions would have to constrain the excesses of popular democracy, not unleash them. Women, meanwhile, had much to lose if the new federation did not extend the suffrage to them.

The practical significance of the first Federal Council remained limited. With an eye on the turn of the century, and an even more careful eye on the political debate about the benefits of federation in his own New South

Wales, elder statesman Henry Parkes attempted to revive the federation movement. His Tenterfield Oration in 1889 made the usual references to other models – 'surely what the Americans had done by war, the Australians could bring about in peace' – and focused on the advantages a 'government for the whole of Australia' would bring to national defence.[15] An Australasian Federation conference was called in 1890 – New Zealand was still a potential partner – and brought together some of the crucial leaders: Parkes, Tasmania's Clark, Victoria's Deakin, Queensland's Samuel Griffith. Parkes assured this audience that Australians had 'made such progress as has excited the admiration of the best of other countries' and that only nationhood could ensure that 'the name of an Australian [will] be equal to that of a Briton'.[16] The conference wrote an address to Queen Victoria, and a wider audience, declaring that 'the best interests and the present and future prosperity of the Australian Colonies will be promoted by an early union under the Crown' and directing each colony to send delegates to a convention to consider a federal compact.[17] This National Australasian Convention met in Sydney in March and April 1891, and adopted a draft constitution: it mixed features of the American and Westminster systems, with a lower house and an upper house, the first made up of members representing districts and the latter of members representing states. The draft also enumerated a list of specific powers that the colonies would cede to the national government.

Yet if Parkes and other federal advocates had hoped to lead a crusade, they were disappointed. The draft constitution failed to tackle significant areas of contention – such as tariff policy – and once the Free Trade and Labor parties allowed it to lapse in the New South Wales parliament, it was not taken up in any other colony. Interest also waned among New Zealanders, who began to think more about the potential disadvantages of political, economic and military union across so many miles. The push for federation remained more vibrant outside the official political process than within it, and the Australian Natives Association and the Federal Leagues revived it at a convention in Corowa in 1893, seeking to ensure popular participation and calling for the election of representatives to a constitutional convention. New South Wales premier George Reid persuaded the other colonial premiers to discuss the issue at a conference in Hobart in 1895, and they accepted the basic principle of a constitution, framed by elected representatives, being put to a popular referendum in each colony. A further People's Federal Convention was held in Bathurst in 1896.

In the end, the people's desire for attachment and for the realisation of what many assumed to be an ordained process of national union sustained the federation process through the delays and wheeler-dealing of colonial politics. The finer details of the draft were hashed out at the Federal Conventions of 1897 and 1898, and a Constitution Bill was written. Referenda were held in June, 1898. Voters in Victoria, Tasmania and South Australia ratified the new constitution by large majorities – more than eighty per cent voted yes in Victoria and Tasmania, as did two thirds of South Australian electors. But in New South Wales, where the political contest over free trade and protection was strongest, and the political elite was most divided, the yes vote, while a majority, fell short of the absolute number of eighty thousand needed for ratification.

New South Wales secured some amendments at a further premiers' conference in early 1899, including a provision that the federal capital would not be Sydney but would be in New South Wales (and therefore could not be Melbourne). The amended constitution bill was sent out again, and huge crowds gathered in Sydney to see the results being posted. This time, it passed in every colony, though the vote was close in Queensland, where the unwillingness of Brisbane and the south-east was outweighed by the strong enthusiasm of people in the northern, western and central areas, who saw federation as their best hope of eventually separating from Queensland. With the significant amendment that the right of appeal to Britain's Privy Council was retained, the British Parliament passed the *Commonwealth of Australia Constitution Act* in

Table 8.3   Votes in the federation referenda

	Number voting	% voting yes
1898		
New South Wales	137,823	52.0
South Australia	53,120	67.4
Tasmania	14,513	81.3
Victoria	122,610	82.0
1899		
New South Wales	190,161	56.5
Queensland	69,484	55.4
South Australia	83,043	79.5
Tasmania	14,228	94.4
Victoria	162,458	94.0
1900		
Western Australia	64,491	69.5

Source: Helen Irving, *The Centenary Companion to Australian Federation* (Melbourne: Cambridge University Press, 2001), p. 416

1900. The dithering of Western Australia, which had persistent concerns about the potential financial costs of union, had delayed the referendum there. So the Act had to make clear that its provisions also related to Western Australia 'should it choose to join'. It did, by a vote of more than two to one, joining the new Commonwealth of Australia almost one month after the British Parliament had officially created it.

THUNDERSTORMS AND FIREWORKS

On 1 January 1901, Commonwealth Inauguration or Federation Day celebrations were held all over the new nation. There were processions, allegorical cars, decorated arches and banners, good and bad poetry and lots of speeches. Sydney's event was spectacular. There had been problems with the tickets, and a good-sized Sydney thunderstorm on New Year's Eve made the morning muggy and discomforting. The great parade set off at 10 a.m., with booming guns and pealing bells. It expressed the colony's hierarchy, in reverse. The parade was led by a trade union section – including thirty mounted shearers, ten silver-miners, and ten slaughtermen and journeymen butchers – which was followed by representatives of the friendly societies, the fire brigades, heads of churches and religious groups (though not the Catholic Cardinal, who would not take part in a parade if it meant giving precedence to the Anglican Archbishop), mayors and political dignitaries, and the ministers of the new Commonwealth, including Edmund Barton, who would be the first Prime Minister. They were followed by police, soldiers and, at the end, the first Governor-General, John Hope, seventh Earl of Hopetoun. Everyone ended up at Centennial Park. Movie cameras recorded the events in flickering film. The thousands-strong crowd sat patiently; there was no amplification, so few heard anything of the prayers, speeches, the Queen's Proclamation and the swearing-in. Four hundred voices sang a *Te Deum*, ten thousand schoolchildren sang *Federated Australia*, and a thousand adults sang Handel's *Hallelujah* chorus, before everyone sang *God Save the Queen*.

There were all kinds of events: aquatic demonstrations and swimming carnivals, displays of 'native' weapons and dancing, and a Grand Commonwealth Continental Concert in Adelaide (which followed a Grand Parade of Illuminated Cycles). Australia was personified by young women, in the main; in Sydney, she stood on a float, surrounded by shearers and gold-diggers, while at Echuca, on the Murray River, a wagon held six girls, one for each of the federating colonies. There was some unkind talk in Melbourne; some Victorians, reported one magazine,

Illustration 8.1   The Chinese Arch and Procession, 1901
Source: LaTrobe Pictures Collection, State Library of Victoria, Accession No.
H96.160/651.

'have returned to Melbourne decidedly the worse for their outing. They
are thinner than when they started. Want of food, want of sleep, and
hot, perspiring weather, have fixed the historical event indelibly in their
memories'.[18] Alfred Deakin of Victoria rose above inter-colonial rivalry
but maintained a slightly ironic air:

> It is certainly a very self-conscious nation that has just made its
> appearance in the centre of the Southern Seas. Platform orators and
> the Press have combined to instruct it as to its present importance and
> future potentialities. The newspapers of late have comprised many
> retrospects and statistical comparisons as to our progress and relative
> resources in population and wealth, all calculated to minister to that
> self-esteem which is by no means wanting among us.[19]

On Federation Day, the *Sydney Morning Herald* welcomed a 'new and
broader nationhood' and an 'outlook so full of dazzling promise', while
the Brisbane *Worker* welcomed the Australian people and the 'glorious
destiny [which] awaits if their hearts are true and their hands strong

and they do not suffer themselves to be betrayed by bribed leaders and corrupt statesmen'. For many Australians, there was still an 'if'. This was now a nation, but a half-confident, anxious one, relentlessly comparing itself with other nations and wondering if they respected it. Still, as the fireworks flared over Sydney and other cities on New Year's night in 1901, it would have seemed a bright tomorrow, and the beginning of a century that could be of and for Australia.

9

· · · · · · · ·

A Protective Nation: 1901–14

In 1901 one of Australia's best-known poets, Banjo Paterson, visited the Sussex home of Rudyard Kipling, who had just published one of his most famous novels, *Kim*. Travelling through the countryside in Kipling's new car, a pastime still a novelty in the early twentieth century, Kipling ordered their driver to stop outside a village butcher's shop in order to perform, in Paterson's words, 'a little Empire propaganda'. Introducing Paterson, Kipling directed the butcher to henceforth buy all his lamb from Australia in order to 'keep the money in the Empire'. The butcher, unaware of his customer's identity, replied: 'The Empire! Ha! My customers don't bother about the Empire, sir. It's their guts they think about!'[1]

Empire might not have mattered to the ordinary Englishman or woman the way it did to Rudyard Kipling, the poet famous for describing colonisation as 'The White Man's Burden'. It weighed a little more heavily on the minds of Australians, albeit with varying degrees of intensity. The vast majority thought of themselves as part of the wider British world, through ties as diverse as family, sport and a shared cultural tradition of books, reading and writing. The question of Australia's Britishness received new urgency in the post-federation years, as people began to wonder what it actually meant, for them, to be at once part of the British Empire and a self-governing Commonwealth.

As with any momentous change, there was anxiety and anticipation. While it might have been difficult to muster broad public enthusiasm for the idea of federation, once the new nation had been formed there was no going back. Nationhood had its responsibilities that could not be overlooked – defence, policies on population and immigration and a response to what was seen as one of the burning questions of the day: how to manage the interests of capital and labour. The last was particularly pressing in Australia, where the political wing of the organised labour movement had met with early electoral success. Coming out of the conflict-ridden and economically disastrous 1890s, there was a sense that a new century and a new nation offered an opportunity to devise novel solutions. It was, potentially, a situation where the old world might learn something from the new.

POLICIES, PROTECTION AND PROGRESS

The old world, 'the mother country' as it was often called, was not rejected in the ambition to experiment. In the decade before World War I, empire remained the touchstone for Australia's early forays into international relations. This was despite a growing awareness in Australia that an assumed commonality of interests was, from the British perspective, often a matter of expedience rather than policy. The advent of World War I has tended to obscure the extent to which, in the years preceding it, Australia had begun to seek out alternative defence relationships and possessed some extra-territorial ambitions of its own. There was a slight recasting of the relationship with the United States during this period although, as David Malouf has put it, Australia's relationship with Britain 'has always been one in which the third term, either open or unstated, is "America"'.[2] By the early twentieth century, Australians and Americans shared an overt interest in their territories as the domain of the white man, which was a point of difference between the Australians and the British, who governed a multi-racial empire.

The growing determination to ensure Australia remained a predominately Anglo-Saxon society was matched by an impulse common in other Western societies a concern to make sure that the 'guts' of ordinary workers were not left entirely dependent on the winds of fate. This was an era when states were becoming more overtly nationalist and belligerent, to be sure, but it was also a period in which intellectuals more openly contemplated the ameliorative capacity of governments. During the course of the nineteenth century, most Western societies had at least moved towards the regulation of industry and industrial conditions, particularly in relation to the employment of children and women. Political theory that had been highly individualistic in emphasis gave way to socialist or liberal philosophies, dramatically different doctrines that nevertheless shared a belief in the necessity of state interference or intervention for the greater good. Australia attracted attention for its willingness to experiment with new schemes and policies designed to alleviate the problems faced by workers who were exposed to the worst excesses of the capitalist system. This reputation for progressiveness reached its high-water mark before the war, although the victory won for ordinary workers was symbolic at best, Pyrrhic at worst. The willingness with which states, including Australia, later sacrificed the lives of young men on the battlefields of Europe should not obscure an earlier, and fundamental, shift in the ways governments thought about the quality of life of their citizens.

There were nine changes of Prime Minister between 1901 and 1914, an instability which belied the coherence of the national agenda which would emerge in this period. It took most of the pre-war decade for Australian federal politics to settle into something resembling a two-party system. Edmund Barton was the first Prime Minister of Australia (1901–3); Alfred Deakin was the second (1903–4). Their party, the Protectionists, led the Parliament for its first four years on a platform of the necessity of growing Australia's economy by protecting Australian industry from external competition. This was a position with which their main rivals, the federal Labor Party, for the most part happened to agree, although Labor's social reform agenda was more radical. The Protectionists often held office with Labor's support, and were pushed further along a progressive path than was perhaps their natural inclination. In 1904, Labor won federal office and Chris Watson became the world's first Labor Prime Minister, although within a year Deakin would be back in the chair again.

The results of such negotiations were often reform initiatives that offered something for both industry and workers, within a framework that privileged the development of capital. This was not Australia as socialist utopia; it was a national reform agenda built upon pragmatic compromise. The other non-Labor party was more identifiably conservative, at first focusing on free trade, and later renaming themselves the 'Anti-Socialist' party. The increasing electoral success of the Labor Party, particularly after 1908, ultimately meant the non-Labor forces in politics combined to form something resembling a broader liberal coalition in order to try and block them. The political groupings of protectionist and free-trade, which had so dominated politics in the lead up to federation, had gone forever. Hence, 'liberal' parties in Australia – of which there have been many variants over time – tended to the right and in general came to oppose the politics of the left, and increasingly so as the twentieth century wore on.

Whatever the hue of their ruling party, strong nations were those which could afford to offer some assistance to their less fortunate citizens. New nations seemed to be those most willing to experiment with what form that assistance might take. Old-age pensions were made available nation-wide in Australia after 1909 (although they had first appeared earlier in some colonies) and invalidity benefits for those over sixteen who were unable to work owing to disablement or blindness were available from

Table 9.1 Key Commonwealth legislation, 1901–14

1901	Immigration Restriction Act
	Customs Act
	Excise Act
	Pacific Island Labourers Act
1902	Commonwealth Franchise Act
1903	Defence Act
	Naturalisation Act
	Judiciary Act
1904	Conciliation and Arbitration Act
1905	Papua Act
	Census and Statistics Act
	Copyright Act
	Representation Act
1906	Australian Industries Protection Act
1908	Invalid and Old Age Pensioners Act
	Quarantine Act
	Surplus Revenue Act
1910	Australian Bank Notes Tax Act
	Seat of Government (Administration) Act
	Naval Defence Act
1911	Commonwealth Bank Act
1912	Maternity Allowances Act
	Commonwealth Workmen's Compensation Act
1913	Navigation Act
	Committee of Public Accounts Act
	Norfolk Island Act
1914	Crimes Act

Source: Commonwealth of Australia Consolidated Acts, at http://www.austlii.edu.au.

1910. One of the distinctive features of these Australian welfare measures was their means-tested but non-contributory nature, which formed a contrast to the contributory schemes developing in Britain and Germany during the same period.

Of particular note to outside observers was the creation of institutions that would mediate the interests of employers and workers. Most international interest centred on the issue of compulsory arbitration which, despite its dull name, meant that employers could be compelled, by a judicial institution, to pay their workers a certain level of wages. In 1911, two legal academics at the University of Sydney, writing for an

American audience, explained that in Australia, free of the prejudices of the 'Old World', 'legislation goes further along the path of the world trend and achieves ends whose attempts in other, older communities would be deemed experimental in a wild degree'.[3] A visitor reporting on behalf of the French Labour Bureau, Albert Metin, called these developments, which he largely attributed to the political success of the organised labour movement, *Le Socialisme sans Doctrines*.[4] Socialism without Doctrine, for Metin, meant labour's willingness to adopt practical measures in relation to wages and industrial disputes, rather than an insistence on a more pure, or doctrinal, socialist principle of collective ownership. Most trade unions warmed to the idea of compulsory arbitration but, contrary to Metin's focus on the activities of the labour movement, middle-class liberals in particular favoured it as the way to restore social harmony after the hard and bitter years of the 1890s.

For the barrister and politician Henry Bournes Higgins, the metaphor of war was not too strong a way of describing what he believed to be an inevitable conflict at the heart of social life. 'The war between the profit-maker and the wage earner is always with us', he wrote, insisting that it produced 'much loss and suffering, not only to actual combatants, but also to the public'.[5] This was a big statement to make in 1914, although Higgins was in the United States when he made it and he could not have foreseen the length and cost of the European war which had just begun. Arbitration was, for Higgins, the path to Australia's peaceful future or, as he put it, 'a new province of law and order'. After federation, industrial disputes that crossed state boundaries could be heard by the Commonwealth Court of Conciliation and Arbitration, which had been established in 1904. Within a few years, Higgins presided over the Court, his optimism for the system undeterred by its strictly interstate jurisdiction. 'Just as bushfires run through artificial state lines, just as the rabbits ignore them in pursuit of food, so do, frequently, industrial disputes', he insisted.[6]

Compulsory arbitration was intimately linked to the key symbolic element that emerged out of this period of social policy experimentation: the basic wage. Labour activists in the United States and Britain had been interested in the concept of establishing a minimum wage for workers, but it was in Australia and New Zealand that the proposal was put into practice. The first bushfire that Justice Higgins had to put out during his presidency of the Arbitration Court cleared the ground for him to define the court's understanding of what constituted a 'fair and reasonable wage'. At the time, this was critical, because legislation had passed through the Federal Parliament in 1906 offering local manufacturing industry the carrot of a tariff on imported goods and the stick of excise duties on their own products. The stick would be spared if employers offered their workers a 'fair and reasonable' wage, which was to be determined by the Arbitration Court. Known as the 'new protection', this was a policy designed to promote Australian industry and to protect the standard of living of the working class. Alfred Deakin had declared in the federal Parliament that a minimum living wage was essential because the 'working creature' was not a 'mere cogwheel in the industrial machine', but a 'man, with sympathies and an immortal soul'.[7]

In 1907, H. V. McKay's Sunshine Harvester Works, a maker of agricultural instruments, claimed exemption from the new excise on the grounds that they paid their employees wages that were indeed fair and reasonable. In his adjudication, Justice Higgins offered a definition: fair and reasonable wages were those that could meet 'the normal needs of the average employee, regarded as a human being living in a civilized community'. The Harvester Judgement, as it became known, considered 'normal needs' to be a life of 'frugal comfort' and the 'average employee' as a man who had a wife and 'about three children'.[8] The idea of workers' entitlement to 'frugal comfort' had come from a Papal Encyclical of 1891. A stream of witnesses, including housewives who detailed exactly how much it cost to house, feed, clothe, insure and educate an Australian working-class household in 1907, led Higgins to determine that a minimum of seven shillings a week should cover a family's most basic costs.

The idea of a basic wage had taken hold and its standards adhered to those which had been outlined in Harvester. Federal protection of manufacturing industry remained in place, but ultimately, it was the individual states that legislated for judicial determination of a minimum wage through their own courts and wages boards. Higgins' talk of the scourge of bushfires and rabbits had been premature – most cases remained within state borders – but his broader belief in wage determination remained a constant of Australian industrial life for at least half a century. By the 1920s, most Australian workers were employed in industries where the rates of pay, hours and working conditions came under 'awards' defined by arbitration tribunals.

Unskilled workers benefited most, but arbitration offered less to those with higher levels of expertise and could not guarantee that which Higgins, Deakin and other liberals of their ilk most desired: harmony between capital and labour. There was still much to be negotiated and strikes continued to occur. Sometimes the root of the conflict was conditions of work and rates of pay, at others it was a more symbolic contest over the rights of workers to exhibit the collective spirit. The most dramatic in this period occurred in Brisbane in 1912, when a dispute involving tramways employees – who wished to wear a union badge when their employer disapproved – escalated into a general strike that shut down the city and led to intense conflict between baton-wielding police and protestors.

One of the ironies of Australia's reputation as a social laboratory was that, whatever measure of protection it may have offered to workers, a willingness for state intervention was of equal, if not greater, benefit to the industries, which remained shielded from external competition. Liberal politicians wanted social cohesion, but they wanted businesses to thrive too. Arbitration was essentially based on the idea that ordinary people had the right to enjoy a decent yet humble standard of living, and knew their place in the broader social order. It was also premised on the assumption of ongoing and strong class-based identities. The belief that most workers would be happy with frugality immediately locates the idea of a basic wage in its historical context: this was the period before the development of mass-consumer society.

Some workers were more equal than others under the system that eventuated. The basic wage was a male wage and hence female wage inequality became institutionalised. In the days before equal pay, even if a woman was responsible for the support of herself and dependents and therefore had no choice but to work, the rate remained the same as if she were single. Men were paid a living wage regardless of the number of their dependents; the assumption was that they had women and children to support, even if they did not. This gave single men a comparatively high standard of living; it impoverished deserted, widowed and abandoned women. In 1912 about twenty per cent of the labour force were women, a figure which remained largely stagnant until the 1960s. Women were paid at approximately half of the male rate until that time, a coincidence between participation and reward that is hard to overlook.

In 1912 Labor Prime Minister Andrew Fisher declared that mothers 'were performing the highest duties of citizenship, and enduring dangers not second to those of war'.[9] The Maternity Allowance he introduced, granting £5 to mothers on the birth of a child, gave a clear message to women that their primary role in the new nation was as mothers to the future Australian population. The 'baby bonus' amount was not insubstantial: it was equivalent to almost a month's wages for a female factory worker. Nor did it discriminate on the grounds of marital status: single mothers were as entitled as married women to receive the payment. The prejudice that lay at the heart of the maternity allowance was linked, instead, to skin colour.

'Asiatic' women and 'Aboriginal natives of Australia, Papua or the islands of the Pacific' were not eligible to receive the baby bonus. White women were to be encouraged to procreate, those of colour were not.

There had been some concern since the late nineteenth century about Australia's falling birth rate, a fate it had in common with other industrialising nations of the Western world. Women did not appear to be unhappy about bearing fewer children; those who turned their mind to the development of the nation saw things differently. In New South Wales, a Royal Commission under the chairmanship of Sir Charles Mackellar had been appointed in 1903 to inquire into this 'grave disorder', which sapped 'the vitals of a new people, dispelling its hopes, blighting its prospects and threatening its continuance'.[10] 'New people' is the key phrase here; the older people, the Indigenous people who had been displaced by the coming of the Europeans, were no longer perceived as an important part of the nation or its future. The Australian Constitution, for instance, had specified that Aborigines were not to be counted as part of the national census.

The exclusion of Indigenous, Islander and Asian women from the baby bonus was typical of the ways in which the new nation sought to limit its most basic citizenship rights. The Australian Constitution contains no Bill of Rights similar to that of the United States. In Australia, ultimately, citizenship is an 'empty category' that is filled only when Parliament passes legislation creating specific entitlements for its citizens.[11] The ostensibly progressive welfare measures of the early part of the twentieth century, such as old-age pensions and invalidity benefits, were subject to the same restrictions as the baby bonus: Indigenous peoples and Asians were not eligible to receive them.

The capacity of the Australian state to give with one hand and take with the other received its most symbolic expression during the passage of the *Commonwealth Franchise Act 1902*. The Act fully enfranchised white women on equal terms with men, a right not achieved at a federal level in the United States until 1920, Britain until 1928 and France until 1944. It simultaneously excluded all 'aboriginal natives' of Australia, Asia, Africa or the Islands of the Pacific except New Zealand from voting in federal elections, unless they already possessed such rights at state level, and most of them did not. This was not white women's votes won at the expense of the Indigenous population – it was not a direct trade in those terms – but rather indicated the ways in which the settler community predicated its unity and sought to secure the nation on racial grounds. A capacity for progressive measures within a racially restrictive framework was a hallmark of the early Australian federal state.

RACIAL RESTRICTION

Protection was a word in frequent use in the first decades of the twentieth century; it had positive implications because in most cases it meant looking after the interests of workers and industry. It was a term that would have entirely different connotations for the Aboriginal population. Until the 1930s, policy makers assumed that the Aborigines were a dying race. Under the terms of the Constitution, the states retained responsibility for their Aboriginal populations and legislated on their behalf. Hence, in 1911 an Act was passed in South Australia 'for the better Protection and Control of the Aboriginal and Half-Caste Inhabitants of the State of South Australia'. Known thereafter as the *Aborigines Protection Act*, the longer title included reference to the control that was the real purpose of the more euphemistic term 'protection'. The transfer of the Northern Territory from the state of South Australia to the Commonwealth after 1911 meant that the federal government also concerned itself with Indigenous affairs from this time. About 20,000 Aborigines lived in the territory compared to fewer than 2000 Europeans.

As a consequence of legislation passed in different jurisdictions, there was considerable diversity in the treatment and conditions faced by Aboriginal people. The most draconian regimes operated in the places where the majority of Aboriginal people lived: Western Australia, Queensland and the Northern Territory. In these regions, government-appointed Protectors exercised enormous powers over the lives of their charges, who were effectively wards of the state. They were able to remove children from the care of their parents, restrict the movements and marriages of Aboriginal people and interfere in the terms of their employment. These were also the states in which Aborigines were increasingly removed from contact with other Australians and confined to institutions, reserves and mission compounds. The South Australian legislation was similarly harsh, but Aborigines there were not forced onto compounds.

In New South Wales, by contrast, Aborigines began to be dispersed from reserves established in the previous century and encouraged to blend into broader white working-class communities. This created vulnerabilities of a different kind, when extended kinship networks were disrupted by the forced removal of Aborigines from places that had been home to them for a long time. A similar situation pertained in Victoria, where the government determined who was 'part' Aboriginal and adopted a policy of retaining reserve accommodation only for compliant 'full-blood' Aborigines. In Victoria and Western Australia, some institutions and reserves were run directly by the Government, but in the majority of cases the state worked in close association with mission and church organisations who staffed the missions, reserves and children's homes.

In almost every state, mixed-race children could be removed from their families by authorities and sent to live in institutions and training schools. 'Rescuing' Aboriginal children had been practised in some states since the nineteenth century, but it was in the early post-federation period that it became a more systematic policy around the country. Legislation paved the way for child removal, but the full force of this policy would be felt when Protectors driven by eugenically inspired racial ideologies were appointed after 1914. The peak removal period was yet to come, but the impact on Aboriginal communities and parents was immediate. One Aboriginal mother wrote to the Chief Secretary of Victoria in 1914, and demanded that she be allowed to see her daughter, who had been taken from her and placed in an institution: 'We not slaves or prisoners of war to be treated like that. How would you like to be in the same place as I am [?] you would feel it'.[12]

Despite the pain behind such pleas, and the continuing presence of an Indigenous population, a white Australia remained the unblushing desire of almost every prominent thinker and activist in early twentieth century Australia, from the liberal protectionist to the most strident labour activist. The belief that the future of Australia lay with its white inhabitants, and that Indigenous people would soon fade away, influenced the treatment that was meted out to its first peoples. It also determined the way in which potential new arrivals were handled. In 1901, at least ninety-five per cent of the Australian population were of British origin, and politicians were determined to keep it that way and to attempt to make it whiter still. The first major piece of policy legislation passed by the federal Parliament was the *Immigration Restriction Act 1901*, which was designed to deny entry to Australia of non-white peoples. More than this, the Act revealed that the 'white Australia policy', as it came to be known, was a founding principle of the new nation. 'At the very first instant of our national career we are as one for a white Australia' the first Attorney-General, Alfred Deakin, told the national Parliament in September 1901.[13] His Labor parliamentary colleagues would have agreed with him. In May of the same year, a white Australia emerged as the first plank in the platform of the newly constituted federal Labor Party, which also included adult suffrage, old-age pensions, a citizen's army and compulsory arbitration.

The arguments made in favour of white Australia in the first Parliament were manifold; dissent was rare. They ranged from comments that vilified the integrity of other peoples and cultures, seeing in them the scourge of disease and the source of moral turpitude, to insistence upon the dangers that non-white labour posed to working conditions, the assumption being that coloured labour worked for less and lowered wages and standards for everyone. In contrast, a few speakers feared the industry and competition of particular groups, such as the Japanese, and saw them as potential rivals to be routed rather than as the harbingers of lower standards. The capabilities of people from cultures other than his own could be acknowledged but could not override Alfred Deakin's more profound belief in the essential precursor to a strong, healthy and successful nation: unity of race. The 'admixture of races' was the certain path to ruin. It led to racial degeneration, corroded democracy and weakened the social fabric. 'Unity of race is an absolute essential to the unity of Australia', Deakin insisted.[14]

The most often-quoted and eloquent spokesman on behalf of white Australia, Deakin was also an admirer of the United States, which for him provided both object lesson and inspiration in matters of national interest and integrity. This was justification for white Australia that rose above local concerns about labour and wages. 'The great republic of the west' had been torn asunder by the legacy of slavery.[15] It was Deakin's opinion, expressed anonymously in one of many articles he wrote under commission for London's *Morning Post* in these years, that '[t]hose States of the American Union which are without a noticeable Negro population are better governed and more efficient members of the Union than those in which there are two separate peoples'.[16] Australia could escape this fate, and become an even better democracy, by preventing the arrival of alien groups. 'The Yankees of the South Pacific are determined to prevent race fissures, babel cities and debased admixtures in their Commonwealth', one American commentator noted. 'They welcome immigration adapted to democratic institutions and 20th century civilization, but will not received adulterated goods'.[17]

Australia might, in another sense, follow the United States' lead and declare its national interests to the region, and the world. In Parliament, Deakin argued that white Australia could be considered 'the Monroe doctrine of the Commonwealth of Australia'.[18] The Monroe doctrine had, since the 1820s, asserted that there should be distinct American and European spheres of power and a concomitant right of the United States to exert influence in the territories of the American continents free from European intervention or any further attempts at colonisation. By invoking the name of Monroe, Deakin sought to underscore the centrality of white Australia to the nation's future path and distinct identity, and to insist on its right to do so without imperial interference. In this respect, white Australia was the beginning of a series of small departures in the imperial relationship, but it was also one of the points at which the interests of Australia began to cohere with other societies which identified themselves as new, democratic and white.

It had been clear since before federation that the British were placed in a difficult position by their settler colonies' desire to restrict immigration to their shores. Canada and South Africa had evinced sentiment similar to Australia's in their desire to limit Asian immigration, in particular. In the scramble to prove themselves worthy inheritors and perpetuators of the Anglo-Saxon tradition, the settler colonies sought to emulate both the institutions and racial composition of the mother country. In whiteness was strength; colour indicated servility and subordinate status. According to the logic of imperialism, governing people of colour and bestowing upon them the benefits of civilisation was the white man's 'burden'. Settler colonies were not interested in adding further to the load they already carried. These aspirations collided with the politics of Empire, which offered ostensible equality before the law to all its subjects, whether they were inhabitants of the self-governing colonies or living under conditions of direct rule. Restricting the free passage between colonies of British subjects made a mockery of imperial citizenship. If immigration restriction posed internal problems, it also raised difficulties for Britain's external relationships. Eager to court the Japanese as Allies, the British were also conscious of condoning the policies of its colonies that discriminated against them and imperiled ongoing friendly relations.

Despite the delicate balancing act forced on the British by the confluence of their Empire responsibilities and international alliances, they were steeped enough in the racial thinking of the day to appreciate and sympathise with the desires of their settler colonies. Secretary of State for the Colonies, Joseph Chamberlain, recommended that the Australians follow the example of the South African colony of Natal, which had recently implemented racially restrictive immigration legislation without mentioning the word race or colour. Following an innovation originating in the United States, another society increasingly set upon seeing itself as a land for the white man, Natal had been able to limit the influx of Asian immigrants by administering a 'dictation test'. Ostensibly a limitation on the grounds of literacy, this was effectively restriction on the grounds of race. Australian legislators took the cue; potential immigrants could be offered a dictation test in 'any European language'. Within two years Alfred Deakin, now Prime Minister, could boast that the 'educational tests which could be applied so as to shut out all undesirables' had 'worked well' because so 'few had managed to survive it'.[19] 'In fact and in effect', he later wrote, 'our colourless laws are administered so as to draw a deep colour line of demarcation between Caucasians and all other races. No white men are stopped at our ports for language or any other tests. ... On the other hand all coloured men are stopped unless they come merely as visitors.'[20]

There had been some voices raised in Parliament about the subterfuge of the test, and implications that it was cowardly to hide behind the smokescreen of literacy when the fire was race. But this was pragmatic politics and the Empire must be seen to save face. Nor was everyone happy about immigration restriction's ugly twin, deportation. The *Pacific Island Labourers Act*, passed in the same year as restriction legislation and considered its essential counterpart, was designed to expel people known then as 'Kanakas', Melanesian islanders from the Solomons and New Hebrides who worked in the sugar industry in northern Australia. Representatives of that industry had been the most vociferous of the few opponents of white Australia. Their motives were driven by self-interest rather than any more developed sense of a common humanity. The legislation was implicit recognition that despite all of the rhetoric, there were regions of Australia that were most certainly *not* all white. The Northern Territory was one such place, northern Queensland was another.

The global sugar industry had been dominated for almost a century by the vast movements of indentured workers from China and India, and profitability was predicated on the availability of this cheap labour. Australian sugar enterprises had sourced or kidnapped cheap labour from their Pacific back yard, but the principle remained the same. This was also an era when the ability of white men to undertake manual labour efficiently in the tropics was in question; the economic development of Australia's northern tropical zone was felt to be in peril. Fears about white man's capabilities in the tropics would continue for several decades, but the sugar industry was able to survive the deportation of Pacific Islanders via the grace of well-timed mechanisation and the boon of industry protection.

The numbers of islanders employed in the industry had in fact fallen since late in the nineteenth century, about the same time that numbers of white workers began to rise as machines performed the work once required of men. The potential losses to employers were offset by generous tariffs, which helped protect their industry and encouraged the production of 'white' sugar. The deportation act was amended in 1906, and introduced a grain of compassion into the debate: Pacific Islanders who had married white women were allowed to stay in Australia. An exception was also made for Japanese pearl divers based in Broome and around the Torres Strait, who risked their lives to fetch the pearl shells that made buttons and belt-buckles for the European and American markets.

A NEW AND GROWING NATION

Despite fears that the general ban on coloured labour would slow the economic development of the country – a cost most people appeared willing to bear – it was time to be optimistic again in the early years of the twentieth century. The economic effects of the severe depression of the 1890s had almost lifted by 1906 and from then until World War I a significant economic recovery was underway. In its wake, there was a slow reshaping of the workforce. Some economic patterns were becoming entrenched that would determine the type of employment available for Australians for much of the twentieth century. The construction and maintenance of railways, trams, roads and bridges, communications and new technologies like electricity: in Australia all were the responsibility of the government, and the state consequently became a significant employer of both professional and unskilled labour. The levels of public-sector employment in Australia remained distinctive throughout the Western world until after World War II.

While the impression abroad that the Australian state was a substantial employer remained accurate, the dominance of pastoral work and rural life in many accounts of Australian life and identity would continue for at least another half a century, despite significant structural changes that would alter this picture forever. The drift to the cities and to urban, manufacturing and service-industry work had begun. Even though the Australian economy depended heavily on agriculture and the export of primary produce, and work in the rural industry was still the main form of employment, from the turn of the century the numbers of people working in primary industry began a slow but steady decline.

By 1911, almost twenty per cent of the workforce was employed in manufacturing, particularly in the clothing, textile and metalworking industries. These were precisely the industries that benefited under the policy of tariff protection, and they grew accordingly. People were drawn to manufacturing work and preferred it to the privatised drudgery of domestic service, which began to reduce in significance as an occupational category. Office and clerical work were also on the rise, and they were occupations that attracted young women, who were seen as naturals with the relatively new typewriter, which seemed to require skills akin to the use of a sewing machine and a piano. Both city and rural workers put in a long week, whatever their occupation. The average in 1914 was a 48 hour week, which for most meant slightly over eight hour days during the week and about half that again on Saturday

Apart from encouraging the growth of manufacturing industries by providing tariff protection, the way forward for the economy was seen to lie in government investment in infrastructure and in population growth through natural increase and immigration. Immigration had slowed to a trickle in the twenty years after 1890, but accelerated again after 1911. Between 1911 and 1914, 234,000 new immigrants arrived in Australia, most from the British Isles. This helped the Australian population reach almost five million people by 1914. Planners did not know it at the time, but these few years before World War I constituted the peak of British immigration to its dominion territories. In the nineteenth century, the United States had been the preferred destination; in the early part of the twentieth century most British migrants wanted to disembark at imperial ports. Australia's population statistics benefited accordingly, but never again in the twentieth century would Britons emigrate – to Australia or anywhere else – with such enthusiasm and in such numbers.[21]

This was a significant change in global migration patterns that would ultimately require a rethinking of immigration policies in places such as Australia, but it took some years before these new patterns emerged. In the meantime, Australian population planners remained focused on Britain as the most desirable source of immigrants for the same reason that the government was willing to reward mothers with an allowance for the birth of a baby: they augmented the white population of Australia. Octavius Beale, Sydney businessman and member of the Royal Commission on the Birth Rate, practised what he preached. The father of thirteen children, Beale was one of numerous voices raised in concern about the need to people the continent of Australia. On a visit to London in 1906, Beale concluded a public speech about 'Imperial Immigration' by quoting a remark by US President Theodore Roosevelt: 'Beware of keeping the northern territory of your continent empty'.[22] For Roosevelt being 'empty' meant an absence of white men willing to defend the territory; the Indigenous people who formed the majority of the population in the north were seen as unreliable and, in any case, irrelevant to the nation's future. A decade earlier, Roosevelt had been impressed by the work of Charles Pearson, a British academic who migrated to Australia and had become influential in university and government circles with his progressive and erudite views on women's rights, democracy and education. When reviewing Pearson's *National Life and Character*, a book that argued that the 'higher races' of British and Europeans were in peril of losing ground to the rapidly multiplying 'lower races', Roosevelt insisted that 'with much of the competition between the races reducing itself to the warfare of the cradle, no race has any chance to win a great place unless it consists of good breeders as well as of good fighters'.[23]

Roosevelt's twin images of the emptiness of the north and the warfare of the cradle had particular resonance for Australians. The vastness of Australia's land mass, the smallness of its population and its geographical proximity to Asia were a combination of factors that led to intense speculation about the type of danger Australia might face in the future. Books like Pearson's, which predicted the rise of Asian populations, appeared to have their basic premise confirmed by early twentieth century. By this time, fears about potential attack from a rival European colonial power had abated. The threats now seemed closer to home, and to the immediate north.

LOOKING OUTWARD: ALLIANCES AND EMPIRES

There had long been discomfort about, and attempts to restrict, Chinese immigration. Indeed, Pearson had predicted it would be the Chinese who would be the power to contend with in the coming century. But the Chinese had not embraced the technological and industrial revolution that had driven European global expansion. Japan had, and by 1895, when Japan defeated China in the Sino-Japanese war, it became clear to military experts that the Asian power to be feared was not China, but Japan. Novelists capitalised on these anxieties, and fired the imaginations of Europeans, Americans and Australians by writing stories that played on fears of invasion, defeat and miscegenation. The geo-political forces at play seemed to matter little in terms of whether it was the Chinese or Japanese cast as villains in these stories. The popular mind rarely distinguished between ethnicities when it came to fears that circulated around the 'yellow' man.

It was therefore with some trepidation that Australians received news of the Anglo-Japanese Alliance in 1902. Keen to ease its defence burden in the Pacific, the British viewed an alliance with the Japanese as potentially neutralising any threat the Russians might pose in the region and as a chance to maintain friendly relations with an emerging naval power.

Despite anxiety about British commitment to Australia's own defence, there was muted support in Australia for Japan in its conflict with Russia over territory in Manchuria and Korea.

In May 1905, when the Japanese roundly defeated the Russians in a decisive battle in the Tsushima Strait, the emergence of Japan as a major new power in the Pacific was confirmed. It unleashed new fears about the rise of Asia and confirmed older ones. Japanese victory in the Russo-Japanese war was the first time in the modern period that an Asian power had been victorious over European military forces. Yet the potential threat Japan might pose to British interests seemed to be contained by the Alliance, and the Japanese Fleet made two friendly visits to Australian ports, in 1903 and 1906. The response was warm and welcoming, the kind of respectful reception given to the visit of one's parents' friends. The Japanese continued to resent their exclusion from immigration to Australia and made complaints at the highest diplomatic level, but there was no change to the white Australia policy.

Friendship was one thing, a sense of brotherhood and communion another altogether, and it was the latter that was the more heartfelt need. At the 1907 Colonial Conference in London, Deakin had sought to convince the British government that a new kind of imperialism was called for, one in which self-governing colonies like Australia could enjoy a more direct relationship with the British government. 'The farther we are removed from the centre the more the union means to us', Deakin told a gathering of Liberals in London during his visit.[24] In increasingly uncertain times, the union meant a great deal to Australians, as Deakin's description of himself as an 'independent Australian Briton' would imply, but at times it felt like a stone in the shoe to the British. Despite their irritation with men like Deakin, there was at least recognition of the desire of its white territories for some distinction over colonies like India that were still subject to direct imperial rule. The self-governing colonies were to remain part of the Colonial Office but they would be known in future as the 'Dominions'.

While the British might have seen the Alliance with Japan as a relief, at least in the short term, the United States viewed the activities of the Japanese somewhat differently. They were views closer to Australia's own, but could be expressed with the force of a nation on the verge of becoming a significant global power. By the early twentieth century the United States had developed its naval resources and was keen to demonstrate its military prowess. President Roosevelt decided in 1907 to send sixteen new battleships, manned by 14,000 sailors, for a leisurely circumnavigation of the globe. The tour of the Great White Fleet was no battle of Tsushima but it was a peacetime display of force designed to impress upon the world that there were regional rivals to Japan's naval power. Deakin, smarting from his recent knuckle-rapping at the Colonial Conference, saw in the Great White Fleet an opportunity to demonstrate his concerns about Australia's defence and his willingness to look outside the imperial relationship to ensure it.

The largest crowds in Australian history, gathered on the heads, along the streets and in pleasure cruisers, greeted and cheered the arrival of the US battleships, which dropped anchor at Sydney, Melbourne and Albany. Deakin was careful during the actual visit to highlight Australia's loyalty to Empire while simultaneously reinforcing the message that there were deep-felt connections with America. 'The crimson thread of kinship', he suggested, invoking a familiar phrase, 'our chief bond of union within the Empire, extends throughout the great republic whose sailors we are about to welcome as guests, and the honoured representatives of this mighty nation are welcomed as blood relations'.[25]

Seeing the grandeur of white-painted battleships gliding into Sydney Harbour in the winter of 1908 had confirmed the desire for Australia to develop its own military forces. The next year Australia introduced legislation that established compulsory military training, but not conscription, for boys and men between the ages of fourteen and twenty. As if to confirm that the recent visit of the Americans had not compromised Australia's primary loyalty, at the end of 1909 Viscount Kitchener arrived in Australia at the invitation of the Commonwealth Government to advise them on defence matters. Considered to be a colonial military expert, Kitchener had led the British to victory in the South African War, and had recently concluded a term as Commander-in-Chief in India. He was incredulous that each state was isolated by different railway gauges, which 'would appear to be more favorable to an enemy invading Australia than to the defence of the country', and proposed a more systematic interior connection. Kitchener's recommendation that the voluntary militia, while proving 'what excellent material existed among the young manhood of Australia', still needed properly trained officers led to the formation of the Royal Military College at Duntroon. Kitchener also believed that 'the danger of want of population and consequent ineffective occupation in many parts of the country' was a very serious state of affairs.[26] Now it seemed that both the President of the United States and one of the British Army's most senior and experienced commanders were worried about the 'empty north'. Within two years the Royal Australian Navy had been established. When offered as support to the United Kingdom at times of war, or when visiting international ports, the new Navy would default to the command of the British Admiralty, a statement of Empire loyalty if ever there was one.

Australia had already proven its willingness to participate in Britain's colonial wars. The colonies sent off representatives to the Sudan, to the Boxer Rebellion in China and to the South African War. They fought under the British flag, but drew attention to their colonial origins with distinctive dress and emblems. The 5th Queensland Imperial Bushmen, for instance, wore a possum fur band around their slouch hat. The commitment continued after federation. Prime Minister Edmond Barton had declared in the first federal Parliament that 'when our empire is at war with any power whatever … it becomes our turn to declare the motto, "The Empire, right or wrong"'.[27] In 1902, a federal contingent set sail for South Africa, as the first military representatives of the new Commonwealth. In total, over 16,000 Australians fought in the South African conflict. George Arnold Wood, a young professor of history at the University of Sydney, thought that love of empire motivated some recruits, but most were enticed 'by sheer love of adventure and the desire to escape from the monotony of bush life'.[28]

Wood was one of the few critics of Australian involvement in the South African War, Henry Bournes Higgins was another, but they did not gain widespread support. There was some criticism that the war was in fact being fought in order for the British to gain control of gold mines on the Rand, rather than in defence of the rights of their settlers and Africans in the Boer-controlled Transvaal and Orange Free State. 'The less we say in Australia about the treatment of the blacks, the better for our self-respect', one Labor politician remarked about claims of Boer inhumanity to Africans, although his reward was ultimately to be removed from public office.[29] As the war dragged on, there was increasing unease about the tactics used by the British. The court-martialing of Australian soldiers and the execution of two was not well received – Kitchener had in fact signed the death warrant of the most infamous, Breaker Morant – but most controversial was the policy of sacking Boer farms and placing Boer women and children in concentration camps.

Some of the Australian forces expressed disquiet about such tactics, at least in private. Hubert Murray, a New South Wales barrister who fitted Wood's profile of a man who went to Africa to escape a life he found tedious, complained to his wife: 'Our principal pastime is burning farms and laying waste to the country generally. My particular job is cattle-lifting and collecting Boer farmers who are all being sent to Pretoria as prisoners. I hate the whole business but shall have to see it through.'[30] Once back in Australia, he described the anti-war movement to his brother Gilbert, a professor of Greek who was a pacifist, as 'a singularly harmless lot, but they are vigorously denounced as traitors engaged in a veiled attack upon the Empire'. Most thought the Empire 'right' in this case, and approximately 600 Australians who died during the fighting were considered to have made a sacrifice on behalf of the motherland. One of them, twenty year old Keith Mackellar, was the son of prominent Sydney physician, politician and businessman Sir Charles Mackellar. In a letter of condolence to the family, a fellow Australian soldier told the family that Keith had 'met his death, as a gallant and true son of Empire'.[31]

NATIONAL SYMBOLS

By the end of the South African war, Australia was preparing to assume some colonial responsibilities of its own in the Pacific region. There were strategic considerations, given that a ring of territories around Australia might provide a defence buffer. Commercial interests played a part too, as Australian businesses wanted to access the land and labour of the South Pacific to further their interests in coconut and rubber. The cheap labour to be had on the islands was considered one way of getting around what one executive called in 1910 'the present white Australia craze', but if capital was to invest it also wanted territorial security.[32] This was something that Australia could not ensure alone, and the British were not interested in supplying. Matters came to a head over Australia's desire for Britain to annex the New Hebrides, when it became clear that without British support no extension of Australia's external territories was possible.

Federation actually provided the opportunity for the British to further distance themselves from Australia's territorial ambitions, because they could now hand over responsibility for the territory of New Guinea, annexed at Queensland's insistence in the 1880s, to the new Commonwealth. The gradual transfer began in 1902. Hubert Murray, not long back from the South African War, arrived in 1904 as Chief Judicial Officer. From 1906, with the passing of the *Papua Act* the territory was renamed and Murray, appointed Lieutenant Governor in 1908, soon led the Australian administration. In the years before World War I, Papua remained a relatively insignificant possession, with a sparse white population intent upon controlling the labour of Papuans who worked the coconut and rubber plantations. It was Murray's job, and inclination, to provide some measure of protection to the 'natives' from other officials

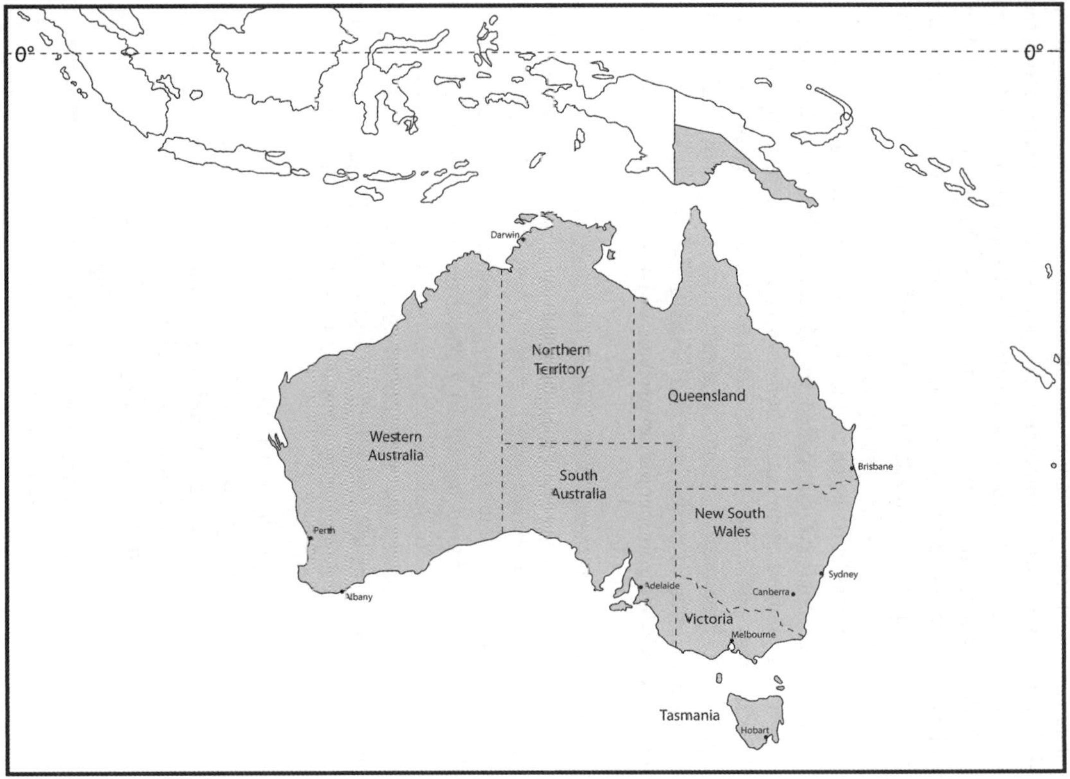

Map 3 Federated Australia, 1911

and settlers, most of whom he considered to be 'men of very bad character'.[33] As a consequence, most of them hated him.

If Australia's colonial ambitions were going nowhere fast, other plans for constructing symbols of nationhood were progressing, albeit slowly and not always smoothly. The longstanding debate about the site of a new national capital was settled with the choice of Canberra in 1908. Sited inland between Australia's two largest cities, Sydney and Melbourne, in part to quell rivalry between them, the design of the new federal capital was made the subject of a competition. In 1912 an American architect, Walter Burley Griffin, a onetime associate of Frank Lloyd Wright, was announced as the winner. The drawings that accompanied his design were completed by Marion Mahony, soon to be his wife and a talented architect in her own right. Influenced by the City Beautiful movement, the Griffins sought to take advantage of Canberra's topographical features to create a planned modern city that would allow for the cultivation of civic virtue and aesthetic beauty. 'It is a grand site for a city,' Griffin commented on arrival, 'Australians do not paint their country as they should'.[34]

These were sentiments with which the poet Dorothea Mackellar, daughter of Sir Charles and sister of Keith who had died in the South African War, might have agreed. After a privileged childhood spent between Sydney, her family's country properties and frequent trips to Europe, Dorothea found herself in London in her late teenage years, suddenly homesick for Australia. She composed a poem, 'Core of My Heart', which captured the expectation that the England of the antipodean imagination would feel familiar. And yet her distance from home called forth a new appreciation of Australia's different aesthetic.

> The love of field and coppice
> Of green and shaded lanes,
> Of ordered woods and gardens
> Is running in your veins.
> Strong love of grey-blue distance,
> Brown streams and soft, dim skies
> I know, but cannot share it,
> My love is otherwise.
>
> I love a sunburnt country,
> A land of sweeping plains,
> Of ragged mountain ranges,
> Of drought and flooding rains.

I love her far horizons,
I love her jewel-sea,
Her beauty and her terror
The wide brown land for me!

First published in London's *Spectator* in 1908, it was soon reprinted and became more familiar to Australian readers as 'My Country'. The first stanza is now largely forgotten, but its second is one of the few pieces of federation-era poetry still familiar today.

The innovations that stemmed from the belief that the key conflict at the heart of social life was that between capital and labour have been less well remembered, in part because the twentieth century would be dominated by conflicts of a different order altogether. Some sensed it coming. Even in the relative isolation of Papua, Hubert Murray confided to his brother in September 1911 that he felt 'rather uneasy' about the prospect of war with the Germans. He imagined that his son Terence 'would be up to his neck in it … for which I suppose I should be glad'. 'It seems humiliating to sit down on this side of the world', Murray concluded 'and have your fate decided in the North Sea'. Murray seemed wary, but not unduly perturbed, about the fate of his son in the event of war breaking out. H. B. Higgins may have lived to regret his almost flippant remark comparing the war in Europe with the issue of industrial arbitration. While Higgins was touring the world lecturing on the role of the Arbitration Court, his son Mervyn enlisted in Melbourne soon after the fighting broke out. On the other side of the world, Rudyard Kipling's son John was also inspired to join up. Kipling had been a vocal supporter of the British in the South African War, Higgins had been a sceptic and critic. In 1914, they agreed about the necessity for Britain to be at war with the Germans in Europe, and soon they would share an understanding of its cost.

10

A Nation at War: 1914–18

The decision in August 1914 to support Great Britain wholeheartedly in its struggle with Germany appeared to offer expansive possibilities for the new Australian nation. In an era when it was widely believed that great nations were either born or forged through the crucible of battle, Australia's peaceful transition to nationhood seemed to lack a certain gravitas. There had been no war of independence, no glorious revolution. Britain had been willing to let the Australian colonies go, even to encourage them on their path to independence. The immediate response to the tense European situation – an offer of 20,000 troops and the Australian Navy placed under the command of the British Admiralty – was a statement of loyalty to Empire. There was a sense too that this was not just an opportunity to stand shoulder to shoulder with Britain at a time of crisis; Australia might be on the cusp of a new chapter in its history, with the word sacrifice written onto the page.

GOING TO WAR

In the early weeks of the war, the concept of sacrifice remained abstract; expression of Empire loyalty was the more dominant theme as community leaders organised patriotic demonstrations at dusty railway sidings, country show-grounds and grand town halls in the major cities. Hats were tossed in the air, the chorus of Rule Britannia rang loud, the King was cheered. The singing and cheering overwhelmed the concern of the small band of Christian pacifists who disliked militarism in any form, and the far left who viewed the conflict as a fight between capitalist powers intent on using working people as cannon fodder. Even those with socialist leanings bowed to the force of popular sentiment and the logic of loyalty. Nettie Higgins (later Palmer), the niece of Judge Henry Bournes Higgins, had first been attracted to socialist ideas during her time as a student at the University of Melbourne. Living in London in the early part of the war, she wrote home to her brother: 'now that the war has begun, I feel that fighting it through is the only way to finish it ... I feel that we must face realities, and that talking against war now is like talking against a thunderstorm when you are in it'.[1]

The Australian government made sure it could control any talk about the war. A newly elected Labor Government, led by Andrew Fisher, introduced the *War Precautions Act* in October 1914. The Commonwealth government now exercised full powers over the economy, introduced censorship, controlled the newspapers, and could prosecute or penalise people it deemed engaged in action prejudicial to the war effort. Uncontroversial at the time, the Act was guided through Parliament by Attorney-General William Morris Hughes. Later, Hughes described it as possessing 'authority that barely stopped this side of absolutism'.[2] The Act was a Trojan horse that 'Billy' Hughes, who within the year would replace the overwhelmed and ailing Fisher as Prime Minister, would use to full effect.

Of Welsh origin, Hughes was a veteran of the Australian labour movement, pugnacious, acid-tongued and a man who had been a strong advocate of compulsory military training. His belief in compelling men to do things that they might rather not would only increase as the war news worsened. Hughes' small stature, deafness and irascibility polarised the politicians and statesmen who worked closely with him, but it went with a single-minded determination to win the war and safeguard Australia's interests that endeared him to soldiers and the electorate. It was a pact that would endure throughout the war but was incapable of surviving much beyond it.

In the early months of the war, men volunteered in droves. They marched for miles to recruiting offices. The sense of excitement and adventure, tinged with escape from an ordinary fate, swelled the ranks of men offering themselves for military service. It was the primary motivation for most who signed up. Yet there were men who enlisted because they felt it to be their duty. A schoolteacher from Toowoomba who had recently won a scholarship to study classics at the University of Queensland, Eric Partridge, felt he could not continue the life of a student in wartime because it made him feel 'little less blameworthy than Nero fiddling while Rome burned'.[3] Whatever their motivation, Australian soldiers would be paid handsomely: six shillings a day, which was a fortune in comparison to the one shilling received by the British troops.

The public soon learned that Australian soldiers would fight as a contingent, in their own divisions, rather than being scattered throughout existing British formations. They were to be led by Major General William Bridges, one of Australia's most senior defence figures. Bridges had most recently overseen the development of the national military college at Duntroon. He chose the title Australian Imperial Force (AIF), a name which stressed the twin themes of empire and nation. The recruiting offices were overwhelmed and could afford to be fussy. It was not a luxury that would endure. Men of small stature were rejected; only those over 5 feet, 6 inches in height were accepted after passing a rigorous medical examination.

The carnival atmosphere and determination to hand-pick the best specimens of Australian manhood underscored the naiveté of most people about what warfare between major industrial powers would be like, or how long it would last. By November 1914, enough men had enlisted to fill 38 troopships carrying 12,000 Australian and New Zealand infantry and the 1st Australian Light Horse Brigade. For the first eight months of the war, Australians would be spared the casualty lists that were causing such torment in Europe. The enthusiasm for war continued. As Eric Partridge put it, when the losses belonged to other, distant people, 'death was invested with glory, not pain, not with bitterness, not with sorrow'.[4]

There were some early Australian casualties close to home. Australia's external territory of Papua shared a border with the German colony of New Guinea. Within days of war being declared the British instructed the Australian government to disable any German communication facilities. By September 1914, the Australian Naval and Military Expeditionary Force, at a cost of six Australian lives, had destroyed the wireless station on the island of New Britain and had occupied the German colonies of New Guinea and Nauru. This war-time military occupation was the beginning of a long relationship between Australia and New Guinea. The shape of things to come was indicated within a few months. In early 1915, Hubert Murray was asked by the government to write a report on the administration of German New Guinea 'assuming that the Commonwealth takes it over'.[5]

The Germans, who had for so long been thought of as Anglo-Saxon cousins (despite their annoying perch in New Guinea), and desirable immigrants for white Australia, had to become the enemy. A few years before the war, the census revealed over 33,000 German-born residents living in Australia. Farming communities of German origin, most numerous in South Australia and Queensland, did their best to be as inconspicuous as possible and largely avoided internment as enemy aliens under the *War Precautions Act*. Business and community leaders of German origin, and those who lost their jobs owing to increasing anti-German feeling, were less fortunate.

The government used events such as the sinking of the passenger liner *Lusitania* by a German submarine and the execution of British nurse Edith Cavell in Belgium as evidence that the German was a barbaric enemy especially prone to attack women and children. They circulated lurid posters of the Hun, hands and swords dripping with blood, holding aloft the bodies of innocent victims. Following the lead of the British Royal Family, which from 1917 ceased to be known as the House of Saxe-Coburg-Gotha and adopted the name Windsor, some Australian towns changed their names to sound less Germanic. By the end of the war, 4500 Australian residents of German origin had been interned and a further 2500 captured in German territories or on German ships were also imprisoned.

ANZAC COVE

The first recruits to the AIF fully expected to engage the German enemy. Their disappointment was palpable when it became clear that instead of training on England's Salisbury Plain, the Dominion troops would go through their paces in the Egyptian desert. Insufficient accommodation in England and the entry of Turkey into the war on the side of the Germans had sealed their fate. The Australian and New Zealand Army Corps trained together and soon became identified with the acronym ANZAC. Decades of rhetoric about white Australia had not made the Australians sympathetic to the cultures and practices of non-Anglo peoples. Complaints about the hot and sandy environment meshed with discomfort with another culture, boredom and resentment of training routines. When finally told that they would be going into action in April 1915, one young wheat agent from Western Australia summed up the feeling: 'you can bet it was like putting a bit of roast meat to a starving man – we sprung to it'.[6] The anticipation was evidence of the troops' inexperience; 'one was twenty years younger in 1915 than in 1917', Eric Partridge recalled.[7]

Eager to eliminate Turkey from the war, in part because it blocked access to India and Russia, the First Lord of the Admiralty Winston Churchill planned an audacious attack. The naval bombardment of the Dardanelles in March 1915 did not deliver Constantinople to the Allies as he had hoped, so an amphibious landing was planned for the following month. Troops stationed in Egypt would be used for the offensive.

The naval activity in effect provided forewarning of the invasion. It also spelled disaster for Turkey's Armenian people, who originated from a region close to Russia and stood accused by their government of disloyalty and conspiring to assist an Allied invasion. On the evening of 24 April 1915, within Turkish borders, the mass killing of Armenian people began. The following morning, at 4.30 a.m. on 25 April 1915, the Anzacs, British and French troops amassed offshore and began a three-pronged assault on the Gallipoli peninsula. The odds were against the Allied troops, who landed on beaches at the base of sandstone cliffs. There were tens of thousands of them, but they were easy targets for the outnumbered Turkish troops entrenched at the top of almost perpendicular cliff faces. In presumption of success, the Allies referred to their landing place as 'Anzac Cove'. Instead of withdrawing, which would have been the most pragmatic strategy, the Anzacs and other Allies were ordered to plough on. They won a little ground and dug in.

Members of old and new Australia commanded the forces. Captain Joe Lalor, the grandson of Eureka legend Peter Lalor, died leading his troops on the first day. Major General Bridges had arrived, surveyed the scene, and argued for an immediate evacuation. He lasted a little longer – a bit more than three weeks – before he was killed. There was a saying common among the soldiers of 'one star, one stunt', but it is unclear whether Australian officers died in proportionally greater numbers than their troops, which was the case in the British Army.[8] The 4th Australian Infantry Brigade was led by an officer who would survive the war, John Monash, an engineer with an interest in military strategy who was an unlikely member of the Melbourne business establishment. His parents, Polish Jews, had emigrated to Australia.

The intensity of fighting waxed and waned. Monash remarked that for the first twenty-two days it seemed to him 'that absolutely the longest period during which there was absolutely no sound of gun or rifle-fire . . . was ten seconds'.[9] By the time Eric Partridge arrived in September 1915, '"Johnny Turk" did not molest them at all at night'.[10] He thought that after the landing, warfare on Gallipoli was 'comparatively innocuous' with 'a few "purple patches" so vigorous to satisfy the most warlike – not that those men were numerous'.[11] The Allies fought with their backs to the sea, dependent on ships for supplies and ammunition; the Turks were reinforced more easily by men and equipment that arrived overland. At enormous cost the Allies remained at Gallipoli for eight months.

As the first major battle of the war in which Australian troops had participated, there was a staggering weight of expectation. 'Australians have been very sensitive to the criticism of Old World visitors – that we were a pleasure-loving people, who only thought of sport, but did not work very hard and in a serious crisis would be found wanting', one returned man, Hugh Knyvett, reminded his readers in 1918.[12] The chance for Australian soldiers to distinguish themselves in battle was an opportunity to silence these implied criticisms. More than that, it was a chance to prove the virility of the race. In an era when it was commonly believed that nations and people were engaged in a battle for the 'survival of the fittest' – an awkward but influential transposition of Darwinian scientific thought to a social setting – strong soldiers became evidence of racial fitness. Hence, Knyvett could write that the Anzacs were 'eager to prove their country's worth as a breeder of men'.[13]

It was therefore with a huge sense of relief and pride that Australians read the first published account of the performance of their soldiers in battle. Describing the almost insurmountable odds that greeted the dawn landing, British war correspondent Ellis Ashmead-Bartlett declared that the Anzacs had acquitted themselves like 'a race of athletes'. He had never witnessed such courage. Ashmead-Bartlett issued the verdict that had been so anxiously awaited; Australians 'had been used for the first time and had not been found wanting'.[14] Soon after, his reports were supplemented by those of Australia's own official war correspondent, Charles E. Bean. The legend of Anzac, of courage under fire, of mateship and egalitarianism, owed much to Bean's reports throughout the war and his compilation of 1916, *The Anzac Book*. The meticulous diaries that Bean kept during his time at Gallipoli and later on the Western Front would go on to form the basis of his *Official History of Australia in The War of 1914–18*, a widely read book that for the first time made the exploits of the ordinary soldier, rather than the tactics of the battlefield general, the focus of interest and inquiry.

Like all mythologies, the Anzac legend grew out of a particular context. Its story of strength emerged from anxiety about weakness. Reports about the physical distinction of Australian soldiers, their bravery and courage, reflected the longevity of fears about the convict stain. What had become of the Anglo-Saxon race in the Antipodes, given its inauspicious beginnings? In 1915, one claim made for Gallipoli, more prominent then than now, was that it demonstrated the strength of Australian 'manhood'. Talk of manliness in the early twentieth century was innately linked to ideas about race; white manhood was the pinnacle of civilisation. The performance of Australian soldiers in war demonstrated that the white race had thrived in the Pacific. The reputation that the troops won as being egalitarian, disdainful of authority, laconic and courageous, may well describe any army in the world, but similar questions had not been asked of them and there was not as much riding on the answer.

An essential part of the Anzac mythology has been the way it celebrates a disrespectful attitude towards authority. Yet disdain for authority did not equate with disdain for all things British, however attractive this prospect may appear to later generations of Australian nationalists. Without question, Australian troops and officers were critical of the decisions made by British generals and battlefield commanders. Originating with the fiasco at Gallipoli, this view continued throughout the war owing to the high death tolls associated with trench warfare. The strategic decisions of Australian officers also came in for similar criticism, and likewise, their authority was not always well-regarded. The merger of all the Australian divisions into an Australian Corps in 1917, and the reputation these troops won under the command of Monash, certainly consolidated a sense of national distinctiveness that was not present before the war. Still, Australians fought on the behalf of the British Empire, and saw themselves as part of the British war effort. Half of the men who joined the AIF had been born in Britain, leading Banjo Paterson to comment that 'the Australian ranks were full of Yorkshiremen, Cockneys and Cousin Jacks'.[15] Like Australian sporting culture, which reflects its northern English antecedents, the egalitarianism that came to typify the Australian military may well have its roots in British working-class culture.[16]

The often-repeated phrase that Gallipoli was 'the birth of a nation', which became more insistent with the passing of time, grew from the belief that blood must be spilt, sacrifice must be made, for a people to become one. Citizenship, in this reckoning, receives its highest expression in sacrifice. Federation had proved that nations could be forged peacefully, with ink. Gallipoli showed that nationalism comes at a higher cost. The Australian nation was not born at Gallipoli; a particular story that placed war at the centre of Australian nationalism was. It was a story that handed the highest form of citizenship to men, and placed them at the scene of the birth, a symbolic move that excluded women from this most enduring element of Australian nationalism. The centrality of war to the story of Anzac also meant that grief and loss and suffering were part of its very core. These emotions, transcendent because they were so widespread, drew those inherently excluded from Anzac into its reach.

As early as 1918, Hugh Knyvett remarked that the Australians were 'no more than half the troops that were engaged in that fated campaign, but it has so caught the popular fancy, that in spite of all historians may do, injustice will be done' to the others who fought alongside them.[17] And there were many others – troops from Allied nations including New Zealand,

Britain, France and their colonies – who outnumbered the Australians by three to one.[18] All participated in a relentless, costly campaign that had caused considerable controversy by its conclusion. Before the landing, Monash had fantasised that he was about to be involved in 'great events which will stir the whole world and go down in history … to the eternal glory of Australia and all who have participated'. By September, he thought that it 'was about time somebody began to ask questions'.[19] That month, inspired by critical reports appearing in the English press, an ambitious young journalist, Keith Murdoch, visited the peninsula. After leaving, he wrote to the Australian Prime Minister insisting that Gallipoli 'is undoubtedly one of the most terrible chapters in our history'.[20]

Although Murdoch's letter has been criticised on the grounds of its hyperbole and factual inaccuracies, the sentiments it expressed struck a chord, and it eventually found its way into the hands of the Allied War Council. It was but one link in a chain of evidence that suggested the Gallipoli campaign had been a strategic disaster bedeviled by tactical errors. By December, a change in command led to a decision to abandon the campaign. Monash described the 'stupendous and paralyzing news' as being like 'a thunderbolt from a clear blue sky'. He predicted a 'howl of rage and disappointment from the troops'.[21] One of them, Eric Partridge, actually thought the evacuation was 'a necessary retreat from an improfitable, equivocal and doubtfully-tenable position'.[22] The troops covered their feet in sandbags and descended to the shore. Not one life was lost in the evacuation. The final death toll for Australia was 8700; the other Allies had lost over 35,000 men. It had been most costly for the Turks, who lost nearly double that number.

FRANCE AND FLANDERS

Worse was to come. Gallipoli looms large in Australian historical imagi-nation of World War I, but it was at the Western Front where the decisive battles of the war were fought. Australians also fought in the Middle East against Turkey, taking part in campaigns in Sinai, Palestine, Lebanon and Syria. The land war in Belgium and France, in which Australia participated from mid-1916, claimed the vast majority of Australian casualties. Hugh Knyvett broke his leg in three places and received twenty other shrapnel wounds when a German bomb rolled into his trench during the Battle of the Somme in November 1916. He would see no further action. Trench warfare utilising heavy artillery, mustard gas, machine-guns and barbed wire became a war of attrition that resulted in nothing but a stalemate for years. It would last until further advances in weaponry and equipment, including aeroplanes and tanks, and strategic innovation solved the problem of how to gain decisive victory and forward movement.

The cost in human life was enormous. British poet John Masefield's depiction of a cat wandering among the carnage eating dead men's brains is a singular image of the extent of inhumanity. War artist Will Dyson thought the men he saw on the Western Front had 'eyes like tired mares'.[23] Being there almost brought Eric Partridge unstuck. Gallipoli had possessed what he could only describe as a 'wild virginity' in comparison to the desolation of the Western Front. Partridge's portrayal of trees like huge skeletons, the 'storm of shells, the rain of pellets, that driving sleet of machine-gun and rifle bullets', the 'sights that would have sickened the keeper of a charnel-house' and the change in his 'whole moral composition' are among the most moving and memorable Australian accounts of the war.[24]

General Sir John Monash, whom King George V knighted in the field, was more vainglorious, both for himself and his troops. In May 1918 he had been appointed the Commander of the Australian Corps. Never noted for his modesty, Monash (who likened the numbers under his command to those controlled by the Duke of Wellington and Napoleon) claimed that 'the Australian corps is the backbone of the Allied Armies'.[25] This was an exaggeration, given that Australian troops never made up more than five per cent of the Allied forces, but Australian brigades did play decisive parts in several key battles that turned the tide of the war in the Allies' favour. Britain's capacity to draw on the resources of Dominion nations like Australia for extra troops and resources, when combined with the entry of the United States into the war on the Allies' side, had been crucial to their ability finally to defeat Germany.

By the end of the war in November 1918 about half of all Australian men aged between 18 and 45 had joined the military forces. A total of 330,000 served overseas. Of that number more than 50,000 died and another 155,000 had been wounded and sometimes maimed for life after losing their eyesight, limbs or sanity. The British had military losses in the order of 723,000, but despite the vast difference in total numbers, there was a broad equivalence when it came to population proportions. The United Kingdom had lost 1.6% of its population; New Zealand suffered the highest losses of any Dominion nation at 1.4%, with Australia running a close second at 1.2%.[26]

Very few Australians remained unaffected by the war. Despite the scale of participation and of loss, grief still came as a shock. Mervyn,

Table 10.1 Australian battle casualties in World War I

Year	Area	Killed*	%	Wounded	%
1915–16	Dardanelles	7,818	14.6	19,441	12.5
1916	France & Flanders	12,541	23.4	28,734	18.5
1917	France & Flanders	20,036	37.4	54,505	35.1
1918	France & Flanders	12,189	22.8	49,101	31.7
1916–18	Egypt & Palestine	973	1.8	3,351	2.2
Total		53,557	100.0	155,132	100.0

* Including those who died of wounds or poison gas
Source: W. Vamplew (ed.) Australians: Historical Statistics (Sydney: Fairfax, Syme and Weldon Associates, 1987), pp. 414–5.

the only child of Justice H. B. Higgins and his wife Mary, was killed by a sniper's bullet in the Sinai Desert in December 1916. He had been one of the few officers of his regiment to survive Gallipoli. Mervyn's cousin, Nettie Palmer, was shattered. 'It was five hours ago I heard the news and ever since then I have been almost howling', she told her brother. 'To think of those bonzer people Uncle H and Aunty M is just ghastly. I have never been so much cut up because of anyone's death'.[27] When one of Mervyn's childhood friends, Elsie Masson, heard the news of his death it compounded an existing sorrow. 'It seemed to me more than ever as if everything of one's youth was being snatched away from one and there was nothing left', she wrote.[28] Elsie's Masson's fiancé, a veterinary surgeon from Western Australia, had died at Gallipoli during the Battle of Lone Pine. She travelled twice from Melbourne to Perth to visit his family. 'In some ways such a visit is a disappointment,' she reflected, 'for again you hope for some unspecified form of relief, for the illusion of being again with the lost one, and you rapidly realize that you will not get it, and that nothing on earth, no people, no place, no thing can ever bring him back'.[29] Higgins would have agreed. 'My grief has condemned me to hard labour for the rest of my life', he lamented.[30]

THE DILEMMA OF CONSCRIPTION

The glowing accounts of the performance of the Anzacs at Gallipoli had boosted the number of recruits to the AIF, which peaked in July 1915.

Thereafter, the number of men presenting themselves for enlistment slowly but surely began to erode. It is impossible to quantify the impact of war-weariness and sorrow. Yet social pressure on men to enlist continued – symbolised by the infamous gesture of handing a white feather to an 'eligible' recruit who appeared to be 'shirking' his duty – and recruitment campaigns stressed the link between military service, masculinity and empire loyalty. By late 1915 a Universal Service League had formed, arguing that the state should introduce compulsory military service to ensure that Australia fulfilled its obligations to the defence of the Empire, and that there was equity in the recruitment process. They were afraid that only the best and brightest would volunteer, draining Australia of its best racial stock. Britain continued to press for reinforcements from its Dominions, and had addressed its own falling numbers by introducing conscription in January 1916.

The wind seemed to blowing in the direction of conscription, and the union movement in Australia began to prepare itself for the storm. They were nervous because the Labor Prime Minister, Billy Hughes, was touring Britain and winning praise from the press as an eloquent spokesman on behalf of the war effort. The flattery might cause him to turn his head. In May 1916, an interstate trade union rally in Melbourne declared that conscription would be used 'as a bludgeon to break down the standard of the industrial classes'.[31] They feared that a conscripted army would be used not merely for defence purposes, but also to break strikes within the country. Women, children and blacks – cheap labour – would be substituted for white male workers, and hard-won working conditions would be eroded. The criticism that capitalists were using the war to their advantage, to smash organised labour and to grow rich on the sacrifice of the working classes, reflected the influence of the radical American organisation Industrial Workers of the World (IWW), or 'the Wobblies'. Membership of the IWW was small in Australia, but its language inflected the conscription debate.

Concern about the importation of coloured labour to replace conscripted white workers was a particularly Australian spin on the issue of compulsory service. Attachment to a white Australia also motivated Billy Hughes, who had begun to believe that Australia's capacity to protect this cherished goal in any peace settlement depended on a full commitment to the Allied war effort. By 1916, for Hughes and many other Empire loyalists, conscription seemed the only way to ensure that commitment. When the War Office requested a further 32,500 men by September 1916, and 16,500 per month until the end of the year, Hughes knew that voluntary enlistment would not supply the numbers. Ultimately, he would submit two referenda on the issue to the Australian public, the first in October 1916 and the second in December 1917.

The United Kingdom, New Zealand (August 1916) and Canada (August 1917) had introduced conscription by an Act of Parliament. The United States introduced conscription within a month of its entry into the war in 1917. The same course was not followed in Australia. This was largely due to the electoral success of the Labor Party. At the time of the first conscription referendum the Labor Party, an organisation that had traditionally opposed conscription, controlled the federal Parliament. Legislation introducing conscription would not have passed the Labor-dominated Senate. Hughes also knew that the conscription issue would be a touchstone for a conflict that had been brewing within the Labor Party for at least a decade. The industrial wing of the Party, which increasingly favoured militant strike action, had become convinced that its political wing was willing to compromise labor principles on the assumption of office. In 1915, to the chagrin of the union movement, the Hughes government had abandoned a planned referendum on the nationalisation of monopolies, and price controls, among other constitutional issues. This pre-existing conflict between the industrial and political wings of the party predisposed it to the dramatic split that would ultimately occur over the conscription issue.

Making conscription a matter of referendum, where individuals must choose to vote 'Yes' or 'No' on that issue alone, was designed to give the government a clear mandate. Yet the starkness of the choice, which so easily lent itself to a dichotomy of life or death, unleashed a depth of feeling rarely seen in the electoral process in Australia. Hughes' attempt to sidestep a fight within the Labor Party transferred the battle to the streets, living rooms and lecture halls. This was an issue that mattered. The major daily newspapers, the Protestant churches, and the academic and professional classes urged a 'Yes' vote. They argued that conscription was a sign of loyalty, both to the Empire and to the Australians already serving abroad. Hughes tried to present his case for conscription as consistent with some of the ideas that the labour movement and trade unions held dear. In order for there to be equality of sacrifice, all eligible Australian men must be considered for military service. To do otherwise was to 'scab' on the men in the trenches, and to be an international 'blackleg' when it came to sharing victory.[32] This was a direct parallel of the unionist argument that every worker benefits from the gains that unions win from employers, therefore all workers should be part of a union. Conscription was also in the nation's self-interest. If Australia expected the protection of Britain for its self-defence, it must reciprocate when Britain itself was in a moment of crisis.

Illustration 10.1 Leaflet produced by the National Council of Women for the Second Conscription Referendum, 1917
Source: Australian War Memorial, RC00319.

Opposition to conscription came from trade unionists, pacifists and, to a more debatable extent, Catholics. Pacifist groups, such as Vida Goldstein's Women's Peace Army, advanced the libertarian argument that the state should not be able to compel men to fight. 'No man is free if he has to go away against his will,' she told a gathering in Bacchus Marsh, her words duly noted by the policeman reporting the event.[33] Adela Pankhurst, who had arrived in Australia after falling out with her famous mother and sister over the tactics to be pursued in order to win women's suffrage in Britain, was another prominent opponent of conscription. Sectarian differences were muted during the first referendum campaign but were among the most divisive of the second. By then, Melbourne's Catholic Archbishop was the Irishman Daniel Mannix, a vehement critic of the British response to the 1916 Easter Rising in Dublin, in which leaders of the rebellion were court-martialed and executed. Mannix, who drew large crowds, insisted that Australia was being forced to participate in a 'trade war' and that 'Australia has done her full share'. Not all Catholics agreed with his stance against conscription, the Archbishop of Perth being one notable critic. Yet in 1916/17 Catholics comprised almost

one-quarter of the Australian population, and most of them had, or identified with, Irish ancestry. They were predominantly working people, and
Mannix's opposition to conscription blended elements of the trade union
position with a criticism of British war aims.

The first referendum, on October 1916, was defeated by a narrow margin
of 72,000 votes. In spite of the government's ability to censor reports of
anti-conscription meetings, to ban their pamphlets, and to fund National
Referendum Councils to spread the message, the Australian public had
rejected conscription. By the second referendum, Hughes had outlawed
the IWW, and pro-conscriptionists had become increasingly vitriolic, the
intensity reaching its peak in a poem entitled 'The Antis Creed' which
contained lines such as 'I believe the men at the front should be sacri-
ficed/ I believe that we should turn dog on them/ I believe that Britain
should be crushed and humiliated'. There was a popular but erroneous
contemporary perception that women had voted against conscription, and
they were particular targets in the second referendum campaign. Anti-
conscriptionists sought to capitalise on their earlier success by publishing
posters such as 'The Blood Vote' which depicted an ashen-faced woman,
reflecting 'They put the dagger into my grasp/It seemed but a pencil then/
I did not know it was a fiend a-gasp/ For the priceless blood of men'.[34]

The second referendum delivered a more resounding 'No' vote than
the first, and was defeated by 167,000 votes. The majority serving in
the front line on the Western Front had voted 'No'. Earlier that year, the
Director-General of Recruiting reported that letters written by soldiers
to their families had influenced the 'No' vote in the first referendum.[35]
Personal connections (with Britain or serving soldiers), pre-existing
political beliefs, fear of undermining white Australia, cultural identifications: all played a role in the outcome of the conscription referenda.
Ultimately, however, the most radical position was the most influential.
'My wife and daughter are working against conscription,' Nathaniel
Jacka declared in 1916. He had two sons at war, one of whom, Albert
Jacka, had won a Victoria Cross and featured on recruiting posters
throughout the land. The family at home believed that 'we should keep
free the land for which our sons went out freely to fight'.[36] For the
Jackas, and many other Australians, freedom meant choice.

One American observer declared that the intensity and passion of the
conscription debates meant that the 'country was in as wild a state as a
pending civil war could produce anywhere'. He felt the outcome was a
good reflection of the Australian character and the strength of its democratic
traditions. On polling day the result was accepted without equivocation.
'Workingmen lay upon the grass of the public domain like seals' and talked

of 'anything but conscription'.[37] Yet its legacy would linger for years, for sectarianism was again a feature of Australian public life.

The Labor Party imploded in the wake of the conscription debates. The Party expelled all of those who supported conscription, including the Prime Minister. At the time, it was said that the Labor Party 'blew its brains out', as many of its most experienced and capable politicians followed Billy Hughes out of the party.[38] Billy Hughes remained in office, but this was only possible by forming a coalition with the opposition. This new alliance, known as the 'Nationalist' or 'Win-the-War' Party, went to a federal election in May 1917, which it won by a handsome majority. Although conscription had been defeated, the victory of the Nationalists suggested that the majority of Australians remained committed to the prosecution of the war itself.

FIGHTING WAR AT HOME

In European countries, World War I was experienced as the first 'total war', where the economy and society were fully geared towards involvement in the conflict. This was not the case for Australia, which was 17,000 kilometres from the major battle zone and in no danger of invasion. Australia did not have, in 1914, a fully industrialised economy capable of producing vast amounts of munitions, armaments and military hardware. The economy was instead driven by the export of primary products from the mining and pastoral industries and economic growth was supported by borrowing large amounts of overseas capital.

War caused major disruptions to world financial markets and shipping, which reduced both Australia's capacity to deliver its export products to market and importers' efforts to replenish their stock. The government passed legislation forbidding trade with Germany and the land war in Belgium and France obliterated European markets. Instead of raising capital overseas, the government sought voluntary loans from its own citizens in order to fund the war effort. By 1919 the Commonwealth was in debt to the tune of £325 million. Gross domestic product had fallen by ten per cent, as the flow of foreign capital ceased.

Structural changes were introduced to enable the country to survive the disruption caused by war, and to preclude any possible cooperation with Germany or German interests. Wheat and wool producers benefited from new government marketing initiatives, in which produce was pooled and then sold on behalf of growers by a central board. Imperial purchase agreements that the government negotiated with Britain during the war meant that exports were in fact paid for (thereby preventing their purchase by the enemy), despite ongoing difficulties with shipping. Effectively, the government now purchased, or directly engineered purchasers for, wheat, meat, sugar and wool. This created an expectation in the rural sector that primary producers were entitled to protection by the government, one which would continue after the exigencies of war had passed.

Another solution was found for minerals, which had assumed sudden strategic importance in wartime. British manufacturers, who before the war had purchased Australian iron for their steel industries, switched from exporting goods to the production of materials for the war. The Australian government seized upon the changed circumstances to bolster domestic steel production, and the Broken Hill Proprietary Company (BHP) witnessed significant expansion of its Newcastle steelworks from 1915. BHP enjoyed a virtual monopoly on the rich iron-ore deposits in South Australia and government contracts ensured that they were not worked without reason. Base metals (lead, zinc, copper, tin) had begun to be processed in Australia before the war but German-owned companies, which possessed technological superiority, dominated the infant Australian base metal industries. Most of the mined lead and zinc had customarily been exported to smelters in Germany and Belgium, a situation that was the cause of great alarm given that munitions were manufactured from them. Consequently, the government passed legislation ensuring that Anglo-Australian interests could wrest control of the existing companies, such as the smelter at Port Pirie. As an added precaution, German businessmen with direct links to the mining industry were interned. The government also created conditions favourable for the expansion of Australian-owned smelting works for lead and zinc to a group of Melbourne businessmen, known as the 'Collins House Group', who enjoyed a virtual monopoly and grew extremely wealthy as a result.

It was a different story for most members of the Australian workforce, who struggled to retain their standard of living as prices increased, wages stalled and the economic slowdown caused unemployment to rise. Big business was accused of profiting from wartime shortages and lining their own pockets. Waves of strikes rolled throughout the country during the war years as workers protested against declining conditions and their reduced purchasing power. Women, who in 1917 outnumbered men for the first time in white Australian history, took to the streets to declare their frustration with wartime conditions, especially the high price of basic foodstuffs.

The British government used the services of women in auxiliary capacities during the war, but the Australian government steadfastly refused the requests of its own female citizens to do so. Nursing was the only direct form of war service available to Australian women, and over 2000 trained nurses joined the Australian Army Nursing Service and worked in field hospitals near the battlefields. Theirs was an extraordinary but atypical war. Grace Cossington Smith's portrait of 'The Sock Knitter' (1915) is the most enduring visual representation of the war work women did perform: preparing 'comfort packs' for soldiers, assisting with their recuperation when invalided, raising money. War did not draw vast numbers of Australian women into non-traditional occupations, as it did in Britain, nor did it give impetus to campaigns for political emancipation, given that Australian women already had the vote.

Some Australian women activists in fact used the wartime exigencies to work for pre-existing political goals related to the protection of women and children, which could now be recast as being of national benefit. The Woman's Christian Temperance Union played a key role in the successful campaign to introduce early closing of hotels, which had been adopted by all states except Queensland and Western Australia by 1916. Anti-German propaganda and the conscription campaigns had positioned Australian women firmly as mothers, wives, daughters and sisters. When combined with the emphasis on manhood that accompanied discussions about Gallipoli and the Anzacs, the war reinforced rather than undermined existing gender divisions.

VERSAILLES AND THE AFTERMATH

The war had also done nothing to shake Billy Hughes' conviction that the future of Australia was white and that Japan remained a threat to its security. This was the wellspring of Hughes' nationalism, and a point of difference between Hughes and the British government. The ongoing Anglo-Japanese Alliance was a source of frustration to Australia, doubly so once the Japanese had occupied a string of islands in the Pacific that had been German territory before the war. Yet tension in the Australia-Britain relationship during the war also stemmed from a familiar source. Australia was a bit-player in a larger British drama, but felt the need to be consulted about the overall direction of the script. Like Deakin before him, Billy Hughes visited London in an effort to persuade the British that realignment of the relationship was necessary. The stakes were higher now. He wanted Australian representation 'right in the middle of the spider's web that was spinning out its thread of death'.[39] But until 1917, there was no official representation of Australia or any other Dominion nation in the British War Cabinet. Even then, after the formation of the Imperial War Cabinet, the British did not consult the Dominions about the peace terms they were negotiating, although Hughes did win separate representation for Australia at the Peace Conference and membership of the British Empire delegation. This level of representation at an international forum would have been scarcely imaginable before 1914.

The war bound Australia more tightly to Britain after a period of experimentation with alternative identifications. The nascent sense of brotherhood with fellow white man's countries such as the United States dimmed as empire patriotism surged during wartime and the United States stood aloof from proceedings. The Presidency of Woodrow Wilson from 1913 also led to a recasting of the relationship. Wilson was interested in the relationship between self-determination and democracy in ways that Theodore Roosevelt, for instance, would never have countenanced. This became clear when Billy Hughes, en route to London, visited the American President in 1916 in order to lobby for Australia's retention of the Pacific Islands at the conclusion of the war. Wilson was, Hughes recalled, as 'unresponsive as the Sphinx in the Desert'.[40]

Wilson remained unmoved by Billy Hughes at Versailles, where the future of former German colonial possessions was decided. The American President was a vocal opponent of annexation, Hughes belligerent in his support for it. The British were disinclined to upset the Americans, whom they knew to be the real victors in the war, in economic if not moral terms. Abusing British Prime Minister Lloyd George in his native Welsh, 'which hit [him] between wind and water', and unfurling a map of Australia and its surrounds before the League of Nations Council in order to make his point about Australia's vulnerability, Hughes was singular in his determination to retain New Guinea.[41] A compromise solution was eventually reached whereby a three-class mandate system, graded by levels of 'development', handed New Guinea to Australia as a C class mandate. This effectively meant Australia ruled New Guinea as an 'integral portion of its territory', with a limited form of oversight by the League. It was as much of a victory that could be expected in the circumstances. The key outcome was that the white Australia policy could be applied as stringently in New Guinea as in any part of the Australian mainland.

Hughes also went on the offensive when it emerged that Japan was lobbying for the inclusion of a racial equality clause in the League of Nations covenant. Convinced that any such development would affect

A HISTORY OF AUSTRALIA

a nation's capacity to pass restrictive immigration laws, Hughes was an outspoken opponent of the clause. 'Our white Australia policy would be a pricked bladder. Our control of immigration laws would be so much waste paper.'[42] He calculated, correctly, that US representatives would share his reservations based on their own desires to control immigration. The racial equality measure was defeated but Japan emerged from the conference as a mandatory power in the Pacific. Concern about Japanese presence there remained a point of connection between the United States and Australia.

International leaders may not have liked his style but Hughes returned home to a hero's welcome. The outpouring of affection that greeted him belied deeper tensions that bedeviled Australian society. Trade unionists had won a symbolic victory with the defeat of conscription, but believed that the war had delayed or even jeopardised improvements to general working conditions. Strikes and industrial disputes increased dramatically in the next decade. There was also the challenge of resettling 170,000 soldiers who had returned from Europe and the Middle East by the end of 1919. For all the public posturing about the manliness of Australian troops, most people knew that those who returned from the war were changed men. As early as 1917, Henry Lawson had observed that men were 'coming back battered, broken, and some with shattered nerves, from the Hell they went through ... coming back, many of them, to broken faiths, lost jobs and billets, and domestic troubles and miseries'.[43] The war had created a new social division, between those who served and those who had not.

11

· · · · · · · ·

A Nation Divided: 1919–39

It has been estimated that every second Australian family was bereaved in World War I. The grief could be intensely personal, but it was also experienced at a broader cultural level. Some feared that the extent of loss had fostered a mindless hedonism, others held that service for the nation gave them privileges that others did not deserve. The divisions that the war engendered in Australia lingered into the 1920s and 1930s. Loyalty – to nation, to Empire – once again became a matter for debate, rather than being an assumption that it was something all Australians shared.

The success of the Bolshevik Revolution in Russia in 1917 unleashed fears of insurrection, menace and contagion in all Western democracies. Australia was no exception. As a country with a strong tradition of labour activism, the anxiety of some observers about Australia's vulnerability to revolution was particularly acute. By the 1920s, the social experimentation that had made Australia's name in the pre-war era, particularly its arbitration and basic wage system, came under increasing scrutiny as the economy foundered. Governments turned to university-trained civil servants and academics for expert advice on how to solve apparently entrenched problems, but politicians could not resist the allure of proposing solutions that assured the country that Australia's prospects knew no bounds. Economists, scientists and population experts were beginning to beat a different drum, and to offer more contained visions of what Australia's future might be like. In the 1920s, it seemed hard to imagine smallness as greatness. By the 1930s, it was hard to imagine any future at all.

Returned soldiers' sense of distinction was countenanced, and thus accommodated, by becoming enshrined as government policy. If the worker had embodied the ameliorating impulse of the Australian state before the war, the soldier took his place thereafter. The Commonwealth created a wide-ranging system of pensions and other benefits relating to health, education, preference in employment and housing for returned servicemen and their dependents. This was among the most extensive of all the Allied nations. Despite the generosity of these entitlements, the incalculable cost of war trauma was borne by individuals and their families for another generation. Returned servicemen's peak organisation, which in time would be known as the Returned Services League (RSL), had direct access to government. Membership of the RSL declined as it links with government grew and its official control of Anzac Day, which was a public holiday in all states by 1927, meant Anzac became a figure of an imperial hue.

The link between war service and entitlement also delayed the development of health and welfare schemes for the broader community, and meant that women's citizenship entitlements in large measure remained tied to the activities of men, just as they had been through the granting of a living wage. By the 1920s, planners had realized that smaller families were probably an irreversible trend – if slower among Catholics – and exhorted women that if they were going to breed less, they needed to clean more. Domesticity and child-care were no longer the natural vocation of women, they were sciences that could be exacted through the advice of infant welfare sisters, psychologists and doctors. The federal government was content to provide advice about motherhood rather than fund child-rearing through any kind of family endowment scheme.

The war, which had crystallised Australian national feeling, also caused it to shift direction. Australian participation on the world stage had narrowed its vision. An earlier generation of Australian politicians had been inspired to build a protective state, which attempted to consider the interests of both workers and business. The results were uneven, but a willingness to experiment was at its core. The 1920s witnessed a contraction of this impulse, and the passing of those who had been central to it. Beginning with Alfred Deakin in 1919, the decade saw the deaths of Edmund Barton, Henry Lawson, Rose Scott, Andrew Fisher and Henry B. Higgins. One of Deakin's last public acts had been a plea on behalf of conscription, but he could not have foreseen that the fall-out over the referenda would have a lasting impact on the tenor of Australian public life. The 'yes' vote may have been defeated, but its supporters successfully cast themselves as the true Australian nationalists, those whose imperial loyalties outweighed any class or sectional interests. There was something very Anzac-like in their capacity to rewrite defeat as moral victory. In the 1920s, Australian nationalism became a defensive project, one that was on guard against the potential corruption of disloyal elements. Innovation gave way to insularity.

SAFEGUARDING AUSTRALIA

Hughes' Nationalist Party retained power after the December 1919 federal election, but Hughes was a wartime leader and his power base eroded quickly in peace. The Party itself was a strange beast, an awkward union of ex-Labor men and conservatives whose shared imperial loyalty momentarily bridged the differences between them. It lacked an ideological core. The only way the alliance could hold together was if a common enemy could be found. By the end of the war, that enemy was the Bolshevik. The foreignness of the term amplified its apparent threat. The Spanish Influenza epidemic of 1919, which caused 12,000 deaths in Australia, only confirmed the growing paranoia about the need to safeguard Australia from external dangers. In the early years after the success of the Bolsheviks in Russia, groups or individuals with even moderate leftist leanings were identified with the revolutionary party that was responsible for the murder of the Russian royal family. The direct assault on the monarchy was anathema to imperially minded Australians, who might have elected the first Labor government in the world but had never evinced any serious interest in revolution.

The Labor Party, which had moved further to the left after the conscription split, ultimately became more moderate as the 1920s progressed, aware that the taint of Bolshevism was inimical to its cause. This suited the Catholic connections of the party, which had been strengthened by a shared attitude to conscription during the war, but could find no point of reference with godless Marxism. In contrast, the industrial wing of the movement found inspiration in the success of their Russian brothers and became more militant. It was a bifurcation that seriously weakened the chances of federal electoral success for the labour movement. This also meant the Nationalist Party no longer needed Billy Hughes, who in the war had channeled votes away from a potential political rival. The disarray of the Labor Party now achieved that purpose single-handedly. In the quarter-century from 1916, Labor would hold federal office only once, for a few years at the beginning of the Depression.

Hughes' background also meant that for conservatives, he always carried the whiff of the other side. The brinkmanship and aggression that were the hallmarks of Hughes' character were an advantage when there was a war to be won, and American presidents to be stared down. When the enemies were internal rather than external, it was a style that suddenly appeared more like a liability than a force for unity. The Nationalist Party self-consciously fostered an ongoing sense of crisis and danger, but they no longer needed a 'Little Digger' to lead them through it. The time was fast approaching for an officer to take charge.

He arrived in the form of Stanley Melbourne Bruce, who had been elected to Parliament in 1918 after returning to his native Australia from war service in the British Army. A wealthy businessman who ran an importing firm, educated at the best private schools in Melbourne before attending Cambridge University, Bruce was no man of the people. To the top end of town, he was heaven sent. Bruce knew the rules and could be trusted. Bruce's key political asset was his capacity to appear patrician and passionless in an era when it was important to give the impression of a firm hand. His rapid transition to the Prime Ministership was facilitated by the entry into politics of a third force, the Country Party.

Formed in 1920 to represent the interests of the growing number of small-scale agricultural producers, the Country Party believed that current protection policies benefited manufacturers and urban workers at the expense of those involved in primary industry. In Australia, the message found fertile ground in rural areas and at the 1922 general election, the new party won enough seats to force the Nationalists into coalition if they wished to continue governing. The leader of the Country Party, Dr Earle Page, was adamant that he would not work with Hughes. In February 1923, Hughes was forced to step aside and Stanley Bruce, who had been Treasurer in the previous government, became Prime Minister, with Page as his deputy. The Bruce-Page government would hold power for the rest of the 1920s.

The inter-war years were a time when there was growing doubt about the ability of ordinary people to know what was best for them. Stanley Bruce firmly subscribed to this view, which blended fear about the potential for subversion from communists with optimism about the capacity of the expert and belief in the superiority of the officer class. One of the legacies of the Bruce-Page government was the creation of a suite of Committees, Councils and Boards to direct public policy, on matters as diverse as immigration, the tariff and scientific research. This certainly drew on the expertise available in the professions and universities, but the advisory bodies were immune from responsibility to the electorate for the advice that they dispensed.

BRITISH TIES AND AMERICAN INFLUENCES

In contrast with the nascent professionalisation of policy-making in the domestic sphere, Australia's international relations continued to be directed by sentimental attachment to Britain. Australia had achieved nationhood in 1901 at the high-water mark of the British Empire. From that point onwards the power of the British Empire began to diminish, as a result of the rise of other industrial powers, the war, and colonial independence movements. Australia resisted this tide of history, and cherished its status as a member of the imperial family even as the heart of Empire itself became more interested in divesting responsibility than incurring it. A telling moment occurred at the 1926 Imperial Conference, when former British Prime Minister and chair of the conference, Arthur Balfour, declared that henceforth the self-governing Dominions were 'autonomous communities within the British Empire, equal in status, in no way subordinate one to another'.[1] Australia, like New Zealand, was more interested in retaining the sense of hierarchy that had always typified imperial relations, because the seniority of the British conferred on them responsibility for the welfare of junior members. 'We need not fear that ... obligations will not be observed', Bruce reassured the federal Parliament after his return from the conference.[2] But of course that is exactly what a country like Australia did fear: that Britain may not exercise its obligation to Australia in defence matters. In 1931, the *Statute of Westminster* recognised the independence of the Dominions within the Commonwealth. Despite these clear signals from London that a Dominion nation like Australia ought to begin planning for its own future, defence and economic ties remained strong in the wake of the war and the message went unheeded.

The attachment to British culture remained firm too, although there was a new warp in the loom which meant that the weave began to look different in the post-war period. American influence became apparent in architecture, where West Coast housing styles such as the California Bungalow and Spanish Mission were popular in the new post-war suburbs. Cultural productions from the United States, particularly film but also music, won an avid following in Australia in the 1920s. As one American commentator put it, 'the movies overnight have become a mammoth industry ... we are suddenly, and actually, exporting not only goods but ideas', and Australia became one of the most important markets for Hollywood film.[3] It was the beginning of a trend that remained throughout the twentieth century: Australians were early and enthusiastic adopters of new communication technologies. The size and scale of theatres built in the 1920s, which were almost palatial in their proportions, testified to the popularity of the cinema, and the sense of escape and excitement it offered to viewers. It was one of the ironies of the age that the cinema in both content and venue dangled a glamorous lifestyle before its audience that, as the decade drew to its close, fewer and fewer of them could hope to emulate.

The 'talkies' and radio were just two of the technological developments which rendered isolation less central than it had been to the unfolding of the Australian story. The founding of the Queensland and Northern Territory Aerial Services (QANTAS) in 1920 was an early statement of optimism about the capacity of air travel as a new form of civil transport that also had the benefit of delivering services such as mail to regional districts. In 1924, Stanley Bruce became the first Australian Prime Minister to travel by air on official business. By 1930, his successor was able to conduct a telephone conversation with the British Prime Minister. Families living in the suburbs benefited from the extension of electric tram and train services. Their homes were increasingly connected to sewerage and mains electricity, which powered new appliances such as electric kettles, toasters, heaters and radios. Access to these items was uneven, as was ownership of motor cars, which increased dramatically and made Australia number six in the world for the number of vehicles on its roads. City dwellers' day trips to the countryside and seaside created a new awareness of Australian fauna and flora. 'The motor car,' one boy later recalled, 'aided our communion with the natural'.[4] The car also created new features in the Australian landscape: the carport in the driveway and small businesses such as garages which sold petrol and repaired or serviced vehicles.

Not everyone was happy about what one magazine in 1927 labelled the 'the tide of red-roof ugliness' that began to seep out from the cities and the new forms of mass entertainment that appealed to their occupants.[5] Even left-leaning artists and writers still looked to England as the centre of civilisation and they, along with other intellectuals, articulated another theme that was to become more prominent as the twentieth century progressed. The distinction between elite and popular culture grew more pronounced in the post-war period, along with a disdain for the tastes of ordinary consumers. Discomfort about perceived vulgarity was often matched by an equally incurious attitude towards the European avant-garde's experimentation with modernist forms. This was another twist in the tale: British artists and writers had begun to experiment with styles that made little impact on the Australian scene. Censorship reinforced ignorance by banning the importation of literature such as James Joyce's novel *Ulysses* and Remarque's *All Quiet on the Western Front*. British and European art and literature of the 1920s had responded to the trauma of war by exploring the themes of decline and alienation. No similar developments occurred in Australia at this time; in fact, the war was conspicuous by its absence in writing of the 1920s and 1930s. Yet the enthusiastic response to the tours of the Ballets Russes in the late 1930s, with its signature music, dance and design (including sets by Picasso), suggested an unmet public appetite for innovation in the arts.

The most ambitious of Australian authors, among them Nettie Palmer and her husband Vance, attempted to inspire a nationalist literature by revisiting the *Bulletin* tradition and infusing it with intellectual rigour. It was not a recipe for commercial success, and even its artistic merit was debatable. The writing of authors like Ion Idriess, who was interested in narrating stories that fantasised about the potential for development to be found in Australia's frontier zones of Queensland, the Northern Territory and New Guinea, found a readier market. Occasionally, violence flared in these territories. The killing of Aborigines at Forrest River in Western Australia in 1926 and Coniston in the Northern Territory in 1928 was a reminder that the new century carried forth the legacies of the old. They also renewed a level of humanitarian concern for Aborigines that had been in abeyance for almost a century.

DEVELOP, DEVELOP, DEVELOP

Development was the mantra of the federal government. Manufacturing industries were given further encouragement to expand in the 1920s, with the introduction of higher protective tariffs. Although the census of 1921 revealed that for the first time more Australians were employed in the manufacturing sector than in primary production, rural development was the cherished object of national development. Other settler nations, such as New Zealand and Canada, also saw their future in similar terms. They, along with Australia, created soldier settlement schemes to reward their returned servicemen by giving them access to land on generous terms in the hope that this would fast-track the development of the agricultural base.

Prime Minister Bruce summed up his theory of economic development in a memorable phrase: Australia, he said, needed Men, Money and Markets. This was a new take on an old formula. Australia was to be developed by attracting millions of immigrants to its shores, borrowing money from overseas lenders to develop the infrastructure necessary to ensure their success as agricultural producers, then selling the produce they created to an overseas market. Britain was central to the plan. It was to be the major market destination for exports, and the source of men and money. The equation also required easy credit and healthy export prices.

Illustration 11.1 Jimmy Clements (1847–1927), Wiradjuri elder, sometimes referred to as 'King Billy', who claimed 'sovereign rights to the Federal Territory' during the celebrations to open Parliament House in Canberra, May 1927
Source: National Archives of Australia, A3560, 3108.

So great was Bruce's faith in Australia's carrying capacity that he made it an element of his speech to open the new Parliament House in Canberra on 9 May 1927. 'Great though our progress has been', Bruce told the assembled crowd, including the King's son the Duke of York, 'Australia is but on the threshold of achievement. In the future millions of the British race will people this land.'[6] British migrants did come in the 1920s, but not quite in the numbers the government had anticipated. The migrants were channeled to rural districts where the land was of marginal quality. The soldier settlers shared their lot, because by the 1920s the most fertile and productive land had already been taken. Instead of attracting millions of migrants, the government spent millions of pounds supporting tens of thousands of people who had very little capital and even less farming experience to develop their land. There were families who managed to turn their farms into successful business prospects, but for some the hardships became too much to bear. By the end of the 1920s, almost a quarter of the soldier settlers had left their plots, and the government was forced to write off £23.5 million in bad debts incurred by the scheme. During the same period, thousands of Italian migrants arrived in Australia, largely owing to the introduction of a quota system that restricted their entry to the United States. The Italians were unassisted immigrants, but their mostly rural background fitted them well for successful incorporation into small but established migrant farming communities in areas like the cane-growing region of northern Queensland.

Australian governments, at both a federal and state level, borrowed heavily to finance immigration from Britain, and to invest in the development of infrastructure such as roads and services for rural communities. The Hydro-Electric Commission of Tasmania was but one of numerous public works projects commenced in the 1920s. By 1927 too many state governments had borrowed too much money for similar schemes, and the federal government consolidated the debt and took it over with the establishment of the Loan Council. The frenzy of borrowing was premised on the assumption that repayment of the loans would be made with funds accumulated from a thriving export market of commodities and agricultural produce. Britain did not preference Australian exports as hoped, other countries began to produce similar goods more cheaply, and export prices collapsed. More money had to be borrowed to make interest payments on existing debts. It was like borrowing money on a credit card to pay the mortgage.

Stanley Bruce was a businessman by training, and he knew that he was in danger of losing the house. The London banks were not happy and warned Australia that its levels of debt were unsustainable. Bruce had never been enamored of the arbitration system and its founding principle of the basic wage. Encouraged by professional economists who believed that politics rather than theory had driven the system, Bruce increasingly focused on arbitration as the cause of Australia's economic woes. This was a parochial response to the economic difficulties of the period, but it drew some of its force from fears of a foreign menace.

The government twice passed legislation directed at industrial agitators in an effort to deport or imprison them. When introducing the anti-Communist *Commonwealth Crimes Bill* to parliament, the Attorney-General declared that there 'was a small but growing body of men in Australia, inspired by foreign ideals, deliberately seeking the destruction of Australian democracy'. He ridiculed the use of the word proletariat. 'There is no proletariat in Australia,' he insisted, 'there is no need to bring here ideas that may have been suited for Russian serfs, who can hardly call their lives or souls their own'.[7] While the government may have tried to insist that the ideas came from elsewhere, the tenacity with which unionists clung to their wage rates and conditions in a worsening economic climate was decidedly local. Frustrated by the continuing industrial action of seamen, waterside workers and miners, Bruce attempted, unsuccessfully, to wrest control over industrial matters away from the courts and into the bailiwick of the federal government. Beleaguered by government attacks and sensing the hardening attitude of employers, the union movement formed a federal executive, the Australian Council of Trade Unions. This peak body, along with the RSL, comprised the two political institutions that emerged from the 1920s whose influence would be keenly felt in Australia for at least the next half-century.

In later life, Bruce reflected that 'My chief advantage as a politician was that I did not give a damn'.[8] Other Australians of Bruce's generation did care about some of the values that had been enshrined in the arbitration system. Bruce's attempt to repeal the *Conciliation and Arbitration Act* in 1929 ultimately saw him swept from office, and a Labor government assumed federal power for the first time since the war. The industrial agitators may not have been so foreign as conservative political forces imagined. Yet Australia's economic fortunes were tied to the international order and its implosion in late 1929 would have a profound effect on the export-driven economy. Australia still had men, and women and children to feed, but the money and markets had dried up.

The economic forecast had been dire for much of the late 1920s. Scientists had further bad news to deliver in this decade, although it was difficult to hear above the clarion-call of development. Former Senator Anthony St Ledger resented scientists using phrases like 'the dead heart of Australia'. 'If statesmanship will but do its work, we can conquer it', with irrigation, immigration and railways, he insisted in 1923.[9] To scientific minds, it was increasingly clear that Australia's climate and geography meant it would never support the hundreds of millions of people originally envisaged as forming a vast new white civilisation in the Pacific. Aridity and poor soil would always limit the carrying capacity of Australia. 'Owing to insuperable natural disabilities Australia cannot continue to absorb any considerable number of immigrants,' warned

British geologist Professor John Gregory, who had spent the earlier part of his career in Australia. He described as a 'fantastic over-estimate' the numbers of immigrants proposed by civil servants and politicians concerned to boost Australia's population.[10]

In disappointment there was relief, too. The decades spent worrying about the attractiveness of Australia to the teeming masses of Asia now seemed to be energy misspent. This was not a continent capable of absorbing excess millions of people, from Asia or anywhere else. The challenge was going to be one of managing unpredictable rainfall, vast tracts of infertile land and the environmental damage caused by introduced species, plants and populations. It would not be one of guarding endless possibilities of agricultural production from hungry hordes standing at the gate. The activities of the Japanese in the early 1940s would temporarily revive invasion anxieties, but from the 1920s it was clear that Australia's destiny would be determined by climate as much as ambition. Another unanticipated consequence of this new scientific knowledge was a nascent appreciation of older modes of existence and environmental management. It was now possible to see Australia through new eyes, as a fragile place that must be tended with care and respect, a knowledge that had always been part of an Indigenous world view.

THE CRASH

The Australian economy was not well by the end of the 1920s. Its lifelines were effectively destroyed by the collapse of American stock markets in October 1929. Direct economic ties between Australia and the United States were not particularly strong. Hence, the Wall Street crash attracted little attention at the time; that recessions tend to follow the downward spiral of the stock market was a lesson learned from the events of the late 1920s and early 1930s. The magnitude of the American economy, and its importance as an investor, meant that a depression there had serious repercussions throughout global markets. Among the hardest hit economies were those of the United States itself, Western Europe, Great Britain and Australia.

Britain was heavily indebted to the United States. Refusal of further credit to British firms had a trickle-down effect for their own investment capabilities. Credit evaporated and in Australia, so too did the government jobs that it funded. As manufacturing declined in the northern hemisphere, demand for Australian export goods plummeted and prices fell. By mid-1931, the prices of Australia's key exports of wheat and wool had fallen 50 per cent from their high point in the mid 1920s. Visions of Australia's future as a predominantly agricultural society meant that its economy had not undergone the diversification that might have provided some protection against falling world markets. The two factors upon which the Australian economy most depended – credit and export prices – had collapsed at one fell swoop.

At the peak of the depression, in 1933, Australia had among the highest unemployment rates in the Western world. With unionists' unemployment at about 30 per cent, Australia's rates matched those of Germany, and were worse than those of Britain at 22 per cent and the United States at 25 per cent. Unemployment figures masked considerable diversity, and there were regions in Britain and the United States worse hit than others. Statistics also provided rough estimates only, and did not take into account the under-employed, those who had withdrawn from the labour market and the school leavers who had not yet had a chance to find work. The extent of unemployment, in Australia and elsewhere, may well have been much higher than statistics suggested.

The crisis was of unprecedented magnitude and severity, and governments around the world struggled to find a solution. The knee-jerk response when the dam burst was to rebuild the walls. Protective tariffs were erected or strengthened in most of the advanced economies,

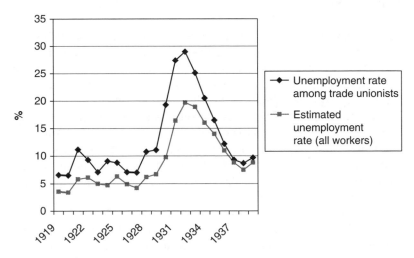

Figure 11.1   Unemployment, 1919–39

Source: W. Vamplew (ed.) *Australians: Historical Statistics* (Sydney: Fairfax, Syme and Weldon Associates, 1987), p. 152.

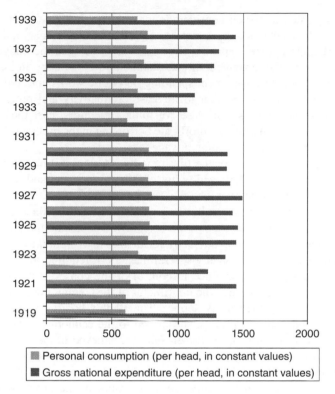

Figure 11.2   Indicators of living standards, 1919–39

Source: W. Vamplew (ed.) *Australians: Historical Statistics* (Sydney: Fairfax, Syme and Weldon Associates, 1987), p. 226.

including Australia. Credit evaporated. This intensified the predicament, because it provided a disincentive to international trade and prevented water from entering the dam at all. The defensive and deflationary measures merely made matters worse.

SEEKING A SOLUTION

During the Great Depression of the 1930s the new federal Labor government in Australia, elected a mere fortnight before the Wall Street collapse, was caught in a cleft stick. The primary political undertaking of the Labor Party was a commitment to maintain the wages and living standards of working people. The economic orthodoxy of the day suggested that such considerations could not be uppermost when it came to counteracting economic depression. Deflationary policies were the appropriate response. The aim was to balance the budget, in order to begin the repayment of unsustainable levels of debt. In essence this meant cutting government spending on public works, and reducing wages and pensions, in order to increase productivity and profit. The British finance houses that were Australia's creditors, cast their eyes south, mindful of Australia's profligate borrowing in the previous decade and its reputation for a minimum wage.

The government, led for the first time by a Catholic Prime Minister, James Scullin, was besieged with conflicting advice and clashing agendas. A self-made man who had run grocery stores and newspapers before entering politics, Scullin had warned Parliament since the late 1920s about the parlous state of the economy. Diagnosing the problems proved easier than finding a remedy for them. Any solution the government devised needed to satisfy several masters. It required the approval of the Senate, which remained in control of the conservative political parties. Scullin also needed the imprimatur of the Commonwealth Bank, which controlled the money supply. The Bank's board, composed of business and financial leaders, subscribed to the economic orthodoxies of the day. Its chairman, Sir Robert Gibson, believed in the axiom of a balanced budget. This bedevilled any attempts to find a more creative solution to the depth of the economic crisis. He was one of numerous advisors, including newly appointed professors in the growing discipline of economics, who argued that Australia's international economic reputation was an essential consideration in the resolution of the crisis. There was no advantage to be gained for Australia if it became known as a nation that defaulted on its commitments. That was a sure path to oblivion. Argentina's decision to do so meant that it was an international pariah.

Following the advice of British bankers appeared to be one way of ensuring international respectability. At the behest of Gibson, the Prime Minister invited representatives of the highest echelons of British finance, including Sir Otto Niemeyer, to visit Australia and consider its current position. 'In recent years', Niemeyer stated in August 1930, 'Australian standards have been pushed too high relatively to Australian productivity and to general world conditions and tendencies'.[11] For 'standards', read 'wages'. His advice to the premiers of all Australian states was stark: cut spending, no further borrowing and balance the budget. Despite ongoing public controversy over Niemeyer's remarks – one Senator described it as 'rot', 'Australians were not prepared to accept rice and a loin cloth in lieu of their present standards' – in August 1930, the Commonwealth and State governments, under the terms of the Melbourne Agreement, took Niemeyer's medicine.[12] Within a few months, the Arbitration Court followed suit, reducing the basic wage by ten per cent. Unemployment rose even further.

If conservative economists had, at times, a blinkered understanding of the remedy for the crisis, their critics oversimplified its origins. Already suspicious of the 'Money Power' of the banks after the depression of the 1890s, many in the labour movement attributed the current economic disaster to a conspiracy engineered by greedy financiers determined to impoverish wage earners. This completely missed the global dimensions of the depression and its systemic nature. Capitalism itself was in crisis, and banks fell alongside businesses. Blaming the banks also lent itself to the age-old vilification of moneylenders that drew some of its strength from anti-Semitism. The visit of Niemeyer, whose German-Jewish origins attracted derision, was a case in point.

Ultimately, the new Labor government could not withstand the pressures brought by internal splits over how to best respond to a financial crisis of such magnitude. The Premier of New South Wales, Jack Lang, even suggested that the debt be simply repudiated, a position that caused further division. The three major options – deflation, inflation and repudiation – were still hotly debated when the Premiers met again in June 1931. The compromise solution, heavily weighted towards deflation, was premised around the notion of 'equality of sacrifice'. Wages for those on Commonwealth awards (who comprised about half the workforce) were cut a further 20 per cent, with the sweetener that interest rates for bond holders would be similarly reduced. Like many compromise solutions, in an effort to provide something for everyone, no one emerged happy. Even John Maynard Keynes was prompted to comment. Wage reduction, he suggested, was a 'double-edged weapon'. 'Expand the internal bank credit and stimulate capital expenditure as much as prudence and courage will allow', Keynes counselled.[13]

SURVIVING THE HARD TIMES

There was not, nor was there ever likely to be, equality of sacrifice. The unskilled suffered the most, concentrated as they were in labouring jobs in the hardest-hit sector of building, infrastructure projects and manufacturing. They were the most likely to hit the road in search of work, or move their families from rented accommodation they could no longer afford to the shanty towns of corrugated iron and hessian bags that began to emerge on city fringes. Rural families, particularly wheat farmers in Western Australia and Victoria, suffered crippling debt repayments and reduced income in the depression years. They at least had the advantage of living off the land, even if their diet was frequently reduced to rabbit, bread and dripping. Those at the beginning and the end of their working life were more likely to be unemployed, as were single men without families to support. In this moment of crisis, preference in employment was given to those in the prime of their lives perceived to be fulfilling their social and familial obligations. Despite these inequalities, there was a shared sense of reduced opportunity. Novelist David Malouf, whose own family circumstances were not dramatically altered by the depression, remembers his 1930s childhood in Brisbane as 'a time of pinched horizons and few amenities'.[14]

Women already had poorly remunerated and confined employment opportunities, even in the good times, and this pattern continued in the depression. Their concentration in areas less likely to falter, such as the light manufacturing of food and drink, when combined with cheaper wage rates, did mean that their jobs were more secure. Others withdrew voluntarily from the workforce. None of these factors prevented women from being accused of taking men jobs, despite plenty of evidence to the contrary. Women might have been less likely to lose an existing job, but they were not replacing male workers in industries that had contracted severely and had no work to offer anyone, of either sex.

Families made pragmatic decisions about survival. Couples postponed marriage and avoided the expense of forming a new household. A key choice for already established families was to limit the number of mouths to feed. The birth rate had in fact been falling since the early 1920s, but declined even further in the depression years. In 1921, an Australian woman bore an average of three children; in the early 1930s she bore only two. There might have be some positives in this decision to limit fertility. Despite the hardship and poverty of the 1930s, infant mortality rates, which had been slowly declining since 1904, dropped significantly in the depression and continued to do so for the rest of the century.[15] School inspectors reported that children maintained a healthy weight and were no more prone to diseases and malnourishment during the depression than they had been before it.

Adults who remained in full time employment may have in fact benefited from the changed economic conditions. Those with jobs enjoyed increased purchasing power, as prices fell. The folk memory of the depression is so coloured by soup kitchens and tramps it is easy to forget that some contemporaries remained ignorant of its impact. People with cash in reserve were able to acquire devalued assets. The generous were able to help out family members and neighbours less fortunate than themselves. Occupations which were necessary for the order and management of society – teaching, policing, communication – were more secure than those associated with a booming economy. Teachers and policemen may not count among society's wealthiest individuals, but they usually enjoy steady work in bad times. That is why so many working-class families, for so long, encouraged their brightest sons and daughters into such occupations. In the era before full employment, job security ensured upward mobility.

White-collar work was not an automatic insulation against unemployment. Professionals such as doctors and lawyers were less affected than architects and engineers, whose work revolved around construction and manufacture. Male clerks suffered a particularly severe contraction in their employment opportunities. Middle-class masculine identity was premised on the idea of breadwinning, as was respectable working-class masculinity by the early decades of the twentieth century. Among these men, the depression's impact was more than financial. It was corrosive of self-confidence. As poet Vincent Buckley would later recall, the depression's 'demons were the shape of acid in the very grass. It meant the whole outside pressing into a man's psychic room, denying his relevance. It was a threat to his manhood and to a woman's sense of possibility. "Nobody wants a man," my father would say despairingly'.[16] Queuing for food rations or enduring invasive questioning by charity workers added insult to injury. Wives and mothers in these households often bore the silent burden of making ends meet. Unskilled labourers had always faced the prospect of seasonal work and trade fluctuations, and there had been plenty of insecurity in the 1920s. The depression's impact on those who least suspected it contributed to the profundity of the changes it would ultimately inspire.

If the depression exposed the shortcomings of orthodox economics, it also revealed the inadequacy of welfare provision in Australia. The old solutions of bags of baby clothes, food rations and blankets could not keep up with the demand. More than this, the extent of need gave the lie to the long-standing distinction between the deserving and undeserving poor. Charities had always operated on a premise that it was important to be alert to imposition. In this view, unemployment was more often than not a choice. Poverty might well be a veneer for laziness. The Great Depression demonstrated, in most dramatic form, that the market was subject to cyclical fluctuations and that unemployment was the consequence of a downturn. It was not a moral failing. The extent of the suffering overwhelmed the charitable. There were too many applicants to investigate thoroughly. Human need outweighed moral prescriptions.

Elements of older understandings about relief lingered in the solutions government devised to meet the extent of the problem. The evaporation of credit meant there could be no massive public works programmes to absorb the vast numbers of unemployed. There was no general unemployment insurance scheme; only Queensland had gone some way towards implementing one in the 1920s. To avoid starvation, state governments introduced 'sustenance' programmes. Soon known colloquially as 'susso', they provided rations and coupons but were reluctant to distribute cash. In Victoria, Tasmania and South Australia 'susso' recipients were forced to work for their relief. Victoria's Great Ocean Road, which winds so majestically along the rugged coastline, is a testament to that labour. 'Susso' never even came close to providing a living wage. In the cities, unemployed single men were seen as potential troublemakers and converts to communism. Consequently, governments created unemployment camps in the country and on the urban fringe to confine single male relief recipients and keep an eye on them.

The unemployed and under-employed resented the conditions of relief and the indignity of distrust and surveillance. They complained, by letter and on foot, in demonstrations outside parliaments and treasury buildings. Police response to such actions was usually swift and often brutal. This was activism born of despair and frustration, rather than any critique of the capitalist system designed to bring it down. Still, communists sensed an opportunity to advance their analysis of the class system. They sponsored the Unemployed Workers Movement, which had a membership of 30,000 in the peak depression years of the early 1930s. The movement assisted people resisting eviction from their homes, and organised protest against the conditions of unemployment relief. Practical help appealed and won support, but relatively few were converted to the communist cause. Party membership climbed to 2000 but there it stayed.

The sight of rioting workers, the theatrics of Lang and even a tiny spike in communist activity was enough to set conservative hearts racing. The most significant political activity in these years, in terms of the sheer numbers engaged in it, lay with right-wing citizens' leagues, not in their nemesis. These organisations, with predominantly middle-class membership, feared that the depression might lead to a Bolshevik-style revolution. Nationalist in inspiration and conservative in politics, they gave themselves names such as the All for Australia League.

They worried about the Labor government's capacity to respond to the crisis. Eric Campbell, the Sydney solicitor who formed one such group, the New Guard, described his organisation as 'grimly determined and fully prepared to stop the state from being Sovietized'.[17] By September 1931, there were 36,000 paid-up members in New South Wales alone.

The citizens' leagues were ripe for political harvest. Their criticisms of the way politicians had handled the economic crisis meant that an alliance with a pre-existing party was unlikely. Much of the debate about the response to depression had also occurred in extra-parliamentary forums, particularly among an influential Melbourne-based consortium of financiers, business and civic leaders known as 'the Group'. They in turn had courted a Labor cabinet member, Joseph Lyons, who had been vocal in his opposition to Lang's ideas about debt repudiation. Lyons' background as a Tasmanian school teacher, his large family of eleven children and frequent caricature as a koala belied his bear-like political instincts. Aware that the Labor Party was riven with conflict over the economic crisis, and attracted by the solutions proposed by the Group, in March 1931 Lyons announced that he no longer had confidence in his own government. He spent the rest of that year courting the citizens' leagues, shoring up the support of the Nationalist Party and cultivating his connections with the financial and business world. The formation of the United Australia Party (UAP) later that year, and its landslide election victory in December 1931, saw Joseph Lyons become the next Prime Minister of Australia. He would remain so until his death, whilst still in office, in 1939.

The election of the UAP government effectively incorporated the citizens' leagues into the mainstream polity and their more secret, armed groups burst like the bubble they had always been. The new Prime Minister was instrumental in orchestrating a series of developments that ultimately led to Jack Lang's dismissal by the Governor of New South Wales. The economic problems continued unabated for several more years, but the intensity of public debate gradually dissipated and the major sources of political destabilisation had been effectively neutralised.

HEROES, VILLAINS AND RIGHTS

During these years, aviation and sport provided welcome distractions from instability and uncertainty. The fear and distrust that permeated the 1930s frequently leaked into the enjoyment of such pursuits, or maybe

193

the danger and suspicion heightened the pleasure derived from them. Although his own business had collapsed during the depression, and he had himself joined the New Guard, the aviator Sir Charles Kingsford Smith continued to organise and endure path-breaking flights to the delight of the Australian public. His activities, alongside other aviators Charles Ulm, Bert Hinkler and Amy Johnson enjoyed extensive press coverage. There was dismay but not surprise when Kingsford Smith perished over the coast of Burma in 1935. Aviation was inherently dangerous and did not frequently invite theories of treachery or conspiracy. The comparatively safe sport of cricket, in contrast, was riven with controversy in the early 1930s. Responses to the Bodyline tour of England's cricket team in the summer of 1932–33 were at once a distraction from the hard realities of the depression, and displaced anger at some of its injustices. The Australians made complaint to the British sporting authorities that the English cricket team was 'unsportsmanlike'.[18] Niemeyer had arrived in a bowler hat and showed no mercy about Australia's indebtedness to England. The English cricket team were more blunt: they tried to undermine the Australians by delivering body blows with a leather ball. Unfairness seemed to rule the day.

Don Bradman, who was rattled but survived Bodyline, became a hero to a generation of schoolchildren, while older Australians also continued to venerate their wartime heroes. When Sir John Monash died in 1931, a quarter of a million people lined the streets to pay their final respects. In his last years, Monash had overseen the development of the Shrine of Remembrance in Melbourne, which was opened in 1934. The inscription read: 'The sacrifice of a nation lies here'. Sydney's Anzac War Memorial in Hyde Park was opened in the same year. Other iconic features of city landscapes were also completed or initiated in the 1930s, including the Sydney Harbour Bridge (opened in 1932) and Brisbane's Story Bridge.

These urban projects expressed a shift of direction in these years that saw a drift away from the hope that Australia would be a predominantly agrarian society. No clearly articulated vision had yet emerged in its place. The UAP continued to expect that recovery would come from the agricultural export sector. International trade barriers quashed that hope, although gold mining in resource-rich states such as Western Australia led it out of depression. By the late 1930s the mining town of Kalgoorlie could boast an Olympic sized swimming pool, bringing water for leisure to the desert as a symbol of its recovery. Wool-growing regions would have to wait longer for their industry to revive. In 1932 the government had negotiated the Ottawa Agreement. This finally achieved a long cherished goal of preferential trading terms for Australian goods in Britain, although not in relation to the critical export of wool. In exchange, British goods were imported to Australia with lower tariffs. Balance of trade figures slowly began to improve.

Heavy manufacturing industries also developed in the mid-late 1930s, benefiting from wage reductions and protection. Partly out of necessity, with credit no longer available, the government entered into agreements with private companies such as BHP and General Motors-Holden. Gone were the days of new state enterprises; the 1930s saw the emergence of a new pattern. Generous leaseholds, concessions, taxation breaks: this was how the state would sponsor industrial development into the future.

It was also becoming apparent that new ways would be needed to approach issues of even longer standing. In the decade since the early 1920s, Aboriginal numbers had climbed by almost 10,000. The anticipated fading away of Australia's Indigenous people had not come to pass. Indeed, by the 1930s there were other signs of renewal, in terms of both white humanitarian concern and Aboriginal activism. Australia's membership of the League of Nations, and its role as a mandatory power in New Guinea, gave international imprimatur to those concerned about the treatment and rights of Indigenous peoples. A number of humanitarian groups, many of them founded by middle-class Christian women, became prominent in their advocacy of improved conditions for Aborigines in this period. Much of their concern centred on Aborigines living in more remote communities in the western and northern parts of the continent. This was in part due to humanitarian connections with prominent anthropologists, whose work focused on tribal Aborigines considered vulnerable in the face of the onslaught of European civilisation. Together, for much of the 1930s, humanitarian groups and anthropologists lobbied government for the segregation and protection of Aborigines.

The inter-war period also witnessed the creation of a host of Aboriginal organisations devoted to improving conditions for their people, among them the Australian Aborigines' League. In the late 1930s, this organisation sponsored two major initiatives, which made claims for Aborigines as the original occupants of the land. The first, a petition addressed to King George V, asked for separate Aboriginal representation in Parliament. The second was a declaration that the sesquicentenary of white settlement in 1938 should be considered a 'Day of Mourning'. The date 26 January 1938 would mark the '150th Anniversary of the Whiteman's seizure of our country', the League insisted. 'We appeal to the Australian nation of today to make new laws for the education and care of Aborigines, and we ask for a new policy which will raise our people to full citizen status and equality within the community'.[19]

Both white humanitarian groups and Indigenous activists campaigned for Aboriginal rights, on the grounds that there were differences between Aborigines and other Australians. In the early 1930s, the newly appointed Professor of Anthropology at the University of Sydney, A. P. Elkin, published an influential pamphlet that took a different view. Elkin argued, in *Understanding the Australian Aborigines*, for a 'positive policy' to be developed in relation to Aborigines. Instead of segregating Aborigines on reserves, they should be encouraged and supported to adapt themselves to the way of life practiced by the mainstream Australian community. As the 1930s progressed, Elkin's influence in government, academic and humanitarian circles grew, as did faith in his assimilationist ideas. The transition from protection to assimilation was a significant shift in policy and practice. It coincided with an increasing focus on 'half-caste' Aborigines, a group previously overlooked by reformers. In 1939, a new government department of Native Affairs was established, largely at Elkin's behest. This confluence of events also contained within it a subtle, but important, shift of emphasis. If Aborigines were to assimilate effectively, they were in need of the civil rights enjoyed by other Australians, not specific rights possessed only by Aboriginal people, who bore a special relationship to that state which had usurped their possession of the continent.[20]

The existence of a substantial 'half-caste' population was common knowledge in inter-war Australia, although it was still considered risqué to raise the topic of sexual relations between Indigenous and non-Indigenous Australians. The novelist Katherine Susannah Prichard had won some notoriety in the late 1920s for her willingness to explore interracial sex in her acclaimed novel *Coonardoo*. In the depression years, Prichard and other writers also shifted direction and began to question the relationship between art and society in new ways. For Prichard this meant turning away from the focus of her earlier work, and an attraction to Soviet-inspired attempts to foster revolutionary consciousness through art. Subsequently Prichard became one of the most well-known practitioners of the social-realist novel in Australia. Such an approach tended to compromise artistic and aesthetic sensibility, and was not one commonly adopted in Australia.

More typically, the depression made the nationalism that had influenced Australian creative life in previous decades seem naïve at best, shallow at its worst. Artists, writers and intellectuals became eager for news from elsewhere, for new ways of making sense of the crisis that had engulfed their society. The scale of suffering in the depression had revealed the fragility of Australian prosperity. Given the impact of global developments on Australian affairs, there was a new urgency to become more informed of their implications, not only in terms of politics, but also in relation to art and culture. Frustration with insularity coalesced around the issue of censorship. In the mid-1930s, writers and academics formed the Book Censorship Abolition League, urging the government to allow Australians access to key political and literary works. 'The object of the league', explained Miss Theo Lucas, 'is to defend the right of Australians to a free selection of intellectual and cultural ideas'.[21] Yet by 1936 there were still over 5000 books on the blacklist, including Aldous Huxley's *Brave New World*. If the 1920s had witnessed a widening gap between popular and high culture, the 1930s opened a rift between intellectuals and government.

It was clear to everyone that the system of protection a previous generation had put in place for breadwinners – the basic wage, arbitration, tariffs for industry – had not sheltered them from deteriorating world-wide economic conditions. If any consensus emerged from the 1930s, it was that the suffering and insecurity endured by so many should not be allowed to occur again. New structures were needed to provide a safety net for the nation and its people. Before these programmes could begin in earnest, developments elsewhere again determined the course of Australia's future.

12
. . . .
Defending Australia: 1939–49

When Britain declared war on Germany in September 1939 the leaders of other Dominion nations, such as Canada and South Africa, consulted their Parliaments about what they might do in response. In Australia, the new Prime Minister, Robert Menzies, who had assumed office upon the death of Joseph Lyons, showed his hand within an hour. In a radio broadcast, he declared that it was his 'melancholy duty' to inform the country that Britain had declared war, and 'as a result, Australia is also at war'.[1] Probably not, but Australian governments had been in denial about the independence that the *Statute of Westminster* had granted them for the best part of a decade and had not yet ratified it. The Prime Minister's declaration of loyalty was soon followed by anxious deliberations about the type of commitment Australia would in fact be prepared to offer. There were several elements in the mix: the parlous state of Australia's own defences, the military activity of the Japanese in East Asia and the lack of enthusiasm for another war. Apart from declaring Britain's enemies as Australia's too, the contrast with the response to World War I could not have been greater. The Prime Minister even went as far as declaring that it would be 'business as usual'.[2]

In the event, it was anything but, particularly after Japan entered the war in December 1941. For the first time Australia found itself on a total war footing, a situation which generated both opportunities and restrictions, particularly on rights and liberties. World War II instigated major and lasting changes to the Australian economy, witnessed the first new national social security measures since 1910, and dramatically increased the powers of the federal government at the expense of the states. The first war was viewed as Australia's opportunity to take part on the world stage; participation in the second emphasised just how small that role would be. Despite enemy action reaching closer to Australia's shores than ever before, it was the shock experienced in the previous decade that would be the most influential driver of post-war planning. Before the depression, the phrase on politicians' lips was 'the basic wage'. After it, 'full employment' was the new mantra. Alongside meeting military and defence commitments, much of the war was spent worrying over how to avoid the depression and instability that had followed the conclusion of World War I. In the early 1940s, people longed for peace while remaining fearful of its consequences.

THE EARLY YEARS OF THE WAR

Initial ambivalence about the new war was reflected in sluggish recruitment rates. With only a small standing army, the government soon announced the establishment of the 2nd Australian Imperial Force. The Minister for the Army made it clear that, despite the continuity in name for the overseas force, very different circumstances prevailed in 1939 when compared to 1914. 'Then', he told the Parliament 'the safety of Australia was not for a moment considered to be in danger'.[3] Now, Japan was no longer a British ally, and it had invaded China in 1937. By October 1939, the government had announced compulsory military training for single men in order to constitute a militia for home defence.

The government studiously avoided reference to the word conscription as it established the militia and felt no compulsion to put the matter to a referendum. The futility and divisiveness of doing so had been amply demonstrated in the last war. To sweeten the pill, it was made clear that no member of the militia would be compelled to serve outside Australian territory. Significantly, this meant it was possible for them to serve in Papua and New Guinea, external territories that fell within Australian borders. The establishment of the militia, when combined with a lack of dramatic war news emanating from Europe within the first six months, in a period known as the 'phony war', meant that voluntary recruitment into the expeditionary force continued at a trickle.

Enough men had enlisted by January 1940 for the first contingent of the 2nd AIF to depart for overseas service. The decision to send them had not been easy. Menzies objected to the British tendency to treat Australia like a colony and argued that the activities of the Japanese must be taken into account when determining Australia's overseas commitment. This nascent sense that Australia's interests may differ from Britain prompted Australia's first independent diplomatic appointments, to the United States, Japan and China, in early 1940. Ultimately, a desire to not appear less loyal than New Zealand, which had offered an expeditionary force, and reassurances from Churchill that fear of the United States would deter Japan from any further military aggression, ended the prevarication about the expeditionary force.

Australian troops were deployed to support imperial defence strategy in the Middle East, which remained Britain's priority over and above any concerns about East Asia. The Suez Canal was an important communication hub, the region was oil rich, and Italy's African colonies were a potential new front in the war. Menzies also made a further military commitment. Australia would participate in the Empire Air Training Scheme, which resulted in the Royal Australian Air Force training over 20,000 airmen to serve with British Bomber Command. The most glamorous of military roles in the war was also among the most perilous, and almost 3500 Australian airmen died as a result of their participation in strategic bombing campaigns. The commitment also seriously weakened Australia's capacity for air defence during the Pacific War.

Following a precedent set during World War I, the federal government did not delay in passing legislation that ensured that it could govern by regulation. There was broad consensus that the *National Security Act* was a necessary evil in wartime, despite the Labor opposition's concerns about the violation of civil liberties. Initially refusing to be part of a wartime coalition government, by mid-1940 the Labor Party agreed to join an Advisory War Council. This was in its own interests, as the government now had complete control over resources, production and the population. The UAP government was dealt a blow when three of its most senior members, including the critical posts of the Minister for Air and the Minister for the Army, along with the Army's Chief of Staff, were killed in an aeroplane accident near Canberra in August 1940. The men were also Robert Menzies' friends. 'I felt that, for me, the end of the world had come', the Prime Minister later reflected.[4] In one sense, it had. An election a month later returned the UAP only with the support of independents. Despite his background as a scholarship boy from the country, Menzies' successful career as a barrister and his facility with language meant that he was a man who did not wear his learning lightly, whose arrogance was a potential source of alienation for the electorate; his leadership of the UAP had always been fragile and became more so as the war progressed.

The fragility of the coalition government belied the relative buoyancy of the early war years. War had given the economy the boost it needed to move forward out of depression. Increased government expenditure and recruitment into the militia and 2nd AIF had reduced the problems of unemployment. The prices of primary export products rose owing to increased international demand. The British bought everything primary producers could offer. The irony that Australia's export industries only regained their prosperity as the world descended into war was not lost on its representative bodies. 'It is saddening to reflect that it was left to human slaughter to solve the problems of over-production and unprofitable prices', one agricultural journal lamented.[5]

After the fall of France in June 1940, recruitment finally received the fillip it needed and three new divisions were raised, two of which were sent to the Middle East. The most well-known action in which Australians served there was during 1941–42 in defence of the Libyan town of Tobruk, earning them a designation as the 'Rats of Tobruk' by the German propagandist Lord Haw Haw. It was a sobriquet that veterans later adopted as a mark of distinction. More controversially, Australian forces also participated in the defence of Greece, a military debacle for the Allied forces which resulted in a retreat to Crete and ultimately defeat, with over 5000 Australians taken POW by the Germans. These military campaigns in Europe, the Mediterranean and the Middle East also meant that British promises about their capacity to defend Singapore in the event of an attack began to recede into the mists of time.

The Greek campaign coincided with Menzies' visit to Britain in the first months of 1941. Recalling that an Imperial War Cabinet had been formed during the last war, Menzies lobbied for greater Dominion representation. There was no support for the idea from any quarter. The South African Prime Minister, Jan Smuts, even told Menzies that 'we Dominion Prime Ministers should mind our own business and leave Churchill to mind his'.[6] Menzies was permitted to attend meetings of the British War Cabinet, but Australia's deepening concerns about Japan could not find an audience when Britain was already strategically overstretched and fearful about a German invasion. Churchill scarcely saw the Dominion nations as separate entities, according to Menzies, and 'the more distant the problem from the heart of empire, the less he thinks of it'.[7] It was not an imagined slight. No inter-Allied conference for the duration of the war included representation from small nations like Australia. This sense of exclusion from decision-making and failure to consider Australia's interests would continue for the remainder of the war. It was a conscious policy on behalf of Britain and the United States. Broad consultation was, according to Churchill, 'the most sure way to lose a war'. 'You have to be aware of the well-known danger of "having more harness than horse"', he told the House of Commons.[8]

Menzies returned to Australia deflated by his harness status, and frustrated by his inability to reveal confidential war cabinet discussions that would have testified to his efforts to represent Australia in relation to the disastrous Greek campaign. Menzies' absence had also allowed internal dissent with his leadership to foment. Billy Hughes, by now almost 80 years old, could still manage a colourful insult, declaring publicly that Menzies 'couldn't lead a flock of homing pigeons'. It was now untenable for Menzies to lead a party so riven with dispute, and he resigned in August 1941. The problems for the UAP were bigger than personality alone, despite Labor leader John Curtin's acute observation that Menzies 'would rather make a point than make a friend'.[9] The UAP was a party that lacked an ideological core: opposition to Labor and imperial loyalty were not enough to see it through the new demands of a wartime government. Menzies' replacement, Arthur Fadden, was short-lived. In October 1941, he too resigned after losing the support of two independents, and Labor's John Curtin formed a new government. Leader of the Labor Party since the mid-1930s, Curtin was a self-educated man from Victoria, a former newspaper editor in Western Australia, and a veteran campaigner on national issues: he had vast experience in the labour movement and knew its measure. He would not let the Australian Labor Party implode as it had done during its previous two terms in office.

THE SHOCK OF WAR

Events in Europe had influenced Japanese ambitions. Two of the key colonial powers in Asia, France and the Netherlands, now had their homelands occupied by Germany. Their colonies, French Indo-China and the Netherlands' East Indies, were newly vulnerable. In addition, the British Navy was heavily committed in the Mediterranean. The British defence strategy for the region, centred on Singapore and premised on naval superiority, appeared shaky. A combination of wilful ignorance and racial arrogance meant that the Japanese were still not taken seriously. Only one Australian division, out of the three raised in 1940, was sent as military reinforcement to Malaya. When the Japanese attacked the United States' Pacific Fleet at Pearl Harbor in December 1941, and soon thereafter sunk the HMS *Repulse* and *Prince of Wales*, the worst-case scenario had come to pass. There was to be a land and air war against Japan, Allied air cover was dangerously thin, and Japan had naval supremacy. John Curtin made a declaration of war against Japan separately from Britain, and told the Australian public that they faced 'the gravest hour in our history'.[10]

The Prime Minister cast his response to Japan's entry into the war in terms of racial and national survival. In mid-December, Curtin reassured

202

the Parliament of his 'determination that this country shall remain for ever the home of the descendants of those people who came here in peace in order to establish in the South Seas an outpost of the British race'. The white Australia policy, he said, was based on 'economic and sound humane reasons' and would not be overturned by an act of aggression.[11] Soon after the British had surrendered Hong Kong on Christmas Day 1941, Curtin made the most famous speech of his political career. 'Without any inhibitions of any kind,' Curtin announced in a New Year's message, 'I make it quite clear that Australia looks to America, free of any pangs as to our traditional links or kinship with the United Kingdom'.[12] Such willingness to fight for Australia's interests won support in some unlikely quarters. Raised on a pastoral property in rural New South Wales, Jill Ker Conway was unaccustomed to hearing her parents praise a Labor politician. 'My parents were rugged individualists who scorned socialism and the Labor Party as the political recourse of those who lacked initiative,' Ker Conway recalled. After hearing Curtin's speech, in which he 'candidly acknowledged our situation ... their spirits soared. They recognised an Australian patriot.'[13]

Curtin's frankness replaced diplomacy in other forums too. In January 1942, he told Churchill in a confidential cablegram that it would be an 'inexcusable betrayal' if Singapore were evacuated after all the promises that had been made about its impregnability. As romantic as the notion of betrayal might appear in retrospect, as an argument it has certain limitations. Australia had not taken due responsibility for its own defences in the inter-war period and wanted to believe British platitudes rather than subject them to searching critique. Furthermore, the British themselves had underestimated the potential threat from Japan. It was also clear, from mid-1940, that the British did not have the military capacity to fight a war in two oceans. Curtin's public announcement of a realignment with the United States at the moment of crisis invested the Australian government with rather more choice than it possessed in the matter. As a small nation, Australia then, as now, must rely on a major ally for its defence. Curtin's speech is better understood as a plea than a declaration.

The plea did not fall on deaf ears. In January 1942, Churchill made a speech in the House of Commons that made clear that responsibility for Australian security was now as much the concern of the United States as it was of Britain. For Churchill, Japan's entry into the war was a cloud with a silver lining: it ended the United States' isolation and delivered him a powerful new ally in the battle against the Axis powers. Australia's defence and security needs were now a matter for discussion, rather than competition, between Britain and the United States; indeed, they agreed

203

upon the course to be followed. Australia therefore 'turned to' the United States with British blessing.

Churchill himself did not mince words, and warned that the Allies could expect 'severe ill-usage at the hands of the Japanese' in 1942. He also declared that the Japanese were unlikely to undertake a 'mass invasion' of Australia; they were more focused on the 'rich prizes' of the Philippines, the Dutch East Indies and Malaya. In due course, Churchill believed, the industrial might of the United States and the combined energies of the Allies would defeat Japan.[14] However prescient this assessment was, it offered cold comfort to Australians at the time. Furthermore, the Australian government was not privy to discussions between Churchill and US President Roosevelt in which they had decided, in December 1941, to 'Beat Hitler First'. Without adequate reinforcement, Singapore fell in February 1942. It was soon followed by the Netherlands' East Indies. Within the space of three months, 22,000 members of the 2nd AIF had been taken POW by the Japanese.

For the first time, Australians coiled barbed wire along the beaches, plastered brown paper to their windows, and dug air raid shelters in their back yards. Petrol had been rationed since 1940, but the new circumstances saw rationing extended to tea, sugar, alcohol and clothing. Told by their Prime Minister that 'the fall of Singapore opens the battle of Australia', there was widespread fear of a Japanese invasion.[15] 'So great was the shock that Australians, the most taciturn of people, had actually been moved to speak about the news to total strangers', Jill Ker Conway remarked.[16] The bombing of Darwin in February 1942, with the loss of 250 lives, added to the sense of vulnerability. So too did the presence of three Japanese submarines in Sydney Harbour. Curtin attempted to translate the need for commitment and sacrifice into a vernacular that most people would understand: 'as things stand today in Australia, brains and brawn are better than either bets or beer'.[17]

In January 1942, the government had issued new manpower regulations, which allowed it to mobilise all workers, reserve occupations and declare certain industries as essential. Society and the economy were now organised for total war. It was an expensive business, and all previous measures to support it, including loan issues and saving certificates, were now inadequate. In order to fund such vastly increased expenditure, the government resorted to a far-reaching decision. Charged with the 'full responsibility of protecting Australia from invasion', the Treasurer Ben Chifley insisted the government 'must be able to command the full resources of the nation in revenue, man-power and efficiency'.[18] From May 1942, only the federal government would levy and collect income

204

tax, a source of revenue previously collected by state governments. Once gained, this power would not be relinquished.

The sense of crisis peaked in March 1942, and heralded the arrival of the United States' General Douglas MacArthur, appointed as Supreme Commander of the Allied Forces in the South West Pacific Area. Curtin's relief was palpable when he stated that 'there is in this country a deep feeling of gratitude to the President and people of United States for this evidence we see around us in terms of men and munitions'.[19] The Americans were henceforth in control of the campaign to defeat Japan. Despite its hosting duties, Australia was the junior partner. By mid-1942, following the naval battles of the Coral Sea and Midway, the immediate threat of a Japanese invasion of the Australian mainland had eased. American intelligence confirmed that the Japanese would not invade Australia, but the sense of urgency and commitment fostered by threat was one the Australian government was eager to maintain. The Japanese, already with a toehold in the islands of New Guinea, continued to press for occupation of Papua.

Interpreting Japanese war aims, and distinguishing an Australian territorial island from the main continent, was a difficult task in an environment so saturated with fear. US and Australian troops, including the conscripted militia, fought a successful campaign to beat back Japanese forces, on the precipitous and dangerous Kokoda track that wound through the Owen Stanley Ranges in New Guinea. It was to become the best-known, and most revered, Australian action in the Pacific war. Efforts to commemorate the battle since then have erased the important distinction between territory and homeland, and discount the argument that the Japanese did not plan to invade mainland Australia. The major Allied offensive against Japan did not occur until 1944–5, and Australian troops were assigned a 'mopping up' role in the wake of American advance forces through the Pacific.

THE IMPACT OF WAR

By the end of the war almost one million American GIs had passed through Australia, initially welcomed by the Prime Minister as kin 'who spring from the same stock as ourselves'.[20] Not so the ten per cent who were of African American descent, and whose presence caused a ripple of discomfort in a country with a white Australia policy. Yet Indigenous Australians admired, as one described it, 'blacks with money in their hands; blacks who were confident and stood up straight and looked you in the eye'.[21] The white women who dated black GIs, according to poet Dorothy Hewett, 'were shunned and talked about as the lowest thing that crawled'.[22] This was the racial overlay on a more general resentment about the interaction between Australian women and American service-men, who were soon known colloquially as 'over-sexed, over-paid and over here'. Thousands of Australian women were to follow their new American husbands back over there, as part of the world-wide 'war bride' migration phenomenon that occurred once the war was over.

The war had the paradoxical effect of both intensifying gender divi-sions and blurring gender boundaries. Criticisms of women's involve-ment with GIs reflected broader discomfort with the more permissive, transient atmosphere associated with wartime exigency. Women were seen to be both its purveyors and potential victims. Albert Tucker's painting *Victory Girls* (1943), with its bare-breasted, skeletal women clutched by soldiers with the faces of pigs, articulated the fear of moral decay. The vision of excessive femininity, of licentiousness, coexisted alongside another concern, that drawing women into occupations previ-ously the preserve of men would de-sex them.

In the early days of the war some Australian women, inspired by the feats of aviatrix and car drivers in the interwar period, formed paramili-tary organisations. The Government initially resisted, as they had done for the duration of World War I, incorporating women into auxiliary services. By 1941, the worsening war situation prompted a change of heart. That year witnessed the establishment of the Women's Auxiliary Australian Air Force, the Women's Royal Australian Navy Service and the Australian Women's Army Service. Nurses could also serve under the auspices of the Australian Army Nursing Service. By the end of the war, 65,000 women had enlisted. Fears that military service and masculine clothing would defeminise women led recruiting posters to emphasise the ongoing heterosexual desirability of female recruits, who retained waistlines and wore lipstick. This material also underscored the point that such jobs were to assist men, and that by the end of the war, women would gladly exchange a wrench for a broom.

The establishment of the Manpower Directorate in 1942 meant that all potential Australian workers, including women, could be mobilised by the state. Some women chose to join the Australian Women's Land Army, a civilian organisation formed to replace male farm workers. Women were also directed into industrial employment, but their overall workforce participation rose by only five per cent. More significant was the shift in the types of jobs women performed. They abandoned domes-tic service for better paid jobs in industry and transport, and would never work in service in such numbers again. Married women entered the work-force part time, and tended to stay there after the war had ended. The government's willingness to support female workforce participation by providing state-funded child-care was to last only for the duration of the war.

Other welfare initiatives introduced at this time signalled a more permanent change. There was a bipartisan commitment to ensure that new social security measures would prevent the suffering of the 1930s. In a global context, these ideas were articulated in the Atlantic Charter, where Britain and the United States agreed that their aims for the post-war world were an 'improved labour standard, economic advancement and social security'. The first new welfare measure to appear in Australia, in January 1941, was a non means-tested, nationwide, child endowment scheme, which would protect families 'from the industrial hazards of their breadwinners'.[23] This was followed by means-tested widows' pensions in 1942, and unemployment and sickness benefits in 1944. In Britain, the Beveridge Report of 1942 laid the basis for the post-war welfare state. In Australia the Joint Committee on Social Security, which began to report from 1941, served a similar purpose. Its first report declared, 'no longer can we sustain the claim that we are the social laboratory of the world'. Poverty continued to exist because 'unemployment has baffled and prevented our efforts to safeguard living standards'. Hence, the aim of post-war policy should be 'the perfecting of our social and economic organisation so that unemployment be abolished or, if that is found impossible, reduced to a minimum'.[24]

In May 1945, the government released a white paper entitled *Full Employment in Australia*, which stated: 'Full employment is a fundamental aim of the Commonwealth government'.[25] The basic or minimum wage had ceded its central rhetorical position in visions of how to create a just society. The harsh lesson of the depression had been that guaranteeing a minimum income did not ensure that there were sufficient jobs available to provide it. Agricultural and rural industries, so long perceived as the motor of economic growth and the country's ultimately destiny, were now refigured as one of the ongoing challenges for the state. They had not provided the security or destiny so long imagined. Employment needed to be plentiful and diverse, and the manufacturing industries that had thrived in wartime conditions were to be encouraged in peace.

The war also drew Indigenous people into new relationships with the state and economy. Approximately 6000 Indigenous Australians and Islanders served in the military forces, irregular services and support units. Discriminatory clauses in the *Defence Act* discouraging the enlistment of anyone who was not of substantially European descent were relaxed after 1942. When the chips were down, Aborigines were considered Australians who would defend their homeland after all. As poet and activist Oodgeroo Noonuccal, who worked as a signaller for the Australian Women's Army Service during the war, put it: 'There was a job to be done ... all of a sudden the colour line disappeared'.[26] Many Aborigines employed in the services and support units received cash wages for the first time since white settlement.

There was a flutter of concern that Aborigines in the north of Australia might be attracted by Japanese propaganda about throwing off the yoke of white colonialism, a fear that proved baseless. More suspicion adhered to people with links to the Axis powers, and early in the war the federal government had established a series of internment camps. Men perceived as sympathetic to European fascist regimes were among their first inmates. As the war progressed, the net was cast wider, and Germans and Italians were interned. Those living in the north of Australia, a zone of high sensitivity after the Japanese entered the war, were particularly vulnerable. Living outside the camp walls provided little shelter from the injuries of malice and fear. One German couple, long-term residents of coastal Victoria, felt so taunted that they closed their kitchen door and gassed themselves.[27]

Australia accommodated a further 8000 enemy alien internees, mostly Germans and Italians, who had been transported to the country from the Netherlands' East Indies, Britain and its territories including Palestine, Iran, Singapore and Malaya. Enemy POWs captured by Allied forces, including Italians and Japanese, were also incarcerated in Australia. The shortage of manpower and Italy's early defeat in the war meant that thousands of Italian POWs were dispersed throughout rural communities as farm labourers. The conflict with Japan was ongoing and all Japanese POWs remained confined. The stigma of imprisonment was too much for some of these men to bear. In 1944 Japanese POWs broke out of their Cowra camp, and over two hundred were killed in the attempt to recapture them.

Almost all people of Japanese origin already living in Australia were confined to the camps. In total, over 7000 residents were interned in Australia during World War II. Among them were the leaders of the Australia First Movement, a nationalist movement critical of Britain and hence perceived to be sympathetic to its enemies. When the fear of Japanese invasion had subsided, its members were released, and a later Commission of Inquiry found that the response had been out of proportion to the threat the movement had posed to security. European internees began to be released towards the end of the war, and were allowed to

Table 12.1 Australian battle deaths in World War II

	Number	%
Killed in action or died of wounds in Europe and Africa	9,307	34.4
Died as prisoner-of-war in Europe or Africa	265	1.0
Killed in action or died of wounds in Asia	9,470	35.0
Died as prisoner-of-war in Asia	8,031	29.7
Total	27,073	100.0
Australian Army	18,713	69.1
Royal Australian Navy	1,900	7.0
Royal Australian Air Force	6,460	23.9
Total	27,073	100.0

Source: W. Vamplew (ed.) *Australians: Historical Statistics* (Sydney: Fairfax, Syme and Weldon Associates, 1987), p. 415.

remain in Australia at the conclusion of hostilities. In contrast, almost all Japanese internees were deported in 1946, even those among them who had been born in Australia to Japanese parents.

At the end of the war, Australia learned about the fate of its own POWs. The figures were most stark for the 22,000 POWs of the Japanese, one-third of whom had perished. In the history of modern warfare, such death statistics in captivity were not without parallel, and not even remotely the worst, but they came as an appalling shock to Australians in 1945. The number of Australian deaths in World War II, at 27,000, was about half that of World War I, and a significant proportion of those had occurred in captivity. Reduced scale did not make individual grief any more bearable. For Maud Edmondson, whose only child died at the battle of Tobruk, a posthumous Victoria Cross was a 'distinction [that] has bucked Will [his father] up wonderfully but I am afraid I can't even think of it. The loss seems far too great to think of. Jack & I were very dear pals'.[28]

Australians had not played anything like a central role in the penulti-mate battles of the war in either Europe or Asia. There was very little from this conflict that paralleled the potential for mythology that had emerged from World War I. The men who fought were the 'sons of Anzac', inheritors rather than progenitors of a military tradition. It was the Prime Minister, John Curtin, the man who had apparently stood up to Churchill, who emerged as one of the most mythologised people of this war. Curtin's death while still in office, a mere month before the successful conclusion

Illustration 12.1 Liberated Australian and British servicemen, who had been held as prisoners of war by the Japanese, an image that received wide circulation in the daily press in September 1945
Source: Australian War Memorial, 019199.

of the war, confirmed the perception that he had worked himself to death on Australia's behalf. It had been a less costly war than the first, in national if not personal terms. The death tolls throughout Asia and parts of Europe, in comparison, were staggering; in Russia alone, twenty-seven million people had died. This displacement in Europe would ultimately reshape Australia, as refugees began to look for a new home.

REFUGEES AND A RECONSTRUCTED NATION

The war had renewed Australia's commitment to an extensive immigration programme, for reasons of defence and economic development. 'If Australians have learned one lesson from the Pacific war', the Minister for Immigration, Arthur Calwell claimed in 1945, 'it is surely that we cannot continue to hold our island continent for ourselves and our descendants unless we greatly increase our numbers'.[29] The preference, as always, was for white immigrants and family groups, and assisted passage schemes were negotiated with Britain. The far greater refugee crisis in Europe, when combined with Australia's determination to join post-war international organisations, ensured that immigration programmes began to take on a different hue. Australia's membership of the International Refugee Organization led to an agreement to receive Displaced Persons from Europe as migrants, with the proviso that they remain in allocated employment for one year. 'We looked forward to emigration', Polish woman Lydia M., who had spent the war in concentration camps and undertaking forced labour in Germany, later recalled. 'We were impatient to go there as quickly as possible and to help build that young country and to forget forever places the remembrance of which would bring tears to our eyes'.[30]

Between 1947 and 1953, over 170,000 people arrived in Australia from eastern and northern Europe. It was the beginning of the massive post-war migration programme that would change the demographic composition of Australia. The presence of European refugees would also ultimately allow Australians to develop an understanding of this war that was more worldly than the meanings which had attached to World War I. One teenager in the 1950s, the son of a former POW of the Japanese, attended an inner-urban Melbourne high school with Latvians, Poles, Russians and Hungarians from a nearby migrant hostel. He recalled that 'they broaden[ed] our horizons with their stories of war-torn and depressed post-war Europe, which put Australia's depression and war into important perspective'.[31]

The Australian government, like that of other small nations, was eager to participate in international forums such as the new United Nations, founded in 1945. Australian involvement in its establishment left an ambivalent legacy. On the one hand, the External Affairs Minister H. V. Evatt had been instrumental in ensuring that a concern for economic and social development was included in the UN Charter. On the other, Evatt insisted that the new United Nations respect domestic jurisdictions of member nations, largely because he was concerned to ensure the white Australia policy was not a matter for debate in the new forum. In the immediate post-war period, there were efforts to distance Australia from some of the more negative international implications of the policy through the cultivation of good relations with newly independent Asian states such as India, Pakistan and Indonesia.

This was a period of halting self-determination in Australian foreign policy: one of the lessons of the war had been that a great and powerful friend might have interests inimical to Australia's own. By the mid-1940s there were tensions in the relationship with the United States, not least over their sense of destiny in the Pacific, an ambition which clashed with Australia's vision of itself as an immanent regional force. At the end of the war, the US desire to fortify a vanquished Japan from the threat of communism further estranged the Australian government, whose ideas about how Japan might be reformed did not accord with the American view. These frustrations led to a renewal of Commonwealth connections, initially through a bilateral treaty – Australia's first – with New Zealand in 1944 and later, as part of the British Commonwealth Occupation Force in Japan from 1946. Ironically, Australian presence in Japan effectively heralded the beginning of the demise of the white Australia policy. One of the first steps towards dismantling white Australia occurred in 1949, when the Minister for Immigration allowed Japanese war brides to enter the country.

Membership of international organisations was also seen as a way to ensure economic stability in the immediate post-war period. Determination to avoid the mistakes of the 1930s, and a desire to prevent the isolation that had compounded its effects, drove Australian participation in international economic agreements such as that forged at Bretton Woods in 1947. The International Monetary Fund and the International Bank for Reconstruction and Development (later the World Bank), presented to the Australian people as 'an attempt for the first time in history to grapple with world economic problems by concerted action on a world scale for the common good', reflected the optimism of the early post-war period in new models of economic management. Australia's economy had come out of depression in 1940, and its expanded manufacturing sector, high levels of immigration and capital investment meant that the country entered a long economic boom where unemployment rarely rose above two per cent for the best part of two decades.

In the four years after 1941, the total war footing of the economy and society had enabled the Labor government to exert greater control over employment and private enterprise. In some cases this was through regulation, in others it was due to the process of nationalisation. Both accorded with Labor's preference for centralised planning and control as the surest path to creating an equitable society. A solution to the acute housing shortage after the war was found in the establishment of a Housing Commission, which advised making federal loans to the states provide low-cost rental accommodation for people unable to purchase a home of their own. Overseas telecommunications and the airlines were nationalised during the 1940s, on the assumption that the public interest was best served when the state oversaw such complex technologies. Efforts to nationalise more familiar concerns, such as the medical profession, met with resistance.

Table 12.2   Key social and economic legislation, 1939–49

1939	Supply and Development Act
	National Security Act
	Aliens Registration Act
	National Registration Act
	Trading with the Enemy Act
1940	National Security Act
1942	Statute of Westminster Adoption Act
	Black Marketing Act
	Widows Pension Act
	Women's Employment Act
	Australian Broadcasting Act
	Income Tax (Wartime Arrangements) Act
	Income Tax Assessment Act
1944	Unemployment and Sickness Benefits Act
	Pharmaceutical Benefits Act
1945	Commonwealth and State Housing Agreement Act
	Hospital Benefits Act
	Banking Act
	Education Act
1947	Pharmaceutical Benefits Act 1947
1948	National Health Service Act
	Nationality and Citizenship Act
1949	Snowy Mountains Hydro-Electric Power Act
	National Emergency (Coal Strike) Act

Source of Data: http://www.nma.gov.au

There would be no full national health scheme, which was established in Britain from 1948, but pharmaceutical benefits and federal subsidies to public hospitals emerged as an acceptable compromise.

The government tried several times throughout the 1940s, via referendum, to prolong its control over employment, housing and primary production by arguing that it would deliver more profound reforms and equity, but the public rejected such moves as redolent of the austerity they sought to escape. The most radical proposal came in 1947, when the Labor government attempted to nationalise the banks, on the premise that banks were conducted primarily for profit, 'and therefore follow policies which in important respects run counter to the public interest'; consequently, 'their business should be transferred to public ownership'.[32] Again, politicians called forth memories of the depression in an effort to justify the policy. Public ownership of the banks would 'assist us to stave off depression and avoid a repetition of the miseries of the 1930s'.[33]

Non-labour political forces, now in opposition for the best part of a decade, spied a fork in the road. Many of Labor's policies were premised on preventing economic catastrophe, but the task seemed to be becoming one of managing prosperity. Since the mid-1940s, former Prime Minister Robert Menzies had been busy reenergising the conservatives. He had been central to the formation of the new Liberal Party in 1944, which identified as its core constituency a group Menzies called 'the forgotten people'. These were the lower middle-classes, people neither rich nor blue-collar, unionised workers. There was a special appeal to women, with a strongly domestic and familial tone to Menzies' compliment that he wished to represent the 'backbone of the nation'.[34] The Liberal Party successfully harvested the optimism of peacetime by deriding the fixation on centralisation as reminiscent of a socialist state. They were assisted in this task by continued economic growth, which seemed to make a mockery of Labor's earnest preparations for its opposite. There was a perception abroad that Labor appeared to be building a fortress, when the forecast appeared fine and a shelter would do.

When preparing for a general election in late 1949, the Prime Minister Ben Chifley, who had been in office for four years since Curtin's death, gave a speech in which he stated that it was the duty of the community to keep an eye on the 'light on the hill' and 'to see our less fortunate fellow citizens are protected from those shafts of fate which leave them helpless and without hope'.[35] It was a noble sentiment out of step with the times. Jill Ker Conway, by now attending school in Sydney, in thrall to the circle of friends who surrounded her older brothers, raced cars and listened to jazz music, described her generation as being 'agog with the excitement of prosperity'.[36] Her mother had admired John Curtin's patriotism in the war years, but that emergency had now passed. Robert Menzies' Liberal Party now seemed the most appropriate manager of state and society: individualist, anti-communist, and encouraging the excitement that Labor sought to contain. Peace should not be feared; it was there to be enjoyed. Banks should not be nationalised; petrol should no longer be rationed. 'Every extension of Government power and control,' Menzies insisted, 'means less freedom of choice for the citizen'.[37] In December 1949, the Australian public chose him as their next Prime Minister.

Map 4 Australia in 1945

13

. . . .

Security: 1949–63

On the evening of June 13, 1951, King's Hall at Parliament House in Canberra was filled with men in dinner suits and women in floor-length ball gowns. The occasion was the Jubilee of Federation Ball, a celebration of fifty years of Australian nationhood. Robert Menzies, then eighteen months into his second term as the country's Prime Minister, called the room to attention just before midnight. There was dramatic news to impart. It was his sorrowful duty to inform the gathering of the death, that evening, of the leader of the Labor Party, Ben Chifley. Never one for dancing, Chifley had decided to spend the evening in his room at a nearby hotel, where he had suffered a massive heart attack. News of his passing brought the Jubilee Ball to a standstill, and the party was over.

For the rest of the decade, there would be little cause for celebration in Labor's ranks. Menzies' political skill, which rested in his capacity to take a value system centred on individual choice and home ownership and transform it into an ostensibly apolitical national way of life, was in part responsible. Internal divisions in the ALP over how to respond to the discrediting of communism in a cold war environment compounded the problem. Although politics played a hand, the main contributor to Menzies' longevity in the role of Prime Minister was the economic long boom of the 1950s and 1960s. Despite the dominant image of the 1950s as an age of security and conformity, this was a more anxious and insecure time than popular memory would have it. There were also some profound social changes underway in this period that would eventually produce new visions of what Australia's future might look like. An emphasis on individualism, when combined with the exhortation to domesticity, ultimately produced a set of contradictions that would be articulated by a better-educated generation who had not experienced the Great Depression, and no longer feared it.

216

THE COLD WAR AND UNCERTAIN FUTURES

There was intense concern about the world the coming generation would inhabit because the early 1950s, especially, were a time when ongoing peace seemed less than a sure prospect. Despite the optimism that had greeted the formation of the United Nations, the conclusion of World War II heralded the onset of deteriorating relations between the United States and the USSR, once wartime allies and now victorious major powers. The Soviets were unwilling to cede large portions of Eastern Europe that they had liberated from German occupation, and the Western democracies were allied in their opposition to any further extension of communist rule, in Europe or anywhere else. The world began to polarise into blocs in support of the two new superpowers; as a capitalist democracy, there was never any doubt that Australia would line up in support of the United States.

It was not yet apparent that this new cold war would be fought in a series of proxy wars and would not spill into another global conflict, a prospect made more terrible by the power of nuclear weaponry. One of the first proxy wars occurred between 1950–3, when over 17,000 Australians served as part of a multinational force stationed in South Korea, which was in conflict with the communist north. The action had UN imprimatur, but it was the initiative of the United States, keen to contain communism in Asia. The Australian commitment in Korea reflected support of the American position on communism, but it was also designed to give leverage to the argument that the United States should consider a Pacific defence agreement along the lines of Europe's NATO pact. At this juncture, Australia was still most anxious about a resurgent Japan, and was relieved when the United States, along with New Zealand, signed the ANZUS Treaty in 1951. ANZUS contained no guarantees, but it did require its partners to 'act to meet the common danger' if one were attacked. Much as Australia had relied on the might of the British navy in the colonial period, in the postcolonial, cold war environment a treaty with the United States was viewed in similar terms. Some of the language had changed – talk was now of upholding democracy, not civilisation – but there were echoes of the old anxiety about the near north and the desire for a powerful friend. This was matched by the now-familiar reluctance to spend much money on its own defence: for all the obsession about the communist menace, Australia's defence spending remained remarkably small in this period, at only a bit over two per cent of gross domestic product.

Growing anxiety about the vulnerability of the region, especially after the communist victory in China in 1949, meant that Australia was willing to join the United States in some of its measures for 'forward defence'. Menzies subscribed to US President Eisenhower's theory, first articulated in 1954, that each nation in the region might be thought of as one in a row of dominos, and if one 'fell' to communism, the rest would quickly follow suit. Hence, Australia also joined the Southeast Asian Treaty Organisation (SEATO) from its inception in 1954, another US-led initiative designed to contain communism to which only two Southeast Asian nations were signatories. Eventually, Vietnam was included as territory under SEATO protection, and it provided the justification for the Australian government to send military instructors to the anti-communist government of South Vietnam in 1962.

The Commonwealth also remained an important organisation through which Australia navigated its way in post-imperial Asia, attempted to establish relationships with newly independent states and engaged in military and diplomatic commitments to strengthen the region against the alleged communist threat. From 1950, the Colombo Plan saw bilateral aid flow from Australia and other Commonwealth countries to South and Southeast Asia in the hope that improving living standards and strengthening economies would insulate the region's new nations from communism. Its best remembered feature was the entry of thousands of Asian students into Australian tertiary institutions. There they interacted with Australian university students, some of whom came to realise that Asian cultures were more complex than they had been led to believe. There was less to fear than there was to learn from these new residents, and this constituted another crack in the wall of white Australia.

The willingness to provide ostensibly humanitarian aid was matched by a readiness to express self-interest through force. From 1950, the British response to communist insurgents in Malaya included members of the Australian Air Force and Army, who remained until a final withdrawal in 1963. Within two years the newly federated Malaysia was in conflict or 'Konfrontasi' with Indonesia, and Australian forces were back again as part of a Commonwealth contingent to repel them. In the mid-1960s, Donald Horne was prompted to remark that all of this activity was evidence that Australia perceived itself as 'some great power's best ally, somebody's brave and resourceful younger brother'. For him, this was a sign that Australians had 'no moral assurance about their place in the world. They are not South Africans. They no longer know who they are.'[1]

WHITE AUSTRALIA IN A POSTCOLONIAL WORLD

Australia's 'place in the world' was difficult to define in the 1950s, as it sought to combine a desire to be part of international organisations such as the United Nations and the 'New Commonwealth' of ethnically diverse postcolonial nations, and to provide for its defence by its role as signatory to treaties with the United States. Moreover, the Menzies government attempted to juggle these commitments while clinging to a defining feature of the Australian nation since federation: the white Australia policy. This was an increasingly hard act to manage. Australians may not have been South Africans, and the government did not endorse the policy of apartheid, but in the United Nations they were reluctant to endorse any interference in the domestic affairs of that nation, given Australia's own immigration policies and its near-colonial administration of New Guinea. Similarly, Australian support for the Dutch retention of West New Guinea, in light of Indonesian claims to the territory, could be interpreted as ongoing support for colonial rule rather than concern for Australian security, given the shared border with New Guinea.

It was difficult to convince members of the new Commonwealth, whose citizens were not allowed to migrate to Australia owing to their racial background, that Australia considered them equals. It was an insult that did not sit well with the ongoing assumption that many of them were also potential communists in need of lessons in democracy. 'We betray those forces in Asia who are our allies and friends', one Melbourne academic warned, 'when we refuse to take adequate steps to correct an impression that racial discrimination is an instrument of Australian government policy'.[2] In the 1950s, small steps were taken to blunt international opprobrium without risking domestic outcry. In private correspondence, the Minister for External Affairs, R. G. Casey, asked the press to drop reference to the term 'white Australia', which had been quietly abandoned as distasteful in government circles. In 1958, the vilified dictation test was replaced with the more bureaucratic process of entry permits. The year before, non-Europeans who had lived in Australia for fifteen years were allowed to become permanent residents. Representatives of the churches, who protested the inequity and inhumanity of the policy, were heartened if still frustrated by such developments, as were students and academics interested in Asian affairs. By 1960, an organisation of which they were part, the Immigration Reform Group, published a pamphlet with a title that did not mince words: *Control or Colour Bar?*

Uncertain about the changing international scene, in which his cherished values of empire, white Australia and the supremacy of Anglo culture were becoming remnants of a pre-war era, Menzies remained a deft hand on the home front. In 1950, he sought to capitalise on the cold war antipathy to, and fear of, communists by attempting to outlaw the Communist Party of Australia and by requiring individuals accused of being communists to bear the burden of proof to demonstrate that they were not. In effect, this would render any opposition or criticism mute by tarring it with the 'communist' brush. When the High Court declared the legislation unconstitutional, Menzies' confidence was unruffled. He took the matter to a referendum in 1951. The 'No' case was spearheaded by the Labor Party, by now under the leadership of H. V. Evatt, who had successfully challenged the legislation in the High Court. The referendum was defeated by a narrow margin, with enough voters convinced that the legislation posed such a serious threat to civil liberties that it ought not to be allowed. Much like the defeat of the conscription referenda in World War I, this was a surprising result in a climate so dominated by anxiety.

Though Evatt had won this battle, the fallout was so costly that it was Menzies who won the war. Elements within the Labor Party were hostile to communism and critical of Evatt's involvement in the defence of communist civil rights. Chief among them was the Catholic organisation known as the Movement, which had been active since the 1940s in forming industrial groups within trade unions that had close affiliations with the ALP. The denouement came in the early 1950s, with an election-eve defection of Soviet diplomat Vladimir Petrov, who alleged that a Soviet spy ring existed in Australia. Convinced this was a conspiracy engineered by Menzies to win the 1954 federal election, a position he pursued at the subsequent Royal Commission into Espionage, Evatt was like a dog with a bone. His ongoing defence of communist sympathisers further alienated him from the strident anti-communist elements within the ALP. Ultimately, the tensions could not be contained, and in 1954 the anti-communist factions of the ALP split from the party, to form a new political force, eventually named the Democratic Labor Party (DLP). Although achieving only five Senate seats by 1970, the real significance of the DLP lay in the preferences of its unsuccessful candidates, which were directed to the Liberal-Country Party Coalition, effectively keeping that party in office for the better part of two decades.

Extraordinary measures were taken in the name of security. The nuclear arms race was conducted on the assumption that possession of weapons acted as a deterrent to attack, yet it did little to calm the fears of the general public. Within the government, old loyalties to Britain were reinforced when it agreed to the testing of nuclear weapons for the British, on islands off the coast and at Maralinga in South Australia in the 1950s. Even older patterns of behaviour were enacted when the people Indigenous to the region, the Pitjantjatjara, were removed from their homeland in order to make way for British interests. One of the most dramatic portrayals of ongoing public concern about the possibility of nuclear annihilation was in English-born and Australian resident Nevil Shute's 1957 novel *On the Beach*. Set in the southern hemisphere after a cataclysmic nuclear conflict in the north, the novel has the Australian government distributing suicide pills to its population in order to prevent a more horrible death from a rapidly descending radiation cloud. 'Was this, I wondered in the late 1950s, all I had to look forward to?', one Tasmanian schoolboy later recalled, 'Would I grow up just in time to die?'[3]

SUBURBAN FUTURES

The schoolboy would thrive and win a Rhodes scholarship to Oxford University, but in the 1950s Peter Conrad was a child whose father worked constructing housing for Tasmanians, and the family spent weekends surveying the father's work. Conrad Senior's attitude to the development of suburban quarter-acre blocks was typical of his generation, who were eager to acquire houses of their own after the delays of depression and war: 'Here where all was new, the old miseries of a poor rural childhood could be forgotten.'[4] The yards, carports, simple but functional homes and new cement paths also lured couples from over-crowded inner-city areas eager to offer their children a better standard of living than their own thus far. Around the edges of major Australian cities, orchards, market gardens, bushland and paddocks were cleared to make way for new suburban subdivisions.

These new suburbs broke the long-standing ties between neighbourhoods and particular industries, and signalled new identities that were more about home and family than they were about work. About a quarter of the new homes were built by owner-builders, with many families prepared to live in a garage while the new dream home was constructed beside it on weekends. In 1947, the home ownership rate was at a low of fifty-three per cent; by 1954 this had increased to sixty-three per cent and in 1961 it had reached seventy per cent. This was much higher than the United Kingdom where, though rates were on an upward trajectory, by 1961 still less than half the population owned their own home. It was also slightly higher than the United States. Since that time, the

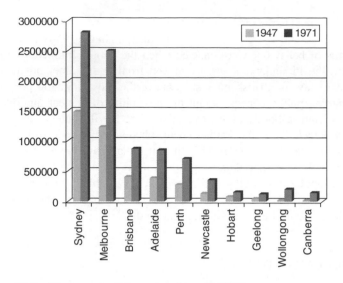

Figure 13.1   The growth of the major cities, 1947–71

Source: Australian Bureau of Statistics, 'Australian Historical Population Statistics, 2006' (3105.0.65.001), at http://www.abs.gov.au.

home ownership rate in Australia has exhibited a remarkable stability; it remained at seventy per cent for the next four decades.[5]

As some families moved out of the inner-city to the suburbs, their place was taken by migrants who brought new forms of community, altered existing architecture to reflect their own aesthetic, and increased the number of shops and restaurants to cater for palates accustomed to different herbs, spices and regional European cuisine. Italians were the most numerous newcomers, but there were substantial numbers of Greeks, Yugoslavs, Germans and Poles. Holocaust survivors were also among their number, and ultimately Australia would become home to the second largest survivor population outside Israel. Between the end of the war and 1963, two million immigrants arrived on Australia's shores, expanding the economy, providing a willing labour force, and enduring the hardships and upheaval of removal from their home country.

Almost 10,000 children were brought from Britain as unaccompanied child migrants. Upon arrival in Australia, some of them found themselves placed in harsh, austere institutions, where they were subjected to exploitation and abuse. Most children arrived in family groups, and there was also a significant number of single men, who called home for wives once they had established themselves in Australia. 'We lived hard two or

Illustration 13.1   A syndicate of 26 British migrant families in NSW engage in a 'spectacular home building scheme', 1957
Source: National Archives of Australia, A12111, 1/1957/21/9.

three years until our families came', Italian migrant Giuseppe reflected when recalling his life of boarding houses, shared rooms and frugality while he supported his family in Rome, and saved up the deposit for a house in Australia.[6] Once arrived, migrant married women were more likely to work outside the home than their Australian-born counterparts, in a double-shift that would become more familiar to Australian women of all backgrounds by the late twentieth century.

No longer could Australia claim to be ninety-eight per cent British. Still, policymakers expected immigrants to assimilate, lose their cultural distinctiveness and adopt an ill-defined Australian way of life. They were 'New Australians', welcomed by Good Neighbour Councils, although their denigration as 'dagos', 'refos' or 'wogs' revealed the resistance that some Australian-born people had to other lifestyles and values. There was also an expectation of gratitude and deference. When Dutch migrant Arian Brandsma, who taught at a school in south-west Western Australia, was asked to speak to a church group in his community, he chose as

223

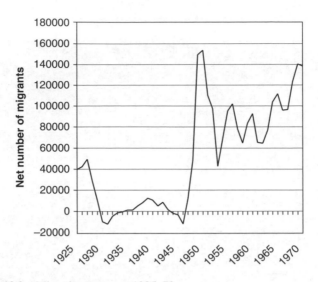

Figure 13.2   Migration patterns, 1925–70

Source: Australian Bureau of Statistics, 'Australian Historical Population Statistics, 2006'
(3105.0.65.001), at http://www.abs.gov.au.

a topic 'Who is my neighbour?' Brandsma detailed the low-level jobs
most migrants undertook, and the poor standard of accommodation many
of them endured; by the following morning his employer had already
received 'three calls saying he had a communist on his staff'.[7] Migrant
groups were resilient in the face of such hostility, and derived strength
from their community groups, sporting clubs and religious organisations.

The greatest rejection was reserved for Australia's Indigenous people:
government policy moved from assuming that the genetics of race mixing
would herald the end of a distinctive Aboriginal society, to a more draconian
system whereby Aborigines would be trained to adopt the 'Australian way of
life'. The Commonwealth Minister for Territories, Paul Hasluck, declared the
aim of the policy of assimilation in 1951 to be that 'all persons of Aboriginal
blood or mixed blood in Australia will live like white Australians'.[8] This
meant the removal of children and their placement in institutions or adoption
by white families and discriminatory legislation that made the privileges of
citizenship dependent on the abandonment of Aboriginal cultural practices.
In the mid-1960s, the poet Oodgeroo Noonuccal pleaded in a poem entitled
'Assimilation – No!': 'Pour your pitcher of wine into the wide river/And
where is your wine? There is only the river.' Earlier she had asked: 'Must
we native Old Australians/In our own land rank as aliens?'[9]

224

There were several occasions in the 1950s and early 1960s when Australians welcomed more temporary visitors to their shores, keen to affirm old loyalties and explore new possibilities in the post-war era. The ecstatic reception given in 1954 to the young Queen Elizabeth II, the first reigning British monarch to tour Australia, represented the high-water mark of faith in the ties of tradition and empire. Two years later Melbourne hosted the Olympic Games; the very act of presenting itself as a modern city possessed of a culture sophisticated enough to offer a welcoming reception to athletes from all around the world began to chip away at the Anglo-Australian dominance of public life. The Queen returned almost a decade after her first visit to a rather more muted response, from the public if not the Prime Minister, who was prompted to quote poetry in praise of his Queen. In 1964 the tour of Britons from an altogether different background prompted near-hysteria in some circles. Approximately 300,000 fans lined the streets to greet the Beatles when they toured Adelaide; the numbers in other Australian capital cities were almost as great. New tastes in music and popular culture were becoming a notable public presence.

THE LONG BOOM

It was only from the mid-1950s, a full decade after the conclusion of the war, that it seemed certain another depression would not come in its wake. Old formulas were applied to boost the Australian economy and, for the time being, they worked. There were echoes of the 1920s, with its twin emphases on development and protection. Manufacturing industry expanded with the assistance of high tariffs and provided jobs for the rapidly increasing population. The rural sector grew strong again around the time of the Korean War, when wool exports surged, but in the long term agriculture was in decline and there were stagnant numbers and falling rates of employment in the rural industries in the post-war period. From the 1950s there was a revival of the coal industry for the production of electricity, and new discoveries of mineral commodities such as iron ore, bauxite and nickel and energy sources such as natural gas. These industries were important sources of export income, particularly given the concentration of manufacturing industry on the domestic market. The rapidly industrialising economies of Asia, particularly Japan, were Australia's most important export market by the late 1960s. The Australian economy remained highly protected and regulated by government, and in a buoyant global market it thrived. Labor MP Clyde Cameron quipped in 1964: 'You could grow bananas at the South Pole if you could get a big enough tariff protection'.[10]

The 1950s built the foundation of the unprecedented prosperity more fully enjoyed in the 1960s, yet it seemed a contingent and uncertain process at the time. There was plenty of work, and wages had doubled between the end of the war and the mid-1960s, but those gains were tempered by the rising cost of living. They were also uneven. The incomes of professionals rose more dramatically and quickly than other sectors of the economy. Migrants, especially those from non-English speaking backgrounds, were concentrated in unskilled process and labouring occupations, and exhibited very little occupational mobility. A taxation system that provided rebates for dependent spouses, and continuing female wage inequality despite an improvement in 1950 (when the Arbitration Court increased women's share to seventy-five per cent of the basic male wage), meant that apart from Aborigines, women solely responsible for dependent children remained among the most disadvantaged members of society. Reserve managers and white employers frequently paid their Aboriginal workers only a proportion of the going rate. Furthermore, many Aborigines living under state Protection Acts had the large part of their wages or welfare benefits withheld from them and pooled in a government-controlled trust fund, and they lived only on pocket money or rations. Just as the practice of child removal was later known as creating a 'stolen generation', activists later referred to the money they believed owed to Aboriginal people as 'stolen wages'.

For most of the population, there were improvements to working conditions and these were more prosperous times than anyone could remember. Employers in the most dangerous occupations, including the coal-mining and timber industries, began to pay some heed to new standards for industrial safety. Continuous employment laid the foundation for economic wellbeing even more surely than wage increases. The 1950s and 1960s also saw the introduction of long service leave and the extension of paid annual leave, up from the 1930s initiative of one week to a previously-unimagined luxury: three weeks paid holiday each year. New opportunities for leisure, such as modest annual holidays at the seaside or in a caravan parked by a lake or river, were extended for people unaccustomed to being able to afford it in terms of time or money.

A CONSUMER SOCIETY

This signalled a more profound shift from production to consumption. The economy was reoriented towards domestic consumption, and instead of being exhorted to restraint and self-sacrifice, as they had been during the depression and war years, Australians were now encouraged to spend more. From 1963, savings banks were allowed to offer personal loans to their customers. Many of the new consumer goods that found their way into Australian homes – refrigerators, washing machines and vacuum cleaners – arrived with the assistance of loans, hire purchase and women's wages. The steady expansion of female workforce participation was dominated by the part-time work of married women, twenty per cent of whom worked outside the home by 1961. The radiant housewife with the tiny waist and apron who beamed from magazine advertisements was a middle-class phenomenon, and one that increasingly had its own frustrations. In the early 1960s, American commentator Betty Friedan labelled the 'problem that has no name': the emphasis on individualism, desire and fulfilment in the post-war era was becoming incompatible with a life lived in the service of others.

Self-denial and prudence, once considered the virtues of good citizens, now seemed decidedly out of step with the times. From 1956, a new medium for conveying these messages of contentment through consumption became available. Within a decade, ninety per cent of Australian homes possessed a television, and the furniture was rearranged to face it. The palatial cinemas that had been such a feature of the urban environment now stood forlorn: in Melbourne alone, one third of the cinemas had closed their doors by 1959.[11] The car further reinforced this privatisation of leisure activity, as Australians abandoned public transport usage – at a high point after World War II – for the privilege of travelling on their own timetable.

The expansion of credit in the mid-1950s, combined with the slower rise in car prices when compared with wage gains, meant that car ownership became a reality for more and more households. In 1953 one in five Australians owned a car; by 1962 this had grown to one in three.[12] It was an addiction that had its costs: in 1951, the Chairman of the Australian Road Safety Council pointed out that since 1945, the number of casualties from road accidents was double the number of military casualties sustained in the war. The road toll was a 'vampire which draws the life blood of the nation'.[13] There were also an increasing number of deaths from another addiction that Australians had developed in the mid-century period: smoking. A little over a quarter of women smoked, a number that gradually increased until it had reached one in three by the 1970s; men's smoking rates had peaked in 1945, when seventy-two per cent of them smoked, but by the late 1960s this had pegged back to a bit less than half the adult male population.[14] Workplaces, banks, entertainment venues, public transport and many homes were filled with smoke and ash-trays.

In a cold-war environment, the notion that the state might compel people to refrain from smoking in public places or wear seat belts was anathema to the idea of freedom.

In keeping with the accent on desire that underpinned the consumption of material goods, the pursuit of sexual pleasure was gaining new legitimacy, although its most appropriate and respectable expression remained within marriage, or at least intended marriage partners (around a quarter of all brides were pregnant on their wedding day).[15] Plays like Ray Lawler's *Summer of the Seventeenth Doll*, which premiered in 1955, had an explicitness about sexual matters that shocked respectable audiences but nevertheless reflected a new willingness to broach the issue. An emphasis on companionate marriage, in which husband and wife were expected to work as a team, and to derive both personal fulfilment and sexual pleasure from it, also encouraged frankness. There was a spike in the divorce rate in the immediate post-war period, as hasty wartime unions or those that had not withstood the pressures of war were dissolved, but by the mid-1950s rates declined again for another decade.

Plenty of jobs and the availability of credit to furnish their homes meant that couples married in unprecedented numbers and at a younger age than ever before. By 1952, the birth rate had finally recovered to its pre-depression levels and then exceeded them. Australia, like most other Western nations, was in the grip of a 'baby boom' which peaked in 1961, when Australian women bore an average of 3.5 children. That year also marked the release of the oral contraceptive pill, which in these early years was most likely to be taken by married women determined to limit the size of their family. The birth rate would never be so high again.

BABY-BOOMERS AND THE COMING GENERATION

This was the era of the overflowing classroom. The existing stock of schools and teachers was barely adequate to cope with the new demand for their services. Enrolments in Australian schools doubled, from 1.5 to 3 million students, in the fifteen years after 1953.[16] 'Until the 1950s no-one in our family had gone to school past the age of fourteen', recalled Don Watson, who was raised on a dairy farm in country Victoria.[17] Three of the four Watson children matriculated and two went on to university. Apart from an extensive programme to build new secondary schools and, from the 1960s, the provision of public funds to private schools, governments also sponsored university attendance. The first beneficiaries were

228

war veterans, followed by bright young students enticed to enter the teaching profession by the offer of university scholarships in exchange for education department service upon graduation. 'Earlier generations of workers' sons have been consigned to the Depression scrapheap, recruited for war or sucked into the factories,' one recipient reflected, 'from my generation, postwar Australia happens to be recruiting teachers for babyboomers'.[18] It was the best time in Australian history to be a bright working-class boy.

The importance of tertiary education to Australia's post-war development had been recognised by the establishment of the Australian National University by an act of the federal Parliament in 1946. Nationwide, about 30,000 students were enrolled in a university in 1955, a figure that would triple by the mid-1960s; but the much greater expansion of the tertiary education system did not come until the later 1960s and 1970s, when the baby boom generation had completed their secondary schooling.[19] Compulsory primary education from the late nineteenth century vastly improved literacy rates; the expansion of the tertiary education sector in the mid to late twentieth century would produce another social change: a growing group of men and women alert to possibility, and able to articulate some of the contradictions that beset their society. For some, new professional employment opportunities would constitute a break with their class of origin, with social mobility offering at once better material prospects and new sources of tension between the generations.

For the time being, university students did not seem particularly troublesome. More worrying to conservative commentators were the groups of 'bodgies' and 'widgies', working-class teenagers who dressed in clothes that emulated the styles of their American rock and roll idols and appeared rebellious, sexualised and potentially delinquent. All sorts of reasons were advanced for this phenomenon – working mothers, high wages, comics, horror films shown in cinemas desperate to recoup the audience share lost to television, popular music – but the moral panic had ebbed by the late 1950s. By then, the fashions worn by the sub-culture had become mainstream, and rock and roll had lost a certain edginess by its incorporation into television music programmes designed for family viewing. There had been no actual increase in juvenile crime and full employment blunted any edge of disaffection. Adolescents remained a growing and visible proportion of the population, and as a demographic they had certainly arrived: teenagers were new and important consumers of popular culture and fashion.

There were some who derided popular culture, and thought the aspiration to live in a small but comfortable house on a quarter-acre block was a sentiment devoid of finer feeling and ignorant of the advantages of urban life. The architect Robin Boyd declared in the early 1950s that the suburbs were 'a material triumph and an aesthetic calamity' and bemoaned their distance from facilities and infrastructure. Boyd represented a developing critique that Menzies' Australia was a place that stifled culture and mocked creativity. Describing his feelings about Australia in 1958, the novelist Patrick White referred to the 'Great Australian Emptiness' in which 'the buttocks of cars grow hourly glassier, food means cake and steak, muscles prevail and the march of material ugliness does not raise a quiver from average nerves'.[20] And yet White, who would be awarded the Nobel Prize for Literature, felt that although there was no appreciation for his work in Australia – 'the dingoes are howling unmercifully' – living in the country was essential to his creative process.

Others felt a growing impatience with the way Australia projected itself to the world, and the need for innovative cultural productions that would give expression to the Australian sense of place and its historical particularities. In the early 1960s, the writer Charmian Clift thought Australians were 'desperate to be redefined' and encouraged them to do so before 'the aspic of overseas conception sets firmly around the jolly swagman and the overlander and condemns us to be served up forever in jellied garnish'.[21] The work of composer Peter Sculthorpe, *The Fifth Continent*, offered something like a redefinition in 1963. One listener to the live broadcast from the Hobart Town Hall felt entranced by the 'Australian accent' of the composition and was spellbound as the European instruments became quiet and the sound of the didgeridoo emerged. 'It echoes from some remote distance in space and time,' he recalled 'and what it chants is the song of the Australian earth'.[22]

14

· · · · · · · ·

Dissent and Social Change: 1964–79

The fifteen years after 1964 were among the most tumultuous Australia had yet witnessed. Introducing conscription in 1964 to assist in the fight against 'aggressive communism' certainly generated dissent, but the social upheavals of these years were private as well as public, enabled in part by the prosperity that had typified the post-war period.[1] Security had encouraged confidence and an ability to ask questions, in short, to imagine a different kind of future. For those who had experienced first the depression, then war, the relative stability of the 1950s was an important achievement. The contradictions implicit to it, especially the tensions between conformity and individualism, might sometimes have been experienced as frustration. For the next generation, now coming to adulthood and with strength in numbers, the ambiguities were more difficult to contain and emerged as a willingness to criticise and sometimes even abandon the way of life their parents had worked so hard to achieve. Here was a generational shift, from acceptance to expectation, from knowing your place to knowing your rights, from finding a safe place to finding your 'self'.

This occurred as the very conditions that had produced such confidence, full employment most particularly, began to evaporate. The challenge for governments in this period was one of managing social change and responding to new expectations and demands, without abandoning the responsibility to ensure that the Australian economy could withstand the pressures caused by the return of global economic instability, recession and unemployment. The erosion of certainty left something more interesting in its wake, a new vitality and willingness to embrace locally-produced art, cinema and writing as having something worthwhile to say about Australian life. A more precarious future and, after three decades of non-British immigration, a less homogenous present, encouraged experimentation and breathed new life into the culture.

THE VIETNAM WAR

The ongoing alliance with the United States drew Australia into the most controversial international issue of the era, the Vietnam War. As Britain began to withdraw from the Asia-Pacific, Australia stepped up its support for US operations in Vietnam. Between 1962 and 1972, almost 60,000 Australians served in Vietnam, with the loss of 521 lives. As always, this was a show of loyalty to a major ally, and a self-interested if hypo-thetical move designed to ensure a reciprocal response in the event of a crisis. Initially, Australian participation in Vietnam was a popular cause, with most of the public convinced that it was an essential step in the forward defence against communism. The visit of US President Lyndon B. Johnson to Australia in 1966 drew large and enthusiastic crowds, spurred on by the Prime Minister's remark earlier in the year that it was 'all the way with LBJ', although anti-war protestors made their pres-ence felt. The introduction in 1964 of national service for men turning twenty years old, targeting precisely those baby boomers nurtured on the language of choice and individualism, had begun to diminish support for the war. There was an inherent contradiction in making it compulsory to fight for someone else's freedom. The controversial tactics employed by the United States, including napalm attacks and the blanket bombing of civilian populations, also tarnished the image of a just war.

Although the anti-war movement would come to be dominated by youth, and particularly by radicalised students at university campuses, it initially grew out of pacifist organisations of longer standing and other groups opposed to national service. One of the earliest and most public demonstrations was staged by a group called 'Save Our Sons', a coalition of mothers protesting against the state's new ability to compel their sons to go to war. Veterans of earlier wars who had now embraced pacifism, some ministers of religion, trade unionists, writers and intel-lectuals also became disillusioned with the conduct and context of the war in Vietnam. There was a growing perception of the conflict as a nationalist, anti-imperial struggle. A realisation that communism was not a monolithic force and that the region was not under incipient threat from China or anyone else allowed this view to flourish.

The domino metaphor no longer held the same purchase as it had twenty years earlier. The loss of Australian as well as Vietnamese lives underscored the war's futility, and lent added emotional force to appeals to end the bloodshed. The image of dead soldiers returning from Vietnam in 'green plastic bags' prompted poet Bruce Dawe to write in 1969 that 'they're bringing them home now, too late, too early'.[2] In 1970

Illustration 14.1 'Union of Australian Women in the May Day Parade', 1965
Source: National Library of Australia, nla.pic-vn4395009.

and 1971 hundreds of thousands of Australians participated in moratorium marches that called for a halt to the war in Vietnam. After meeting a Lithuanian girl at the Moratorium march in Melbourne, protestor Val Noone realised the reach of the movement: 'Australia really was changing ... when the children of Eastern European refugees, whose parents had fled communism, were turning out to march'.[3] The United States had already begun a staged withdrawal in 1969, with the Australian government following its lead. Most of the troops had already returned by 1972, when the newly elected Labor Prime Minister called home the few who remained and abolished conscription.

BEING DIFFERENT

Participation in the Vietnam War was divisive and controversial, but it was not alone responsible for breaking the long hold of the conservatives on federal political power in Australia. After Menzies' retirement in 1966, the Liberal Party had chosen an able successor, Harold Holt. He wasted little time in removing some of the shackles of the Menzies era, and began by quietly introducing changes to the *Migration Act* that allowed greater

233

numbers of non-Europeans to remain permanently in Australia. The Labor Party had dropped white Australia from its platform the previous year. Holt's disappearance while swimming at an isolated Victorian beach in the summer of 1967 left a leadership vacuum from which the Liberals did not recover.

The Labor Party was on an opposite trajectory. In 1967 they had elected a dynamic and ambitious barrister, Edward Gough Whitlam, to lead the party forward. Whitlam sensed that the demographic and economic changes in Australia since the end of the war had created constituencies that the Labor Party needed to capture if it were to win office. There were new cultures less focused on class or religion or indeed, on anti-communism, as the basis of political identification. By 1972, almost a third of all employment in Australia could be classified as professional or white-collar work. The old language of working-class solidarity and union strength was unlikely to appeal to them. They were more likely to respond to a political programme commensurate with their upwardly mobile aspirations, such as educational opportunities for their children, dignity in retirement, proper medical treatment and services and infrastructure that would improve the standard of living. Whitlam made clear in 1969 that he believed these opportunities could only be provided by government 'and increasingly in Australia the national government must initiate those opportunities'.[4]

These were still prosperous times and there was no real sense that the economy was in trouble, a frequent trigger for a change of government. For all the jobs and houses and new suburbs that the post-war economic boom had delivered, the government had set little aside for the development of infrastructure. Many of the new suburban subdivisions lacked amenities like footpaths, street lights, kindergartens, libraries and public transport. The need to maintain the parks, gardens, streets and facilities in inner suburbs had been similarly overlooked. Although the suburbs had been mocked in the 1950s by commentators like Robin Boyd, most people continued to live in them and may well have agreed with the view expressed by Adelaide academic Hugh Stretton in 1970: 'Instead of despising the suburbs we should work to improve them'.[5] It was also becoming clear that the boom years of the 1960s had not been kind to everyone. In the midst of prosperity, there were ongoing pockets of poverty, particularly among the aged, invalids, single parents, recent migrants and Indigenous people. Social welfare expenditure had not been a priority for governments of the 1950s and 1960s, and its proportion of the national budget fell throughout the period. Existing benefits, such as child endowment, did not keep pace with inflation.

Grievances about inattention to the services that help make communities more functional combined with mounting frustration that the government simply did not know how to make Australia a better place to live. Donald Horne expressed this critique most famously in 1964 when he described Australia as a 'lucky country run mainly by second-rate people'.[6] Such thinking was also behind the desire among those who viewed themselves as creative, artistic or intellectual to leave what they saw as the stifling mediocrity of Australia for the more cosmopolitan and diverse cities of Europe and the United States. 'In Australia,' one of Barry Humphries' theatrical characters exclaimed, 'we've got culture up to our freckles'.[7] While there was a greater critical mass of people in London and New York interested in new forms of music, art and writing, they made similar criticisms of the pre-war generation's hold on power, the pressure to be 'straight' and the vacuity of consumerism.

Closer to home, the expansion in the numbers of students enrolled in tertiary education exposed them to the ideas of the New Left prominent in academic circles. As the strident anti-communism of the cold war years lifted, some scholars employed neo-Marxist analyses to explain not just the conflict in Vietnam, but also ongoing inequalities in their own society. There was a surge of activism on university campuses throughout the Western world, and Australia was no exception, as students embraced these critiques of capitalist and consumer society and searched for alternative structures. The black rights movement in the United States and the women's liberation movement were also important influences.

Those in authority, who were often maligned in this period as 'the establishment' – the government, the education system, churches, the older generation – were seen to have squandered the opportunity to produce a better world, and had instead created a society riven with continuing violence, inequality, hypocrisy and exploitation. Oppression could assume many forms, and alongside the militarism that was derided by the anti-war movement, consumerism, racism, sexism and homophobia emerged as important topics on the reform agenda. Exploitation could also extend to the natural world, and concern about the environment received resurgent interest. An extended campaign in the late 1960s and early 1970s to stop the inundation of Lake Pedder in Tasmania was unsuccessful, but it did herald the arrival of the world's first 'green' political party. The lessons learned in this campaign contributed to victory in their next, which ultimately prevented the building of the Franklin Dam in Tasmania in the early 1980s. Photographic images of the Tasmanian wilderness were used extensively in the campaign, and contributed to the development of Australians' appreciation of their natural environment.

With an established narrative about the shortcomings of their society, it now became much more possible to choose to live differently from one's parents. Couples increasingly chose to live together before marriage, and divorce rates rose throughout the 1960s to the point where one in three marriages contracted in the early 1970s ended in divorce.[8] Gay men and lesbian women lived more openly than they had in the past, and their communities were a more visible public presence, especially in the inner cities. In other respects, there was a return to some of the demographic patterns of earlier times, with a rising age at marriage and at least one in five people choosing not to marry at all. Near universal marriage at an early age turned out to be a post-war generational quirk, not the harbinger of future trends.

There was a rediscovery of the inner city by those whose parents had abandoned it, and a new appreciation for its more diverse cultures and streetscapes. Extended, shared households were formed there, and with the help of the contraceptive pill greater sexual freedoms were explored outside the confines of marriage, although a frequent complaint among female members in these circles was that gendered assumptions about housework and child-care were difficult to shift. There was also greater experimentation with illicit drugs, although this too could have its costs. 'For a while the fires die down in you,' Sydney poet Michael Dransfield reflected, 'until you die down in the fires'.[9] Helen Garner's *Monkey Grip* (1977) gave literary expression to these new lifestyles, and provided a window on to them for the majority who still lived a more domestic, suburban existence.

At its heart, this was still a capitalist, consumer society, and the clothing, hairstyles and aesthetic that accompanied the counter-cultural lifestyle were trends not missed by large corporations, who soon filled boutiques and department stores with all the requisite accessories. There were plenty of suburban parties in the 1960s and 1970s where people wore caftans, admired macramé owl wall-hangings and sat on tie-dyed cushions without ever dreaming of calling the hostess a bourgeois capitalist bitch. Yet the counter-culture was not merely style without substance, it was an aesthetic and world view flexible enough to have its softer edges absorbed by the broader society. This was a more relaxed time, when standards of dress, entertaining and domestic life became less formal and when difference was more likely to be viewed as an expression of individuality than deviance. Changing fashions, which moved from the tight bodices and collars and ties of the 1950s, to fabrics and styles that moved with the body, reflected some of the new freedoms. Personal grooming changed too, with the tidy sets and short back and sides of the 1950s giving way to free-flowing locks and, for men, facial hair.

Living collectively, with friends or a lover, without excessive devotion to material goods, was also easier to celebrate and maintain when it was a conscious choice rather than the consequence of thwarted opportunity or endemic poverty. This was accompanied by a recognition that an alternative lifestyle was to some extent a matter of choice, but that broader inequalities relating to sex and race, for instance, would require structural change in order to be addressed. The new generation ultimately arrived at the same conclusion as older challengers to the established order. It would require legislative change – action by the state – for marginalised groups to achieve equality. Moreover, the state may also have a role to play in ensuring a better standard of living for all its citizens. This wasn't exactly a return to Metin's socialism without doctrine, but it was a renewed willingness to embrace the ameliorative capacities of the state after decades of cold-war inspired demonisation of anything that faintly resembled it.

THE WHITLAM YEARS

A social democrat rather than a trade unionist, a federalist, and a man who excelled at articulating how Australia had changed, Whitlam's appeal to the 'men and women of Australia' saw him win office in December 1972. A television advertisement with pop singers and actors belting out 'It's Time', and Whitlam's appearance on the campaign trail in slacks and a tight T-shirt with the same slogan emblazoned across his chest, signaled the sense of generational change that his victory embodied. The fact that Whitlam himself was already middle-aged, and looked a bit awkward in the T-shirt, simply underscored how long the previous government had clung to power.

Apart from swift action in relation to ending Australia's commitment in Vietnam, the new government moved quickly to establish its programme of reform. It increased federal funding to schools, abolished tuition fees for university, officially repudiated the white Australia policy, significantly increased government spending on Indigenous affairs, recognised China, introduced equal pay for women and passed legislation providing for no-fault divorce. The rapidity of the changes was as impressive as their reach; in terms of women's earnings, for example, Figure 14.1 shows something of the immediate impact. It was nowhere near equality, but it was better than ever before. There was also

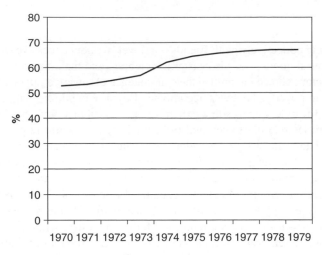

Figure 14.1 Women's average weekly earnings as a percentage of men's, 1970–9

Source: W. Vamplew (ed.) *Australians: Historical Statistics* (Sydney: Fairfax, Syme and Weldon Associates, 1987), p. 157.

money for urban renewal and suburban infrastructure, funding assistance for community organisations, pensions for single parents, and the introduction of a universal health plan known as Medibank. It was a programme premised on continued economic growth, and one that in some, but certainly not all, respects built upon incremental but significant changes to policy initiated by the previous government.

The economy held good for the first few years of Labor's tenure. There had been developments in the 1960s that began to impact on the precarious formula that held Australia's economic equation together. The growing strength of the European Economic Community (EEC), with preferential trade terms for member organisations (which included, after 1973, the United Kingdom) and policies that encouraged overproduction, began to limit the markets for Australia's export goods and drive prices down. Australian manufacturing industry, relying as it did on high protection tariffs, was increasingly inefficient and internationally uncompetitive. Economists acknowledged that this structure had a use-by date that was fast approaching. There had been efforts to review and reform the policy of industry protection since the 1960s, but governments were reluctant to upset vested manufacturing interests, despite the disadvantage to other sectors, such as rural industries, that resulted from it. Several industries still enjoyed extremely high levels of protection that had been put in place to survive the economic crises of the early 1930s, and had not been reviewed since.

The Whitlam government, elected on a reform platform, took the advice of economists who had long recommended a reduction in the tariff. Like many other actions of this government, this was a dramatic change: in 1973 there was a twenty-five per cent reduction in tariffs across the board. Combined with an upwards revaluation in the dollar and wage gains, it was a heady brew. Imports became cheaper, and firms unused to competition began to cut jobs. There were plans in place to deal with the inevitable unemployment that would result from reform, but the situation spun out of control. The timing of economic reform could not have been worse; 1973 was also the year that the long boom of the post-war period ended. The US economy began to unravel, beset first by inflation in the wake of the Vietnam War, and then by an energy crisis prompted by the Organization of the Petroleum Exporting Countries (OPEC) in the Middle East. Embargos on oil in response to Western support for Israel in the Yom Kippur War of 1973, followed by price hikes of over 100 per cent, drove oil-dependent economies into an inflationary spiral. Recession followed, and the combination of a stagnant economy and rampant inflation saw a new term enter the language, 'stagflation'. The profound disruption to trade and investment networks had serious repercussions for an export-driven economy dependent on foreign investment, such as Australia's, despite its virtual self-sufficiency in fossil fuels. Unemployment, virtually unknown for a generation, returned.

The dire economic situation was a combination of poor timing and belated recognition of the extent of the crisis; the political catastrophe Labor found itself in by late 1975 was the combination of a hostile Senate and some problems that were more of its own making. Whitlam's leadership style was both the key to his political success and a factor in his downfall. Uncompromising, domineering, a visionary who thought detail beneath him, once in office Whitlam was unlikely to consult with key stakeholders in ways that may have soothed some of their concerns about rapid change or led to fruitful compromise. One of Whitlam's ministers described the style as 'Government by tantrum', and it did not facilitate a strong sense of either a leadership or a ministerial team. Consequently, several ministers operated as lone wolves and found themselves embroiled in scandals that undermined confidence in the government. When this extended to an attempt to raise financial loans without parliamentary approval, the Opposition triggered a crisis.

239

Throughout its two brief terms in office, the Labor government faced a Senate dominated by the Liberal-National Country Party coalition. The Opposition was tireless in its hostility to the programme Whitlam sought to implement, and struggled to accept the Labor Party as a legitimate national government with a mandate to implement its reforms. By 1975, its leader was Malcolm Fraser, an Oxford-educated career politician with family links to the pastoral industry. He initiated a long parliamentary stalemate, in response to the loans scandal, in which the Coalition refused to pass bills that would give the government the revenue it needed to function. Refusing to accede to a demand for an election, Whitlam was removed from office when he was, contrary to all constitutional precedent, dismissed by the Governor General.

The sacking of an elected head of state by the unelected official representative of the Queen sent shockwaves around the country. Television footage of Whitlam standing on the steps of Parliament House, surrounded by cheering supporters, glowering with defiance and declaring 'Well may we say God save the Queen, because nothing will save the Governor General' conveys some of the shock and anger the dismissal generated. Outrage in some circles was not enough to overcome the perception in many others that this was a failed government, and Fraser was voted in as Prime Minister with a landslide election victory to the Coalition.

RIGHTS AND WRONGS

Some of the changes that had been made in the Whitlam years drew on incremental shifts in policy and public understandings that had a longer gestation. The Aboriginal civil rights movement, which had been established in the inter-war years, for instance, had continued to be active in the 1950s and 1960s, and drew new supporters from the ranks of white university students. Wary of attracting unwanted international attention for their racial policies, the federal government granted voting rights to Aborigines in 1962. Five years later over ninety per cent of Australian voters agreed at a referendum that the two references to Aborigines in the Australian Constitution should be deleted, thereby giving the federal government power to legislate for Indigenous people and to count them in the census. Although the 1967 Referendum did not grant Aborigines citizenship, a commonly held misconception, it did perform important symbolic work by including them in the Australian nation. Its consequences for the daily lives and future prospects for Aboriginal people were less clear. Most states (apart from Queensland) had by that time dismantled discriminatory legislation. In 1966 the Arbitration Commission granted equal pay to Aboriginal pastoral workers, although many lost their jobs, and by extension their residence on traditional lands, when employers in the cattle industry phased out Aboriginal labour as a consequence. That same year the Gurindji people from Wave Hill in the Northern Territory walked off in protest at their wages and conditions, and rolled a land rights claim into their wages case by insisting on the double injustice of exploitation and dispossession. A petition they presented to the Governor General stated: 'Our people have lived here from time immemorial and our culture, myths, dreaming and sacred places have evolved in this land ... we feel that morally the land is ours and should be returned to us'.[10]

Land rights began to displace civil rights as the focus of the Aboriginal protest movement as the 1960s progressed. The Gurindji and Yolgnu people from the Gove peninsula in Arnhem Land became central to campaigns in the late 1960s and 1970s to restore 'tribal land' to Aborigines living in remote regions of Australia. This focus meant the issue of restitution for Aboriginal people living in the southern parts of Australia, who had found it more difficult to retain ongoing associations with their land in the face of dense white occupation, remained an open question. A land rights petition organised by the Federal Council for the Advancement of Aborigines and Torres Strait Islanders in 1969 managed to gather 100,000 signatures. The hopes of this campaign were dashed in 1971, when the Northern Territory Supreme Court ruled that the Yolgnu people did not have a propriety interest in the land on the Gove peninsula because Australian common law had never recognised native title to the land.

The following Australia Day an Aboriginal Tent Embassy was set up on the lawn in front of Parliament House in Canberra to protest the ongoing denial of land rights to Indigenous people. 'While this nation does not recognize and make substantial compensation and land restoration gestures to Aborigines', the Aboriginal activist Kevin Gilbert insisted in 1973, 'then in the minds of all blacks, the Australian claim to nationhood continues to rest on injustice and hypocrisy'.[11] Gilbert embodied a new strand of activism in the Aboriginal protest movement, a younger generation inspired by the identity politics of the era and the 'black power' movement in the United States, who began to foreground cultural identification as an essential element in the politics of Aboriginal protest. There was a concomitant interest in self-determination, and henceforth white involvement in Aboriginal political movements became more problematic and difficult to negotiate.

241

While the courts continued to deny native title, some steps were taken by the federal government to address Aboriginal grievances. Legislation was passed in 1976 that allowed Aboriginal groups to make claims if they had ongoing 'traditional associations' with their land in the Northern Territory. The Wave Hill claim had been settled the previous year, when Gough Whitlam met the Gurindji leader Vincent Lingiari and poured into his hands 'part of the earth itself as a sign that this land will be the possession of you and your children forever'.[12] It was still only a small part of the Australian earth that could be subject to claim by Aboriginal groups, and the larger issues of native title, self-determination, restitution and the socio-economic condition of Indigenous people remained the subject of intense debate and concern. In the mid-1960s Aboriginal infant mortality was among the highest in the world, and although the creation of Indigenous health programmes and services saw some improvement, by the early 1980s Indigenous infant mortality was still two and a half times that of the Australian average. Despite a commitment in 1973 to raise the health standards of Indigenous people to the level enjoyed by the rest of the Australian population within a decade, average life expectancy for Indigenous men and women remained at least twenty years lower than anyone else in the country, and Figure 14.2 gives an indication of what seemed an intractable economic disadvantage.[13]

A recasting of the relationship with Indigenous people in Australia's external territory was more rapid and, by some reckonings, conducted with undue haste. Since World War II Australia had governed Papua New Guinea under a trusteeship agreement with the United Nations, until such time that the territory was considered fit for self-government. There had been significant subsidies for the territory's development, and reforms in wages, education and health, but the economy was frail and the legacies of long colonial rule ran deep. In the post-war period there was bipartisan agreement on the need for self-determination in Papua New Guinea but the timetable was unclear. Whitlam's rise to power hastened the path to independence. 'The whole world believes that ... we run one of the world's last colonies,' he told a gathering at Port Moresby in 1971, concluding that this leaned 'heavily indeed on the world's goodwill and on Australia's credibility'.[14] Within two years, Whitlam's government had granted Papua New Guinea self-government and it achieved full independence in 1975. This was a mixed blessing. In 2010, the Australian government still contributed aid that accounted for twenty per cent of the national budget, well over a third of the population lived below the poverty line, and the country had the highest HIV/AIDs rates in the region.[15] It was a profile not uncommon among countries struggling to overcome their colonial past.

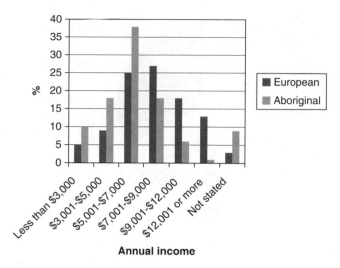

Figure 14.2   Annual personal income for European and Aboriginal men, 1976
Source: John S. Western, *Social Inequality in Australian Society* (Melbourne: Macmillan, 1983), p. 208.

Very few Papua New Guineans entered Australia after the white Australia policy was relaxed in the 1960s, and by that time the supply of immigrants from eastern and southern Europe was about exhausted. Asians with professional and technical skills had been welcomed since 1966, although they still formed a small proportion of the whole. Turks, Syrians and Lebanese began to arrive in Australia in greater numbers, although as Figure 14.3 shows they still formed a small proportion of the whole. By 1971, Australia's population had reached almost 13 million people, and migrants and their children born in Australia accounted for about 60 per cent of the population growth since the end of the war.[16] While officially abandoning white Australia was an important symbolic change to immigration policy, the seeds of a more ethnically diverse Australia had been sown well before that, by the sheer volume of non-British people who had arrived in the 1950s and 1960s. The post-war migration programme had transformed Australia, and it was clear by the mid-1960s that the policy of assimilation was effectively marginalising new immigrants and not catering to their needs.

Deficiencies with English language, in particular, meant that education, health care and dealing with bureaucracy were difficult for migrants and their children. In addition, these services contained no recognition

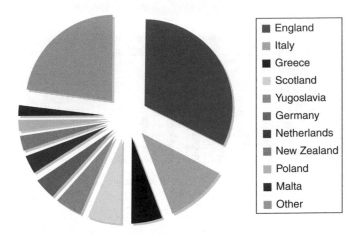

Figure 14.3   Birthplaces of the foreign-born population, 1971

Source: Australian Bureau of Statistics, 'Australian Historical Population Statistics, 2006' (3105.0.65.001), at http://www.abs.gov.au.

that cultural difference may preclude participation in certain practices or events. By the early 1970s, the new Labor government decided that a term originally coined in Canada, 'multiculturalism', with its implication that ethnic and cultural diversity were welcome features of national life, was a more positive approach to a large and continuing migrant presence. There was now greater representation for peak migrant bodies, interpreter services, and funding for initiatives to assist people from 'non-English speaking backgrounds' in their new home. To reinforce their message that racial discrimination should not be tolerated and was now, in fact, illegal, in 1975 the Parliament passed the *Racial Discrimination Act*, finally ratifying a UN convention to which Australia had been signatory nine years earlier. Legislation outlawing racial discrimination did not mean that it disappeared from the daily lives of migrants and Indigenous people, or even from their interactions with officials, but it did send an important message to the community that they should not assume absolution for intolerance.

The 1970s were the twilight years of a feature that had dominated Australian immigration programmes since the early twentieth century: the provision of assisted passages to immigrants in order to boost Australia's population. In the early 1970s, fifty-eight per cent of immigrants still arrived with government assistance; by the end of the decade less than a quarter did so.[17] This was a time when demographers and scientists who had long questioned Australia's carrying capacity, given the relatively low proportions of fertile land and its susceptibility to drought, began to receive a greater public hearing. The unlimited population growth was no longer necessarily considered a good thing, and indeed the Whitlam government abolished the two per cent annual population growth target that had been policy since the end of World War II. There has never again been an explicit goal for population growth in Australia, although some growth is assumed through annual immigration targets. The death knell of the extensive assisted immigration programme, however, came with the return of worldwide economic recession in the early 1970s. Despite the Whitlam government's reputation for the reform of immigration policy and procedure, immigration fell substantially during Labor's term in office. Since that time, there has been no long-term, clearly articulated population building strategy in Australia, and immigration policy is more subject to changes in the economic climate, refugee crises and the ideologies of particular governments.[18]

By the end of the 1970s, the immigration programme began to assume some of the features that would predominate for the rest of the century, most particularly family reunion and the admission of people as refugees and on humanitarian grounds. The Fraser government did not reverse the decision to end white Australia; indeed after the end of the Vietnam War in 1975, it oversaw the first large-scale Asian immigration of the twentieth century, with 90,000 Indo-Chinese refugees settling in Australia by the early 1980s. The majority of Vietnamese migrants arrived on aeroplanes, although it was the 'boat people', who had endured a hazardous journey across the oceans, who captured the public imagination. The new government also embraced the policy of multiculturalism. It expanded the ethnic radio stations introduced under Labor by establishing the Special Broadcasting Service in 1978, in order to provide multilingual radio and television services for the now substantial numbers of people from non-English speaking backgrounds.

An official toleration for difference was matched by a new nationalism, apparent on film and television in particular, that reasserted the central Anglo-Australian values of egalitarianism and mateship. The arts were revived with a substantial injection of government funding and the formation, in 1975, of the Australia Council and the Australian Film Commission. Some films, such as *My Brilliant Career*, *Breaker Morant* and *Gallipoli,* chose historical topics to pursue contemporary questions about gender relations, imperialism and militarism. Films exploring race relations, such as *The Chant of Jimmie Blacksmith*, did not enjoy the box office success of movies that portrayed Australians in a more sympathetic light. By the end of the 1970s, television mini-series like *Against the Wind* reprised the nation's convict origins in ways that were more in accordance with Australians' view of themselves as heroic battlers. For the time being, the most public and successful of these cultural productions spoke to the concerns of Anglo Australia. Even if they countenanced a reasonable dash of self-deprecation, these films still failed to consider what the experience of those on the periphery might say about the centre, or how they contributed to the evolution of it.

Music, dominated by imported products for most of the post-war years, reflected a new confidence that Australian audiences may wish to hear the vernacular. On radio, the music of the Masters Apprentices, Daddy Cool, AC/DC, and Skyhooks – whose album *Living in the 70s* evoked Australian youth's experiences of drugs and sex with references to haunts in Sydney and Melbourne – expressed the variety of styles that appealed to the vast youth market. Live bands in pubs and clubs were their preference for entertainment; those who preferred classical music, and who could afford the seats, enjoyed the new arts centres that opened throughout the country in this period, the most notable of them the Sydney Opera House in 1973.

By the end of the 1970s the culture was flourishing but the economy was floundering. After 1977, unemployment did not fall below five per cent for the rest of the decade. 'Australia stands poised on the threshold of the 1980s,' declared Robert J. Hawke, the President of the Australian Council of Trade Unions, 'more uncertain of the future ... than at any other period in its history'. A unionist of academic rather than shop-floor pedigree, Hawke argued that 'full employment was the cement that held our society together' and predicted that as the cement crumbled 'it is not difficult to perceive the emergence of two societies – the employed and the unemployed'.[19] While the metaphor may have been dramatic, Hawke was not wrong when he identified unemployment as an issue that would dominate the next decade and then some.

15

$\cdots\cdots\cdots$

Global Nation: 1980–2010

In September 1980, the heads of government of sixteen Asian and Pacific Commonwealth countries met in New Delhi to discuss international political issues, world economic trends and the potential for regional cooperation. Prime Minister Malcolm Fraser represented Australia. Fully expecting to discuss his position on Kampuchea, where Vietnamese forces had recently deposed the Pol Pot regime, and his attitude to the Soviet presence in Afghanistan, Fraser instead found himself defending Australia's highly protected economy. The Prime Minister of Singapore, Lee Kuan Yew, accused Fraser of being 'too narrow minded' on the issue of industry protection, and chided him that Australians would become the 'loafers of the South Pacific' unless they opened up to economic competition.[1] The same year, two futurists published a book, *Will She Be Right? The Future of Australia*, which argued that Australia was in danger of becoming the 'poor white trash of Asia'.[2]

Loafers, white trash: the visions of Australia's future offered up in the early 1980s were a nightmare inversion of the optimistic images of a racially strong, economically secure working people that dominated public discussion at the start of the twentieth century. The challenges of the 1980s and 1990s were to reform the economy, renegotiate regional relationships and reconcile with the nation's Indigenous people. Becoming a global nation required local pain, as the economy adjusted to structural changes. By the 2000s, anxiety about terrorism in the wake of the attacks on the United States in September 2001 meant that a new paradigm emerged about the need to maintain national security, in ways that reignited debate about cultural diversity and territorial integrity. While the global financial crisis of 2007 plunged the economies of the United States, Europe and the United Kingdom into dire straits, Australia's economic reforms of the prior twenty years saw it weather the financial storm without the unemployment and institutional collapses that engulfed other societies.

Reimagining Australia as an Asia-Pacific nation, a rethinking of its past and concern about its present, prompted questions about what it meant to be Australian. Internationalisation of the economy, new communication technologies such as the Internet, and the increasing affordability of overseas travel meant that Australia and Australians were not as isolated as they once had been. Owing to its long and successful immigration programme, Australia by the late twentieth century was one of the world's most diverse societies, at least in its cities, which is where most of its people lived. Still, in the era of globalisation, the persistence of localism was a notable feature. In Australia, one form this took was the return of the country's military history to the centre of nationalist sentiment.

ECONOMIC RATIONALISM

In the early 1980s, both unemployment and inflation in Australia were running at over ten per cent. Australia's ongoing economic woes opened the door to new ways of thinking about the economy and the market emanating from the United States and the United Kingdom, economies that were also in difficulty at this time. On a visit to Australia in 1981 the feted American economist Milton Friedman was overtly critical of the highly protected Australian economy: 'What sense does it make for the Australian to pay twice as much as the world price for automobiles?', he asked. Imported vehicles would be cheaper to consumers than locally produced cars. Hence, economic reform was in Australia's self-interest. 'Of your own free will, you are condemning yourselves to a lower standard of life than you need have', Friedman concluded.[3]

As the long boom ended across the Western world, the post-war faith in a strong public sector and direct government intervention in fiscal policy as the best path to prosperity crumbled. Furthermore, the development of data processing technology at this time meant that national borders became increasingly irrelevant to money markets, as capital moved more freely and quickly around the globe than ever before. Neoliberal economic theories emerged as the clarion call for a new era in global finance. An embellishment of older-style laissez-faire economics, tempered by an assumption that there would always be market fluctuations and accompanying unemployment, neo-liberalism saw a return to free-market economics. Trade liberalisation, deregulation and the privatisation of state-owned enterprises were some of the key features of a rejuvenated faith in the private sector as the driver of efficiency and economic growth. This was a theory, just as much as Keynesianism had been, no matter how much its adherents presented it as the gospel truth. Exactly how equity was to be maintained under these new models remained an open question. In Britain, this way of thinking and operating was called Thatcherism, in the United States, where Milton Friedman was a key advisor to government, it was known as Reaganomics. In Australia, it was called 'economic rationalism'.

One of the ironies of the era was that economic rationalism, which in the United States and Britain found its greatest advocates in conservative politicians, was a programme implemented in Australia by a Labor government. Given the state of the economy, the Liberal–National Party Coalition could not retain government when it went to the polls in 1983. That election was won by the ALP, led by the charismatic and personable 'Bob' Hawke, whose years running the Australian Council of Trade Unions gave him extensive contacts in both the business world and with union leaders. Suited up, tanned, his infamous lick of silver hair tamed for the cameras, Hawke was still remembered by the Australian public as the campaigner who appeared on TV like a 'retired bodgie, all checks and stripes' and sideburns, with a broad accent and passion for consensus.[4] Hawke was more of an everyman than was Fraser, his potentially alienating intellectual pedigree as a Rhodes scholar mitigated by his student beer-drinking record. The clever larrikin is a difficult act to pull off, but Hawke managed it.

Further developing the 'two nations' metaphor he had used in 1979, Hawke led the ALP to victory with the slogan 'Bringing Australia Together'. Along with his Treasurer, Paul Keating, Hawke believed that the only way to ensure Australia's economic future was to accommodate both labour and industry in the process of reform and restructuring. In this, they differed from the course pursued in Thatcher's United Kingdom, where the 1980s was dominated by intense conflict between the government and unions and bitter and disabling strikes. Wary of Whitlam's reputation for ineptitude in relation to the economy, the new ALP government was keen to appear cutting-edge and informed in relation to economic challenges.

In an effort to bring inflation under control, and to model its consensus approach to change, the new government sponsored a series of summits and councils designed to negotiate changes to the economy, the tax system and industrial relations. The first of these, the National Economic Summit held in April 1983, Hawke described as 'a first step towards our great national goals of national reconciliation, national reconstruction and national recovery'.[5] In the 1980s, 'reconciliation' was not about

Australia's Indigenous population, but meant an attempt to end to the decade-long disputes between unions and employers. The unions had been persuaded to accept a Prices and Incomes Accord in which they agreed to restrict strikes and demands for wage rises in exchange for an improved social wage, which included increased government spending on welfare, education and health. The government reinstated a universal health insurance scheme, Medicare, much as Whitlam had intended the original Medibank, in distinct contrast to the United States, where health care remained firmly in the private sector and with accompanying problems of access and affordability.

The early Accords reconfirmed the importance of centralised wage fixing to the management of industrial relations in Australia, yet within a decade that too was seen as a model too restrictive if Australia wished to maximise its economic competitiveness. A distinctive feature of Australia's economic system was about to be dismantled. Talk about productivity, flexibility and efficiency replaced an older language about the basic wage and the dignity of labour. Industry-wide, standardised wage deals were now seen as unable to distinguish between productive and under-performing workers, and to contribute to inflationary pressures by pushing up wages across the board. Wage rises must be linked to productivity improvement, and this could only be determined if each enterprise made its own arrangements with its own workers. By 1991, this process was known as enterprise bargaining, and it began to replace industry-wide agreements. These were still collective agreements, after a fashion, because unions most often represented employees in their negotiations, but the centralised system that had dominated Australian industrial relations for almost a century had gone.

THE 1980S: BOOM AND BUST

As the 1980s progressed, Australia signalled to the rest of the world its desire to participate more fully in the global economy. The abandonment of exchange controls in December 1983, known as the 'floating of the dollar', meant that the market rather than the government would henceforth determine the value of the Australian dollar in relation to the world's key currencies. Once the domino of exchange controls had fallen, other key features of the highly regulated financial system followed in quick succession. Until the 1980s, Australian banks were restricted in the amount of money they could lend to customers. The bank manager was an important figure in the local community, and most often a trusted financial adviser. After the float of the dollar, foreign banks were allowed into the country and banks began to more aggressively compete for business. By the end of the decade, this had led to a decline in lending standards, a bewildering array of products, and an excessive expansion of credit, some of it in foreign currency. With the newly fluctuating value of the Australian dollar, this was, potentially, an incendiary situation. Justice Andrew Rogers of the NSW Supreme Court later described foreign currency loans as 'greed fuelled by ignorance'.[6]

There was an expectation in Australia, and in other Western nations, that the high inflation of the 1970s would continue. This contributed to a boom in asset prices, on the assumption that inflation would erode the real value of borrowed money, but increase the value of assets acquired through debt. In the United States the ethos of the 1980s was encapsulated in the Hollywood film *Wall Street*, in which the main character contended that 'greed, for the want of a better word, is good'. The more relaxed fashions of the 1970s gave way to the power suits, high collars, taffeta dresses, big hair and dramatic make-up that reflected the new emphasis on consumption and artifice. In Australia, the helicopters, lavish parties and exponential expansion of the businesses of men like Alan Bond and Christopher Skase were typical of some of the decade's excesses. Bond bankrolled Australian victory in the 1983 America's Cup yacht race, ending 132 years of American dominance, and unleashed a wave of nationalist sentiment set to the tune of Men at Work's popular 1981 song 'Down Under'. Victory was symbolic for a small nation keen to take on the world, and a good news story during a period in which the benefits of economic reform seemed uncertain, and rural residents of eastern Australia suffered through a crippling drought. Struggling farmers were among those who would live to regret refinancing their properties by taking out a foreign currency loan.

Asset bubbles are bound to burst and when this one did, both internationally and within Australia, following the stock market crash of 1987, the creditors came calling. In some cases, the fall of the entrepreneurs was as spectacular as their rise. Financial failure was widespread and fed into the recession of 1990-91. The inability of major borrowers to repay loans led to the collapse of several merchant banks, and the state banks of Victoria and South Australia, among others. In the previous few years, interest rates had climbed as high as 18 per cent, as monetary policy was tightened in an effort to curb the spree. These were not, in fact, unprecedented rates, nor even the highest the country had seen, but in a deregulated sector the increases now flowed through to household mortgages. Unemployment rose as business strained under the pressure of high interest rates and faltering confidence. Although he was pilloried for describing this as the 'recession we had to have', and there was much debate about interests rates staying too high for too long, Paul Keating had been correct in identifying the recession as marking the end of almost two decades of high inflation.[7] In the 1980s inflation averaged eight per cent; by the 1990s it had fallen dramatically to an average of two per cent.[8]

The recession also contributed to the declining popularity of Bob Hawke, who faced a strong internal challenge from Keating, an ambitious career politician who had played an important role in the restructuring of the Australian economy. Eager to implement his broader vision for Australia, what he would come to call the 'big picture', Keating was installed by his party as Prime Minister as the result of a leadership challenge in December 1991. Keating believed that despite the recession, Australia should 'keep up the pace of change'. The nation's economic future would be secured by establishing more binding economic and cultural ties within its own Asia-Pacific region.

In order to facilitate more extensive trading relationships, Australia had begun lowering tariffs on imported goods. There was already an Association of Southeast Asian Nations (ASEAN) designed to foster economic growth in the region, but it did not include Australia or the powerful economies of the United States and Japan. In the name of trade liberalisation, in 1989 there was an initial Asia-Pacific Economic Cooperation (APEC) forum meeting in Canberra, where ministers from eight Asian nations, including Japan, Indonesia and Korea, and Australia, New Zealand, Canada and the United States met to discuss the possibility of greater collaboration. By the early 1990s, the APEC economies conducted more than half their trade with each other, and increasingly perceived it to be mutually beneficial to form a common position in relation to the size and scope of the EEC and to enter into a multilateral trading system.

The rapidly industrialising economies of Indonesia, Taiwan and Korea were important markets for Australia's commodities exports, but Australia was keen to export products and services to Asia beyond raw materials. Malaysian President Mahathir was circumspect about the aims of APEC, and his refusal to attend the 1993 summit in Seattle prompted Prime Minister Keating to label him a 'recalcitrant', an insult that soured relations between Australia and Malaysia.[9] In 1994, at Bogor, Indonesia, this hurdle was overcome, and APEC members signed a 'declaration of common resolve' rather than a binding treaty, in which they agreed to work towards 'free and open trade and investment in the Asia-Pacific'.[10] Through economic reform and strengthening regional trade relationships, Australia avoided its predicted fate as the 'white trash' of the South Pacific, and had arrived at the position where its Prime Minister was photographed, along with other APEC leaders, wearing a batik shirt at Bogor.

INTERNATIONALISING THE ECONOMY

By the early 1990s, most industry protection had been phased out to minimal levels, and by the end of that decade Australia had been transformed into one of the world's most open trading economies. This led to productivity gains and greater choice for consumers, who were now able to purchase an increasing number of imported consumer goods more cheaply than ever before. Households were now more likely to have washing machines, microwave ovens and television sets made in Korea or China rather than in Australia by a local manufacturer. The acquisition of new consumer goods was not the event it had been as recently as the 1970s, when all the children in the street would know if a household had acquired a colour television set. Multi-national corporations began to replace independent businesses as local shopping strips and shopping centres hosted an ever-increasing number of outlets for retail, service and food franchises. This was a society that on the one hand expanded choices, and on the other narrowed the number of businesses that actually offered them. The independent retailers that remained recast themselves as boutique, alternative or family-run, in order to differentiate themselves from the chains and to inspire custom based on a dedication to diversity and difference.

The privatisation of formerly state-owned enterprises like banks, telecommunications authorities, airports and utilities continued apace on the assumption that competition encouraged efficiency. Customers everywhere faced a new and bewildering range of contracts for basic services like telephones and electricity. The savvy might cut themselves a good deal, but the elderly, infirm, or poorly educated now had a new capacity to make bad choices that might cost them dearly. State-owned enterprises may have been slow and inefficient, but they possessed a certain transparency and commitment to affordability that with hindsight seemed valuable. Universities continued as federally funded institutions, but in keeping with the user-pays philosophy, fees were reintroduced for domestic tertiary students in 1989 as a contribution to the cost of their education. Full fee-paying places for international students had become available in 1986, and the number enrolled in education institutions had reached almost 200,000 by the end of the 1990s.[11] International students made a significant contribution to the income, diversification and internationalisation of the Australian higher education sector, and transformed it into one of Australia's largest industries.

In the 1990s, most of these international students came from the Asian 'tiger' economies of countries such as Singapore and Hong Kong. Yet globalisation had an uneven impact on the region. Many more people in the Asia-Pacific worked in the industries that supplied Australia with its new consumer goods in conditions that came under increasing scrutiny as the century drew to a close. By that time, an international anti-globalisation movement was critical of the growth of large, multi-national corporations, which exploited the human and natural resources of the less well-regulated and highly indebted economies of the developing world.

The costs of economic reform were local as well as global. Even though reconstruction of the economy had been essential for effective Australian participation in global markets, there was a price to pay. Unemployment most particularly affected workers in industries that had been deregulated and subject to significant reforms, such as white goods, clothing, textiles and footwear. The Gissing clothing factory, which had operated in the regional town of Maitland for over forty-five years, shut its doors and retrenched its workforce in late 1991, after deciding to shift its production base to the Philippines, where workers were paid six dollars a day.[12] It was a situation repeated in regions and towns throughout the country. Manufacturing industries that involved a large metals component, such as the car industry, were also hard hit. The decline of manufacturing in the north-east of the United States had led to its designation as a 'rust belt'; by the early 1990s this was a term also applied to the southern states of Australia, particularly Victoria, South Australia and Tasmania, where much of this industry was located.

After falling for much of the 1980s, by the early 1990s unemployment peaked again at eleven per cent, the highest rate since the Great Depression. In December 1991, almost a third of school leavers registered for unemployment benefits.[13] That year, newspapers published league tables of the worst-hit states, suburbs and regions. Increased work intensity, wage restraint and significant growth in part-time and casual work saw unemployment rates fall again to about six per cent by 2000. Profit share for employers increased under these conditions, so that the 1990s also witnessed increasing inequality between the profits drawn by employers and the wages they were willing to pay to employees. The 1990s were a decade when the rich got richer.

In keeping with the economic rationalist model that dominated thinking on the economy, Australia's welfare system was subject to a full-scale review in the 1980s. There had been only ad hoc and incremental welfare changes since the early post-war period, and very little ongoing monitoring of the system. The invalid pension programme, for instance, had been virtually unchanged since 1908. The return of unemployment meant an upsurge in demand for income assistance, known colloquially as 'the dole', and a rethinking of the terms upon which it was distributed. Several ministers in the Fraser government had contributed to a perception that there were 'dole bludgers' who did not work because they did not want to, in contrast to the 'taxpayers' who supported them. By the time unemployment had reached ten per cent this was a difficult claim to sustain, but the new Labor government was as committed as its predecessor to tightening up eligibility requirements. A small minority of people collected the dole to support their experiments with alternative living or creative careers, but by the late 1980s, their days were numbered.

In the wake of the 1986 report of the Social Security Review, income support programmes were henceforth linked with training and job placement assistance in order to encourage a return to employment and a reduction in welfare dependence. Many of these services were now subcontracted out to private providers. By the late 1990s, a 'work for the dole' programme had been introduced for jobseekers who had been on benefits for twelve months or more. The effect was to introduce greater monitoring of welfare recipients, to tighten access and to improve benefits in some cases. Families with children made the biggest gains in this period, with the introduction in 1987 of a family allowance supplement, which led to higher rates of payment per child and significantly expanded the numbers of families able to access the benefit.

Given that one of the concerns in this period was growing youth unemployment, increased child payments were also designed to encourage parents to keep their children at school longer, and indeed by the early 1990s the proportion of children completing their secondary education had doubled. An emphasis on education dovetailed with a desire to increase the productivity and flexibility of the workforce, and tertiary education participation rates also increased. One of the most notable features of these expanded participation rates was the increasing educational levels of women, who by 1987 were attending university in numbers equal to men.[14] These women, like those with lower educational attainments, pursued employment as much through necessity as choice. Continued high levels of migration throughout the 1990s and 2000s put pressure on existing housing stock, which meant that house prices doubled in this period, and most families now required two incomes to sustain a reasonable standard of living.

AN AGEING SOCIETY

Children were now dependent on their parents for a longer period and were a smaller proportion of the Australian population than they had ever been. By 2000, they constituted only one-fifth of the nation's people, whereas a hundred years earlier children had comprised more than a third.[15] The baby boom had temporarily interrupted a long-term population trend of declining fertility. Between 1972 and 1987 fertility dropped by almost a third, so that by 2000 the total fertility rate was fewer than two children per woman, a trend in keeping with rates in Europe, North America and Japan.[16] Continuous waves of immigration had ensured that Australia was a relatively youthful society for much of the twentieth century. Immigration also contributed to Australia's overall population, which increased by 50 per cent in the thirty years after 1980 to reach 22 million people by 2010. It was also among the most diverse Western nations, with almost a quarter of the population born overseas by 2000, a rate second only to Israel.

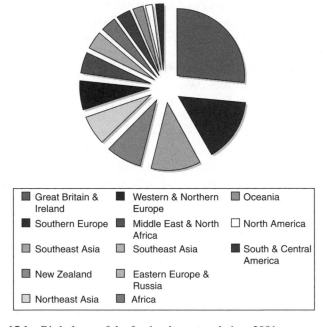

■ Great Britain & Ireland	■ Western & Northern Europe	■ Oceania
■ Southern Europe	■ Middle East & North Africa	☐ North America
▨ Southeast Asia	☐ Southeast Asia	■ South & Central America
■ New Zealand	▨ Eastern Europe & Russia	
☐ Northeast Asia	■ Africa	

Figure 15.1   Birthplaces of the foreign-born population, 2001

Source: Australian Bureau of Statistics, 'Australian Historical Population Statistics, 2006' (3105.0.65.001), at http://www.abs.gov.au.

Table 15.1 Vital statistics, 1851, 1901, 1947 and 2001

	1851	1901	1954	2001
Population	437,665	3,773,801	8,986,530	19,529,274
Number of births	15,784	102,945	193,298	246,394
Birth rate (per 1,000 people)	36.1	27.3	21.5	12.6
Number of deaths	5,878	46,330	81,788	128,544
Death rate (per 1,000 people)	13.4	12.3	9.1	6.6
Number of marriages	4,677	27,753	77,298	103,130
Marriage rate (per 1,000 people)	10.7	7.4	8.6	5.3
% of population female	41.3	47.6	49.4	50.4
% rate of annual population growth	8.0	1.6	2.1	1.3
% population aged 0–14		35.1	28.6	20.5
% of population aged 15–29		27.8	21.1	20.9
% of population aged 30–64		33.1	42.0	46.1
% of population more than 65		4.0	8.3	12.5
Infant mortality rate (per 1,000 births)		103.6	22.5	5.3
Life expectancy at birth (women)		58.8	72.8	82.8
Life expectancy at birth (men)		55.2	67.1	77.8

Source: W. Vamplew (ed.) *Australians: Historical Statistics* (Sydney: Fairfax, Syme and Weldon Associates, 1987), pp. 26, 44–5, 50–1 & 56; Australian Bureau of Statistics, 'Australian Historical Population Statistics, 2006' (3105.0.65.001), at http://www.abs.gov.au.

As fertility declined and Australians lived for longer, the age profile of the population began to trend upwards. The ageing of the population presented new challenges to government, largely in relation to how the elderly were to be supported in their retirement. Non-contributory old-age pensions had been introduced in the early twentieth century as a mark of a civilised society, one that embraced a responsibility to support people after a lifetime's labour. Yet the pension provided no more than a spartan existence; before the 1980s more generous superannuation incomes were available only to a minority of employees. The restriction of especially lucrative superannuation schemes to existing members meant that early retirement, like early marriage, would be another distinctive experience for the baby-boom generation. Throughout the 1980s and 1990s, the government made changes to superannuation laws in an effort to make individuals and industry bear more of the cost for retirement. The access of low-income, casual and part-time employees was thereby improved, although it did not entirely solve the problem of how rapidly growing numbers of elderly without adequate retirement income could be supported.

Increasing life expectancy also accounted for the growing number of older people. Between 1901 and 2000, life expectancy had increased from 55 to 78 for men, and from 59 to 83 for women.[17] By the end of the century, Australians were most likely to die from cancer or circulatory disease and almost never from infectious or parasitic diseases, which had constituted a quarter of all deaths in 1907. Improved sanitation and the increased use of antibiotics from mid-century also meant that children were much more likely to survive into adulthood. These figures obscured the ongoing lower levels of life expectancy for Indigenous people, which in 2000 was still almost twenty years lower than the level for non-Indigenous Australians. This disparity was almost twice that of comparable nations with an Indigenous population, such as New Zealand and Canada.[18]

INDIGENOUS CHALLENGES

Indigenous issues assumed unprecedented prominence in Australia during the final decades of the twentieth century, and initiated a broader public discussion about Australia's history as a settler colony. The commemoration of the bicentennial of British settlement in 1988 concentrated attention on the question of Indigenous dispossession, as Aboriginal activists insisted that 'white Australia has a Black History' and suggested 26 January 1788 should be renamed 'Invasion Day'. In 1992, decades of activism around the question of land rights received an important symbolic victory when the High Court declared in the *Mabo* judgement that native title existed in Australian common law, and that the source of native title was a traditional connection to or occupation of the land.

The significance of *Mabo* lay in its rejection of the doctrine of *terra nullius*, which had deemed that the land had belonged to no one at the time of European arrival. Critically, the court also ruled that native title could be extinguished by legislative or executive action, without the requirement for consent or compensation. This effectively meant that much of the Australian land mass could not be subject to a native title claim and the original native title holders could not be compensated for its loss. 'How many times must it be said that no private land in Australia is under threat as a result of the Mabo decision?', the Minister for Aboriginal Affairs remarked in 1993, in the face of ongoing anxiety about the implications of the decision.[19] In 1996, when the *Wik* decision held that native title could co-exist with pastoral leases, there was a further flurry of alarm, although in the case of any conflict of interest it was clear that the pastoral lease would extinguish native title rights.

The judges in both court cases made implicit comment on the dispossession of Indigenous peoples. Justices Deane and Gaudron had commented in *Mabo* that Australia had 'a national legacy of unutterable shame'.[20] The fate of Indigenous Australians also received new attention as an essential part of the 'big picture' politics Paul Keating practised during his tenure as Prime Minister between 1991 and 1996. In the wake of a Royal Commission finding that 'the legacy of history goes far to explain the over-representation of Aboriginal people in custody, and thereby the death of some of them', a Council for Aboriginal Reconciliation was established in 1991, in order to improve both the economic and social prospects for Aboriginal people and to acknowledge the 'unfair and often inhumane treatment' that had been meted out to them.[21] In a speech at Redfern Park in late 1992 to launch the forthcoming International Year for the World's Indigenous People, Paul Keating stressed that failing to acknowledge Australia's shortcomings in its treatment of the nation's Indigenous people had 'degraded all of us'. Reconciliation would only begin with recognition. 'Recognition that it was we who did the dispossessing. ... We committed the murders. We took the children from their mothers.'[22] Keating's use of the pronoun 'we' implied a contemporary acceptance of collective responsibility for the actions of the past.

The visit of Queen Elizabeth II and the fiftieth anniversary of the fall of Singapore in the first few months of Keating's leadership were unrivalled opportunities to make clear other elements of his big picture: Australia's place in Asia and the increasing irrelevance of the ties with Britain. At a welcome reception for the Queen at Parliament House, Keating said there had been a 'profound change' since the Queen's first visit to Australia in 1954. 'These days we must both face the necessities of a global economy and global change. ... We must also face regional realities', Keating insisted. 'Just as Great Britain some time ago sought to make her future secure in the European Community, so Australia now vigorously seeks partnerships with countries in our own region.'[23] Coming only weeks after an Australia Day suggestion that the flag be changed, and that Australia begin the process of moving towards a republic, these sentiments were criticised by the Liberal-National Party coalition as disrespectful and extreme. Only a few hundred people had showed up to greet the Queen when she arrived at Sydney Airport, suggesting that Keating's views on the monarchy, at least, were not so out of step with those of the electorate. In the Parliament, Keating berated the coalition's leadership as 'yesterday's men' caught in the 'cultural cringe' values of the 1950s.[24] It was less clear if Keating's views on Australia as part of Asia and his emphasis on the need to reconcile with Indigenous Australians had widespread support.

A new interpretation of Australia's history stood at the centre of Keating's 'big picture'. The views Keating espoused were not unfamiliar to academic historians, one of whom, Don Watson, had found a new career as Keating's main speech-writer. The critical histories that emerged from the new social movements of the 1970s – focused on women, the environment, Indigenous people and ethnic minorities to name a few – had a political impact in all liberal democratic societies, not just Australia. 'There are those who gnaw away at our national self-respect, rewriting history as centuries of unrelieved doom, oppression and failure', declared Margaret Thatcher in Britain in 1979.[25] Until the mid-1990s, Australia's political leadership, by giving public imprimatur to a critical view of the national past, swam against the tide of successful conservative political parties that dominated Britain and the United States.

These views endeared Paul Keating to the progressive middle-class, but that was not a demographic large enough to ensure ongoing electoral success. Keating declared his federal election win in 1993 as a 'victory for the true believers', but it was more accurately a defeat of the Opposition's electoral platform: a consumption tax, zero tariffs and the reduction of unemployment benefits. While the Opposition pushed for further reform of the economy, Keating saw it as time to pull back and reiterate older Labor traditions of social democracy that centred on fairness and compassion. He thereby successfully deflected some of the anger about the cost of economic rationalism onto the Liberal Party, and denigrated their leader, the economist and banker John Hewson, as a 'feral abacus' intent on pushing Australia to extreme free-market economics at the expense of working people. By 1995, the Liberal Party had elected a formal federal Treasurer from the Fraser ministry, John Howard, as Leader. Despite the formidable handicap of his record with economic management in the high-inflation, high-unemployment early 1980s, as a career politician Howard was deeply versed in the traditions of liberalism, and saw a rejuvenation of that political philosophy as the best way to differentiate himself, and his party, from the ruling ALP.

THE HOWARD YEARS: MAINSTREAM AUSTRALIA AND 'MINORITY' INTERESTS

By the mid-1990s, the economic reforms of the previous decade began to bear fruit, but the memory of their costs ran deep, and meshed with a growing sense of grievance that 'minorities' were the government's key concern. In reference to Paul Keating's roots in suburban Sydney, and to growing wage disparities, Howard declared in 1995 that 'the battlers have taken a fearsome battering from the boy from Bankstown'. 'There is a frustrated mainstream in Australia today,' Howard continued, 'which sees government decisions increasingly driven by the noisy, self-interested clamour of powerful vested interests with scant regard for the national interest'.[26] 'Powerful vested interests' did not mean big business or manufacturing industry, as it might have in political rhetoric from an earlier part of the century, nor did it include 'spontaneous, community-based organizations'. Rather, for Howard it meant identity-based 'interest groups' who held the ear of government and created division rather than unity in national life. The key rhetorical elements of Howard's political programme were laid out in this speech: the Liberal party would represent 'the battlers' and 'mainstream Australia' and would not be hostage to 'vested interests'.

Howard's political skill was to resuscitate the idea that Labor governed on behalf of sectional interests. Where once Labor was accused of pandering to the working class and the unions, now Howard suggested they gave preference to 'minorities'. In 1996, he won office with a campaign that declared that a Coalition would govern 'For All of Us'. The frustrations that Howard articulated also created space for the election to Federal Parliament of Pauline Hanson, who offered a less mannered critique of 'reverse racism', 'political correctness' and 'multiculturalists'.[27] The perception that Aborigines and migrants had prospered at the expense of 'mainstream Australia' could not be supported by even simple economic analysis, but it was one that the new federal government did not challenge, thereby allowing a new politics of bitterness to have an uneasy legitimacy in Australian public life. As part of a host of public sector reforms, the new government abolished agencies such as the Office of Multicultural Affairs, and reduced the funding of ethnic organisations. Despite publicly distancing itself from the multicultural policies of the previous government, there was a significant increase in immigrant intake between the late 1990s and 2005, and substantial funding for programmes to assist migrants in their transition to residence in Australia.

At the end of the twentieth century, Australia's history rather than its future occupied centre stage in public debate. The election of John Howard as Prime Minister deepened, rather than concluded, contests over the nation's past. At stake were the issues of shame and responsibility. Howard derided a 'black armband view' of the nation's history that constructed 'little more than a disgraceful story of imperialism, exploitation, racism, sexism and other forms of discrimination'. He insisted that 'we have achieved much more as a nation of which we can be proud than of which we should be ashamed'.[28] In this view, pride in the past restored responsibility for previous wrong-doing where it rightfully belonged: previous generations. This narrative was given dramatic focus in 1997, when the report of the National Inquiry into the separation of Aboriginal and Torres Strait Islander children from their families, *Bringing Them Home*, suggested that Australian government policies had been tantamount to genocide, and recommended a formal apology. 'Australians of this generation should not be required to accept guilt and blame for past actions and policies over which they had no control', Howard insisted.[29] The focus should be on addressing contemporary problems, not apportioning blame for actions of the past.

The depth of Howard's opposition to an apology had derailed the reconciliation process by the late 1990s, although it did inspire a counter-movement of public support. By 2000, the Walks for Reconciliation in major Australian cities had seen hundreds of thousands of Australians take part in public calls for a renewal of the process. Similarly, the opening and closing ceremonies of the Sydney Olympics featured the themes of apology and reconciliation. Although non-Indigenous Australians were prepared to act out their support in this way, the hard work of reconciliation – in terms of a possible treaty, restitution, compensation and reconstruction – remained elusive. The devil was also in the detail of a referendum for Australia to become a republic, which proposed a Presidential model that caused division in republican ranks, and ultimately failed when it was put to the vote in 1999.

The search for a positive spin on Australia's history settled on the mythology of Anzac. The unspoken context for its celebration in the early decades of the twentieth century was a desire to overcome the nation's convict origins, to prove that the Anglo-Saxon race had thrived in the south. Its revival at the century's end also offered a path out of murky origins. As celebrating Australia Day became more and more problematic in light of its association with the original act of dispossession, the focus for a point of origin turned off shore, and settled on a rugged bit of Turkish coastline, referred to as a 'little piece of Australia' by Prime Minister Hawke when he visited Gallipoli to commemorate the seventy-fifth anniversary of the landing in 1990.[30] The media contingent accompanying him picked up the cue. 'For the Australians', who had made the long journey to Turkey, this was 'a return to the foreign birthplace of Australian nationhood'.[31] Anzac Day was increasingly celebrated as the national day, the qualities of mateship, egalitarianism and resourcefulness as the defining features of a national identity. Politicians attempted to elide the association between Anzac and militarism, so problematic in the Vietnam era, by insisting that war was the mere context for the substance of national character to emerge. Anzac was 'a legend not of sweeping military victories so much as triumph against the odds, of courage and ingenuity in adversity,' Prime Minister Keating insisted in his speech to mark the funeral service of an unknown Australian soldier in 1993.[32]

The rebirth of Anzac had a long gestation under successive Labor governments of the 1980s and 1990s; the election of John Howard as Prime Minister ensured that it would thrive. The federal government directed significant resources to promoting the commemoration and visibility of Australia's wartime heritage at memorials and schools, and the success of these initiatives was measured by the characterisation of opposition to them as being 'un-Australian'. The mythology of Anzac resonated particularly with the young, whose responsiveness to the tragedy of young lives lost was in part ensured by the knowledge that they would be most unlikely to be placed in a similar position.

The increasing parochialism of national identity was matched by a recasting of Australia's place in the Asia-Pacific region, as the conflict between Australia's history and its geography was reintroduced into political discussion. In 2000, when visiting Beijing, Foreign Minister

263

Illustration 15.1 'All our historical research, Prime Minister, indicates that …', 2000

Source: National Library of Australia. nla.pic-vn5017482.

Alexander Downer distinguished between the necessity for 'practical regionalism', which revolved around trade, and a 'cultural or emotional regionalism' that was more problematic for a country like Australia. Less troubling for the Coalition government was its relationship with the United States, in which Australia was eager to embrace the role of 'deputy', particularly after the success of Republican George W. Bush in the November 2000 Presidential election. As the new century began, Australia stood poised, ready to support the United States in its future endeavours. When hijacked aeroplanes flew into the Twin Towers in New York and the Pentagon on 11 September 2001, it was clear that Australia would stand shoulder to shoulder with the United States when it declared a 'War on Terror'.

AUSTRALIAN MILITARY COMMITMENTS

The 'War on Terror' ended several decades of relative quiet in terms of Australia's military commitments. In the early 1980s the return of tension between the Soviet Union and the United States had not required the Australian government to commit any troops in support of US military activities. The most noteworthy public effect of the new cold war in Australia had been to increase concern about the threat of nuclear weapons, with the annual Palm Sunday anti-nuclear rallies attracting hundreds of thousands of participants in the mid-1980s. By the end of that decade, Mikhail Gorbachev's leadership of the Soviet Union heralded a new détente with the West, important agreements to reduce nuclear warheads, and his pursuit of the reform policies of *glasnost* and *perestroika*, which would ultimately result in the dissolution of the USSR. The ensuing spirit of cooperation between the superpowers refocused attention on the role of the United Nations' Security Council to defend its member states against aggression. Iraq's invasion of Kuwait in 1990 drew international opprobrium, and Australian military personnel were part of the multinational force deployed in the first Gulf War to enforce the United Nation's January 1991 deadline for Iraq's withdrawal.

There were ongoing blind spots in Australia's foreign policy. Largely owing to its recent implementation of a treaty with Indonesia to exploit the natural resources of the Timor Gap, the Australian government looked the other way when Indonesian troops massacred pro-independence demonstrators in Dili, East Timor in 1991. Yet by 1999 Australian Major General Peter Cosgrove had been appointed to lead the United Nations-mandated International Force for East Timor (INTERFET) to oversee the withdrawal of Indonesian forces after the East Timorese people had voted overwhelmingly in favour of independence. Australian command of INTERFET was made possible by the diplomatic and material support of the United States, which led to a revitalisation of an alliance that had lost some of its closeness after the United States had been defeated in Vietnam and withdrew from the Asian mainland.

The brief Gulf War aside, for much of the 1990s the Australian military participated in the United Nation's increasing number of peace-keeping missions and humanitarian interventions, designed to protect civilians during civil wars, to provide support in the face of disasters, and to assist in the process of rebuilding in post-conflict societies. The Australian defence forces and federal police were involved in major UN missions to provide aid to famine and drought victims in Somalia, to oversee Cambodian elections in 1993 and to assist recovery in post-genocide Rwanda. Rich in the symbolism of international cooperation, such activities did not require the commitment of vast numbers of personnel and resulted in very few casualties.

Engagements like that in East Timor reflected the new space created for middle powers like Australia in the post-cold war environment.

'Middle powers are not powerful enough in most circumstances to impose their will,' Gareth Evans, the influential Minister for Foreign Affairs between 1988 and 1996 insisted, 'but they may be persuasive enough to have like-minded others to see their point of view, and to act accordingly'.[33] It was now more possible to realise the liberal internationalism that underpinned 'middle power diplomacy'. The approach adopted a multilateral, coalition-building role in international relations. Some of Australia's foreign policy initiatives in the period included a significant role in negotiating the peace process in Cambodia after the end of the Vietnamese occupation, and a central role in pursuing international agreements about nuclear testing, chemical weapons and disarmament. A 1996 bid for Australia to become an elected member of the UN Security Council failed, however, in part owing to the perception that a newly elected Coalition government would, as the new Foreign Minister Alexander Downer put it in the 'Sydney Statement', return to a more bilateral approach and prioritise the 'vital friendship' with the United States.[34]

A willingness to join international campaigns against terrorism in the 2000s saw Australia once again step up its military commitments. From 2001, after terrorist attacks on the mainland United States, Australian defence forces contributed to what ultimately became the NATO-led International Security Assistance Force in Afghanistan. The Department of Defence described the war against the Taliban as intending to 'bring security, stability and prosperity to Afghanistan' with the aim of 'preventing the country from again becoming a safe haven for international terrorists' such as Al Qaeda, the group which had claimed responsibility for 11 September.[35] A different branch of militant Islam, Jemaah Islamiyah, was responsible for a 2002 terrorist attack closer to Australian shores, on the Indonesian island of Bali, in which 202 people, including 88 Australians, were killed. In 2003, Australia joined the United States and Britain in the 'Coalition of the Willing', which invaded Iraq on the justification that Saddam Hussein's regime possessed 'weapons of mass destruction' and hosted terrorist groups such as Al Qaeda. The participation of 14,000 Australian defence personnel in this conflict attracted controversy until the final withdrawal of Australian combat troops in 2008, because the invasion of Iraq had gone ahead without UN Security Council endorsement, and no weapons of mass destruction were ever found. Although there were no combat-related deaths in Iraq, 23 Australian defence personnel were killed in Afghanistan during a decade of involvement, and in 2010 there were 1,500 personnel on active duty.

REFUGEES AND ASYLUM SEEKERS

Australia also continued to fulfil some of its international obligations through its planned admission of refugees and other humanitarian cases, although as the 1990s progressed and numbers increased, some of its policies came under increasing scrutiny. The global refugee population soared in the final decades of the twentieth century, from an estimate of 5.3 million refugees in 1980, to 12 million by 2000 and a further 21.8 million people the UN High Commission on Refugees designated as 'persons of concern'. Despite having no official refugee policy until the late 1970s, the Indo-Chinese crisis had prompted the Australian government to develop a more comprehensive approach, and there was a steady intake throughout the 1980s. Substantial numbers of Asian migrants reignited some debate about the desirability of non-European migration, and there was unease in some quarters about an 'Asian invasion'. Yet this was an echo of earlier concerns about Australia's racial composition, rather than a forceful or influential restatement of them. In the ten years from 1992, almost half of over 100,000 refugees and other humanitarian cases admitted to Australia were from Europe, most often as a consequence of the break-up of the former Yugoslavia and the ethnic and religious conflicts engendered by it.[36]

Concern about the resumption of 'unauthorised' arrivals by boat to remote regions of Australia in the late 1980s ultimately led to a change of policy about people who attempted to arrive in Australia without following strict immigration procedures. The 'boat people' of the 1970s had largely been from Asia. 'Asylum-seekers' of the 1990s were more likely to come from the Middle East and Afghanistan, where autocratic regimes and war had displaced millions of people. The *Migration Reform Act 1992* legislated for the mandatory detention of 'unlawful non-citizens', that is non-citizens without a valid visa. In the early 1990s a new detention facility was opened at Broome, followed by another at Woomera in 1999. The remoteness of the facilities, the length of stay of their inmates and the conditions of their detention prompted a domestic and international protest movement about mandatory detention. Asylum seekers themselves drew attention to the delays in visa processing, and the harshness of their detention in 2002, when 58 inmates at Woomera sewed their lips together in protest at their treatment.

Concerns about the increase of boat arrivals from the late 1990s built on an older rhetoric of invasion and encouraged politicians to experiment with dramatic gestures in the name of national sovereignty. In August 2001, a Norwegian freighter, the MV *Tampa*, was refused permission to enter Australian waters, despite carrying over 400 Afghans rescued from a sinking ship. When it did so, the government ordered Special Air Service troops aboard the ship. In the national Parliament, John Howard described the *Tampa* as a 'metaphor for the dilemma this country faces', and insisted on the government's 'sovereign right to determine who will enter and reside in Australia' and that 'something has to be done to stop that flow of humanity'.[37] On talk-back radio the refugees were admonished as 'queue jumpers' by members of the government, which introduced legislation that excised some of Australia's territory from the migration zone. Subsequently, refugees attempting to enter Australia by boat were intercepted and taken to off-shore detention centres on Nauru, Manus or Christmas Island, in what became known as the 'Pacific Solution' to dealing with unauthorised arrivals.

The terrorist attacks on the United States increased the political purchase of concerns about asylum seekers, who were predominantly Muslim, and led to a recasting of the issue as one of national security. The Defence Minister, Peter Reith, justified his government's policies of border protection by insisting on a responsibility to ensure that the boats were not a 'pipeline for terrorists'.[38] That the asylum seekers were refugees from the regimes that Australia was fighting in the 'War on Terror' did not seem to disrupt the logic or flow of some media commentary, and demonstrated the ease with which security issues became conflated with other political concerns. One of these was the policy of multiculturalism, which came under renewed criticism as a potential path to segregation, with Australians of Muslim or Arabic background identified as people with the potential for divided loyalties, particularly given the popular associations between Islam and terrorism.[39] The final years of the Howard government were marked by a retreat from an emphasis on cultural diversity as a key to nation building, to a growing emphasis on 'national unity' and the need to articulate a 'coherent set of national values' to 'protect Australia in these uncertain times'.[40] From 2007, applicants for Australian citizenship were required to sit a test that examined their knowledge of Australian institutions and values.

THE RUDD GOVERNMENT

Concerns about border protection effectively ensured the Howard government's re-election in 2001, and the electorate's uncertainty about brusque Labor leader Mark Latham saw the Coalition victorious again in 2004. In 2006, a former diplomat and MP since 1998, Kevin Rudd, published an essay entitled 'Faith in Politics'. In it, Rudd identified himself as a social democrat who believed in the 'progressive values of equity, community and sustainability'.[41] He discussed what he saw as the Howard government's shortcomings in relation to asylum seekers, climate change and industrial relations, among others. By the end of the year, the ALP had elected him its federal leader.

Apart from increasing criticism of the harshness of Australia's Pacific Solution, both within Australia and internationally, the Howard government also faced backlash against its WorkChoices legislation, which came into effect in 2006. Exempting small business from unfair dismissal laws, and dramatically altering workplace conditions and entitlements, the final dismantling of Australia's industrial relations system was perceived to unfairly target the most vulnerable members of the workforce. WorkChoices contributed to a perception of Howard and his ministers as aggressive in pursuit of economic competition and insufficiently attentive to issues of equity.

Howard was also a noted climate change sceptic, and his government's refusal to ratify the Kyoto Protocol on greenhouse gas emissions further contributed to an impression of favouring the interests of business over the bigger picture. Environmental conditions in Australia in the 2000s began to undermine public confidence in this approach. By the mid-2000s much of the eastern seaboard was in drought, a not unprecedented development, but one of exceptional intensity. Within a few years the country was so dry that drought's unwelcome companion, bushfire, began to wreak its havoc. The most extreme occurred in Victoria in February 2009, when 173 people lost their lives in the intense fires and thousands were left homeless.

The future of the environment and the impact of climate change had become a global concern by the 2000s, and a particular interest for younger voters, who had not gained much during the Howard years. The welfare initiatives of the 1990s and 2000s were directed towards the middle-aged and couples with children, who benefited from tax breaks targeted at superannuation contributions and single-income families, increased child-care rebates, and a baby bonus. Howard's biggest disadvantage, however, was his age and incumbency. Already in his late sixties, Howard would not confirm when he would step aside for his clearly eager deputy, Treasurer Peter Costello. It began to appear to the electorate as if Howard wanted power for power's sake. In office for eleven years, the Liberal-National Party coalition seemed devoid of policy initiatives, in comparison to the policy deluge issuing forth from the ALP on topics from education to federalism. Howard lost the 2007 federal election, and his own seat, to the ALP.

269

The Rudd government acted quickly to reverse some of the more controversial elements of its predecessors' rule. In the first session of the new federal Parliament, in February 2008, Kevin Rudd issued an apology to the Australia's Indigenous people for the 'laws and policies of successive Parliaments and governments that have inflicted profound grief, suffering and loss on these our fellow Australians'. He made particular mention of the policies of child removal, and the 'suffering and hurt' of the Stolen Generations and their families, and proclaimed: 'for the indignity and degradation thus inflicted on a proud people and a proud culture, we say sorry'. The new government also withdrew its troops from Iraq, abandoned the Pacific Solution to the asylum-seeker issue but did not end mandatory detention, ratified the Kyoto Protocol and introduced significant funding for school infrastructure as part of an 'education revolution'. It acted quickly in response to the global financial crisis, by providing an economic stimulus package and bank guarantees, but Australia's mineral wealth, and the regulations that had remained in the financial system after the reforms of the 1980s and 1990s, made the Australian economy less vulnerable to the dramatic collapses and bail-outs necessary in other parts of the world. The crisis initiated a new international discussion about the possibility that neo-liberal economics had gone too far.

These initiatives saw Rudd and his government ride high in the opinion polls, but when Rudd did not succeed in introducing legislation to establish a carbon emissions trading scheme, and ran up against mining interests when he tried to negotiate a new resources super profit tax, the numbers plummeted. Fearing a catastrophic defeat after only one term of government, the ALP installed a new leader to stem the tide. In June 2010, factional ALP politics delivered Australia its first female Prime Minister, former lawyer Julia Gillard. Keen to hold the Prime Ministership with the legitimacy only an election could provide, Gillard went to the polls within months of assuming the mantle.

Emerging victorious, but only just with the support of several independents and the first Greens politician elected to the House of Representatives, Gillard's biggest challenges early in her Prime Ministership resulted from the forces of nature, rather than politics. The long drought broke in the spring and summer of 2010–11, when record rainfall caused extensive flooding in New South Wales, Victoria and Queensland, where over sixty per cent of the state flooded, including the capital city of Brisbane. Farmers who had celebrated the arrival of rain watched as their crops disappeared beneath a torrent of water. Further damage was to come as Cyclone Yasi, a storm large enough to almost cover the land mass of the United States, tore up crops and infrastructure, and caused further flooding throughout the eastern states.

Droughts, floods, bushfires and cyclones had been a feature of Australia's past, and will remain a part of its future. As an arid continent, subject to El Niño and La Niña events, Australia faces multiple challenges. Scientists argue that climate change and global warming will increase the intensity of extreme weather, in ways that will confront disaster experts, population planners and the economy. Other issues that will play out in the twenty-first century are less easy to identify. History is a discipline of hindsight. Historians need to be modest about their capacity to tell the story of the most recent past, let alone predict the future. They look for patterns of change and continuity, and they need the balance that comes only from a degree of distance. As did the people of the past, we advance into the future with serious issues and challenges on our minds. But the people of the future will be better served for knowing something of the past. As with every history, it is to them that the story now turns.

Notes

1 FIRST PEOPLE

1. The *Endeavour* Journal of Joseph Banks 28 April 1770, 1 May 1770 and 4 May 1770, at http://www2.sl.nsw.gov.au.
2. Historical accounts of the Australia of the first people now rest upon an increasingly rich and broad-ranging scholarship in archaeaology, ethnography and history; the synthesis presented in this chapter draws in particular upon Bruno David, Bryce Barker and Ian J. McNiven (eds), *The Social Archaeology of Australian Indigenous Societies* (Canberra: Aboriginal Studies Press, 2006), Josephine Flood, *Archaeology of the Dreamtime: The Story of Prehistoric Australia and its People* (Adelaide: JB Publishing, 2004), Ian Keen, *Aboriginal Economy and Society: Australia at the Threshold of Colonisation* (Melbourne: Oxford University Press, 2004), Harry Lourandos, *Continent of Hunter-Gatherers: New Perspectives in Australian Prehistory* (Cambridge: Cambridge University Press, 1997), Adam Brumm and Mark W. Moore, 'Symbolic Revolutions and the Australian Archaeological Record', *Cambridge Archaeological Journal*, 15 (2005), pp. 157–75, Harry Lourandos and Anne Ross, 'The Great "Intensification Debate": Its History and Place in Australian Archaeology', *Australian Archaeology*, 39 (1994), pp. 54–63, John Mulvaney and Johan Kamminga, *Prehistory of Australia* (Sydney: Allen & Unwin, 1999), and Tim Murray (ed.), *Archaeology of Aboriginal Australia: A Reader* (Sydney: Allen & Unwin, 1998).

2 THE GREAT SOUTH LAND: 1500–1800

1. Pedro Fernandez de Queiroz, cited in George Collingridge, *The First Discovery of Australia and New Guinea, Being the Narrative of Portuguese and Spanish Discoveries in the Australasian Regions between the Years 1492–1606* (Sydney: William Brooks, 1906), p. 48.
2. T. D. Mutch, *The First Discovery of Australia, With an Account of the Voyage of the "Duyfken" and the Career of Captain Willem Jansz* (Sydney: T. D. Mutch, 1942), p. 21.
3. William Dampier, *A New Voyage around the World* (London: James Knapton, 1697), p. 464 and *A Voyage to New Holland, &c, in the Year 1699* (London: James Wharton, 1703), pp. 147–8.
4. *The London Gazette*, Number 118, 26 August 1768.
5. W. J. L. Wharton (ed.), *Captain Cook's Journal During His First Voyage Around the World* (London: Elliot Stock, 1893), at http://ebooks.adelaide. edu.au/c/cook/james/.

6. Ibid.
7. The *Endeavour* Journal of Joseph Banks, 15 July 1770.
8. 'Australian Canoes', at http://ebooks.adelaide.edu.au/c/cook/james/.
9. The *Endeavour* Journal of Joseph Banks, 20 April 1770.
10. Joseph Banks, 'Some Account of that Part of New Holland now Called New South Wales', at http://www2.sl.nsw.gov.au/banks.
11. The *Endeavour* Journal of Joseph Banks, 28 April 1770.
12. 'Some Account of New Wales', at http://ebooks.adelaide.edu.au/c/cook/james/; Banks, 'Some Account of that Part of New Holland'.
13. 'Australian Natives', at http://ebooks.adelaide.edu.au/c/cook/james/.
14. Banks, 'Some Account of that Part of New Holland'.
15. Matthew Flinders, *A Voyage to Terra Australis* (London: G. and W. Nicol, 1814), vol. 1, p. iii.

3   BRITAIN'S PRISON: CONVICTS, SETTLERS AND INDIGENOUS PEOPLE, 1788–1802

1. Instructions from the Home Secretary, Lord Sydney, to Captain Arthur Phillip, 25 April 1787, at http://www.foundingdocs.gov.au.
2. Arthur Phillip, *The Voyage of Governor Phillip to Botany Bay* (London: John Stockdale, 1789), pp. 66–7.
3. Ibid., pp. 122–3.
4. David Collins, *An Account of the English Colony in New South Wales*, vol. 1 (London: T. Cadell Jun and W. Davies, 1798), at http://www.gutenberg.org.
5. Instructions to Captain Arthur Phillip, 1787, in *Historical Records of New South Wales*, Vol. 1, Part 2 (Sydney, 1892), p. 90.
6. *Cable [Kable] v. Sinclair*, July 1788, Court of Civil Jurisdiction Proceedings, 1788–1814, at http://www.law.mq.edu.au/scnsw.
7. *Historical Records of New South Wales*, Vol. 1, Part 2, p. 88.
8. Watkin Tench, *A Complete Account of the Settlement at Port Jackson* (London: G. Nicol and J. Sewell, 1793), at http://ebooks.adelaide.edu.au/t/tench/watkin/settlement.
9. Watkin Tench, *A Narrative of the Expedition to Botany Bay* (London: J. Debrett, 1789), http://ebooks.adelaide.edu.au/t/tench/watkin/botany.
10. Phillip, *The Voyage*, p. 139.
11. Ibid., p. 69.
12. David Collins, *An Account of the English Colony in New South Wales*, vol. 2 (London: T. Cadell Jun and W. Davies, 1802), http://www.gutenberg.org.

4   FREE AND UNFREE: REFORMING NEW SOUTH WALES, 1803–29

1. *Governor Hunter's Remarks on the Causes of the Colonial Expense of the Establishment of New South Wales* (London: J. Hunter, 1802).
2. Letter to Miss Kingdon, 29 January 1807, cited in *1808: Bligh's Sydney Rebellion* (Sydney: State Library of New South Wales, 2008), p. 12.

NOTES

3. John Oxley, *Journal of Two Expeditions into the Interior of New South Wales* (London: John Murray, 1820), pp. 113, 104.
4. Governor Darling to Hay, 10 February 1827, *Historical Records of Australia*, Series 1, Vol. 13, pp. 105–6.
5. Governor Brisbane's memorandum to R. Wilmot-Horton, Under-Secretary of State for War and the Colonies, *Historical Records of Australia*, Series 1, Vol. 11, pp. 552–4.
6. Anne Bartlett, 'Launceston Female Factory', at http://www.launcestonhistory. org.au.
7. Cited in John Gascoigne, *The Enlightenment and the Origins of European Australia* (Melbourne: Cambridge University Press, 2002), p. 53.

5   NEW AUSTRALIAS: 1829–49

1. Charles Sturt, *Two Expeditions into the Interior of Southern Australia* (London: Smith, Elder & Co., 1833), at http://en.wikisource.org/wiki/Two_expeditions_into_the_interior_of_Southern_Australia.
2. Ibid.
3. George Grey, *Journals of Two Expeditions of Discovery in North-West and Western Australia*, vol. 1 (London: T. & W. Boone, 1841), at http://www.gutenberg.org.
4. John Batman, Journal, 30 May 1835, MS13181, State Library of Victoria, pp. 34–5, 36.
5. Sandra Taylor, 'Who Were the Convicts?', in C. T. Stannage (ed.), *Convictism in Western Australia* (Perth: University of Western Australia Press, 1981).
6. Extract from Governor Richard Bourke's Despatch No. 76, to the Secretary of State for the Colonies, 30 September 1833, in *Votes and Proceedings of the Legislative Council During the Session of the Year 1836* (Sydney: Government Printer, 1847), p. 460.
7. Cited in Douglas Pike, *Paradise of Dissent: South Australia, 1829–1857* (Melbourne: Cambridge University Press, 1967), p. 130.
8. *Votes and Proceedings 1836*, p. 461.
9. Cited in Gascoigne, *The Enlightenment*, p. 27.
10. Batman Journal, 6 June 1835, p. 60.
11. Cited in M. J. L. Uren, *Land Looking West: The Story of Governor James Stirling in Western Australia* (London: Oxford University Press, 1948), p. 270.
12. Despatch from Arthur, 7 January 1832, in *Correspondence and Other Papers Relating to Aboriginal Tribes in British Possessions*, vol. 23 [1834] (Shannon: Irish University Press, 1968), pp. 162–3.
13. 'From a Correspondent', *The Perth Gazette and Western Australian Journal*, 1 June 1833.
14. *Launceston Advertiser*, 26 September 1831, cited in Henry Reynolds, *Dispossession: Black Australians and White Invaders* (Sydney: Allen & Unwin, 1989), pp. 11–12.
15. *R. v. Kilmeister and others (No. 2)* [1838], New South Wales Supreme Court 110, at http://www.law.mq.edu.au/scnsw.

16. Application of the Committee of the Aboriginal Protection Society for the admission of native evidence, 30 July 1839, at http://www.law.mq.edu.au/scnsw.

17. *Report of the Parliamentary Select Committee on Aboriginal Tribes (British Settlements). Reprinted, with Comments by the "Aborigines Protection Society"* (London, 1837), pp. 4 & 125.

18. G. A. Robinson, *A Journey Through the Western District*, 15 May 1841, 20 May 1841, 27 May 1841, 6 July 1841.

19. Henry Meyrick, letter, 30 April 1846, cited in Don Watson, *Caledonia Australis: Scottish Highlanders on the Frontier of Australia* (Sydney: Collins, 1984), p. 170.

20. Peter Cunningham, *Two Years in New South Wales* (London: Henry Colburn, 1827), vol. 2, pp. 53–4.

21. *The A. B. C. of Colonization, In a Series of Letters, by Mrs Chisholm* (London: John Ollivier, 1850), p. 25.

22. James Mudie, *The Felonry of New South Wales* (London: Whaley & Co., 1837), p. 220.

23. Ibid., pp. 13, 20.

24. John Dunmore Lang, *An Historical and Statistical Account of New South Wales, Both as a Penal Settlement and as a British Colony* (London: Cochrane and McCrone, 1834), vol. 2, p. 433.

25. 'The Renewal of Transportation', *The People's Advocate*, 1849.

26. *Port Phillip Patriot*, 21 November 1844.

27. *Sydney Morning Herald*, 6 June 1849.

6   THE GOLDEN LANDS: 1850–68

1. Governor LaTrobe to Lord Grey, Secretary of State, 10 October 1851, cited in Geoffrey Serle, *The Golden Age: A History of the Colony of Victoria, 1851–1861* (Melbourne: Melbourne University Press, 1963), p. 22.

2. John Sherer, *The Gold Finder of Australia: How He Went, How He Fared, and How He Made His Fortune* (London: Clarke & Beeton, 1853), p. 9.

3. James Bonwick, *Australian Gold Diggers' Monthly Magazine* (1853), cited in David Goodman, *Gold Seeking: Victoria and California in the 1850s* (Stanford: Stanford University Press, 1994), p, 153.

4. Sherer, *The Gold Finder of Australia*, p. 10.

5. *The Argus*, September 13 1855.

6. Patricia Clancy and Jeanne Allen (eds), *The French Consul's Wife: Memoirs of Céleste de Chabrillan in Gold-Rush Australia* (Melbourne: Melbourne University Press, 1998), p. 96.

7. Robyn Annear and David Bannear, 'The Proclamation of the Miner's Right', at http://www.egold.net.au.

8. *Report of the Select Committee of the Legislative Council on the Subject of Chinese Immigration* (Melbourne, 1857), p. 1.

9. E. K. Silvester (ed.), *The Speeches in the Legislative Council of New South Wales on the Second Reading of the Bill for Framing a New Constitution for the Colony* (Sydney: Thomas Daniel, 1853), p. 34.

10. *Argus*, 6 October 1852.
11. Daniel Deniehy, 'The Constitution, the Elections, and the Squatting Interest', *Goulburn Herald*, 13 October 1855.
12. Entry for 5 June 1859, in William Hardman (ed.), *The Journals of John McDouall Stuart* (London: Saunders & Otley, 1865), at http://ebooks. adelaide.edu.au.
13. *Guide to the Intercolonial Exhibition of 1866* (Melbourne, 1866), pp. 3, 9.
14. *Argus*, 25 October 1866.
15. *Freeman's Journal*, 12 October 1867.

7 AT THE FOREFRONT OF THE RACE: 1868–88

1. Cited in Cathy Dunn, 'The Attempted Assassination of Prince Alfred at Clontarf, 1868', at http://www.historyaustralia.org.au.
2. Ibid.
3. The poem was written by Richard Whately, Archbishop of Dublin and is in E. Jane Whately (ed.), *Life and Correspondence of Richard Whately, D.D., Late Archbishop of Dublin* (London: Longmans Green, 1866), vol. 2, pp. 109–10.
4. Marcus Clarke, *The Future Australian Race* (Melbourne: A. H. Massina & Co., 1877), p. 22.
5. 'Will the Anglo-Saxon Race Degenerate?', *Victorian Review*, vol. 1, no. 1, November 1879, pp. 114–23, p. 122.
6. George Bennett, *Acclimatisation: Its Eminent Adaptation to Australia* (Melbourne: Acclimatisation Society of Victoria, 1862), p. 5.
7. http://www.rzsnsw.org.au.
8. Frederick McCoy, cited in H. J. Frith, *Wildlife Conservation*, 2nd edn (Sydney: Angus & Robertson, 1979), p. 138.
9. Rolf Boldrewood, 'The Australian Native-Born Type', *In Bad Company and other Stories* (London: Macmillan, 1901), pp. 358–9.
10. Alexander Sutherland, *Victoria and its Metropolis* (Melbourne: McCarron Bird, 1888), vol. 1, p. 29.
11. Report of the Select Committee on the Aborigines, cited in Reynolds, *Dispossession*, p. 193.
12. Board for the Protection of Aborigines, *Annual Report* (1875), at http://museumvictoria.com.au.
13. *Victorian Parliamentary Debates*, 1876, at ibid.
14. Edward Curr, *The Australian Race* (Melbourne: Government Printer, 1886), vol. 1, p. 105.
15. Sutherland, *Victoria and its Metropolis*, vol. 1, p. 29.
16. R. E. N. Twopeny, *Town Life in Australia* (London: Elliot Stock, 1883), p. 188.
17. H. Mortimer Franklyn, *A Glance at Australia in 1880* (Melbourne: Victoria Review Publishing, 1881), p. 166.
18. J. E. Neild, cited in Milton James Lewis, *The People's Health: Public Health in Australia, 1788–1950* (Westport CT: Praeger, 2003), p. 56.
19. At http://www.slv.vic.gov.au.
20. A. G. Austin (ed.), *The Webbs' Australian Diary 1898* (Melbourne: Pitman & Sons, 1965), p. 66.

21. Henry Parkes, 'An Australian Nation', *Melbourne Review*, October 1879, p. 327.
22. *The Age*, 29 May 1883.
23. Cited in Helen Irving, *The Centenary Companion to Australian Federation* (Melbourne: Cambridge University Press, 1999), p. 27.
24. H. T. Burgess, *The Future Position of Australia Among Nations* (Sydney, 1888).

8 A TRULY NEW WORLD: 1888–1901

1. William Lane, *The Workingman's Paradise: An Australian Labour Novel* (Sydney: Edwards, Dunlop & Co., 1892), p. 265.
2. Henry Lawson, 'Australian Loyalty', *The Republican*, 1887.
3. Henry Lawson, 'Star of Australasia' [1895], in *Collected Verse, Volume One* (Sydney: Angus & Robertson, 1967), p. 294.
4. Joseph Furphy, *Such is Life-Being Certain Extracts from the Diary of Tom Collins* [1903] (Sydney: Angus & Robertson, 1945), p. 41.
5. Bernard O'Dowd, 'Australia', at http://www.poemhunter.com.
6. A. G. Stephens, 'A Word for Australia', *The Bulletin*, 9 December 1899.
7. House of Representatives, 12 September 1901, in Sally Warhaft (ed.), *Well May We Say . . . The Speeches That Made Australia* (Melbourne: Black Inc., 2004), p. 220.
8. H. A. Dugdale, *A Few Hours in a Far-Off Age* (Melbourne: McCarron Bird, 1883), p. 99.
9. Louisa Lawson, 'That Nonsensical Idea', *The Dawn*, vol. 3, no. 2 (June, 1890).
10. Rose Scott, cited in Patricia Grimshaw, Marilyn Lake, Ann McGrath and Marian Quartly, *Creating a Nation* (Melbourne: McPhee Gribble, 1994), p. 185; Louisa Lawson, 'Woman's Part in Evolution', in Olive Lawson (ed.), *The First Voice of Australian Feminism: Excerpts from Louisa Lawson's The Dawn, 1888–1895* (Sydney: Simon and Schuster, 1990), p. 120.
11. *The Bulletin*, 21 July 1883.
12. W. G. Spence, *The Ethics of New Unionism* (Crestwick: Martin & Grose, 1892), p. 10.
13. *Boomerang*, 7 April 1888.
14. 'Federal', *Tocsin* [1898], in Hugh Anderson, *Tocsin: Radical Arguments Against Federation, 1897–1900* (Melbourne: Drummond, 1977), p. 12.
15. *Sydney Morning Herald*, 25 October 1889.
16. *Official Record of the Proceedings and Debates of the Australasian Federation Conference* (Melbourne: Government Printer, 1890), p. 40.
17. Ibid., p. 26.
18. *Table Talk*, 10 January 1901.
19. *Morning Post*, 8 January 1901.

9 A PROTECTIVE NATION: 1901–14

1. A. B. Paterson, *Happy Dispatches: War Memoirs* (Sydney: Angus & Robertson, 1934), Chapter XI: Rudyard Kipling.

2. David Malouf, *Made In England: Australia's British Inheritance* (Melbourne: Black Inc., 2003), p. 4.
3. Philip S. Eldershaw and Percy B. Olden, 'Industrial Arbitration in Australia', *Annals of the American Academy of Political and Social Science*, 37:1 (1911), pp. 203–4.
4. Albert Metin, *Le Socialisme sans doctrine: la question agraire et la question ouvrière en Australie et Nouvelle-Zelande* (Paris: F. Alcorn, 1901).
5. Henry Bournes Higgins, 'A New Province for Law and Order: Industrial Peace through Minimum Wage and Arbitration', *Harvard Law Review*, 29:1 (1915), p. 13.
6. Ibid.
7. *Argus*, 23 March 1904, p. 8.
8. *Ex Parte* H. V. McKay, pp. 3, 4. The 'Harvester Judgement' is available online at www.aph.gov.au.
9. *Argus*, 7 December 1912, p. 23.
10. *Royal Commission on the Decline of the Birth Rate and on the Mortality of Infants in New South Wales*, (Sydney: Government Printer, 1904), vol. 1, p. 53.
11. John Chesterman and Brian Galligan, *Citizens without Rights: Aborigines and Australian Citizenship* (Melbourne: Cambridge University Press, 1997), p. 3.
12. Elizabeth Jennings to Secretary Board of Protection for Aborigines, 17 November 1914, in Elizabeth Nelson, Sandra Smith and Patricia Grimshaw (eds), *Letters from Aboriginal Women of Victoria, 1867-1926* (Melbourne: University of Melbourne, 2002), p. 71.
13. *Commonwealth Parliamentary Debates [CPD]*, House of Representatives, 12 September 1901, repr. in Francis Crowley (ed.), *Modern Australia in Documents 1901-39* (Melbourne: Wren, 1973), p. 16.
14. Ibid.
15. Ibid.
16. J. A. La Nauze (ed.), *Federated Australia: Selections from Letters to the Morning Post 1900–1910* (Melbourne: Melbourne University Press, 1968).
17. Frank Parsons, 'Australasian Methods of Dealing with Immigration', *Annals of the American Academy of Political and Social Science*, 24 (1904), p. 211.
18. *CPD*, House of Representatives, 12 September 1901, repr. in Crowley (ed.), *Modern Australia in Documents 1901–39*, p. 17.
19. Deakin at Ballarat, 29 October 1903, in Parsons, 'Australasian Methods of Dealing with Immigration', p. 219.
20. La Nauze (ed.), *Federated Australia*.
21. Jay Winter, 'Migration, War and Empire: the British Case', *Annales de demographie historique*, 1 (2002), pp. 143–60.
22. Octavius Charles Beale, 'Imperial Immigration', *Journal of the Society of Arts*, February 16 1906, 354.
23. Theodore Roosevelt, 'National Life and Character', *Sewanee Review*, 2:3 (May 1894), p. 13, at http://teachingamericanhistory.org.
24. Deakin cited in Gavin Souter, *Lion and Kangaroo: The Initiation of Australia 1901–1919* (Sydney: Collins, 1976), p. 131.
25. *Times*, 20 August 1908, p. 3.

NOTES

26. Report on the Defence of Australia by Field Marshal Viscount Kitchener, 1910, NAA A463, 1957/1079.
27. Cited in Anthony Burke, *Fears of Security: Australian Invasion Anxiety* (Melbourne: Cambridge University Press, 2000), p. 31.
28. R. M. Crawford, *A Bit of A Rebel: The Life and Work of George Arnold Wood* (Sydney: Sydney University Press, 1975), p. 212.
29. Cited in Morris Graham, 'Newcastle rallies to the flag: February 1902. Arthur Hill Griffith and opposition to the Boer War', *JRAHS*, 89:1 (2003), p. 55
30. JHPM [Hubert Murray] to Tab [his wife Sybil], 9 September 1900, in Francis West (ed.), *Selected Letters of Hubert Murray* (Melbourne: Oxford University Press, 1970), pp. 28–9.
31. Cited in Craig Wilcox, 'Our other unknown soldier', *Australian Army Journal*, 3:2 (2006), p. 162.
32. Burns Philp executive quoted in Ken Buckley and Ted Wheelwright, *No Paradise for Workers: Capitalism and the Common People in Australia 1788–1914* (Melbourne: Oxford University Press, 1988), p. 248.
33. JHPM to George [Murray], 14 March 1905, in West (ed.), *Selected Letters of Hubert Murray*, p. 7.
34. Quoted in Souter, *Lion and Kangaroo*, 175.

10 A NATION AT WAR: 1914–18

1. Nettie Higgins to Esmonde Higgins, cited in Souter, *Lion & Kangaroo*, p. 213.
2. W.M. Hughes, *Policies and Potentates* (Sydney: Angus & Robertson, 1950), p. 140.
3. Eric Partridge, *Frank Honywood, Private: A Personal Record of the 1914–1918 War*, introduced and annotated by Geoffrey Serle (Melbourne: Melbourne University Press, 1987), p. 25.
4. Ibid., p. 21.
5. Hubert Murray to George Murray, 8 March 1915, in West (ed.), *Selected Letters of Hubert Murray*, p. 85.
6. Cited in Bill Gammage, *The Broken Years: Australian Soldiers in the Great War* (Canberra: Australian National University Press, 1974), p. 44.
7. Partridge, *Frank Honywood*, p. 39.
8. Ibid., p. 34.
9. Monash to his wife, 16 May 1915, in F. M. Cutlack (ed.), *War Letters of General Monash*, (Sydney: Angus and Robertson, 1935), p. 36.
10. Partridge, *Frank Honywood*, p. 45.
11. Ibid., p. 55.
12. Capt R. Hugh Knyvett, *"Over There" With the Australians*, 2nd edn (London: Hodder and Stoughton, 1918), p. 97.
13. Ibid.
14. *Sydney Morning Herald*, 8 May 1915, at http://www.nla.gov.au.
15. A. B. Paterson, *Happy Dispatches: War Memoirs* (Sydney: Angus & Robertson, 1934).

279

NOTES

16. Tony Collins, 'Australian Nationalism and working-class Britishness: The Case of Rugby League Football', *History Compass*, 3 (2005), AU 142, 1–19.
17. Knyvett, *"Over There"*, p. 95.
18. Joan Beaumont (ed.), *Australia's War 1914–1918* (Sydney: Allen & Unwin, 1995), p. xx.
19. Monash to his wife, 23 April 1915, in Cutlack (ed.), *War Letters of General Monash*, p. 32.
20. Murdoch to Andrew Fisher, 23 Sep 1915, at http://www.nla.gov.au.
21. Monash to his wife, 12 December 1915, in Cutlack (ed.), *War Letters of General Monash*, p. 92.
22. Partridge, *Frank Honywood*, p. 49.
23. Poem in Will Dyson, *Australia at War: A Winter record made by Will Dyson on the Somme and at Ypres during the campaigns of 1916 and 1917* (London: Cecil Palmer and Hayward, 1918).
24. Partridge, *Frank Honywood*, pp. 64–94.
25. Monash to his wife, 18 October 1917, in Cutlack (ed.), *War Letters of General Monash*, p. 202.
26. Winter, 'Migration, War and Empire: the British Case'.
27. Nettie Palmer to Esmond Higgins, cited in Souter, *Lion and Kangaroo*, p. 262.
28. Elise Masson to Bronislaw Malinowski, undated letter, in Helena Wayne (ed.), *The Story of Marriage Volume 1: The letters of Bronislaw Malinowski and Elsie Masson* (London: Routledge, 1995), p. 6.
29. Ibid.
30. Cited in Pat Jalland, *Changing Ways of Death in Twentieth-Century Australia: War, Medicine and the Funeral Business* (Sydney: University of New South Wales Press, 2006), p. 85.
31. J. M. Main, *Conscription: The Australian Debate 1901–1970* (Sydney: Cassell, 1970), p. 37.
32. Newsreel, Australian Labor Government 1916 Conscription Referendum Campaign: *Referendum Bullets* 1916, at http://aso.gov.au.
33. Miss Pankhurst and Miss Vida Goldstein. 1 November 1917, NAA MP11/1/0, 1915/3/1371.
34. Reprinted in Main, *Conscription*.
35. Report by Mr Donald Mackinnon, repr in ibid.
36. Nathaniel Jacka quoted in Damian Powell, 'Annotation: Albert Jacka VC and the Conscription Debate', *Latrobe Journal*, 63 (1999), p. 3.
37. Sydney Greenbie, 'The Pacific Triangle', *North American Review*, 211 (1920), p. 342.
38. Minister for Work and Railways, Mr Watts, during the election campaign in 1917, *Argus*, 3 April 1917, p. 8.
39. Hughes, *Policies and Potentates*, p. 156.
40. Ibid., p. 229.
41. Ibid., p. 238.
42. Ibid., p. 244.
43. Henry Lawson to Miss E. S. Abbott, 4 June 1917, in Colin Roderick (ed.), *Henry Lawson: Letters 1890–1922* (Sydney: Angus & Robertson, 1970), pp. 355–6.

11 A NATION DIVIDED: 1919–39

1. Balfour Declaration, Imperial Conference (1926), at http://www. foundingdocs.gov.au.
2. *CPD*, House of Representatives, 3 March 1927.
3. Charles Merz, 'When the Movies Go Abroad', *Harper's Monthly Magazine*, 151 (1925), p. 159.
4. Donald Horne, *The Education of Young Donald* (Sydney: Angus & Robertson, 1967), p. 10.
5. *Advance Australia*, Sydney, 1 Sep 1927 repr. in Crowley (ed.), *Modern Australia in Documents 1901–39*, p. 248.
6. *Age*, 10 May 1927.
7. *CPD*, House of Representatives, 28 Jan 1928.
8. Bruce, Stanley Melbourne, quote number B0265 in Stephen Murray-Smith (ed.), *The Dictionary of Australian Quotations* (Melbourne: Heinemann, 1984), p. 30.
9. A. St Ledger, 'Keeping Australia a White Man's Country', *Current History*, 18:3, (1923), p. 475.
10. J. W. Gregory, 'Capacity of Australia for Immigration', *Contemporary Review*, 136, (1929), p. 476.
11. *Brisbane Courier*, 22 August 1930, p. 13.
12. *Brisbane Courier*, 19 November 1930, p. 15.
13. *Sydney Morning Herald*, 27 June 1932, p. 10.
14. Malouf, *Made In England*, p. 9.
15. ABS Statistics Cat No. 3105.0.65.001, Australian Historical Population Statistics.
16. Vincent Buckley in Joy Hooten (ed.), *Australian Lives: An Oxford Anthology* (Melbourne: Oxford University Press, 1988, p. 35).
17. *Sydney Morning Herald*, 23 July 1931, p. 10.
18. *Canberra Times*, 19 January 1933, p. 1.
19. *Sydney Morning Herald*, 27 January 1938, p. 1.
20. Bain Attwood, *Rights for Aborigines* (Sydney: Allen & Unwin, 2003), pp. 92–3, 101, 117–8.
21. *Sydney Morning Herald*, 11 July 1935, p. 10.

12 DEFENDING AUSTRALIA: 1939–49

1. *Canberra Times*, 4 September 1939, p. 2.
2. *Sydney Morning Herald*, 6 September 1939, p. 15.
3. *CPD*, House of Representatives, 19 September 1939, vol. 161, p. 677.
4. David Lowe, 'Australia in the World' in Joan Beaumont (ed.) *Australia's War 1939–45* (Sydney: Allen & Unwin, 1996), p. 88.
5. *Land*, 15 Sep 1939 in Crowley (ed.), *Modern Australia in Documents 1901–39*, p. 11.
6. Department of Foreign Affairs and Trade, Historical Documents No 41, Mr R. G. Menzies, Prime Minister, to Mr S. M. Bruce, High Commissioner in the United Kingdom, Cablegram unnumbered CANBERRA, 13 August

1941, MOST IMMEDIATE URGENT CONFIDENTIAL AND PERSONAL TO MR BRUCE, at http://www.info.dfat.gov.au.

7. Paul Hasluck, *Government and the People 1939–41* (Canberra: Australian War Memorial, 1952), p. 347.

8. *Hansard*, House of Commons, 27 Jan 1942, vol. 377, p. 610.

9. Howard Beale, *This Inch of Time: A Memoir of Politics and Diplomacy* (Melbourne: Melbourne University Press, 1977), p. 106.

10. *Sydney Morning Herald,* 9 December 1941, p. 6.

11. *CPD*, House of Representatives, 16 December 1941, Vol. 169, p. 1074.

12. *Sydney Morning Herald*, 29 December 1941, p. 7.

13. Jill Ker Conway, *The Road from Coorain* (Melbourne: Heinemann, 1989), p. 69.

14. *Hansard*, House of Commons, 27 January 1942, vol. 377, p. 617.

15. *Argus*, 17 February 1942, p. 3.

16. Conway, *The Road from Coorain*, p. 67.

17. *Argus*, 17 February 1942, p. 3.

18. *CPD*, House of Representatives, 15 May 1942, vol. 170, p. 1286.

19. *Argus*, 19 March 1942, p. 3.

20. Ibid.

21. E. Daniel and Annette Potts, *Yanks Down Under 1941–1945: the American Impact on Australia* (Melbourne: Oxford University Press, 1985), p. 404.

22. Joanne Penglase and David Horner, *When the War Came to Australia* (Sydney: Allen & Unwin, 1992), p. 120.

23. *CPD*, House of Representatives, 27 March 1941, vol. 166, p. 388.

24. *Commonwealth Parliamentary Papers [CPP]*, 1940–43, vol. 2, p. 759.

25. *CPP*, 1945–46, vol. IV (Part 2), p. 1195.

26. Interview with Oodgeroo Noonuccal, 20 October 1986, in Robert A. Hall, *The Black Diggers: Aborigines and Torres Strait Islanders in the Second World War* (Canberra: Aboriginal Studies Press, 1997), p. 69.

27. Inga Clendinnen, *Tiger's Eye: A Memoir* (Melbourne: Text Publishing, 2000), p. 158.

28. Maud Edmondson to Mr Gibson, 4 August 1941, included in item about John Edmondson available at http://www.australiansatwar.gov.au.

29. *Argus*, 1 November 1945, p. 3.

30. 'Lydia M: From war and slave camp to freedom and peace', in John Lack and Jacqueline Templeton (eds), *Bold Experiment: A Documentary History of Australian Immigration since 1945* (Melbourne: Oxford University Press, 1995), p. 34.

31. John Lack, 'Melbourne: In and Out of my Class', *Australian Historical Studies*, 27:109 (1997), p. 163.

32. *CPD*, House of Representatives, 15 October 1947, vol. 193, p. 798.

33. Joseph Chifley, *Things Worth Fighting For: Speeches*, selected and arranged by A. W. Stargardt (Melbourne: Melbourne University Press, 1952), p. 121.

34. Robert Menzies, *The Forgotten People: A Broadcast Address delivered Friday May 22, 1942 through 2UE Sydney, 3AW Melbourne* (Melbourne: Robertson & Mullens, 1942).

35. Chifley, *Things Worth Fighting For*, p. 85.

36. Conway, *The Road from Coorain*, p. 509.
37. *Sydney Morning Herald*, 11 November 1949, p. 4.

13   SECURITY: 1949–63

1. Donald Horne, 'Australia Looks Around', *Foreign Affairs*, 44:3 (1966), p. 446.
2. Quoted in Henry Ablinski, 'Australia Reviews her Asian Exclusion Policy', *Far Eastern Survey*, 28:11 (1959), pp. 161–7.
3. Peter Conrad, *Tales of Two Hemispheres: Boyer Lectures 2004* (Sydney: ABC Books, 2004), p. 11.
4. Peter Conrad in Hooten (ed.), *Australian Lives*, p. 56.
5. Tom Kryger, 'Home Ownership in Australia – data and trends', Research Paper, Parliamentary Library, 1 February 2009, no. 21 (2008–09), ISSN 1834-9854, http://www.aph.gov.au.
6. 'Giuseppe A: Comparing social life in the 1950s and 1970s', in Lack and Templeton (eds), *Bold Experiment*, p. 99.
7. Quoted in Bill Bunbury, *Caught in Time: Talking Australian History* (Fremantle: Fremantle Arts Centre Press, 2006), p. 136.
8. *Canberra Times*, 19 October 1951, p. 4.
9. Kath Walker, *The Dawn is at Hand: Poems* (Brisbane: Jacaranda Press, 1966).
10 Wray Vamplew (ed.) *Australians: Historical Statistics* (Sydney: Fairfax, Syme & Weldon, 1987), p. 183.
11. Statistics in Michelle Arrow, '16 September 1956: "It's Here at Last": The Introduction of Television to Australia', in Martin Crotty and David Andrew Roberts (eds), *Turning Points in Australian History* (Sydney: University of New South Wales Press, 2009), p. 148.
12. Graeme Davison, *Car Wars: How the Car Won Our Hearts and Conquered Our Cities* (Sydney: Allen & Unwin, 2004), p. 15.
13. Chairman's Report, Ninth Congress, Australian Road Safety Council, 1951, MS5933/1/1 Records of the Expert Group of Road safety, MS Collection, NLA. Federal Office of Road Safety, *The history of road fatalities in Australia* (Canberra: Australian Government Printing Service, 1998), p. 3. References thanks to Marianna Stylianou.
14. http://www.quit.org.au.
15. Peter McDonald, Lado Ruzicka and Patricia Pyne, 'Marriage, Fertility and Mortality', in Vamplew (ed.), *Australians: Historical Statistics*, p. 43.
16. ES 169–180, 'Kindergartens, Schools and Technical Colleges, Enrolments and Teachers by state, 1963–1969', in ibid., 341.
17. Don Watson, *Recollections of a Bleeding Heart: A Portrait of Paul Keating PM* (Sydney: Random House, 2002), p. 9.
18. Lack, 'Melbourne: In and Out of My Class', p. 165.
19. Alison Booth and Hiau Joo Kee, 'The University Gender Gap in Australia: A Long-Run Perspective', at http://econrsss.anu.edu.au.
20. Patrick White, 'The Prodigal Son', *Australian Letters*, 1:3 (1958), pp. 37–40.

NOTES

21. Charmian Clift, 'Images in Aspic', 1965 in Nicholas Jose (ed.), *Macquarie PEN Anthology of Australian Literature* (Sydney: Allen & Unwin, 2009), pp. 716–7.
22. Conrad, *Tales of Two Hemispheres*, p. 34.

14 DISSENT AND SOCIAL CHANGE: 1964–79

1. Robert Menzies, *CPD*, House of Representatives, 5 November 1964, pp. 2517–724.
2. Bruce Dawe, 'Homecoming', in Jose (ed.), *Macquarie PEN Anthology*, p. 785.
3. Val Noone, cited in Peter Cochrane, *Australians at War* (Sydney: ABC Books, 2001), p. 249.
4. Gough Whitlam, *Into the Seventies with Labor: 1969 Policy Speech* (Sydney: Australian Labor Party, 1969).
5. Hugh Stretton, *Ideas for Australian Cities* (Adelaide: by the author, 1970), p. 4.
6. Donald Horne, *The Lucky Country: Australia in the sixties* (Melbourne: Penguin, 1964), p. 209.
7. Les Patterson, 'At least you can say you've seen it', 1974, in Murray-Smith (ed.), *The Dictionary of Australian Quotations*, p. 124.
8. Peter McDonald, Lado Ruzicka and Patricia Pyne, 'Marriage, Fertility and Mortality', in Vamplew (ed.), *Australian Historical Statistics*, p. 43.
9. 'Fix', in Michael Dransfield selected by John Kinsella, *Michael Dransfield: A Retrospective* (St Lucia: University of Queensland Press, 2002), p. 14.
10. Gurundji Petition to Lord Casey, Governor General, 1967 repr. in Jose (ed.) *Macquarie PEN Anthology*, p. 630.
11. Kevin Gilbert, *Because a White Man'll Never Do It* (Sydney: Angus & Roberson, 1973), pp. 40–1.
12. Whitlam speech, 16 August 1975, at http://www.abc.net.au.
13. M. C. Gray, B. H. Hunter and J. Taylor, *Health Expenditure, Income and Health Status Among Indigenous and Other Australians* (Canberra: Australian National University E-press, 2004), p. 7.
14. Whitlam, January 1971, in Murray-Smith (ed.), *Dictionary of Australian Quotations*, p. 281.
15. http://www.undp.org.pg/.
16. W. D. Borrie, 'Immigration Patterns since 1972', in James Jupp (ed.), *The Australian People: An Encyclopedia of the Nation, its People and their origin* (Melbourne: Cambridge University Press, 2001), p. 111.
17. Ibid., p. 113.
18. Gavin Jones, *An Australian Population Policy*, Parliamentary Research Paper 17, 1996–7, at http://www.aph.gov.au.
19. R. J. Hawke, *The Resolution of Conflict* (Sydney: ABC, 1979), pp. 33, 38.

15 GLOBAL NATION: 1980–2010

1. *Age*, 8 September 1980, p. 8.
2. Herman Kahn and Thomas Pepper, *Will She Be Right? The future of Australia* (St Lucia: University of Queensland Press, 1980).
3. *Sydney Morning Herald*, 7 April 1981, p. 9.

4. *Sydney Morning Herald*, 29 August 1984, p. 12.
5. Mr Hawke, 'National Economic Summit Conference,' Ministerial Statement, *CPD*, House of Representatives, 3 May 1983, p. 90.
6. Andrew Rogers, 'Developments in Foreign Currency Loan Litigation', *Journal of Banking and Finance Law and Practice*, 1:3 (1990), p. 201.
7. *Sydney Morning Herald*, 30 November 1990, p. 1.
8. http://www.treasury.gov.au.
9. *Sydney Morning Herald*, 24 November 1993, p. 14.
10. APEC Economic Leaders Declaration of Common Resolve, Bogor, November 1994, at http://www.apec.org.
11. http://www.aei.gov.au.
12. *Sydney Morning Herald*, 21 December 1991, p. 2.
13. *Age*, 11 December 1991, p. 6.
14. Alison Booth and Hiau Joo Kee, 'The University Gender Gap in Australia: A Long-Run Perspective', at http://econrsss.anu.edu.au.
15. Ruth Weston, Lixia Qu and Grace Soriano, 'Ageing Yet Diverse: The changing shape of Australia's population', *Australian Family Briefing*, 10 (2001), at http://www.aifs.gov.au/.
16. Australian Bureau of Statistics, *Yearbook Australia: Issue 77* (Canberra: Commonwealth of Australia, 1994), p. 102.
17. Australian Institute of Health and Welfare, 'Australian trends in life expectancy', at www.aihw.gov.au.
18. Ibid.
19. *Age*, 1 July 1993, p. 3.
20. Mabo v. Queensland No. 2 [1992] HCA 23; (1992) 175 CLR 1, paragraph 50, at http://www.austlii.edu.au.
21. Royal Commission into Aboriginal Deaths in Custody, Volume 1, at http://www.austlii.edu.au.
22. Paul Keating, 'Redfern Park Speech', 10 December 1992, at Australian Launch of International Year for World's Indigenous People, at http://www.austlii.edu.au.
23. *Age*, 25 February 1992, p. 1.
24. *CPD*, House of Representatives, 27 February 1992, p. 373.
25. Quoted in Mark McKenna, *Different Perspectives on Black Armband History*, at http://www.aph.gov.au.
26. John Howard, 'The Role of Government: Headland Speech', 6 June 1995, at http://australianpolitics.com.
27. *CPD*, House of Representatives, 10 September 1996, p. 3860.
28. Cited in McKenna, 'Different Perspectives on Black Armband History'.
29. Cited in Maryrose Casey, 'Referendum and Reconciliation Marches: What Bridges are We Crossing', *Journal of Australian Studies,* 30:89 (2006), pp. 137–48.
30. Cited in Bart Ziino, 'Who Owns Gallipoli? Australia's Gallipoli Anxieties 1915–2005', *Journal of Australian Studies* 30:88 (2006), pp. 1–12.
31. *Sydney Morning Herald*, 27 April 1990, p. 5.
32. Paul Keating, Remembrance Day Speech, 11 November 1993, at http://www.awm.gov.au.
33. Gareth Evans and Bruce Grant, *Australia's Foreign Relations in the World of the 1990s* (Melbourne: Melbourne University Press, 1991), p. 323.

34. Alexander Downer, 'Australia and the United States: A Vital Friendship', 29 May 1996, at http://foreignminister.gov.au.
35. http://www.defence.gov.au.
36. Barry York, *Australia and Refugees 1901–2002: Annotated Chronology, Based on Official Sources: Summary*, 2003, at www.aph.gov.au.
37. *CPD*, House of Representatives, 29 August 2001, p. 30569.
38. Cited in Peter Mares, *Borderline: Australia's responses to refugees and asylum seekers in the wake of the Tampa* (Sydney: University of New South Wales Press, 2001), p. 143.
39. Elsa Koleth, *Multiculturalism: A Review of Australian Policy Statements and Recent Debates in Australia and Overseas*, Research Paper no. 6, 2010–11, at www.aph.gov.au.
40. G. Hardgrave (Minister for Citizenship and Multicultural Affairs), *Australian Citizenship: then and now: speech to the Sydney Institute by the Hon. Gary Hardgrave, MP: Sydney: 7 July 2004*, http://parlinfo.aph.gov.au.
41. Kevin Rudd, 'Faith in Politics', *The Monthly*, no. 17 (2006).

Further Reading

PRE-COLONIAL

Blainey, Geoffrey *Triumph of the Nomads: A History of Ancient Australia* (Melbourne: Sun Books, 1978).

Butlin, N. G. *Economics and the Dreamtime: A Hypothetical History* (Cambridge: Cambridge University Press, 1993).

Clendinnen, Inga *Dancing with Strangers: Europeans and Australians at First Contact* (Melbourne: Cambridge University Press, 2005).

David, Bruno, Barker, Bryce and Ian J. McNiven (eds) *The Social Archaeology of Australian Indigenous Societies* (Canberra: Aboriginal Studies Press, 2006).

Flannery, Tim *The Future Eaters: An Ecological History of the Australasian Lands and People* (Sydney: Reed New Holland, 1998).

Flood, Josephine *Archaeology of the Dreamtime: The Story of Prehistoric Australia and its People* (Adelaide: JB Publishing, 2004).

Gascoigne, John *The Enlightenment and the Origins of European Australia* (Cambridge: Cambridge University Press, 2002).

Keen, Ian *Aboriginal Economy and Society: Australia at the Threshold of Colonisation* (Melbourne: Oxford University Press, 2004).

Lourandos, Harry *Continent of Hunter-Gatherers: New Perspectives in Australian Prehistory* (Cambridge: Cambridge University Press, 1997).

Martin, Jed (ed.) *The Founding of Australia: The Argument about Australia's Origins* (Sydney: Hale & Iremonger, 1978).

Mulvaney, D. J. *Encounters in Place: Outsiders and Aboriginal Australians 1606 1985* (Brisbane: University of Queensland Press, 1989).

Mulvaney, John and Johan Kamminga *Prehistory of Australia* (Sydney: Allen & Unwin, 1999).

Murray, Tim (ed.) *Archaeology of Aboriginal Australia: A Reader* (Sydney: Allen & Unwin, 1998).

Smith, Bernard *European Vision and the South Pacific*, 3rd edn (Melbourne: Oxford University Press, 1989).

Stanner, W. E. H. *The Dreaming & Other Essays* (Melbourne: Black Inc. Agenda, 2009).

COLONIAL

Atkinson, Alan *The Europeans in Australia: A History* (2 vols, Melbourne: Oxford University Press, 1997–2004).

Atkinson, Alan and Marian Aveling (eds) *Australians 1838* (Sydney: Fairfax, Syme & Weldon, 1987).

Attwood, Bain & S. G. Foster (eds) *Frontier Conflict: The Australian Experience* (Canberra: National Museum of Australia, 2003).

Banivanua-Mar, Tracey *Violence and Colonial Dialogue: The Australian-Pacific Indentured Labour Trade* (Honolulu: University of Hawaii Press, 2007).

Banner, Stuart *Possessing the Pacific: Land, Settlers and Indigenous People from Australia to Alaska* (Cambridge MA: Harvard University Press, 2007).

Blainey, Geoffrey *The Tyranny of Distance: How Distance Shaped Australia's History* (Melbourne: Sun Books, 1966).

Bonyhady, Tim *The Colonial Earth* (Melbourne: Melbourne University Press, 2002).

Boyce, James *Van Diemen's Land* (Melbourne: Black Inc., 2008).

Broome, Richard *Aboriginal Australia: A history since 1788*, 4th edn (Sydney: Allen & Unwin, 2010).

Butlin, N. G. *Forming a Colonial Economy: Australia 1810–1850* (Melbourne: Cambridge University Press, 1994).

Butlin, N. G. *Investment in Australian Economic Development, 1861–1900* (Cambridge: Cambridge University Press, 1964).

Carter, Paul *The Road to Botany Bay: An Essay in Spatial History* (London: Faber & Faber, 1987).

Cochrane, Peter *Colonial Ambition: Foundations of Australian Democracy* (Melbourne: Melbourne University Press, 2006).

Crotty, Martin *Making the Australian Male: Middle-Class Masculinity 1870–1920* (Melbourne: Melbourne University Press, 2001).

Daniels, Kay *Convict Women* (St Leonards: Allen & Unwin, 1988).

Davison, Graeme *The Rise and Fall of Marvellous Melbourne* (Melbourne: Melbourne University Press, 1978).

Davison, Graeme, McCarty, J. W. and A. McCleary *Australians 1888* (Sydney: Fairfax, Syme & Weldon, 1987).

Garton, Stephen *Out of Luck: Poor Australians and Social Welfare, 1788–1988* (Sydney: Allen & Unwin, 1990).

Goodman, David *Goldseeking: Victoria and California in the 1850s* (Stanford: Stanford University Press, 1994).

Griffiths, Tom *Hunters and Collectors: The Antiquarian Imagination in Australia* (Melbourne: Cambridge University Press, 1996).

Grimshaw, Patricia, Lake, Marilyn, Quartly, Marian and Ann McGrath *Creating a Nation* (Melbourne: McPhee Gribble, 1994).

Haebich, Anna *Broken Circles: Fragmenting Indigenous Families 1800–2000* (Perth: Fremantle Arts Centre Press, 2000).

Hirst, J. B. *Convict Society and its Enemies: A History of Early New South Wales* (Sydney: George Allen & Unwin, 1985).

Hirst, J. B. *The Strange Birth of Colonial Democracy: New South Wales 1848–1884* (Sydney: Allen & Unwin, 1988).

Inglis, K. S. *Australian Colonists: An Exploration of Social History 1788–1870* (Melbourne: Melbourne University Press, 1993).

Irving, Helen *To Constitute a Nation: A Cultural History of Australia's Constitution* (Melbourne: Cambridge University Press, 1997).

Jalland, Pat *Australian Ways of Death: A Social and Cultural History 1840-1918* (Melbourne: Oxford University Press, 2002).

Karskens, Grace *The Colony: A History of Early Sydney* (Crows Nest: Allen & Unwin, 2010).

Kingston, Beverly *The Oxford History of Australia, Vol. 3, 1860–1900, Glad, Confident Morning* (Melbourne: Oxford University Press, 1988).

Kociumbas, Jan *The Oxford History of Australia, Vol. 2, 1770–1860, Possessions* (Melbourne: Oxford University Press, 1992).

Markus, Andrew *Fear and Hatred: Purifying Australia and California, 1851–1901* (Sydney: Hale & Iremonger, 1979).

McCalman, Janet *Sex and Suffering: Women's Health and a Woman's Hospital* (Melbourne: Melbourne University Press, 1998).

McGrath, Ann (ed.) *Contested Ground: Australian Aborigines under the British Crown* (Sydney: Allen and Unwin, 1995).

McGregor, Russell *Imagined Destinies: Aboriginal Australians and the Doomed Race Theory* (Melbourne: Melbourne University Press, 1997).

McKenzie, Kirsten *A Swindler's Progress: Nobles and Convicts in the Age of Liberty* (Sydney: UNSW Press, 2009).

Mulvaney, D. J. *Encounters in Place: Outsiders and Aboriginal Australians 1606–1985* (Brisbane: University of Queensland Press, 1989).

Neal, David *The Rule of Law in a Penal Colony: Law and Power in Early New South Wales* (Melbourne: Cambridge University Press: 1991).

Nicholas, Stephen (ed.) *Convict Workers: Reinterpreting Australia's Past* (Melbourne: Cambridge University Press, 1988).

Oxley, Deborah *Convict Maids: The Forced Migration of Women to Australia* (Cambridge: Cambridge University, 1996).

Reid, Kirsty *Gender, Crime and Empire: Convicts, Settlers and the State in Early Colonial Australia* (Manchester: Manchester University Press, 2007).

Reynolds, Henry *Frontier: Aborigines, Settlers and Land* (Sydney: Allen & Unwin, 1996).

Reynolds, Henry *The Law of the Land* (Melbourne: Penguin, 2003).

Reynolds, Henry *The Other Side of the Frontier: Aboriginal Resistance to the European Invasion of Australia* (Sydney: UNSW Press, 2006).

Rickard, John *Australia: A Cultural History* (Melbourne: Longman Chesire, 1988).

Robson, L. L. *The Convict Settlers of Australia* (Melbourne: Melbourne University Press, 1965).

Russell, Penny and Richard White (eds) *Pastiche I: Reflections on Nineteenth-Century Australia* (Sydney: Allen & Unwin, 1994).

Serle, Geoffrey *The Golden Age: A History of the Colony of Victoria, 1851–1861* (Melbourne: Melbourne University Press, 1963).

Souter, Gavin *Lion and Kangaroo: The Initiation of Australia*, 2nd edn (Melbourne: Text Publishing, 2000).

Statham, Pamela (ed.) *The Origins of Australia's Capital Cities* (Melbourne: Cambridge University Press, 1989).

Thompson, Roger C. *Australian Imperialism in the Pacific: The Expansionist Era 1820–1920* (Melbourne: Melbourne University Press, 1980).

Walker, David *Anxious Nation: Australia and the Rise of Asia 1850–1939* (St Lucia: University of Queensland Press, 1999).

Ward, Russell *The Australian Legend* (Melbourne: Oxford University Press, 1958).

NATIONAL

Anderson, Warwick *The Cultivation of Whiteness: Science, Health and Racial Destiny in Australia* (Melbourne: Melbourne University Press, 2002).

Attwood, Bain *Rights for Aborigines* (Sydney: Allen & Unwin, 2003).

Beaumont, Joan (ed.) *Australia's War 1914–1918* (Sydney: Allen & Unwin, 1995).

Beaumont, Joan (ed.) *Australia's War 1939–1945* (Sydney: Allen & Unwin, 1996).

Bolton, Geoffrey *The Oxford History of Australia, Vol. 5, 1942–1988, The Middle Way* (Melbourne: Oxford University Press, 1990).

Brett, Judith *Robert Menzies' Forgotten People* (Sydney: Macmillan, 1992).

Brett, Judith *Australian Liberals and the Moral Middle Class: From Alfred Deakin to John Howard* (Melbourne: Cambridge University Press, 2003).

Burgmann, Verity *Power, Profit and Protest: Australian Social Movements and Globalisation* (Crow's Nest: Allen & Unwin, 2003).

Carey, Hilary *Believing in Australia: A Cultural History of Religions* (St Leonards: Allen & Unwin, 1996).

Chesterman, John and Brian Galligan *Citizens Without rights: Aborigines and Australian Citizenship* (Melbourne: Cambridge University Press, 1997).

Damousi, Joy and Marilyn Lake (eds) *Gender and War: Australians at War in the Twentieth Century* (Cambridge: Cambridge University Press, 1995).

Darian-Smith, Kate and Paula Hamilton (eds) *Memory and History in Twentieth Century Australia* (Melbourne: Oxford University Press, 1994).

Davison, Graeme *Car Wars: How Cars Won our Hearts and Conquered our Cities* (Sydney: Allen & Unwin, 2004).

Dutton, David *One of Us? A Century of Australian Citizenship* (Sydney: UNSW Press, 2002).

Edwards, Peter *A Nation at War: Australian Politics, Society and Diplomacy During the Vietnam War 1965–1975* (Sydney: Allen & Unwin/Australian War Memorial, 1997).

Gammage, Bill *The Broken Years: Australian Soldiers in the Great War* (Melbourne: Penguin, 1974).

Gammage, Bill & Peter Spearitt (eds) *Australians 1938* (Sydney: Fairfax, Syme & Weldon, 1987).

Ganter, Regina *Mixed Relations: Asian-Aboriginal Contact in North Australia* (Perth: University of Western Australia Press, 2006).

Garton, Stephen *The Cost of War: Australians Return* (Melbourne: Oxford University Press, 1996).

Gregory, R. G. and N. G. Butlin (eds) *Recovery from Depression: Australia and the World Economy in the 1930s* (New York: Cambridge University Press, 1988).

Hutton, Drew and Libby Connors *A History of the Australian Environment Movement* (Melbourne: Cambridge University Press, 1999).

Jupp, James *From White Australia to Woomera: The Story of Australian Immigration* (Cambridge: Cambridge University Press, 2002).

Grey, Jeffrey *A Military History of Australia* (Cambridge: Cambridge University Press, 2008).

Hirst, John *The Sentimental Nation: The Making of the Australian Commonwealth* (Melbourne: Oxford University Press, 2000).

Inglis, K. S., with J. Brazier *Sacred Places: War Memorials in the Australian Landscape* (Melbourne: Melbourne University Press, 2008).

Lack, John and Jacqueline Templeton (eds), *Bold Experiment: A Documentary History of Australian Immigration since 1945* (Melbourne: Oxford University Press, 1995).

Lake, Marilyn *Getting Equal: The History of Australian Feminism* (Sydney: Allen & Unwin, 1999).

Lowe, David *Menzies and the 'Great World Struggle': Australia's Cold War 1948–1954* (Sydney: UNSW Press, 1999).

Macintyre, Stuart *The Oxford History of Australia, Vol. 4: The Succeeding Age, 1901–1942* (Melbourne: Oxford University Press, 1986).

McCalman, Janet *Journeyings: The Biography of a Middle-Class Generation, 1920–1990* (Melbourne: Melbourne University Press, 1993).

McKenna, Mark *The Captive Republic: A History of Republicanism in Australia 1788–1996* (Cambridge: Cambridge University Press, 1996).

McMullin, Ross *The Light on the Hill: The Australian Labor Party 1891–1991* (Melbourne: Oxford University Press, 1992).

Meredith, David and Barrie Dyster *Australia in the Global Economy: Continuity and Change* (Cambridge: Cambridge University Press, 1999).

Murphy, John *Imagining the Fifties: Private Sentiment and Political Culture in Menzies Australia* (Sydney: UNSW Press 2000).

Murphy, John *Harvest of Fear: A History of Australia's Vietnam War* (Sydney: Allen & Unwin, 1993).

Nugent, Maria *Botany Bay: Where Histories Meet* (Sydney: Allen & Unwin, 2005).

Peel, Mark *The Lowest Rung: Voices of Australian Poverty* (Melbourne: Cambridge University Press, 2003).

Spenceley, Geoffrey *A Bad Smash: Australia in the Depression of the 1930s* (Ringwood: McPhee Gribble, 1990).

Tavan, Gwenda *The Long Slow Death of White Australia* (Melbourne: Scribe, 2005).

Twomey, Christina *Australia's Forgotten Prisoners: Australians Interned by the Japanese in World War Two* (Melbourne: Cambridge University Press, 2007).

Waterhouse, Richard *Private Pleasures, Public Leisure: A History of Australian Popular Culture since 1788* (Melbourne: Longman, 1995).

Waterhouse, Richard *The Vision Splendid: A Social and Cultural History of Rural Australia* (Perth: Curtin University Books, 2005).

White, Richard *Inventing Australia: Images and Identity 1688–1980* (Sydney: Allen & Unwin, 1981).

White, Richard and Penny Russell (eds) *Memories and Dreams: Reflections on Twentieth-Century Australia: Pastiche II* (Sydney: Allen & Unwin, 1997).

Index

Democratic Labor Party, 220
Deniehy, Daniel (writer), 81, 82
Department of Defence, 266
Desceliers, Pierre (cartographer), 15
Desliens, Nicholas (cartographer), 15
Dharrug people, 37
diet, drink and food, 30, 64, 97, 126
disasters and accidents, 101, 269,
    270–1
  Federation Drought 122, 123
disease and health, 65–6, 95, 177,
    227–8, 238, 250, 258
Djan'kawu (ancestral being), 10
Downer, Alexander (politician), 264,
    266
Drasnfield, Michael (writer), 236
Dromemerdeenne (ancestral being),
    10
Dufresne, Marc-Joseph Marion 18
Dugdale, Henrietta, (feminist and
    writer), 112, 119
Dumont d'Urville, Rear Admiral
    Jules, (explorer), 51
Dyson, Will (artist), 164

Earle, Augustus (artist), 90
East Timor, 265
Echuca (VIC), 130
economic conditions, 65, 83, 102,
    103, 146–7, 170–1, 181–4, 201,
    246, 270
  1890s depression, 122–3
  1930s depression, 185–93
  long boom, 225–8, 234, 238–9
  restructuring in the 1980s and
    1990s, 248–55
Edmondson, Maud (mother), 209
education and literacy, 83–4, 95, 97,
    228–9, 237, 255, 270
  denominational and private schools
    54–5, 64, 84, 102, 228
  mechanics institutes, 65
  universities, 218, 228–9, 235, 237,
    253–4, 255
Education Act (Victoria, 1872), 84
Egypt, 159
El-Niño-Southern Oscillation, 4, 117,
    271
Electoral Reform Act (1858), 82

elections, federal, 140, 170, 177, 178,
    193, 200, 214, 240, 249, 260,
    261, 268, 269, 270
Elizabeth II, Queen, 225, 260
Elkin, A. P. (anthropologist), 196
emancipists and exclusivists, 40,
    46–7, 63, 68
Emerald Hill (VIC), 74
Encounter Bay (SA), 23
Endeavour, HM Bark, 19–21
entertainment: cinema 179–80, 227,
    231, 245; television 227, 229,
    245–6, 253
Entwistle, Ralph (convict), 45
environment and landscape, 89–91,
    113–4, 184–5, 269, 271
  conservation and environmentalism
    113–4, 235
Eora people, 3, 26, 31, 35–6, 37–8
European Economic Community, 238
European exploration, 15–21, 23, 42
    49–50, 63–4, 86, 106
Evans, Gareth (politician), 266
Evatt, H. V. (politician), 211, 220
Everingham, Matthew (convict), 27
exhibitions, 86–7, 103, 109
Eyre, Edward (explorer), 63–4

Fadden, Arthur (politician), 202
families and family life, 95, 190–1,
    228, 229, 236, 256
Favenc, Ernest (writer), 111
Fawkner, John Pascoe (settler), 51
Federal Council for the Advancement
    of Aborigines and Torres Strait
    Islanders, 241
Federation, 74, 83, 106–8, 110,
    126–32
  Referenda, 129–30
feminism *see under* women
Fiji, 90, 106, 107
First Fleet, 24–5, 27, 32
Fisher, Andrew (politician), 139, 157,
    176
Flinders, Matthew (explorer), 18, 23
Flinders Island (TAS), 62, 94
flora, gardens and botany 6, 86, 90,
    114
Forbes (NSW), 72